Seeking the Light

AMERICA'S MODERN QUEST FOR PEACE, JUSTICE, PROSPERITY, AND FAITH

Seeking the Light

AMERICA'S MODERN QUEST FOR PEACE, JUSTICE, PROSPERITY, AND FAITH

BARRY L. CALLEN

Evangel Publishing House
Nappanee, Indiana 46550

Cover Design: Tracey Owen

Cover Photograph: The Statue of Liberty/Pete Saloutos, Tony Stone Images, Chicago

Photo credits: 2, author; 17, Archive Photos; 23, 24, 30, author; 43, Thornton/Archive Photos, New York; 47, Archive Photos; 49, American Stock/Archive Photos; 59, 60, Lambert/Archive Photos; 67, 69, 82, 84, 86, 90, 92, 93, 94, 96, Archive Photos; 103, Tames/New York Times/Archive Photos; 113, Frank Driggs/Archive Photos; 120, 126, author; 133, Morgan Collection/Archive Photos; 141, 151, Archive Photos; 152, Popperfoto/Archive Photos; 157, 165, CNP/Archive Photos; 174, Glen Pierce; 177, 179, Archive Photos; 191, Ed Dubrowsky/Archive Photos; 194, Kent State University Libraries/Dept. of Special Collections; 201, 208, Archive Photos; 209, Foto International/Archive Photos; 223, Robert Kusel/Tony Stone Images; 241, Jim Wells/Archive Photos; 242, Sara Krulwich/New York Times/Archive Photos; 247, Dan Coleman/Archive Photos; 266, Lambert/Archive Photos; 271, Reuters/David Brauchli/Archive Photos; 275, Bernard Gotfryd/Archive Photos; 288, Reuters/Mike Theiler/Archive Photos; 297, Reuters/NASA/Archive Photos; 305, Archive Photos; 312, Reuters/Paul Hackett/Archive Photos; 312, Reuters/Sunil Malhotra/Archive Photos; 314, Reuters/Jeff Christensen/Archive Photos; 320, Reuters/Blake Sell/Archive Photos; 327, Chris Smith/Archive Photos.

ISBN: 0-916035-79-4
Library of Congress Card Number: 98-70165

Printed in the United States of America
9 0 1 2 3 4 EP 10 9 8 7 6 5 4 3 2 1

DEDICATION

To Emily Elizabeth Callen, beloved granddaughter, one of scores
now related to the Jackson-Milton High School class of 1959.
Emily has not lived through the final decades of the
twentieth century, but will face the challenges and
opportunities of living in its wake. May she and
they, recipients of the troubled world shaped
by others, lead new generations into
better paths of peace, justice,
prosperity, and faith.

HONORED MEMORIES

In loving memory of five members of the Jackson-Milton High
School class of 1959 who shared our lives, but not long enough
to see this book or the dawn of the twenty-first century. May the
paths they wandered, as well as our own, be blessed with a sense
of direction toward a better future. May the lives they knew, and
those of the rest of the class, have meaning that will light the way
for others.

Charles Creque, d. 1972; Jeannette Grove, d. 1974;
Irving Carnes, d. 1985; Dallas Cribley, d. 1994;
Virginia (Hetzel) Bertram, d. 1994.

CONTENTS

List of Tables ix

Introduction 1
    One Cultural Cycle
    Amnesia Our Common Ailment
    Somewhere in Ohio
    The Theme of Light

1. At the Crossroads 15
    Past and Future
    Everysmalltown, U.S.A.
    A Window on the World

2. Born in the Shadows of War (1940s) 37
    A World Ignited By War
    Peace and Worldwide Change
    Awkward Transitions At Home
    A New Social Landscape
    A Cockeyed Optimist

3. Kids in the Bright Years (1950s) 79
    Ominous, But Upbeat
    Really Good Times
    New Worries, Fresh Hope
    Separate and Unequal
    Seeds of Change
    A Fragile Stability
    Around Our High School
    Forever In Tomorrowland

4. Parenting in the Glare of Many Fires (1960s) 129
    For One Brief Shining Moment
    High Hopes and Higher Education
    Putting On the Country's Uniform
    Dramatically Changing Times
    Rights for All
    Is Anything Nailed Down?
    Faith, But Faith In What?
    By the Light of the Moon

5. Deaths in Quest of Dawns (1970s) 183
    A Sandwiched Decade
    The Chaos Recedes And Rises
    Peace with Dishonor
    Candor and Conservatism
    The Giant Slumps, Conservatives Multiply
    Frontiers and Frustrations
    Life Is Not Forever

6. In Search of Enlightenment (1980s) 235
    The Prime Directive
    Mixing Nostalgia, Escapism, and Faith
    Dying Social Assumptions
    Menace of Global Anarchy
    When All Foundations Crumble
    Living Is Serving

7. The Dim Horizon (1990s) 281
    Military and Economic Storms
    A Volatile Political Climate
    The Market Up, Absolutes Down
    What Is Worth Remembering?
    What Do We Tell Our Grandchildren?
    The Century (and World?) At Its End
    Unfinished Journey

Appendix: "We Hold These Truths" (1997) 337

Select Bibliographies of Recent American History 343
    General
    Religious Perspectives
    Northeastern Ohio Region
    Oral Histories

Index of Persons and Subjects 353

List of Tables

1. Ideals of the United States of America 6

2. The American Experiment: Unrestrained by Tradition 8

3. North Jackson As the Crossroads 11

4. Proud Land of Immigrants 16

5. Religion and American Life 18

6. Foundations for Reconstruction 48

7. Preamble to the Charter of the United Nations 50

8. Births of the Baby Boomers 63

9. Milestones of the Decade (1940s) 72

10. *Brown v. Board of Education* (Supreme Court, 1954) 100

11. Membership of Religious Bodies in the United States 111

12. Milestones of the Decade (1950s) 114

13. Milestones of the Decade (1960s) 144

14. Letter from the Birmingham Jail (Martin Luther King, Jr., 1963) ... 158

15. Milestones of the Decade (1970s) 210

16. Freedom of Religion and for Abortions 216

17. Dying "Modernist" Assumptions 238

18. Painful Economic Realities (1978-1984) 244

19. Milestones of the Decade (1980s) 258

20. Recent Presidents of the United States
    (Franklin Roosevelt to William Clinton) 277

21. Preamble, North American Free Trade Agreement 286

22. A Prayer of Brother Joe (1996) 292

23. Competing Absolutes in the America of the 1990s 300

24. Milestones of the Decade (1990s) 316

Introduction

These pages explore the recent decades as they have been experienced in the United States. Meaning in the present and wisdom for the future require some attention to what already has been. People gain identity as they find themselves part of some ongoing story of a community and then choose to claim that story, that flow of experience, as their own—or bolt its borders and join some other narrative of existence as their adopted heritage and destiny. To be an American with a self-conscious identity as an American requires dealing somehow with the story told here.

In focus here is the complex, fascinating, and often troubled story of the United States, especially as it has evolved in the last half of the twentieth century. The social, political, and religious dimensions of the nation's story are woven together, the way real life usually is. It is assumed that matters of faith are fundamental to the meaning of this story—so that tracing the country's quest for peace, prosperity, and justice since the 1940s is not to be separated from the visions, beliefs, and deepest self-understandings of this particular people. It is important to look behind the headlines, which often treat only the political and economic dimensions of current events. One always finds just beneath the surface a significant religious dimension. As a nation believes, so is its destiny. Americans traditionally have been believers both in an overarching perspective on reality itself and in their own special place in a divine plan for the world. In fact, issues of church and state on occasion have been called the largest subject in the history of the Western world.

The Question of Bias

Understanding comes best when the nation's story is told both in its broad sweep and in the particulars of a group of representative real people who have actually lived the story. Thus, in these pages particular reference is often made to the experiences of members of one high school class, the 1959 class of Jackson-Milton High School in Northeast Ohio. This class of some five dozen "typical" men and women was born at the beginning of World War II and now has become a collection of near sixty-year-olds who have lived through the last decades of national expansion, turmoil, glory, and soul-searching. Yours truly is president of this class and is in debt to nearly all of its members who have endured my frequent letters and calls, submit-

The 1959 class of Jackson-Milton High School at its 1989 class reunion.

ted to long taped interviews, and encouraged me to reflect with them on how their lives have developed and what our nation has become. When individuals are cited by first name only, they are members of this class whose life-journey information has been given willingly for use here. Last names are avoided to maintain their rightful privacy. Occasional illustrations of changing life in Northeast Ohio are offered to help understand this class and represent trends in the nation as a whole.

Parallel to this one high school class is the rather different journey of another, the Palisades High School class of 1965 from California. Occasional reference is made to this class, enabled by the studies of Michael Medved and David Wallechinsky. Frequently noted also across the decades in view is the "babyboomer" generation in general. It has been a population bulge that has impacted the six decades of the 1940s through the 1990s like a large egg that has traveled quite visibly down the whole length of the nation's snake-like life. See the bibliography at the end of this work for a selection of major published sources consulted. It is divided into four parts: general; religious; regional; and oral. History is looked at in both macro and micro ways, in its surface events and in its in-depth meanings. Questions are provided at the end of each chapter to help focus for the reader subjects worth careful thought alone or with a group.

Should the reader be looking for a book on recent American history that is without "bias," it hardly will be found here (or anywhere else!). There is truth in the common statements that where you stand depends on where you first sit and what you see depends on the lens through which you are looking. Even so, complete relativism is not necessarily the only option. Wisdom can emerge when the story of America's recent past is retold by a writer who both seeks to be open about his own bias and is willing to provide the reader with a range of the available alternatives. Since no recalling of history is a neutral exercise free of assumptions, this particular recalling admits to a religious bias. The "new world" colonies from their beginning were saturated with the general worldview and values of the Judeo-Christian tradition. In fact, Thomas Jefferson thought that the Great Seal of the U.S. should portray the children of Israel led by a pillar of light.[1] Likewise, the modern American quest for peace, justice, prosperity, and faith will be served best by a thoughtful and grateful return to key elements of this national foundation and treasure. The Christian faith, rich in Jewish tradition, has been a key player in the American journey and now finds itself on a demanding journey of its own as the nation shifts to much more of a pluralistic stance toward acceptable life values and honored faith communities. The concern found in these pages includes the need to raise serious questions about the appropriateness of aspects of this pluralistic shift.

Reviewing the history of the United States since the 1940s through the metaphor of ancient Jewish experience enables one to understand better the subtle shifting of a modern nation's foundations. It is an exercise in memory on behalf of a better future. The ancient Jewish paradigm of liberation and journey is helpful. To recall this biblical record is to learn of a people who found their way to Egypt, languished there in slavery, were liberated to inherit the "milk and honey" of a promised Canaan land, lost their way in the midst of riches and power, were overcome by fears and forces beyond their imagination, and finally sought to recover the heart of their heritage after the humbling heartbreak of forced exile in a hostile land. They always were to have been a "light to the nations," God's special servant people living in the full reality of this world without being merely more of it. They were and still are to be a special sign of hope, not just more of the common self-seeking, power-grabbing, and despair.

This Jewish memory lends understanding to the dilemma of American Christians who have lived in the final decades of the twentieth century and hope not to have lost their own way in the middle of much milk and honey, riches and power. There has been a shift from Christians being the dominant faith community of the American culture to their frequent anxiety at now being only one of several faith communities currently being tolerated by a

---

[1]Gilbert Chinard, *Thomas Jefferson: The Apostle of Americanism* (Ann Arbor, 1929, reprint 1957), 428.

proud, pluralistic, and quite secular society that has become less sure of its roots and more anxious about its identity and future.

I have written extensively in an earlier volume about the distinctive nature of the faith of Christians.[2] There I explained the two central tasks of Christian theology. One is to be securely rooted in the biblical tradition, to remember with care and appreciation, so that the faith remains true to the essence of its authoritative origins. The other is to be sensitively aware of the culture in which one now lives and with which one hopes to communicate effectively the good news confidently believed to be in Jesus Christ. My previous volume focused on the first task; this book focuses on the second. So the religious bias is here—and so are the competing alternatives. These pages are written by a social "conservative" with select "liberal" sympathies who continues to see relevant substance for the nation's life in the classic Judeo-Christian tradition. Maybe along the way the meaning of words like "conservative" and "liberal" will gain some definition. Whatever they mean, faith ought to lie at their base.

Faith in what is understood to constitute ultimate reality, personal happiness, and true community is foundational for any people. For a nation to be truly and effectively one in the midst of its diversity, some commonality of belief, some shared vision, is vital. Without it, people do "their own thing" and the nation's ideal of freedom becomes rootless, socially chaotic, even destructive. Without it, justice is little more than a balance of power. Prosperity becomes an all-consuming materialistic quest that finally is unable to bring fulfillment, even when seemingly achieved for a time. While hardly fashionable in the 1990s, Nicholas Wolterstorff is right. It is

> ...unacceptable to say that freedom, understood as self-determination, is the overarching goal of our social endeavors. We human beings are a mixture of good impulses and bad, amongst these latter being even on occasion the impulse to do what one knows one should not do. The Christian reads these impulses as having, at bottom, the character of sin: hostility toward God and one's fellows. But if this is true, then obviously the goal for each cannot be self-determination, maturation, removal of all external influence and all internal inhibition. Our sinful impulses ought not to be satisfied but to be conquered, inhibited—dominated, if you will. To acknowledge the presence of sin in our existence is to acknowledge that we have no choice but to engage in the difficult task of *normative reflection*, asking, among other questions, which impulses of the self are to be satisfied and which suppressed.[3]

---

[2]Barry Callen, *God As Loving Grace: The Biblically Revealed Nature and Work of God* (Nappanee, Ind.: Evangel Publishing House, 1996).

[3]Nicholas Wolterstorff, *Until Justice and Peace Embrace* (Grand Rapids: William Eerdmans, 1983), 52.

While this is a book of recent social history and not religious indoctrina-
tion, such issues as good and evil, right and wrong, fear and faith are not
avoided as though they do not exist or are not proper and crucial to acknowledge and address. An Appendix is included at the end to further focus the
current clash in America of moral conscience, the Supreme Court, democratic government intended to be by the people, and the Constitution of the
United States.

One Cultural Cycle

There is helpful perspective in the assumption that the lives of organizations and nations tend to run in broad cycles. While this is not to suggest
some social determinism, as though a *common* pattern is a *necessary* pattern,
to see the general cycling pattern helps understanding of the present and
anticipation of the likely character of the times just ahead. One recent reading of American history, for instance, judges that a cultural cycle lasts about
one long human lifetime and is composed of four phases or "turnings," each
lasting about twenty years.[4] The 1940s through the 1990s comprise the most
recent cycle. It is paralleled and illustrated by the human lifetimes of one generation that has lived and helped define this cycle—and is anxious to know
and be part of shaping what probably comes next. The 1959 high school classes were born in 1940-1941 and are nearing sixty years old as a millennium
concludes and a cultural cycle appears to be nearing its end (and another one
thus beginning).

What are the four phases or turnings of this American cycle that began in
the 1940s and likely will end soon after the 21st century has begun? Briefly
put, they are: (1) A high period of confident expansion as a new order takes
root; (2) An awakening characterized by spiritual exploration, experimentation, and rebellion against the now-established new order; (3) An unraveling
during which individualism triumphs over the now-crumbling national
institutions and traditional values; and finally (4) A cultural crisis, the fourth
turning, when some dramatic and even dangerous starting over is dared
(leading back to another new ordering of things). This is history's apparent
"seasonal rhythm," with about twenty years each of growth, maturation,
entropy, and finally a rebirth. As William Strauss and Neil Howe read
America's recent decades: (1) The "American High" was 1946-1964; (2) The
"Consciousness Revolution" was 1964-1984; (3) The "Culture Wars" is 1984-
2005?; with (4) The "Fourth Turning" then to follow—some new ordering of

---

[4]William Strauss and Neil Howe, *The Fourth Turning: An American Prophecy* (N.Y.:
Broadway Books, 1997).

Ideals of the United States of America

We the People of the United States, in Order to form a more perfect Union, establish Justice, insure domestic Tranquility, provide for the common defense, promote the general Welfare, and secure the Blessings of Liberty to ourselves and our Posterity, do ordain and establish this Constitution for the United States of America.

Preamble to the Constitution of the U.S.A.

I pledge allegiance to the United States of America, and to the Republic for which it stands; One nation, under God, indivisible, with liberty and justice for all.

U.S.A. Pledge of Allegiance

Fourscore and seven years ago, our fathers brought forth upon this continent a new nation, conceived in liberty and dedicated to the proposition that all men are created equal. Now we are engaged in a great civil war, testing whether that nation—or any nation, so conceived and so dedicated—can long endure. We are met on a great battlefield of that war. We are met to dedicate a portion of it as the final resting place of those who have given their lives that that nation might live. It is altogether fitting and proper that we should do this. But in a larger sense, we cannot dedicate, we cannot consecrate, we cannot hallow, this ground. The brave men, living and dead, who struggled here, have consecrated it, far above our power to add or to detract.

The world will very little note nor long remember what we say here; but it can never forget what they did here. It is for us, the living, rather, to be dedicated, here, to the unfinished work that they have thus far so nobly carried on. It is rather for us to be here dedicated to the great task remaining before us; that from these honored dead we take increased devotion to that cause for which they here gave the last full measure of devotion; that we here highly resolve that these dead shall not have died in vain; that the nation shall, under God, have a new birth of freedom, and that government of the people, by the people, for the people, shall not perish from the earth.

President Abraham Lincoln
Gettysburg Address
November 19, 1863

TABLE 1

things not yet clear.[5] To the degree that such a view of social change is generally accurate, it helps to emphasize the now common perception that the years immediately ahead for the United States are crucial ones. The nation must refind its "soul" and somehow reform the core beliefs and structures which make it one people in the midst of its now vast diversity. Failure in this task likely will lead to highly undesirable ends.

World War II (1941-1945 for the U.S.) was the traumatic and pivotal time that resulted in the political reorganization of the world into the way it would be until the collapse of the Berlin Wall in 1989 and the disintegration of the Soviet Union in 1991. The decade of the 1940s, then, is a good place to begin if one wants broad perspective on the 1990s and beyond. It was the launching of the new cycle, the beginning of a "new age." The last half of the twentieth century has been both frightening and exhilarating. In terms of war (a truly sad way to track human history), this observation is appropriate. Although the period between World Wars I and II was distressingly brief, the fifty-three years since World War II, while dominated for the most part by a "Cold War" and numerous regional conflicts, at least to date have avoided World War III and have sustained general economic stability. Within this broad stability, for the U.S. there has proceeded a "consciousness revolution" and now a period of "culture wars."

Our challenge in these pages is to follow the twisting path made by the United States since World War II as the country has sought to find the light of life, the way that leads a people to fulfillment and joy in this modern world of ours. The persisting subjects are *peace, justice, prosperity*, and *faith*. Among the ongoing struggles have been the society's need to define these subjects, discover their proper priorities and interrelationships, and, of course, to actually approach achieving their ideals in the realities of the nation's everyday life. How can world peace be maintained? What constitutes social justice? How is justice essential to peace? How important is prosperity to a nation's well-being? How can prosperity be assured—and what human cost can be tolerated in the process? What is left in this "postmodern" world in which one can believe for life's meaning, fulfillment, and final destiny? What is essential for effective national life? Does it any longer exist?

The "good life" is the typically stated goal of most Americans, with the right to its pursuit a fundamental of the Constitution of the nation (see Table 1). Too often in recent decades, however, this goal of "goodness" in life has been reduced to little more than the production and consumption of goods and services. Such reductionism flies in the face of the essence of the

---

[5]Strauss and Howe, 145-302.

nation's traditional heritage that goes well beyond a robust economy that allows most people to gorge on self-gratification. The really good life surely involves some proper combination of peace, justice, prosperity, and faith. Any one of these without the right relation to the others is shallow, shortlived, and usually brings human misery. Over the course of this nation's recent history, each of these has been pursued, perverted, undermined, idealized, idolized, and realized in part. This complex process has been especially rapid and dramatic in the most recent decades. If one thinks in terms of historical cycles, the U.S. is now in the turmoil time that soon will result in some fresh cultural face-off. Ours is now a world of rapid change that is looking for the foundations of a fresh stability.

The American Experiment: Unrestrained By Tradition

'Tis fine to see the Old World, and travel up and down
Among the famous palaces and cities of renown,
To admire the crumbly castles and the statues of the kings—
But now I think I've had enough of antiquated things....

I know that Europe's wonderful, yet something seems to lack;
The Past is too much with her, and the people looking back.
But the glory of the Present is to make the Future free—
We love our land for what she is and what she is to be.

Excerpts from *America For Me*
by Henry Van Dyke (1852-1933)

The American and Industrial Revolutions began about the same time. From the start Americans have rejoiced in and profited from technological change. For the most part, innovation was unrestrained by custom, tradition, or timidity. Ralph Waldo Emerson (1803-1882), a quintessential American, said: "I simply experiment, an endless seeker, with no Past at my back." The U.S. has been an "experiment." Its founders were trying to do something new under the sun.

Ralph Waldo Emerson (1803-1882)
Circles

TABLE 2

Amnesia Our Common Ailment

An attribute lacked by too many Americans these days, one more prominent in earlier decades when the class of 1959 was born and growing up in
the 1940s and 1950s, is a culture-shaping *social memory*. Voluntary amnesia
is a common ailment today, one in which some "modern" people even take
pride. Maybe this is because change has come so fast, so dramatically, especially since mid-century. The average person knows far more "facts" about the
world than Isaac Newton ever did, although that person may possess less
social vision, personal happiness, and awareness of overarching "truth."
Americans now play games that feature their recall of *trivia*; they may be playing such games because trivia is all they really know or even consider important. Maybe this collective forgetting has slowly eroded the nation's sense of
place, time, and meaning.[6] To forget is to lose identity and risk living in
ignorance of what is most important. Have Americans now reached the time
when they should abandon the cult of what-is-new-is-always-best, leave
behind the heresy that "history is bunk," and get themselves *located* again? Do
we remember the defining story of the United States? Does it need refreshed
and revised? Are we willing to get involved?

Much in the past obviously will not stand the test of the 21st century. Even
so, as C. S. Lewis is quoted as having said in 1949: "We need something to set
against the present, to remind us that the basic assumptions have been quite
different in different periods and that much which [now] seems certain. . .is
merely temporary fashion." To forget is to lose identity and maybe destiny. To
repeat thoughtlessly any past assumptions is to lose credibility in the eyes of
a questioning world. Nothing is acceptable other than what seriously and
simultaneously engages the hard questions of context, tradition, and transition.

The United States has had a series of crucial self-understandings that at
various times have guided its dreams, celebrations, and public policies.
Americans have seen themselves and their nation as the "new world," a fresh
Israel called from the old bondages of Europe to the freedom and challenge
of a new Canaan flowing with milk and honey. In the late nineteenth century,
Frederick Jackson Turner said that this marvelous land, stretching from sea
to sea, seemed to have unending frontiers that kept calling the people to new
beginnings and seemingly limitless opportunities and resources. There also
has been a recurrent sense of the nation's "manifest destiny" that has sent

---

[6]Studs Terkel, *The Great Divide: Second Thoughts on the American Dream* (N.Y.: Avon
Books, 1988), 1-2.

American diplomats, missionaries, and military forces across the continent and around the world to fulfill an apparently God-given duty to make things right for others.[7] More recently, the U.S. has been pictured as the worldwide savior of democracy and the only remaining "super-power" in the world.[8] These and other national self-images have helped make Americans what they are, or at least what they have understood that they are intended to be.

What is the United States as a nation, as a people in the world, maybe even *under God*? Obviously any answer requires complexity and a recognition that national identity always is a fluid thing. One crucial variable is knowing the primary characteristics of the current time of the nation since the nation inevitably is shaping its current reality in part by its responses to how it perceives that things now are. And how are things now? Catherine Keller recognizes the current "utopian burnout" of the United States and reports that it is left with a sad trail of "battered aspirations and obscene satisfactions." The people "strain after the glimmering of a decent collective life for the future." While realism forces doubt about the probability of its realization, Americans nonetheless "stubbornly, like parents, protect its possibility— against the odds, the trends, the projections, against our fears."[9] Thus, this present rehearsal of America's *Seeking the Light* begins with a chapter on the "shadows of war" (1940s) and ends cautiously with a chapter on the nation still in search of at least "a dim horizon" (1990s).

Somewhere In Ohio

An American literary classic by Sherwood Anderson was published in 1919, the year that many of the parents of the graduating classes of 1959 were just being born. Called simply *Winesburg, Ohio*,[10] this book opened a window on national life at the time by viewing at close range the complex and often troubled lives of the residents of a small Ohio town. Winesburg was a place of dreams, illusions, bursts of joy, and long trails of sadness. It was a revealing mirror of real life in thousands of towns that were different only by the

---

[7]See Conrad Cherry, *God's New Israel: Religious Interpretations of American Destiny* (Englewood Cliffs, N.J.: Prentice-Hall, 1971). The phrase "manifest destiny" apparently was first used in an editorial supporting the annexation of Texas by the U.S. (*United States Magazine and Democratic Review*, July/August, 1845).

[8]On the other hand, nations like Iran have thought of the U.S. as the "Great Satan."

[9]Catherine Keller, "Pneumatic Nudges: The Theology of Moltmann, Feminism, and the Future," in Miroslav Volf, et. al., eds., *The Future of Theology* (Grand Rapids: William Eerdmans, 1996), 142.

[10]Sherwood Anderson, *Winesburg, Ohio* (The Viking Press, 1919).

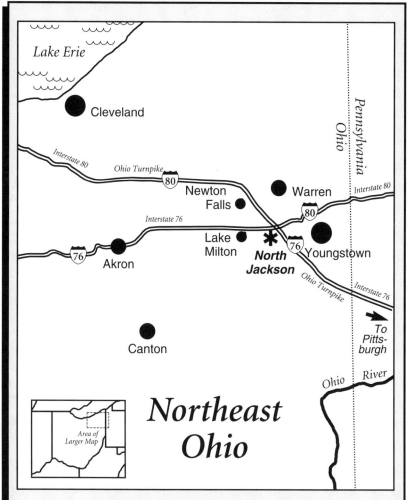

Lake Erie

Cleveland

Ohio

Pennsylvania

Interstate 80

Ohio Turnpike

80

Newton Falls

Warren

Interstate 80

80

Interstate 76

Lake Milton

North Jackson

76

Youngstown

Akron

Ohio Turnpike

Interstate 76

To Pittsburgh

Ohio River

Northeast Ohio

Area of Larger Map

North Jackson As the Crossroads

Numerous locations and establishments in the Northeast Ohio area speak of it as a crossroads of the nation. For instance, Canton, Ohio, near North Jackson, was chosen for the founding of the Hall of Fame of the National Football League in 1962. Two reasons for the choice were prominent. The league originated in Canton in 1920 and the site was within easy driving distance of several large cities and adjacent to several transcontinental highways. One of the nearby cities is Akron, known as the Rubber Capital of the world.

TABLE 3

incidentals of location and name. So it is with North Jackson, Ohio, the location of the high school which graduated the 1959 class highlighted here.[11] Where is North Jackson? It is somewhere in Ohio, not far from Youngstown, Warren, Akron, Cleveland, and Pittsburgh. In many ways it is all over Ohio and quite typical of thousands of other small towns in states nationwide. In fact, given its proximity to several major cities where many parents of class members worked in heavy industry or defense establishments, it may be typical of more than small towns.

Knowing about the last sixty years of the real life experiences and beliefs of this one high school class from this ordinary small town is to know much about a whole generation that has lived through changes unparalleled in human history. Sixty years is just long enough to perceive all four "turnings" of a typical cultural cycle, as well as the full lifespan of a human generation. To know these fifty-eight people is to know much about oneself as a contemporary American. Seen in this one mirror is a typical reflection of what has been—and might soon be—for most of us who call ourselves Americans.

Studying U.S. culture in part by tracking the life journeys of a high school class has been done at least once before, but with a significant difference. *What Really Happened to the Class of '65?*[12] was an interesting look ten years after graduation at a particular kind of class. It was from Palisades High School, a place for the privileged from suburban Los Angeles. This class made the cover of *Time* magazine since it was said to represent teenagers "on the fringe of a golden era," youth of the 1960s, "smarter, subtler, and more sophisticated kids" who then were graduating from a few experimental schools designed and funded for the elite.[13] This "elite" class is noted occasionally in the chapters that follow; but it is hardly the class of 1959 from Jackson-Milton High School. The little Ohio school was underfunded, much more rural-industrial than plush suburban, more blue-collar heartland than the exotic canyon overlooking the Pacific Ocean where Palisades High School was situated. Maybe, however, Jackson-Milton was and still is a better reflection of how it has been for most people in this country. Hardly "on the

---

[11]Part of the research for this book was a seven-year process (1992-1998) of contacting and interviewing in person most of the living members of the Jackson-Milton class of 1959, gathering their life stories, their current reflections on matters relevant to the nation and their own families, always seeking to learn about their memories of the past and their fears about and faith for the future.

[12]Michael Medved and David Wallechinsky, *What Really Happened to the Class of '65?* (N.Y.: Random House, 1976).

[13]"Students: On the Fringe of a Golden Era," *Time* magazine (January 29, 1965).

fringe" of anything elite and privileged, this school's class of 1959 probably has been somewhere in the middle of what has been typical reality for the vast majority of "ordinary" Americans.

In very practical and symbolic ways, this one small area of the country, Northeast Ohio, and this one high school class of 1959 that graduated from Jackson-Milton some forty years ago, may be a useful means of gaining some wisdom. In a way, the members of this class *are* us all. We learn best by sampling life as it actually has been experienced in the harsh and sometimes wonderful realities of this dramatically changing world. The intent here, of course, is much more than following the trail of one high school class in the midst of America's turbulent life. Primarily it is to remember the experience of a whole nation since World War II and to find some broad perspective, to discover a little wisdom, to distill from the morass of these volatile times some shreds of enduring meaning—maybe even a modest level of hope and faith for the future, for that crucial cultural turning that probably is just around the corner.

The Theme of Light

Why use the theme of *light* as the organizational principle of this book? One reason is that light has become a common metaphor for eras of human history. Note the popular designation "Dark Ages" that was followed by the centuries of "Enlightenment" that now appear to be fading into some new darkness.[14] Light serves well to picture the most recent decades of both American and world history. Despite dramatic technological developments, these years have been dimmed by the persistent shadows of prejudice and violence. The stumbling still goes on in the perennial human search for the light that can unveil true wisdom and bring love and justice into human relationships. What, for instance, might be the continuing relevance of Elie Wiesel's sobering autobiographical account titled *Night*?[15] What of this dramatic statement from the ancient world? "I *am* the light of the world" (spoken by Jesus of himself, John 9:5).

---

[14]I offer a brief explanation of the Enlightenment worldview and the "postmodern" mentality rapidly replacing it in the 1980s and 1990s (see Barry Callen, *God As Loving Grace*, Evangel Publishing House, 1996, 44-50). Also see Gene Edward Veith, Jr., *Postmodern Times: A Christian Guide to Contemporary Thought and Culture* (Wheaton, Ill.: Crossway Books, 1994).

[15]Elie Wiesel, *Night*, 1960, is a perennial bestseller, a terrifying book about a young Jew caught in the horrors of Nazi Germany. The author implies that, in the concentration camps along with the Jews, death also came to faith and hope, especially hope as conceived for humankind in the "enlightened" West of the twentieth century.

The following pages trace the American experience since the 1940s. Once this story is told, it may be that the reader will come to share the writer's general conclusion, namely that humanity is at a crossroads as the twentieth century ends. Civilizations appear to follow cycles of birth and decay. The seasons of recent American history have seemed to move from the warm birthing spring of the late 1940s to the winter's chill of cultural death being experienced by so many in the late 1990s. The length of days and the brightness of the light were greater when the members of J-M class of 1959 were children than now when they are grandparents. The 1940s saw the deep shadows of world war, the 1950s the bright lights of national expansion in a time of a shallow peace, the 1960s the glare of many revolutionary fires, the 1970s the near demise of classic illuminations, the 1980s the search for any new enlightenment amid the greedy flow of wealth, and the 1990s the deepening but fragile hope that some horizon, still seen only dimly, now will bring the rise of a sun that can sustain humankind into the twenty-first century.

Modern American history has been a complex and difficult path. The journey is far from over, and its end is not guaranteed to be positive. We join the journey in these pages, recalling cautiously what George Bush announced about the twentieth century to the Republican National Convention in 1988: "This has been called the *American* century because in it we were the dominant force for good in the world. We saved Europe, cured polio, we went to the moon, and lit the world with our culture." Yes, we did! But the culture that has illumined the world has not always brought a welcome light. The journey, proud but not untarnished, is yet unfinished.

Chapter One

At the Crossroads

———

A massive intellectual revolution is taking place that is
perhaps as great as that which marked off the
modern world from the Middle Ages.[1]

———

I am of the opinion that my life belongs to the whole
community and, as long as I live, it is my privilege to do
for it what I can.... Life is no brief candle for me. It is
sort of a splendid torch which I have got hold of for
a moment and I want to make it burn as brightly
as possible before handing it on to future generations.[2]

———

The heritage of so many Americans makes looking at the past both essential and problematic. The United States is an immigrant society and has been since the beginnings of its European settlement in the late sixteenth century (see Table 4). This fact of immigration lies behind America's occasional worship of origins, its intense piety about the past which often combines in a perplexing way with its frequent readiness to ignore history's lessons and focus only on the present and future. The United States can be defined as a people idealizing a distant yesterday while always championing the central theme of progress and newness.[3]

The end of the twentieth century is a time when newness is everywhere and remembering the right things may be urgently needed if justice and peace are to be known in a nation with meaningful roots in the past and viable visions for the future. The whole world now seems to be shifting.

---

[1]Diogenes Allen, *Christian Belief in a Postmodern World* (Louisville, Ky.: Westminster/John Knox Press, 1989), 2.

[2]George Bernard Shaw, quoted in Studs Terkel, *Coming of Age: The Story of Our Century by Those Who've Lived It* (N.Y.: The New Press, 1995), xiii.

[3]See, e.g., Richard Hughes and C. Leonard Allen, *Illusions of Innocence: Protestant Primitivism in America*, 1630-1875 (Chicago: University of Chicago Press, 1988).

This apparent earthquake of human experience is exciting, confusing, often frightening and dangerous. There is much despair in today's world and at least a few shafts of light that are managing to keep hope alive. The whole human family seems to be at a crossroads. Brian Mulroney, then Prime Minister of Canada, put it this way as the decade of the 1990s opened: "The pace

Proud Land of Immigrants

More people have immigrated to the United States than to any other nation in history. Millions of immigrants (mostly European) entered the United States through New York Harbor in the nineteenth and early twentieth centuries, all being thrilled by the first sight of the Statue of Liberty (erected in 1886). Placed on its pedestal in 1903 were these soon famous and beloved *New Colossus* words of Emma Lazarus written in 1883:

> Not like the brazen giant of Greek fame,
> With conquering limbs astride from land to land;
> Here at our sea-washed, sunset gates shall stand
> A mighty woman with a torch, whose flame
> Is the imprisoned lightening, and her name
> Mother of Exiles. From her beacon-hand
> Glows worldwide welcome; her mild eyes command
> The air-bridged harbor that twin cities frame.

> Give me your tired, your poor, your huddled masses yearning to breathe free, The wretched refuse of your teeming shore, Send these, the tempest-tossed to me: I lift my lamp beside the golden door.

Sample Numbers of Immigrants to the United States

	Total Number	Rate*
1881 to 1890	5,247,000	9.2
1891 to 1900	3,688,000	5.3
1901 to 1910	8,795,000	10.4
1911 to 1920	5,736,000	5.7
1921 to 1930	4,107,000	3.5

Annual rate of immigrants per 1,000 of U.S. population at the time.

In these five decades, a high percentage of all immigrants came from Great Britain and countries on the European continent. By comparison, in the decade 1981-1990, the total of immigrants was about 7,340,000, with about 42.6% coming from North America (especially Mexico), 38.4% from Asia, and only 9.6% from Europe.

TABLE 4

*European immigrants see
the Statue of Liberty as
they arrive at Ellis Island
in New York harbor.*

of change in international politics is straining mankind's capabilities of assimilation and assessment."[4] This still is true in other areas of human experience. Where do we go from here? Maybe the prior question is, How did we get here in the first place? Now is a time for a careful balancing of the paradox of past and future. America's journey, its quest for peace, prosperity, justice, and faith, appears to be at a crucial crossroads.

Past and Future

In the United States of the nineteenth century, landscape was almost a national religious symbol. The painter Albert Bierstadt (1830-1902) built a successful career on the belief that the landscapes west of the Missouri River made America unique among the nations. His style dramatized a spectacle of grandeur. In his 1867 painting *Emigrants Crossing the Plains*, one sees displayed lavishly on canvas the covered wagons roll forward into a sunset so wonderful that surely God is beckoning them on to a national greatness never known to humans before. Their difficult trail is covered in the golden glow of one day ending and a brighter one surely yet to dawn. That was the "manifest destiny" of the nineteenth century. But what of the volatile time when the twenty-first century dawns? What frontiers are left? Where does God now beckon? Is belief in God basic or optional? What constitutes national greatness? As we try to recall, what do we foresee? How are looking back and looking ahead best connected?

---

[4]Brian Mulroney, "The Future Has Started," in *Britannica Book of the Year: 1990.*

While things shake and shift, it certainly can be argued that we humans are at a crucial point of major cultural change. The twentieth century is ending. What path will a new century take? Memory is an essential component of any thoughtful assessment and projection. All wheels do not need to be reinvented, nor do already failed experiments need to be tried again. Some

---

Religion And American Life

As to religion, I hold it to be the indispensable duty of all government to protect all conscientious professors thereof, and I know of no other business which government has to do therewith.... For myself, I fully and conscientiously believe that it is the will of the Almighty that there should be diversity of religious opinions among us. It affords a larger field for our Christian kindness.... On this liberal principle I look on the various denominations among us to be like children of the same family, differing only in what are called their Christian names.

Thomas Paine, *Common Sense*, 1776

Of all the dispositions and habits which lead to political prosperity, religion and morality are indispensable supports. In vain would that man claim the tribute of patriotism who should labor to subvert these great pillars of human happiness—these firmest props of the duties of men and citizens. The mere politician, equally with the pious man, ought to respect and to cherish them. A volume could not trace all their connections with private and public felicity. Let it simply be asked, Where is the security for property, for reputation, for life, if the sense of religious obligation desert the oaths which are the instruments of investigation in courts of justice? And let us with caution indulge the supposition that morality can be maintained without religion. Whatever may be conceded to the influence of refined education on minds of peculiar structure, reason and experience both forbid us to expect that national morality can prevail in exclusion of religious principle.

President George Washington, *Farewell Address*, 1796

I have ever judged of the religion of others by their lives.... It is in our lives, and not from our words, that our religion must be read. By the same test the world must judge me. But this does not satisfy the priesthood. They must have a positive, a declared assent to all their interested absurdities. My opinion is that there would never have been an infidel, if there had never been a priest. The artificial structures they have built on the purest of all moral systems, for the purpose of deriving from it pence and power, revolt those who think for themselves, and who read in that system only what is really there.

President Thomas Jefferson, in a letter to Mrs. M. Harrison Smith
August 6, 1816

TABLE 5

sources of wisdom for personal and social life have served well and probably can continue to do so. Some light, once known to be light, might well continue to be light. Some shadows, once known to be nothing but shadows, will continue to dim our view of the light and, if allowed, will continue to lead us even closer to an intolerable darkness. Much is new; but not all has changed. Human aspirations for peace, justice, prosperity, and faith are perennial, although how to define and reach these lofty goals now present fresh challenges.

To recall with care the most recent six decades of American history is a sobering task. Why even try? One reason is that this nation appears to be at a crossroads where perspective is especially crucial. Traditional values are being tossed aside. Assumptions about living standards are being revised forcibly as companies "downsize" and computerize. The future seems so uncertain, so fluid, so frightening, so new and unknown, so full of possibility. The shadows of doubt and the acids of cynicism are gathering fast. There often are wide differences between the thinking and acting of "Depression Babies" and "Baby boomers." It is an ideal time to remember and maybe even learn together. One lesson already being learned is that, as the twenty-first century dawns, a particular way of thinking is tending to lose its grip on Western cultures.

Diogenes Allen reports that a "massive intellectual revolution" is taking place, one that perhaps is "as great as that which marked off the modern world from the Middle Ages."[5] Our "modern age," the one now coming to a close, may be said to have lasted 200 years, from the fall of the Bastille in 1789 to the fall of the Berlin Wall in 1989.[6] The French Revolution in 1789 keyed the launching of the "Enlightenment." Longstanding feudal loyalties and spiritual hierarchies were guillotined. The "rights of man" prevailed and human reason was elevated, sometimes to the functional position of God. Then, 200 years later in 1989, the collapsing of the Soviet Union signaled the ending in failure of this grand and pretentious experiment in human idealism and arrogance. Reality turns out to be more complex than the logical categories available to human rationality. Intellectual know-how and good intentions have not delivered the good life to most of the world's population. So now the door is again open for exercising faith in something beyond human greed and unwarranted self-confidence. We humans are at a crossroads, the changing of eras, where fresh light is needed. The search is on.

---

[5]Diogenes Allen, 2.

[6]Thomas Oden, *Two Worlds: Notes on the Death of Modernity in America and Russia* (Downers Grove, Ill.: InterVarsity Press, 1992), 32.

George Washington, first president of the U.S., insisted that "reason and experience both forbid us to expect that national morality can prevail in exclusion of religious principle" (see Table 5 and Appendix). Even so, since the nation's beginning there have been two opposing ideals of the nation's identity and purpose. One has been called the "Orthodox Vision" and the other the "Progressivist Vision." James Hunter refers to the first of these "mythic origins of the republic" as a "cultural conservatism" represented today by Evangelical Christians and others, but with a long history from John Adams and Patrick Henry to the fiction of Herman Melville, the poetry of Walt Whitman, the rhetoric of William Jennings Bryan, and the political oratory of presidents Abraham Lincoln and Woodrow Wilson.[7] This vision sees America as the product of divine plan and action. Biblical principles form its very fabric.[8] America was to be a nation of exemplary obedience to God's laws, an elect people with a divinely-given role in the world.

The other vision rarely relies on any assumption of the divine for identifying the nation's origin or nature. The "Progressivist" approach follows the view of Henry Steele Commager that the American mind from the outset has been pragmatic, optimistic, and secular.[9] Likewise, many now argue that the core American mentality is by nature and tradition skeptical, irreverent, pluralistic, and relativistic. Thus, rather than assuming that biblical laws formed the basis of the U.S. Constitution and Bill of Rights, the nation's founders are thought to have created a "living Constitution" that cannot be straightjacketed by any assumptions of a preindustrialized society or religious tradition. The nation's central documents (or at least their interpretation and application) are to change as the society changes. Fundamental among this people's shared values is a celebration of diversity and a healthy respect for the belief or non-belief of all other citizens. This vision of the nation, enormously influential in U.S. history, is rooted in sophistic and hedonistic strands of ancient Greek philosophy, made more contemporary by Thomas Hobbes and John Locke. Sometimes called "utilitarian individualism,"[10] its central under-

---

[7]James Hunter, *Culture Wars: The Struggle To Define America* (N.Y.: BasicBooks, HarperCollins, 1991), 109-116.

[8]See, e.g., *Tim LaHaye, The Battle for the Mind* (Old Tappan, N.J.: Fleming Revell Co., 1980). LaHaye's historic assertion is set in the context of his current concern that "humanism," the arrogant wisdom of humans, now controls the United States.

[9]Henry Steele Commager, *The American Mind: An Interpretation of American Thought and Character Since the 1880s* (New Haven: Yale University Press, 1950).

[10]See Robert Bellah and Phillip Hammond, *Varieties of Civil Religion* (N.Y.: Harper & Row, 1980), 169.

standing of proper human motivation focuses on a maximization of self-interest.

From the country's beginning, and especially as the twentieth century ends, these two competing visions or philosophies of America's public life have created a sometimes subtle and sometimes very open culture war. The more "humanistic" vision has gained strength in recent decades. Today, reason too often is being replaced by only emotion, and morality by an all-out relativism. Tolerance is heralded as the great virtue. Truth is seen as merely what a people make it to be and what works for them. Instead of reestablishing older faith systems like Judaism and Christianity as significant in defining the U.S., "postmodern" societies are seeking to "deconstruct" and operate on a minimum of assumptions. This day may be new, but the struggle is old. Richard Neuhaus explains with this simple parable:

> Two ships, both without a compass, are drifting on a night as dark as pitch. The one captain is resigned to having lost his way. The other searches, perhaps desperately, for a glimpse of the North Star. The second is looking for an authoritative point of reference, while the first assumes there is none. The merits of their behavior cannot be determined by reference to different personality types. One is not autonomous and mature while the other is dependent and authoritarian. Our judgment of their different attitudes depends on whether we believe that, in fact, there is such a star that can provide an authoritative point of reference and direction.[11]

Numerous Americans have believed in such a star ever since the early Puritans first moved into New England (1630). The Puritans implanted a sturdy work ethic and belief in the primacy of religion. They featured a focus on newness, living in expectation of something very big yet arising—Christ's reign on earth, the millennium. In fact, "newness was to Americans what antiquity was to Europeans—a sign of integrity, the mark of a special relationship to history and to God. It affirmed the idea of American exceptionalism."[12] Here was a kind of newness that grew from the sturdy soil of a believing community.

It may not be fashionable, but in these pages it nonetheless is assumed that belief should persist both in a "North Star" and in the importance of a nation not being captured by the dominance of any present context or by the constant claims that immediacy is singularly relevant, even apart from

[11]Richard Neuhaus, *The Naked Public Square: Religion and Democracy in America* (Grand Rapids: William Eerdmans, 1984), 18.

[12]*Time* magazine (Spring 1997), special issue on "American Visions," 76.

historical perspective. In Christian perspective, "God is the Power of the Future who lovingly holds close to himself every past moment as he leads us through the present to the promise of what is to be."[13] If "politics" is the pattern of how a people chooses to function together, then politics is "most importantly a function of culture, and at the heart of culture is religion, whether or not it is called by that name…. The secular wisdom can put up with religion that is private, individualistic, subjective. Such religion is an idiosyncrasy in which almost any number can indulge without impinging upon 'the authentically political.'"[14] But faith worthy of its name embraces and directs all of life, including the believer's chosen role in public life.[15]

The parents of the high school classes of 1959 were children in the "roaring" twenties just following World War I and then faced young adulthood in the middle of the Great Depression of the 1930s. Their children were born at the beginning of World War II, were children in the quiet and playful 1950s, and then faced young adulthood in the middle of another national travail, the civil rights and Vietnam struggles of the 1960s and 1970s that stressed the very soul of the nation. As the parents of the classes of 1959 began to die in the 1970s and 1980s, so these class members are now "maturing" themselves as the 1990s and the millennium come to a close. Surely in all this living, dying, and remembering there is some crucial wisdom for the next generations. These pages hope to make at least a modest contribution to such wisdom.

Everysmalltown, U.S.A.

All books start somewhere. This one started in a reflective discussion among about sixty of us in 1994. The group was comprised of members and spouses of the Jackson-Milton High School class of 1959 who had gathered for a class reunion thirty-five years after graduation. We were sitting in a big circle in the upstairs banquet room of Wranglers Olde Country Restaurant in North Jackson, Ohio. Our reunion dinner was over and the group picture already had been taken. The "old" high school building sat just two blocks away, looking about the same as when we roamed its halls and filled its classrooms in our much younger days decades earlier. For many who had

---

[13]Neuhaus, 3.

[14]Ibid., 190.

[15]A strong impulse in several countries today is toward one faith tradition, frequently Islam, dictating all of private and public life, even by use of violence if necessary (e.g., Iran). Christians in Europe often did much the same in earlier centuries (the crusades and Inquisition). Sturdy conviction can lead to very negative results when its perspectives are forced on non-believers. Such forcing is not espoused here.

The Jackson-Milton high school about 1960.

traveled from far away to be present at this nostalgic gathering, the school was very familiar—and yet a little different than we remembered. Some classmates certainly were different!

This group of former school friends (some of whom had not seen each other since 1959) were both ordinary and extraordinary in each other's eyes. Their significance for the relatively few people immediately involved was beyond question. For countless others whom they represent, others who have similar memories and meanings, they are also significant. Their lives and the life of the nation in which they have lived tell a story worth everyone remembering. Often good perspective on the whole comes from the careful understanding of a sample. We who sat in that 1994 circle are typical enough to represent significant perspective for others. We are the Jackson-Milton High School class of 1959, a group of ordinary Americans born as the United States was entering World War II and now proud grandparents and reflective "seniors" as this country and the world enter a new century.

Today North Jackson, Ohio, is a small community of about one thousand people clustered around the crossing of Route 45 (north/south) and Mahoning Avenue (Route 18, west/east). It sits about eleven miles west of Youngstown, nine miles south of Warren, and five miles east of Lake Milton. The surroundings appear primarily agricultural, but the immediate area is heavily industrialized. At least in general, things appear to have changed little since 1959. The town is in Jackson Township, named in honor of Andrew Jackson. It is part of the old "Western Reserve" of the state of Connecticut. The initial charter had given Connecticut residents claim to a strip of land as wide as that

The intersection of Routes 18 and 45 in North Jackson, Ohio, about 1960.

state (fifty miles) and stretching westward to the Pacific Ocean! By the 1780s, when the sheer magnitude of this land claim was known and then negotiated, Pennsylvania had gained legal claim to its present share of the strip and all else went to the federal government—except for some 3.5 million acres around present-day Cleveland, Ohio.

North Jackson lay in this remaining "reserve" of Connecticut. The township of Jackson thus came to combine the lure of the western frontier and the traditionalism of the original American colonies. It is bounded on the north by Lordstown, on the east by Austintown, on the south by Berlin, and on the west by Milton. When a history of the area was published in 1882, there was only one village in the township. Its first settlers were nearly all Scotch-Irish who were migrating westward from Pennsylvania.[16] Even though situated in the center of the township, the village's post office was called "North" Jackson to distinguish it from the many Jacksons in the nation. While the village never has gained any particular recognition by the nation at large, the 1959 class from its high school now has a voice worthy of some hearing.

---

[16]*History of Trumbull and Mahoning Counties*, vol. 2 (Cleveland: H. Z. Williams & Brothers, 1882), 146-147. Also see John R. Balog, with editor Mary Ann Abey, *The History of Jackson Township* (Boardman, Ohio: Pub. privately, 1992).

John Young, a land speculator from New York, came in 1797 to facilitate the sale of land to farmers who were moving west. He had no idea that, in laying out "Youngstown" on the flat lands on the north bank of the Mahoning River, he was founding the heart of what eventually would be one of the great industrial centers of the world. There could not have been a better location. It indeed was a crossroads between the old world and the new, and between a rural existence and the coming urbanization and industrialization of the modern world. Youngstown would become a center of culture that would actively influence the whole nation.

During the nineteenth century the McGuffey Readers, written in the Youngstown area, taught millions of young Americans how to read. William McKinley, the conservative Republican elected president of the United States in 1896, grew up in nearby Niles. The beloved Christian hymn "The Old Rugged Cross" originated in the Youngstown area early in the twentieth century. On the more uncomfortable side, Youngstown has scored certain national firsts about which some are proud and others are ashamed. They at least show that Youngstown is where much of the action has been in America's heartland. The firsts include:

> ...the first strike by nurses in the country, and the first strike by teachers; the first school system in the nation to close due to a lack of money; during the 1950s, number one in gangland car bombings, and today [1981], first in the number of unsolved gangland murders; and the largest plant closing in the nation's history....[17]

Literature, politics, labor justice, crime, and religion, all key aspects of contemporary human life, have flourished in this locale. Here is a good place to test the changing meanings and partial realizations of national ideals like peace, justice, prosperity, and faith.

More recently, in 1995 Bruce Springsteen began singing a sad song that he simply called "Youngstown." It is a mournful ballad about one key city that made the cannon balls to help the Union win the Civil War and rolled out massive quantities of steel that later helped make the difference in America's more recent wars. But when the GIs returned home to Youngstown from World War II, what Hitler couldn't destroy—national purpose and pride—some local residents found dying of its own accord. Americans had been helped to be rich and victorious by Youngstown's great productivity, but they were beginning to grow cynical about some of the nation's new directions. Springsteen's musical lament reads: "We sent our sons to Korea and Vietnam, Now we're wondering what they were dyin' for." Youngstown is ide-

---

[17]"Another Youngstown First," *Warren Tribune*, Nov. 9, 1981.

alized here as the symbol of the nation's industrialized might, with "smoke-stacks reachin' like the arms of God, Into a beautiful sky of soot and clay." Times now were changing, however, and the sad singer is "sinkin' down" in today's Youngstown, drained by the greedy and ungrateful. He claims in wistful memory that, in order to feel at home after death, he hopes the devil will come and take him "To stand in the fiery furnaces of hell." Yes, Youngstown tells—and really is—the story of the nation, conquering the world and struggling to save its own soul.

The Youngstown area, including the modest agricultural town of North Jackson lying just to the west of the city, has been a national crossroads. The crossing, however, is to be defined in geographic as well as cultural terms. The Mahoning River is part of the Mahoning-Shenago River system that drains south into the nearby Ohio River. In the early 1800s it also was connected by a portage to the Cuyahoga River that flowed north into Lake Erie. The site of John Young's new town (Youngstown) was about equidistant from Cleveland on Lake Erie to the northwest (at the mouth of the Cuyahoga) and Pittsburgh to the southeast (at the headwaters of the Ohio River). By 1839 Youngstown was linked to a growing canal system giving it direct water access to Lake Erie northward and to the Ohio River southward. Following the Civil War, Youngstown also became a major railroad city. Soon this town of Young's and its immediate vicinity would be known by the nation as the "Steel Valley" or just "The Valley." When the St. Lawrence Seaway opened for ocean-going traffic in 1959, the Northeast Ohio area was even a new American "seacoast" facing the whole world.

Ohio auto license plates for 1997 featured the state slogan "The Heart of It All!" That is certainly how it was earlier in American history. As the premier route to the great West, the Ohio River was the nation's first "interstate high-way," providing an avenue for settlement and development. From Pittsburgh, where the Allegheny and Monongahela Rivers merge to form the Ohio, it flows west for nearly one thousand miles to Cairo, Illinois, then turns south as the Mississippi River to go all the way to the Gulf of Mexico. Throughout the twentieth century, steel factories and other industries powered by coal mined from the Ohio Basin have contributed mightily to U.S. strength as a world power. Three-fourths of the nation's coal has come from the Ohio Valley.[18]

---

[18]See Walter Havighurst, *River to the West: Three Centuries of the Ohio* (N.Y.: G. P. Putnam's Sons, 1970) and Robert Reid, ed., *Always a River: The Ohio River and the American Experience* (Bloomington: Indiana University Press, 1991).

With these natural resources, transportation routes, and industrious immigrant populations, the Pittsburgh-Youngstown region grew up as "an American counterpart to the Ruhr Valley in Germany."[19] In 1900 local investors created Youngstown Iron Sheet and Tube Company (later dropping the "Iron"), a company which grew rapidly into the largest locally owned steel company in the United States. People from many countries, particularly from eastern and southern Europe, flooded "the Valley" to provide labor for this and a series of other large steel mills and related industries. They joined earlier immigrants from Wales, Ireland, and Germany, and the even earlier colonial settlers from Connecticut. Later the area would experience an influx of African Americans, Puerto Ricans, and others. Over several generations, then, the Mahoning Valley became an important crossroads of the nation and even the world.[20]

In contrast to Pittsburgh, Cleveland, and Chicago, Youngstown was hampered by its relatively limited water supply that came principally from the Mahoning River. Water was crucial for cooling and dumping at the many mills, and for the domestic use of a rapidly growing population. In addition, spring floods and dry summers occasionally affected adversely vital production schedules at the big plants. Following the particularly severe flood of March 1913, a natural disaster that did significant damage in Youngstown itself, the public came to appreciate the need for increasing and controlling the water of the Mahoning River. By 1916, work finally was progressing on the building of a new dam in Milton Township to form Lake Milton on the upper Mahoning.[21] This lovely lake, about one by three miles in size, was for flood control and also would serve as a recreational outlet for the wealthy citizens of Youngstown and other area cities.

By the end of World War I, then, with local steel production booming, there was situated immediately to the west of Youngstown the little town of North Jackson, with the beautiful new Lake Milton just five miles to its west. Local residents sometimes call North Jackson "The Crossroads" since supposedly it sits halfway between Chicago and New York City. It was an agri-

---

[19]Alvin Skardon, *Steel Valley University: The Origin of Youngstown State* (Youngstown: Youngstown State University, 1983), 1.

[20]Nearby, of course, were Akron, rubber capital of the world, as well as Cleveland and Pittsburgh, major industrial and transportation centers of the nation.

[21]North Jackson soon would be flanked by reservoirs designed for flood control and to provide water for the area industries. While Lake Milton lies a few miles to its west, just to its east toward Youngstown also now lies Meander Reservoir. For the story of its construction in 1928-32, see John Balog, *The History of Jackson Township*, 63-70.

cultural and now recreational fringe of Youngstown. One publisher referred to it as "Everysmalltown, U.S.A."[22] This town, really little more than an enlarged crossingpoint of two state highways, is now surrounded by farms and factories, recreational lakes and super highways.

Of particular significance is the resort lake called Lake Milton. It lies five miles west of North Jackson and seventeen miles west of Youngstown. Since its creation in 1915-17, it has been a playground for many Youngstown residents and home to a few hundred people (including Barry who grew up on the lake's western shore in the tiny Village of Craig Beach and became president of the J-M class of 1959). In recent decades the high school located in North Jackson has been Jackson-Milton High School, serving students from both communities and the many farms between.[23] This high school represents well the complex reality that now is the United States. It is in the industrial heartland, a part of the nation's breadbasket, a longtime center for new immigrants from many lands, and most recently a struggling part of the great "rust bowl." Summarizes a recently published history of Youngstown and Mahoning County (in which both North Jackson and Lake Milton lie):

> From salt licks to shopping malls, the history of the city and county have typified the passage of this area from wilderness to agricultural settlement, from canal town to iron manufacturer, from steel producer to post-industrial urban center.[24]

The local population certainly is a diverse one, mirroring the increasing ethnic diversity and cultural pluralism of our present times. To be specific:

> The mining of coal and the making of iron in the nineteenth century attracted northern Europeans, while the steel industry of the twentieth century added those of southern and eastern Europe along with African

---

[22]See Dominic Billett, *20 Years at the Crossroads* (N.Y.: Carlton Press, 1973). Billett was a barber in North Jackson, Ohio, for two decades beginning in 1952, thus including all the high school years of the Jackson-Milton High School class of 1959.

[23]The joint Jackson-Milton Local School District was formed in 1935-36, in part to attract additional support from the state in economically very difficult times. Separate elementary schools were maintained in the two townships, but high school students were centralized in the building in North Jackson. It was first built in 1913, with additions in 1924 and 1935 (to accommodate the merger). Another addition was built in 1950, with a fine new gymnasium finished in 1954—just before the arrival of the class of 1959. In 1957-58 the school enrollment in North Jackson (grades 7-12) had swelled to 1,023.

[24]Frederick Blue, et. al., *Mahoning Memories: A History of Youngstown and Mahoning County* (Virginia Beach, Va.: The Donning Company Publishers, with the Mahoning Valley Historical Society, 1995), 7.

Americans from other parts of the United States. In recent years Arab, Asian, and Hispanic migrants have joined these earlier settlers.[25]

A high school class with roots in this place, roots that now have spread across the nation and also now stretch across the last half of the twentieth century, surely reflects much of what the nation has been and done over these very eventful decades. This class is urban and industrial Youngstown, rural and suburban North Jackson, and recreational Lake Milton. The Jackson-Milton graduating class of 1959 is an important window on our world.

A Window on the World

That 1994 reunion dinner in North Jackson ended with an hour of all the people sitting in a big circle of chairs sharing in conversation that was sometimes hilarious and sometimes quietly reflective. After all, the J-M class of 1959 had come to remember and get reacquainted after thirty-five years.[26] By then, there are many derailed dreams in our worlds, youthful visions that never made it to reality. High school yearbooks often list one dream for each new graduate. But what about thirty-five years later? Some dreams have come true; many have not; some should not, could not, still might. Something tends to happen to many of us along the way. One writer reports: "Convictions to change the world downgrade to commitments to pay the bills. Rather than make a difference, we make a salary. Rather than look forward, we look back. Rather than look outward, we look inward. And we don't like what we see."[27] It is easy to settle for the mediocre as the life-cycle of an individual or a nation ages. Life often pushes people quietly downward. Was this true of this class?

We went around the big circle. As class president, Barry asked each member of the class to share a brief self-introduction—necessary since in many cases hair had changed colors or fallen out, one hundred pounds had become two hundred (or the reverse), spouses had changed, and memories needed to be refreshed. It was fun to listen to good friends from the past bring the rest up-to-date. Betty recalled especially enjoying the question Mike posed before his personal comments— "What am I doing here with all these old people!?" A few of the people were shy, not knowing exactly what to say. Some comments brought outbursts of laughter or an "I remember when you..." tossed

---

[25]Ibid.

[26]There had been only two previous reunions of this class, at the eighteenth and the twenty-ninth years.

[27]Max Lucado, *When God Whispers Your Name* (Dallas: Word Publishing, 1994), 14.

The 1994 reunion of some members of the Jackson-Milton class of 1959.

in from somewhere around the big circle. It was hard to stay on any particular subject, but nobody cared since the real subject was just being together again. What could be learned from the many roads these lives had taken? They had been so together in the late 1950s, and so apart ever since. Would being together again, even just briefly, shed light on anything of importance? Could remembering yield a little wisdom for the rest of this life and even beyond?

Barry teased that maybe it was time to have a little fun by being belatedly honest. If there had been secret crushes between classmates decades earlier, attractions unvoiced and long gone, now was the time to break the news in front of the whole class. One woman glanced toward a bearded man across the circle and said that she had something to confess. She used to think he was so handsome. His wife seemed amused, he looked a little mystified, and everyone roared. Then it happened. Virginia got serious. Few had any idea of the family burdens Virginia was carrying (a new grandmother in a sad set of circumstances related to her daughter). She observed that life is precious and obviously moving on for us. Some others picked up on her more somber mood and spoke quite candidly of the economic anxiety caused by their employment instability, usually the result of numerous companies "downsizing" and repositioning themselves in the rapidly changing marketplace of the 1990s. Several were physically disabled. Others were thinking about when they would retire and how they could manage to afford it. The group decided to stand in a circle of silence as the names of our four already deceased classmates were read aloud. One, Dallas, had died suddenly just two months before this reunion. He had never had a sick day in his life, it was said. He just collapsed and it was over. In 1994, life surely was getting more serious for the J-M class of 1959.

No longer was idealism untested or death only an abstract and distant reality. Most members already had lost one if not both parents. The end could come quickly for anyone now that each was pushing senior citizen status. In fact, Virginia, who had set the serious tone for the evening, would herself, with no warning, collapse and die before that year was out. She became number five in the class archives of precious memories. A lot of life already had been seen. There now was known to be much more to life than fun and games, like the teenage pranks and teachers' quirks that were so much fun to recall on this special reunion day. So an idea got on the floor, the one that led to this book.

While about America in general, this book was conceived to be rich in illustrations of a generation that grew up in the 1940s and 1950s, finished high school in 1959, and now was approaching the end of the century as new senior citizens. So much has been written about the "baby boomers," those who grew up in the turbulent 1960s and often are characterized as rootless experimentalists who always are seeking for something.[28] But the classes of 1959 have lived through everything the boomers have known, have been endowed with a somewhat more stable cultural base, and draw from a clearer memory of once having been "home" in a more traditional and secure culture.

Is, then, this class less rootless than the boomers, more wise and steady as life has twisted and turned? Are we who are a little farther along in life, now beyond our mid-life crises, ready both to look back over our lives and to move forward with sobered wisdom into a fast-changing world? Are you, the reader, ready to look back reflectively and then launch forward with us? We, the class of 1959, have lived and learned. So much has happened in the United States since our births around the time Pearl Harbor was bombed and the United States entered World War II. There has been so much hurt in the world and so much joy and disappointment in our own lives. In fact, we are like millions of others who have lived through the final decades of the twentieth century. Maybe to know a few of the stories of the North Jackson, Ohio, class of 1959 is to know a great deal about life in the nation generally.

---

[28]See, e.g., Wade Roof, *A Generation of Seekers* (San Franciso: Harper, 1993) and Craig Miller, *Baby Boomer Spirituality: Ten Essential Values of a Generation* (Nashville: Discipleship Resources, 1992).

Beyond a little nostalgia, maybe there exists here some insight, comfort, even hope. As the nation's recent story is told, some of the life stories of this class will be mentioned along the way. The first tool in the arts of healing and growing is the will to listen. People in pain need to tell their stories and need to know that they are heard by someone who cares. There has been much hurting in the lives of this high school class, some sixty men and women now beyond mid-life. There also is much happiness and faith. Soon the class will be marking its forty-year reunion after those high school days of long ago. It is time for some perspective for us all.

The Bible views the nature of humanity as both essentially good, created as such by God, and significantly impaired, forced this way by destructive human choice. On the negative side, life—especially in its immaturity, sin, and pain—has a way of isolating people. They cope by covering reality. The tendency is to deny ignorance, greed, or addiction. As we face the twenty-first century, for instance, some of us want to wish away the Holocaust, saying it never happened. Some of us finally put our faith in education—if only we were adequately informed, we argue, most of us would act appropriately. Some of us long for financial security—if only we had enough money, we assume that we could relax and be truly happy. Already, within its own ranks, the J-M class of 1959 has had to face suicide, disease, social dislocation, multiple divorces, the joy of love, the glory of grandchildren, the loss of faith, the thrill of new or renewed faith, and much more. It all is our story, and yours too. Like the ancient Hebrews known to us in the biblical story, a people survive with integrity and strength only as they are willing to remember the past, including the hand of God seen in the best and worst of times.

How should one approach a remembering and analysis of the last half of the twentieth century in the United States? There probably should be a review of the century's statistics, a scanning of its charts, and extensive surveys and sociological analyses of its people, events, and trends. Some of that is found below. But, while helpful and informative, such is not the only task undertaken here. This is more a book of memories and perspectives and less a cold compilation of facts and statistics. Our time is up to its neck in data. What it needs are roots, context, meaning, vision. So these pages record a process of listening, of real living, of testimony rather than mere treatise, of memory more than theoretical analysis. They tell about how it really has been for a nation and a given group of people within it, one high school class that has lived through all these decades with the nation. Here we tell real stories. We remember, listen, learn, try to gather perspective and momentum for tomorrow. We, the generation of the class of 1959, now hold much of the wealth of the nation. Do we also hold a treasure of life's wisdom that deserves a hearing? If we do not, who does?

Our Western minds immediately want to be scientists and not artists, technicians of social history rather than listeners and carers, healers and learners, visionaries and community builders. But, as a tumultuous century comes to a close, the public now is beginning to hear about the urgent need to be "post-modern." Whatever this proves to mean, it at least will seek to reintroduce some poetry into the bland prose of our materialistic lives[29] and help us to hear again the music of faith and experience again the sense of community in the midst of the shambles of misdirected technology and corrosive individualism.

The members of this one high school class and their families (now including numerous children, grandchildren, spouses, and ex-spouses) have known a wide range of pain and joy, all experienced in the midst of the many rapid and dramatic changes in the larger American society since their high school years (1956-59, the relatively quiet and even playful 1950s). The desperate 1930s and frightening 1940s had set the scene. The sensitive 1960s, the struggling 1970s, the expansionist 1980s, and the retrenching and reassessing 1990s were all ahead.[30] This class, in the middle of it all, may not have captured public attention like the "25 most intriguing people" featured annually in *People* magazine. No, they are not the public's fascination. They *are* the public. Rather than Princess Diana, Ted Turner, and Bill Clinton, they are just Betty, Delores, Barry, Charles, Charlotte, Jane, Jerry, Frank, Patty, Ian, Judy, Richard, and four dozen more. However, hearing their (our) stories is to learn much of the story of our times. Listening carefully may even generate a little wisdom worthy of note for those who soon will face the unknowns of life in the twenty-first century.

Of course, what is seen is influenced considerably by the angle of view and how well that view gets broadened by other keen observers. Therefore, throughout this research, reflection, and writing process, I have turned to others. The extensive footnoting throughout the book reflects the best of what recognized historians and social analysts have had to say. The bibliography at the end gathers many of these various sources. Special appreciation is extended to Ian Worley and Judy Rickenbrode Ahart, valedictorian and salutatori-

---

[29]See Walter Brueggemann, *Finally Comes the Poet* (Minneapolis: Fortress Press, 1989).

[30]These decade-defining adjectives for the 1930s, '40s, '50s, '60s, and '70s are borrowed from Howard Aley, *A Heritage To Share: The Bicentennial History of Youngstown and Mahoning County, Ohio* (Youngstown: The Bicentennial Commission, 1975), 293, 367, 420, 451, 500.

an of the Jackson-Milton High School class of 1959, who graciously and critically read the whole manuscript and made constructive suggestions. Others like research librarian Barbara Hoover of Anderson University and editor Glen Pierce of Evangel Publishing House have added their keen eyes. Emily Elizabeth Callen, one of my beloved grandchildren, is the wonderful young person to whom this book is dedicated.[31] I thank her in advance for what she will mean to this world.

The beginning of recent times was what followed the "good war," World War II.[32] Members of the J-M class of 1959 were just kids then. Much was ahead for the country and for them. No one could anticipate it all, of course; but now it can be seen in more perspective. It really was a time of new beginning. All who care about life in the United States—past, present, and future—can benefit by sharing these memories of yesterday and joining in the resulting visions of tomorrow.

---

[31]An earlier book of mine, *God As Loving Grace* (Nappanee, Ind: Evangel Publishing House, 1996) was dedicated to her brother, Ian Patrick Callen.

[32]See Studs Terkel, *The Good War: An Oral History of World War II* (N.Y.: Pantheon Books, 1984).

Taking Time To Reflect

1. Do you agree that our world seems to be at a crucial crossroads? How great is our loss as the known past slips away from us—and never was known at all by new generations? Does the future seem hopeful to you?

2. Is "truth" to be found only in the world of abstract ideas, or can there be wisdom in looking closely at the real lives of ordinary people? Does truth exist objectively, quite apart from our "creating" it as a tool of power against other people?

3. Can the remembering of older people be more than just sentimentality? Will today's young take seriously the wisdom offered to them by an older generation?

4. Do many of us today really want to wish away the past? When, for example, some people deny that the Holocaust in Nazi Germany ever happened, does such a denial not encourage such horrible things to happen again? Is history more than just "bunk"?

5. Give one example of how the American "culture war" now rages between the "Orthodox" and "Progressivist" visions of how American public life should be defined.

6. Do the words of President George Washington (farewell address, 1796) sound like an unusually contemporary warning? Does loss of "religious principle" in public life lead to serious consequences? What about the associated cautions of Thomas Paine and Thomas Jefferson?

Chapter Two

Born in the Shadows of War

1940s

In 1945 the United States inherited the earth…. At the end of
World War II, what was left of Western civilization passed into
the American account. The war had also prompted the country
to invent a miraculous economic machine that seemed to grant
as many wishes as were asked of it. The continental United
States had escaped the plague of war, and so it was easy enough
for the heirs to believe that they had been anointed by God.[1]

Those conflicts and disputes among you, where do they come
from? Do they not come from your cravings that are at war
within you? You want something and do not have it; so you
commit murder. And you covet something and cannot obtain
it; so you engage in disputes and conflicts. You do not have,
because you do not ask. You ask and do not receive,
because you ask wrongly, in order to spend
what you get on your pleasures. (James 4:1-3)

Many observers have sought to probe the "American mind." Here is one
characterization of the U.S. mentality of the nineteenth century:

Nothing in all history had ever succeeded like America, and every
American knew it. Nowhere else on the globe had nature been at once
so rich and so generous, and her riches were available to all who had the
enterprise to take them and the good fortune to be white. As nature and

---

[1]Lewis Lapham, "America's Foreign Policy: A Rake's Progress," *Harper's*, March,
1979.

experience justified optimism, the American was incurably optimistic. Collectively, he had never known defeat, grinding poverty, or oppression, and he thought these misfortunes peculiar to the Old World. Progress was not, to him, a philosophical idea but a commonplace of experience: he saw it daily in the transformation of wilderness into farm land, in the growth of villages into cities, in the steady rise of community and nation to wealth and power.[2]

The 1940s, however, hardly opened with the temptation for most Americans to get lost in their pleasures and traditional optimism. The years of the 1930s had been very hard for most people. Even so, the decade of the 1940s would end with a return of the common temptation to believe that the U.S. had been anointed by God to inherit the earth. Between its awkward opening and its more optimistic ending, the 1940s was to be dominated by the struggle of world war.

President Franklin D. Roosevelt is a towering figure in all of American history. Just as Abraham Lincoln stood in the gap in the wrenching years of the nineteenth-century Civil War, so Roosevelt stood firm and led in remaking his beloved country in the twentieth-century crucibles of the Depression and World War II. Even in the direst moments, he exuded an absolute confidence in the American future, a confidence that was essential for economic recovery and then military victory. It had not been inevitable that the downward spiral of the economy would be stopped in 1933 or that in December 1941, the United States would recover from the disaster of Pearl Harbor and go on to win a worldwide conflict. But Roosevelt made it seem that recovery and victory were inevitable because the causes were just, humane, and truly American. His legacy has thrown its gentle shadow over the whole era from the 1930s through the 1990s.

Without question the years 1940-1949 made up one of the more momentous decades in the whole history of the world. War divided and defined this decade. The year 1945 finally saw the welcome end of the biggest world conflict of human history and the cautious beginning of the structuring of the modern era. For the United States, World War II was seen as a completely "just war," if there ever is such a thing. The "Good War"[3] brought the nation together in what was seen almost universally as a righteous cause. World War I had been fought "to make the world safe for democracy" and at its end in 1918, it was referred to prematurely as "the war to end all wars." On the

---

[2]Henry Steele Commager, *The American Mind: An Interpretation of American Thought and Character Since the 1880s* (New Haven: Yale University Press, 1950), 5.

[3]See the large oral history of World War II by Studs Terkel titled *The Good War* (N.Y.: Pantheon Books, 1994).

80th anniversary of the 1917 U.S. entrance into World War I, this was how World War II was remembered: "In World War II the whole nation rose together with one voice to defend our country and fight against tyranny. What was at stake was nothing less than freedom for the entire world."[4]

World War II was a cataclysmic conflict that remolded the world. Charles de Gaulle of France called it "the greatest revolution the world has ever known."[5] The war killed 40 million soldiers and civilians, wounded millions more, hastened the collapse of European colonialism, and birthed dozens of unstable new nations in Asia, Africa, and the Middle East. The mighty Europe was devastated by its second civil war within a generation, leaving a world-wide power vacuum quickly filled by two nations that had been second-rate powers in 1939, the United States and the Union of Soviet Socialist Republics. In 1945 these two new "superpowers" divided the world between them. The U.S. was the world's greatest economic machine and had a monopoly on the most destructive weapon in human history, the atomic bomb. The U.S.S.R. had the largest land army in the world's history. When the guns finally fell silent, there was high hope that a new world order now could be constructed, one based on international cooperation, with a permanent peace the result. It was not to be.

Technological advances in the awful art of mass killing had developed quickly during the war and made frighteningly clear that the human race had arrived at a wholly unprecedented crossroads. Would the bombing of the Japanese cities of Hiroshima (approx. 140,000 dead) and Nagasaki (approx. 80,000 dead) be the end or only the beginning of previously unimaginable destruction rained on some humans by others? The search would have to begin for a new world order that could avoid atomic annihilation of civilization itself. The keynotes of public sentiment in the United States after the military victory in 1945 were joy, relief, hope, and gratitude. Yes, 1945 marked a very welcome end and an urgently needed beginning.

A World Ignited By War

In the course of the 19th century a few countries, mostly bordering on the northern Atlantic Ocean, had conquered and sought to "civilize" the rest of the non-European globe. These few Western countries, especially England, Holland, France, Germany, Spain, and Portugal, established themselves as the

---

[4]Ossie Davis, during the televised National Memorial Day Concert, Washington, D.C., May, 1997.

[5]Gordon Wright, *The Ordeal of Total War, 1939-1945* (N.Y.: Harper & Row, 1968), 234.

colonial lords of most of humankind.[6] However, time, the human spirit, and especially the worldwide economic depression of the 1930s destabilized political controls and became the soil of coming conflict and massive change. Germany, Italy, and Japan were seeking aggressively to expand their empires by 1940; but by the end of the 1940s, with the possible exception of the Soviet Union, most of the world had rid itself of the dominance of foreign empires. The age of colonialism had waned.[7] The imperial era was largely over. It was a dramatic change that reorganized the world into the general structure we all have lived in ever since.

The Great Depression that staggered world economies in the 1930s also nearly crippled the United States. A prominent but rare example of national power and pride in these difficult years was construction of the Hoover Dam (1930-1936) at Boulder Basin in Arizona. Here was at least one rallying point for American self-confidence, a vast wall of concrete higher than the Pyramid of Cheops, a modern engineering marvel holding back the Colorado River which had carved out the Grand Canyon. Even so, the Depression was hard on industrial centers like those of Western Pennsylvania and Northeast Ohio. Newton Falls, part of the Mahoning Valley chain of plants and near the North Jackson High School, was a typical example of the readjusting being experienced worldwide. Newton Steel moved its plant to Monroe, Michigan, in 1931, throwing hundreds of Newton Falls families into unemployment. In 1934 there were 3,500 local residents. The census of 1940 showed a decrease to 3,100. Understandably, leaders welcomed the end of "the terrible thirties" and were confident in 1940 that "we are facing better times and a more settled world."[8] Hopeful signs included the relocation to Newton Falls during 1939 of the Ideal Foundry. It came from Beaver Falls, Pennsylvania, because of a fire that had destroyed the plant there. With that relocating plant came Charles VanArsdale and his family, including grandson Barry who later would become president of the nearby Jackson-Milton class of 1959.

Prosperous times indeed were just ahead for this area and for the whole U.S. economy, but for a less than ideal reason. The world was again about to

---

[6] Note Eric Hobsbawm, *The Age of Extremes: A History of the World, 1914-1991* (N.Y.: Vintage Books, Random House, 1994, 1996), chapter 7, "End of Empires."

[7] In 1997, when Great Britian finally returned Hong Kong to China after more than 150 years of colonial rule, the once vast British Empire that had ruled India, South Africa, and some fifty other now independent nations had been reduced to thirteen little colonies. After Bermuda and the Cayman Islands, they were mostly small islands no one else particularly wanted.

[8] *Newton Falls Herald*, January 5, 1940.

be nearly consumed with war—a sad but great stimulus to American industry. It would be a global war that would alter national boundaries, end empires, and change the rules of social life for most people on the planet. American business and industry in the 1940s was dominated by preparation for World War II, then by the war itself, and finally in the late years of the decade by the new "Cold War." A terrible negative was the fact that 300,000 Americans would be dead on the world's battlefields. The ironic silver lining to this ugly storm was the positive effect of war on the American economy and its related technological innovation, and thus on the everyday lives of nearly all Americans. In the 1930s the nation struggled in the mire of the Great Depression. By 1950, at least in economic and external terms, most Americans were better off than ever before.

At first Americans had tried to stay away from the brewing problems abroad, hoping for the best. The 1939 New York World's Fair was staged as an upbeat antidote to the Great Depression that by then had debilitated world economies for years. The Fair "glowed with visions of plenty, beauty, and social harmony, all brought within America's grasp by the wondrous alchemy of science and technology."[9] Millions visited "The World of Tomorrow," listened to Albert Einstein, peeked into the mysterious new world of a TV studio, and saw machine-made lightning. The Fair's president dismissed mounting tensions in Europe and gave assurances that there would be no war. Unfortunately, he was wrong. In March of that very year Hitler annexed part of Czechoslovakia, signed the Pact of Steel with Mussolini of Italy, and launched an invasion of Poland in September. It was just the beginning.

On New Year's Day of 1940, even though Germany now had clamped an iron fist around Central Europe and Japan was brutally occupying China, most Americans still were peaceably preoccupied with their own hometown affairs. True, some big trouble was brewing overseas, but the U.S. public was determined not to get involved in another war. After all, there were two broad oceans protecting America from any sparks flying from the ancient hatreds among various "foreigners." Peace, at least at home, was thought to depend on avoiding any premature involvement in the violent quarreling of others far away. Hopefully isolationism could still succeed in the world of the mid-twentieth century.

President Franklin Roosevelt sensed the danger, however, and stepped up military spending at home. Germany began isolating and seeking to destroy

---

[9]Edmund Harvey, Jr., ed., *Our Glorious Century* (Pleasantville, N.Y.: The Readers Digest Association, 1994), 180.

England, especially by its waves of submarine attacks that sought to cut off and starve an island nation heavily dependent on shipping. Soon the Lend-Lease act was passed in the U.S. Congress, allowing the greatly increased sending of nation-saving materials to beleaguered England. In September of 1940 the Selective Training and Service Bill became law, calling for the first peacetime military draft in United States history. While many nervous Americans accused Roosevelt of being a "warmonger," he won a third term in the White House. Would he have to lead the nation into active involvement in a world conflict? Taking no chances, he increased preparations at home and began sending urgently needed war materials abroad, calling America the "arsenal of democracy."

In 1940, with conflict already blazing in Europe, the Ravenna Ordnance Plant, the local "Arsenal," was established by the federal government on 24,000 acres just outside Newton Falls, Ohio. During World War II some 17,000 people were employed there in making small arms ammunition, artillery primers, and detonators. During America's coming involvement in this world conflict, Barry's mother worked at the Arsenal, as did Delores' father. The fathers of J-M 1959 classmates Harry and Larry worked at the nearby Lordstown Army Depot. The United States finally could not manage to avoid large scale military involvement. The J-M class of 1959 was born in the shadows of America's final preparations for all-out war.

The year 1941 saw much more than the births of most members of the class of 1959. It also saw dramatic sporting records set, including baseball's Ted Williams hitting .406, Joe DiMaggio putting together his 56-game hitting streak, and a sensational thoroughbred colt named Whirlaway winning the Triple Crown and the hearts of racing fans everywhere. It was quite a year, but these births and sporting highlights turned out to be the least of the drama for Americans. This also was the fateful year that the dreaded war finally began to affect directly millions of American homes. On December 7, 1941, Commander Fuchida led 183 carrier-based fighters and bombers of the Japanese Navy on a surprise attack of the U.S. naval base at Pearl Harbor on the Hawaiian island of Oahu. Within minutes 2,403 Americans were dead. So was America's isolationism. In 1940 the top ten bestselling nonfiction books in the U.S. had included no "war books"; but 1941 would be very different. Led by William Shirer's *Berlin Diary*, there also were *The White Cliffs* by Alice Duer Miller, *Out of the Night* by Jan Valtin, and *Blood, Sweat and Tears* by Winston Churchill. The public knew now that it was in a great struggle.

The destruction rained on America's Pacific Fleet that day was great, but it was a strategic Japanese blunder in the long run. The Fleet's three aircraft

The deaths of the 2,403 Americans killed by the Japanese surprise attack on Pearl Harbor suddenly ended America's isolationism.

carriers were not there and so escaped damage. Even more significant, Pearl Harbor quickly unified the American people in a crusading zeal that sustained them all the way to eventual military victory in both the European and Pacific theaters of war. President Roosevelt the very next day called on Congress to declare war on Japan, saying that December 7 was "a date which will live in infamy." Three days later Germany and Italy declared war on the United States. It had begun. War was now a worldwide preoccupation. The early months of 1942 marked the low point of the war for the U.S. That year the bestselling book of fiction was *The Song of Bernadette*, evidencing the strong appeal of a religious theme in a time of national stress (over 900,000 copies sold in two years). That same year seven war books dominated the top-ten list of nonfiction bestsellers. *The Robe* by Lloyd C. Douglas, another novel with strong religious content, sold so well in 1943 that the publisher had difficulty meeting the demand because of the paper shortages caused by the war.

A key reason World War II would end in victory for the nations now "Allied" against the "Axis" powers of Germany, Italy, and Japan was the amazing ability of the United States to produce the war goods needed for such a vast conflict. America quickly became the largest arms manufacturer in world history. In a five-year period Americans built nearly 300,000 planes, 400,000 pieces of artillery, 47 million tons of artillery ammunition, 86,000 tanks, 44 billion rounds of small arms ammo, and 6,500 ships. The greater Youngstown, Ohio, area was a major center of steel and arms production. *Time* magazine named General George Marshall "Man of the Year" for 1943 because he was the one who led in arming the Republic for war. He came from Uniontown, Pennsylvania, a coal center just south of Pittsburgh. It was a time when "the flood of events was so enormous and so deep that …men wandered in an unfamiliar waste of circumstance, scanning the horizons for some marker, some direction point…. Their need was not for fascination and awe, but for competence and integrity. Looking at George Marshall, Americans were content."[10]

Amidst all the manufacturing and fighting, a significant source of humorous relief for American GIs was the traveling of comedian Bob Hope. Born in England and reared in Cleveland, Ohio, he became a beloved entertainer of the troops abroad, both in World War II and then in other conflicts in coming decades. In 1944 his book *I Never Left Home* was at the top of the nonfiction bestseller list, selling over a million copies. Hope described in these pages his 80,000 mile trip to various Army camps abroad, his shows in those places, and the reactions of "the boys." He "never left home" in the sense that the American military people everywhere had kept home with them. Bob Hope was a tireless troubadour of brash, corny, and very welcome humor. Observed one reviewer of this book: "Hope is the closest nature could get to a personification of corn without growing silk from his ears!" The reason soldiers needed to laugh so much was chronicled by Ernest Pyle in his *Brave Men* (bestselling nonfiction book of 1945). These very sober pages were based on the author's dispatches from the American fronts in Sicily and France, from the landing in Sicily (June 1943) through the liberation of Paris in September 1944. Pyle was scared and so were most of the soldiers. Few other correspondents captured so well in cold print the hot hideousness of actual war. Through his writings the soldiers had a voice and the folks at home were helped to really understand.

One American company determined to represent home to U.S. service persons wherever they had to be in the world. In 1941 Coca-Cola was bottled in forty-four countries. Once the U.S. entered the war, the company pledged

---

[10]*Time*, January 3, 1944, 17.

to keep the price at five cents per bottle regardless of where it was bottled and bought. During the next four years, Coca-Cola constructed sixty-four new bottling plants on foreign soil. About 250 company employees were given quasi-military status as technical observers following the troops everywhere. They also were given Army uniforms and even officer's ranks. Enemy prisoners often were used as willing workers in the plants. The world learned that Coca-Cola is indeed "the pause that refreshes."[11] Here was American ingenuity at work.

Many fathers of members of the Jackson-Milton class of 1959 saw action in the armed forces of the United States. There were some fathers not involved with the military (like those of Richard and Delores). Even so, rarely was there an extended family that did not have someone in uniform. Harry's father was a Marine who was lost for months behind enemy lines in the Philippines— an unspeakable experience little understood even by his own family because he would not talk about it after the war. Barry's father was a carpenter who sailed around the world as a Merchant Marine carrying war supplies. Ian's father spent time in rural Haiti assisting with the growing for the U.S. government of a replacement supply of rubber. Japanese expansion had depleted the usual sources available to the Allies. Larry's father was a pioneer in the development of radar for military purposes. He was active on the east coast of the U.S., outfitting units to hunt and kill the German submarines that were terrorizing shipping on the Atlantic Ocean. While these fathers risked their lives in national service, their young children played at home as normally as possible, with little comprehension of the consuming conflict now in progress.

War brought to the United States new jobs, anxiety about the safety of loved ones, and considerable social mobility. People with no work packed up and headed to factories, shipyards, and aircraft plants. An estimated 15.3 million Americans relocated. Housing was at a premium; defense-related jobs were not. America's defense industry represented about two percent of the nation's total industrial output in 1940. That rose sharply to a stunning forty-five percent by 1944. Opened prior to the U.S. entry into World War II, the Youngstown Municipal Airport provided the area with a facility for modern air passenger service. Soon it would be enlarged with the construction of a U.S. Air Force base. Construction and production for war was now much of the nation's life.

---

[11]For detail, see V. Dennis Wrynn, *Coke Goes To War* (Missoula, Mont.: Pictorial Histories Publishing Company, 1996).

Many younger American teenagers of the early 1940s now had work and money and were "feeling their oats." Many older teenagers were suddenly far from home and directly in harm's way. Popular music featured songs like "Praise the Lord and Pass the Ammunition" (1942) and "Comin' In on a Wing and a Prayer" (1943). Would enough gunfire do the job? Would the crippled plane land safely? Could praying make a difference when life and even national survival were on the line? Soldiers and sailors, now stationed far away and very much in danger, longed for home and family. They were touched in 1942 when Bing Crosby began singing Irving Berlin's soon beloved song, "White Christmas." Film star Marlene Dietrich came to Youngstown, Ohio, to support the war effort by promoting War Bond sales. The war would be won only if those millions now in uniform were driven by an intense patriotism and those at home invested themselves fully in support of the great enterprise on behalf of world justice and peace.

One relief from wartime tensions on the homefront was the new rage, the foot-stamping gyrations of jitterbug dancing. In 1944 some 700 riot police were required to keep order as 30,000 young fans—mostly teenage girls—tried to get into the 4,000 seat Paramount Theatre in New York City to hear silken-voiced Frank Sinatra, a young man who had started his crooning career in 1943. Classified 4-F because of a punctured eardrum and thus not a fighting soldier or sailor, Sinatra surely did provide some diversionary relief at home. Sounds of war are harsh; Sinatra became the "King of Swoon" with a voice that some said sounded like the cry of a love-sick loon. His would be a very long and eventful career in the entertainment world. In 1943-45 the nation needed some soothing sounds.

The big war dominated American life for almost four years. In April 1945, the country and much of the world was saddened by the death of President Roosevelt. But the heart and leadership he had given the nation in years of economic and then military crisis would carry on. Finally, on May 8, 1945, the welcome news was announced. The European war was officially won and ended. Many large German cities were little more than rubble from relentless Allied bombing. Paris finally had been liberated. Hitler was dead by his own hand. A grateful world went wild with celebration on this joyous V-E Day. Then on August 6 it happened. The "it" was an American B-29 bomber over Hiroshima, Japan, releasing the first-ever atomic bomb, with a second falling on Nagasaki three days later. An estimated 220,000 Japanese died in just those two bombings in those fateful four days. Ironically, Captain Mitsuo Fuchida, commander of the Pearl Harbor attack, flew into Hiroshima Airport just after the American bombing there and was surprised to find himself fac-

A GI celebrates the end of the European war with two WACs (Women Army Corps).

ing "a procession of people who seemed to have come out of Hell." Those local residents who still could walk were burned, filled with radiation, and badly disoriented with extreme shock.

The Japanese Emperor, himself shocked by the unprecedented destruction caused by this previously unknown weapon, finally had had enough of war.[12] On September 2, 1945, V-J Day, eleven Japanese leaders boarded the American battleship Missouri, anchored in Tokyo Bay, to sign the final surrender. Ian, member of the J-M class of 1959 then living near Warren, Ohio, though very young at the time, remembers hearing church bells ringing and seeing people riding on firetrucks joyously celebrating and yelling "the war is over!" It had been the deadliest conflict in human history.

---

[12]Ever since the dropping of the atomic bombs, there has been a debate about whether or not such a devastating act was absolutely necessary. A land invasion of Japan likely would have resulted in much dying on both sides. The Japanese had been warned that bombing was to be expected (as opposed to the unwarned Americans at Pearl Harbor in 1941), but their leaders had not conceived of the level of destruction that would be caused by atomic bombs. Are there any "rules" in war other than winning?

Foundations For Reconstruction

In the great and moving drama of our age, the prologue has been completed. For a generation our ablest prophets have told us that we are living at the end of an age and now we know that this analysis was correct. We have lived in "the end of our time" and we can date it. The date was August 6, 1945....

As the dramatic movement at the middle of the twentieth century begins, we can be reasonably sure that the long dominance of Europe is over, just as, five hundred years ago, the long dominance of the Mediterranean lands was over....

The logic of the situation which the atomic bomb symbolizes is as follows. Though the atomic bomb is the fruit of science, the solution of the problem is not a matter of science, since it is admitted that there is no technological defense. The only hope, therefore, lies in world organization. Only world organization can insure that the fearsome invention is used by those forces concerned with justice and not by the lovers of irresponsible power. But since the world organization is dependent upon the trustworthiness of those concerned, the ultimate question is ethical rather than merely scientific or even political. *The only answer to atomic power is moral power....*

We in the twentieth century have inherited a morality, but we have not thought deeply about it as we have thought deeply about scientific research.... The Ten Commandments constitute the most memorable and succinct extant formulation of the ethical creed of the West. For that reason they provide a convenient statement of the fundamental basis of recovery and reconstruction.... What we have is not an outworn set of specific prohibitions, but positive principles of such a nature that a good society cannot be constructed or reconstructed without reference to them.... The most profound argument for democracy is the realization, fundamentally Biblical in origin, that the love of power is so pervasive and so inordinate that democracy, which means a system of mutual checks, even upon the ruler, is the only alternative to injustice and oppression.... Democracy is necessitated by the fact that all men are sinners; it is made possible by the fact that we know it.

Select quotations from Elton Trueblood,
Foundations for Reconstruction
(N.Y.:Harper & Brothers, 1946), pp. 1-2, 8, 10, 104-105.

TABLE 6

An American atomic bomb fell on Nagasaki, Japan, in August 1945, hastening the end of the war in the Pacific, and beginning the horror and the scientific potential of the "Atomic Age."

World War II indeed was over. While the United States and the whole world now would try to return to a more normal existence, little would ever be the same again. In fact, August 6 was the end of one age and the stunning beginning of a new one—the atomic age. Peace had been bought at great price. Democratic ideals presumably had prevailed. A new world would have to arise from all the rubble and the death. The United States had risen to the place of world leadership. Could the exhilaration of victory be transformed into a vision and a faith in a better future that would come to feature peace, justice, and prosperity? Only time would tell. Already, Joseph Stalin had gained many concessions from Allied leaders that gave the Soviet Union control over vast areas and the chance to seek its own domination of the world's future.

Peace and Worldwide Change

Looking back from the vantage point of the end of the 20th century, it is clear that World War II soon was to become *the* watershed event of our times. With this "great war" came a rapid end of the economic depression that

PREAMBLE
to the
CHARTER of the UNITED NATIONS

WE THE PEOPLES OF THE UNITED NATIONS DETERMINED
to save succeeding generations from the scourge of war, which twice in our lifetime has brought untold sorrow to mankind, and

to reaffirm faith in fundamental human rights, in the dignity and worth of the human person, in the equal rights of men and women and of nations large and small, and

to establish conditions under which justice and respect for the obligations arising from treaties and other sources of international law can be maintained, and

to promote social progress and better standards of life in larger freedom.

AND FOR THESE ENDS

to practice tolerance and live together in peace with one another as good neighbors, and

to unite our strength to maintain international peace and security, and

to ensure, by the acceptance of principles and the institution of methods, that armed force shall not be used, save in the common interest, and

to employ international machinery for the promotion of the economic and social advancement of all peoples,

HAVE RESOLVED TO COMBINE OUR EFFORTS TO
ACCOMPLISH THESE AIMS

Accordingly, our respective Governments, through repesentatives assembled in the city of San Francisco, who have exhibited their full powers found to be in good and due form, have agreed to the present Charter of the United Nations and do hereby establish an international organization to be known as the United Nations.

TABLE 7

had plagued the U.S. and the world for years. The horrors of this world war, now often romanticized in movies, soon yielded to Allied victory. Then came the heroic rebuilding of whole societies and the freeing of half the population of the world from colonial rule. The long dominance of Europe was over, just as several hundred years earlier the dominance of the Mediterranean world had ended. Both the horror and heroism of this global conflict touched nearly every human being on the planet. The aftermath realigned the world politically, economically, and technologically, setting the scene for what the U.S. would come to enjoy and endure in the decades that now have followed.

For the United States, a long distance had been traveled from its national self-image after the Revolutionary War to the one after World War II. In the late 1700s, the new-born nation had won its little place in the sun of the world's independent countries. In the late 1940s, the now matured United States tended to think of itself *as the sun*. Others were to draw their inspiration and strength from the world's protector of freedom, peace, justice, and prosperity. The post-war American euphoria included an easy faith in the nation that had stood in the gap and drove out the great tyrants plaguing humanity. There now were grand expectations that the United States could create a better world abroad and a happier society at home. In fact, the 1940s launched decades in the United States that would be crowded with complexities and contradictions. Hope was high, successes were many and usually glorified, although failures and even national disgraces soon would be present too.

Most of the members of the U.S. high school classes of 1959 were born just months before the Japanese bombs fell on Pearl Harbor in 1941. They were just ahead of the "baby boomers" in the social chain. They had to live their very first years in the midst of a world convulsing in all-out world war. In 1945, when it finally ended, they were still fun-loving and innocent, certainly not understanding the increasing complexities and imminent dangers of world affairs. These affairs, however, would help shape the future, even as the war had and still would shape nearly every person living on the planet.

Amid all the turmoil and then victories of this great war, the United States acquired a leading role in international affairs. The strength of America was militarily and economically superior—and also was claimed to be obvious by the supposed moral superiority of American democracy. This superiority was openly in question, however, because racial segregation and inequality, for instance, were still the social norm. Much work lay ahead if the democratic ideals were to be realized by all citizens. The rhetoric of *justice for all* comes easily from the lips; however, it comes all too slowly when requiring reluctant actions of the self-righteous who hold for themselves a society's reins of power—even in the United States.

President Franklin D. Roosevelt insisted that the United States would have to continue to be active in international affairs if the world were to remain safe for human rights and democracy. As the world war moved to a conclusion, hundreds of diplomats and politicians met in 1944 and 1945 to draft a charter for a new world organization, the United Nations. Millions in the world had endured occupation, death camps, even attempted genocide of whole peoples, and now were calling for self-government and a respect for humanity. The attitude of governments ranged from enthusiasm to passive acceptance to quiet ideological hostility. Joseph Stalin, after all, had put to death millions of his own Russian citizens and the British under Winston Churchill were concerned that too much talk about democracy could threaten the fragile status of their empire, especially India. But the watershed of this great war would spell the ending of many empires and spawn new structures as attempts at international cooperation.

In the 1941 Atlantic Charter, Roosevelt and Churchill had looked forward to a "permanent system of general security." In 1943, the U.S. Congress passed a resolution favoring "international machinery with power adequate to establish and to maintain a just and lasting peace." The end result was a gathering of officials from fifty countries in San Francisco, California, in June 1945, to adopt the Charter for the new United Nations organization. It proclaimed that any lasting international peace and order requires respect for human rights and that the promotion of such rights is an internationally expected obligation of all governments. While there was no way to force member nations of the new UN to comply with such an expectation, it now was an established international standard that at least had a formal vehicle for its proclamation. The permanent home of this new world body was to be New York City in the United States.

Christian philosopher David Elton Trueblood applauded this international development as a prime example of possibly the only way to insure "that the fearsome invention [atomic bomb] is used by those forces concerned with justice and not by the lovers of irresponsible power." But he cautioned that "the ultimate question is *ethical* rather than merely scientific or even political. The only answer to *atomic* power is *moral* power." In his *Foundations for Reconstruction* (1946), Trueblood insisted that central elements of the Judeo-Christian tradition like the Ten Commandments "come to us again with startling relevance."[13] Peace must rest on justice. The quest for material prosperity and the possession of raw power are not enough. For a viable modern society, there must be faith in and obedience to a vision that is believed to have eternal foundations. Fully agreeing was Corrie Ten Boom, whose imprisonment by the Nazis and then her attitude of forgiveness moved millions.[14] A young Christian minister, Billy Graham, became a full-time evangelist the very year World War II ended. He would reflect on this time from the perspective of decades later:

> In the uncertainty of those times [post-war 1940s], many people were ready for a message that pointed them to stability and lasting values. In the providence of God, we were able to take advantage of the spiritual hunger and search for values that marked those years.[15]

Joining the religiously inspired Trueblood, Ten Boom, and Graham was a Trappist monk, Thomas Merton, who would have much to say indeed.[16] Having lived an orphaned, socially "wild," and educationally privileged early life in Europe and the United States, his life changed during Easter week, 1941, when he visited the Abbey of Gethsemani monastery in rural Kentucky. Merton was accepted into that spiritual community, his new-found home. His autobiography, *The Seven Storey Mountain*,[17] was released in 1948. The following year, to help celebrate the occasion of his ordination as a priest, the publisher presented him with copy number 200,000 of this hardback bestseller. Following a reprint edition in 1951 and two paperback editions to follow (1952 and 1970), that impressive sales volume would grow dramatically. The personal saga of one man's fulfillment in solitude, strict discipline, real faith in Jesus Christ, and committed community obviously had touched a nerve in post-war America.

---

[13]D. Elton Trueblood, *Foundations for Reconstruction* (N.Y.: Harper & Brothers, 1946), 8, 11. In the 1960s this Quaker philosopher/theologian would become a beloved mentor of Barry, one member of the Jackson-Milton class of 1959. The vision gained by Barry from this relationship is one key reason that this present book came to be written.

[14]See the story in her bestselling book, *The Hiding Place* (1971).

[15]Billy Graham, *Just As I Am: The Autobiography of Billy Graham* (Harper/San Francisco, Zondervan, 1997), 729.

[16]Thomas Merton would be a prolific writer until his tragic death in 1968, more widely read than any monk in all history. Later it would take a hardback book of 220 pages just to list the published books, poems, letters, journals, and essays written by, with, or about him (Frank Dell'Isola, Thomas Merton: *A Bibliography*, Kent State University Press, 1975).

[17]Thomas Merton ("Father Louis"), *The Seven Storey Mountain* (N.Y.: Harcourt, Brace, 1948).

From the beginning of post-war reconstruction, however, there were more than shattered lives and a spiritual hunger and search. There was the world and national politics that ranged from fragile to fickle to sometimes really frightening. World leaders Joseph Stalin, Winston Churchill, and Harry Truman—then President of the United States for only three months—had to decide how to administer a defeated Germany. As Truman prepared to travel to Potsdam, a suburb of Berlin, he wrote to his mother and sister: "I have to take my tuxedo, tails...high hat, low hat, hard hat.... I have a briefcase filled with information on past conferences and suggestions on what I'm to do and say. Wish I didn't have to go." He had reason to hesitate. Already Russians and Americans were eyeing each other warily. The "hot" war may have ended, but a fresh chill was in the air that soon would be called a "Cold War."

An ironic symbol of what now had to be done worldwide emerged in Washington, D. C. The U.S. presidential family had not been forced to vacate the White House since the James Madisons left quickly in 1814 before the home was burned by the attacking British. Harry Truman's surprising upset of Thomas Dewey in 1948 was followed by the Trumans having to move into Blair House. Signs of serious structural weakening of the White House had appeared, especially on the second floor that was still supported on wooden beams set in place in 1816. The problem of post-war recovery, of course, was greater outside than inside the United States. While no bombs had fallen on American cities, much of Europe was devastated. Europeans, victors and vanquished alike, were exhausted. The very beams on which their societies had been supported had been blasted out of place.

Europeans were hardly prepared to listen to naively innocent talk about progress and a bright future for people of goodwill. There were millions of homeless and displaced persons. Industrial production in Italy stood at twenty percent of pre-war levels. In Germany, whole cities would have to be rebuilt. France faced growing communist movements within. The unusually severe European winter of 1946-47 added food shortages to the other causes of mass human misery. President Harry Truman, in part fearing growing influence of the Soviet Union in Europe, announced the "Truman Doctrine" in 1947. It committed the U.S. to defending governments threatened with communist subversion. George Marshall, Truman's Secretary of State, soon was heading up the "Marshall Plan" that between 1947 and 1951 would spend about 12.5 billion American dollars on the economic recovery of Europe. It was a massive humanitarian effort, one often justified by insisting that it was an effective way of containing communism by the use of America's economic might—and was advantageous to many exporters in

America. Marshall was named 1947's "Man of the Year" by *Time* magazine, the second time for him to receive this high honor during the decade.

These efforts at international cooperation were extended because of a crisis. Tensions flared dangerously in 1948 when the Soviet Union blockaded all land routes to West Berlin and tried to force Western nations to abandon it. The response was a dramatic Berlin Airlift lasting 321 days. In 1949 the blockade finally was relaxed, the first victory of the "cold war." Formation of the North Atlantic Treaty Organization (NATO) now appeared absolutely necessary if Western Europe were to be safe from communism. Formalized in 1949, this alliance has been a Western military mainstay ever since. It and the Marshall Plan went a long way to restabilizing and realigning Western Europe.

Regaining the stability of the nations of Western Europe, however, did not include securing for them their previous empires. The heyday of European colonialism had crumbled, an irreversible watershed of the great war. Governments that before the war had managed vast empires now could not even manage their own internal affairs. By 1947 two million British industrial workers were unemployed. India's demand for full independence from Great Britain could no longer be stopped. The name of Mahatma Gandhi (1869-1948) and his campaign of non-violent resistance now was known worldwide.[18] Then in August 1947, it was finalized. The Indian subcontinent was divided into two new nations, the Muslim Pakistan and the Hindu India, resulting in the greatest human migration in history as masses moved to one or the other for continuing identity and personal safety. The British were relieved of the stigma of colonialism with some dignity and India was to become the second largest democracy in the world.[19]

The following year, another new nation was born as a direct result of the great war. "Zionism" had arisen in response to the persecution of Jews in many lands, especially the unspeakable Holocaust at the hands of Nazi Germany during World War II. The call was for a new homeland for the gathering of Jews to a place where they could enjoy safety and sovereignty over their own lives. It would be the state of Israel, a place open to the immigration of Jews from all countries of their long dispersion, especially at first from

---

[18]Gandhi's social vision and self-sacrificing life of prayer and fasting led millions of Indians to revere him as a saint. They called him "Mahatma" (Sanskrit for "great soul"). In the 1950s and 1960s he would become an inspiration for both minister Martin Luther King, Jr., and monk Thomas Merton as they gave guidance to the civil rights struggle in the United States.

[19]These dramatic events were featured in *Gandhi*, the film that won the Oscar for best movie of 1982.

central and eastern Europe. The end of the British mandate over the area and
the proclamation of Israeli independence came in May 1948. The United
States was the first country to grant it formal recognition and still remains its
champion and supporter. These developments were countered immediately
by the invasion of Israel by five Arab armies, only the beginning of seemingly
unending political and military struggle in the Middle East. Approximately
400,000 Palestinian Arabs fled, many becoming refugees in neighboring
Arab states. So a new diaspora people emerged, setting the stage for a series
of conflicts in the Middle East that would create world headlines for the rest
of the century. They also would create considerable speculation among many
Christians about possible fulfillment of biblical prophecies of end times.

Awkward Transitions At Home

As major developments marked the international scene, society in the U.S.
was also shifting significantly. In 1945 about fifty-two percent of U.S. farm
dwellings, housing some 25 million people, still had no electricity. Demo-
graphically and culturally, the country in many ways was still a land of farms,
small towns, and modest-sized cities. Most Americans still lacked health
insurance or company pensions. Mailing a letter cost three cents. More than
half the population said they belonged to a formal religious group, nearly all
representing the Judeo-Christian tradition (roughly 43 million in Protestant
denominations, 23 million Roman Catholics, and nearly 5 million Jews—a
key reason for the strong support of the U.S. for the new Israel). People now
were living in an increasingly "secular" world, but at least belonging to a
church or synagogue was still very much the American thing to do. Religious
books did pour from the presses, but popular novelists were not focusing frequently on the role of religion in modern life. While most Americans were
still formally Christian, and large numbers of them saw fit to maintain a
nominal connection with some church, "few admitted any categorical connection between religion, church, and morals."[20]

The nation had emerged from the war as an industrial giant, but there
were social and environmental costs at home. Pittsburgh, Pa., the large population and industrial center neighboring Youngstown just over the Ohio line,
became a prime example. This place of high energy and productivity came
out of World War II as a tired, rundown, and overcrowded city. Its pressing
problems were housing, roads, dirt everywhere, and especially smoke in the

---

[20]Henry Steele Commager, *The American Mind* (New Haven: Yale University Press,
1950), 426. The author adds: "The moral instructors of the new generation were the
movies, the radio, and the press...." (426).

air. Heavy industry and the widespread use of coal for home heating was choking a proud city. Soon, however, there began a massive smoke-control program and what would become the exemplary renaissance of a city. When the grime and smog finally were removed, the streets, rivers, and hills of Pittsburgh would comprise one of the more beautiful cities in the land.[21] The war, now won abroad, somehow had to be won again with such social victories at home.

Every American serviceperson had a dream of what to do when the war was finally over and home was safely reached. Some men claimed they would grab and passionately kiss the first girl they saw (there is the famous photo of a sailor doing just that in New York City's Times Square). Others planned to sleep for a month, getting up only for home-cooked meals, or they might decide instead to blow their separation pay on the longest binge of their lives. Robert, Barry's father, dreamed of developing a fishing camp on a beautiful lake (replacing the wild and dangerous oceans), earning a living doing something he loved as an outdoor sportsman. He and Barry's mother, Charlotte, ended up buying a summer cottage on Lake Milton in northeast Ohio, having to winterize it so that it was habitable for a family of four to use all year. Although always having a fishing boat on the lake, Robert stayed too busy working in the mills of Youngstown for the next twenty-eight years to ever develop a camp of his own. James and Jenny, parents of Shirley, moved from their home in Martins Ferry, West Virginia, to Youngstown, Ohio, to go where work was available. When Jim returned from military duty in 1946, he soon decided that he preferred not living in Youngstown. In 1948 this family also moved to Lake Milton, remodeling another summer house into a winterized dwelling. About 1950, Judy's family came from Pennsylvania. Her uncle became active in sponsoring various rides and concessions in the amusement park at Craig Beach.

The heroes of war immediately had to face the hardships of finding a job and especially a place to live. Few new civilian dwellings had been built during the war years and living space for veterans was a major problem at first. Winterizing simple cottages and even former garages into serviceable homes was one answer. In nearby Cleveland, Benny Goodman's band played a benefit at which grateful citizens pledged rooms for rent instead of money. In Newton Falls, a town of about 5,000 people neighboring North Jackson, the "Project" had been constructed—looking like rows of Army barracks forming a new community of private residence duplexes to help house employees

---

[21]See Stefan Lorant, Pittsburgh: *The Story of an American City* (Lenox, Mass.: Authors Edition, 1964, rev. 1975).

of the nearby "Arsenal" during the war. After the war, it was joined by mobile homes in housing some of the local veterans.

Economic foundations had to be laid for postwar prosperity. The United States had been spared any bombing destruction, had a pent-up demand for consumer goods, and certainly had the capacity to produce them. Even so, it was a great challenge. In August 1945, there were more than twelve million Americans in uniform, nearly all male. That was about two-thirds of *all* American men aged 18 to 34! Seven million of them were still overseas. After two years of demobilization, the number in uniform had dwindled sharply. By war's end, a series of big corporations dominated the American economy. The public generally approved of the close partnership of these companies with the federal government since government revenues for war materials had finally ended the Great Depression and now seemed the obvious way to avoid any return to economic despair. Industrialist Charles E. Wilson suggested that the government create a "permanent war economy." Does peace and prosperity require war—or at least the constant threat of coming conflict?

Although most of the military was demobilized, an unprecedented two million remained under arms. By 1947 large military expenditures had resumed. Public prosperity had become tied to permanent production of weapons for some war constantly assumed to be just around the corner. A chilling new arms race was on with a former ally. The Soviet Union had paid dearly for its resistance to the Nazis—25 million dead, with major cities in ruins. But the communist giant remained and still had the largest army on earth, even if it was poorly equipped. Its very existence threatened the West's postwar agenda of creating a new world order of democratic governments and free-market economies.

Even though the problems of creating a new world order preoccupied some U.S. politicians and military planners, most Americans now were focusing on the practical aspects of their private lives. The huge influx of GI's into the workplace strained an economy trying to shift to a peacetime footing. Price controls were lifted and prices soared. Almost no one expected economic growth in the U.S. after the war—some even feared a return to serious depression. But, beginning in 1947, there was what one historian calls "the most awesome economic growth ever seen in human history."[22] The economy bottomed out with a gross national product of $231 billion in 1947. Then it rose to $258 billion in 1948 and reached $285 billion in 1950.

---

[22]Michael Barone, *Our Country: The Shaping of America from Roosevelt to Reagan* (N.Y.: The Free Press, Macmillan, 1990), 197.

Sprawling new communities of look-alike homes sought to address the urgent post-war housing shortage in the U.S.

In the twenty years following 1948, the American gross national product, adjusted for inflation, grew at an average rate of four percent annually.[23] For the first time in history, leisure became a major social problem. Prosperity and machinery were beginning to make possible a degree of self-indulgence previously unknown except for a ruling elite.

For the large numbers of American soldiers, the war had changed their idea of how they wanted to live when they finally got home. They had risked much, seen much, delayed much. Now their sights were set high and their patience levels were low. The search for housing, at first an ordeal for many veterans, soon was relieved by a dramatic growth in the construction of new single-family homes. Why not adapt to housing the assembly-line production techniques of the auto industry? The result often was big new suburban areas of modest look-alike houses. No matter. With low-cost loans provided through the GI Bill to help millions with the finances, young families were making their dream a reality—owning their own homes!

Women increasingly were spending their time in these new homes, having children and again playing the more classic roles of mother and house-wife. Large numbers of women had entered the workplace for the first time

---

[23]*Historical Statistics of the U.S., Colonial Times to 1970*, 2 vols. (Washington: U.S. Bureau of the Census, 1975), 1:226-229.

American women joined the workforce to help win the war by building airplanes, ships, and other war-related materials. One result was the reconsideration of the appropriate role of women in American society.

to support the big war effort. Irving Berlin, composing for the 1946 musical *Annie Get Your Gun*, had Annie Oakley sing this about women in comparison to men: "Anything you can do, I can do better." A Norman Rockwell cover of *The Saturday Evening Post* featured a powerful-looking woman, Rosie the Riveter, whose air of confidence proclaimed that American women could be counted on to do anything they set their minds and muscles to accomplish—including building airplanes and ships. After the war these women had to decide whether to return to "more traditional" female roles or keep working outside the home.

The war had been a driving social force for change in women's lives, but its end now brought a sudden change for many. By early 1946, some 2.25 million American women had quit their wartime jobs. Another million were laid off as many industries cut back sharply on their production schedules. Sex-segregated employment became the norm for those women who stayed in the workplace: "Rosie the Riveter had become a file clerk."[24] Most women who had been U.S. pilots supporting military operations during the war could not get jobs as commercial pilots after the war.[25] They were relegated to being only stewardesses (if they met the age and beauty requirements). Said Eleanor Roosevelt, "a wind [is] rising throughout the world of free men everywhere,

---

[24]Cynthia Harrison, *On Account of Sex* (Berkeley, 1988), 4-5.

[25]Several hundred women in the U.S. were trained as pilots during the war. Their primary task was to ferry war materials and deliver new aircraft from the factories to distribution points in this country and abroad. Generally, their record for efficiency and safety was excellent. Their treatment by the commercial aviation industry after the war appears to be because of the gender stereotype then common in the society.

and they will not be kept in bondage." American women were key parts of this rising wind, although it was rising slowly. Many American men still kept their traditional ideas about their own wives and daughters, and women's magazines of the time typically still presented the image of women as "daily content in a world of bedroom, kitchen, sex, babies, and home." Even so, *Life* magazine presented a 13-page spread in 1947 on the "American Woman's Dilemma." For women, there was home and the world beyond home, but there was little cultural support for real independence from traditional gender patterns.

The Bureau of Labor Statistics reported in 1947 that nearly half of the adult female population of the U.S. was idle (meaning only that they were not employed outside the home). Nearly 20 million women over 40 years old were not employed in the marketplace, had no children under 18, and were neither aged nor infirm. They were said to make up a restless army of ladies who whiled away days and evenings serving on committees, joining social clubs, celebrating cultural events and causes, discussing peaceful uses of the atom, fighting communism and overweight, and playing a great deal of the card-game called Bridge.

Even though there were big social shifts and recurring stereotypes, there surely was a stimulating relief that the big war was over—and there was a strong drive to get on with life at home. In August 1944, Hollywood producer Samuel Goldwyn had been leafing through *Time* magazine when he noticed a photograph of eleven travel-soiled soldiers hanging from the window of a grimy Pullman car, some smiling, some bewildered, all longingly expectant. Below the train window were the words: "Home Again!" A shrewd business man, Goldwyn saw the potential market in those faces; after all, about 15,000,000 men and women would be back in the U.S. once the war ended. The result of this observation was the best motion picture in 1946, *The Best Years of Our Lives*, winner of nine Academy Awards. This was a classic postwar drama of three returning veterans and their readjustments to civilian life. While it ended on an upbeat note, the veterans were depicted as encountering, sometimes bitterly, what appeared to them a shocking lack of patriotism and runaway materialism in postwar American society. Interprets one historian about this film: "Though the ending is schmaltzy, there was bite enough in the film to distinguish it from a Norman Rockwell vision of the nation."[26] The sentimentality was more apparent in the 1946 film *It's a*

---

[26]James T. Patterson, *Grand Expectations: The United States, 1945-1974* (N.Y.: Oxford University Press, 1996), 15. Even so, Joseph Goulden used it as the inspiration for the title of his major book on the period, *The Best Years: 1945-1950*, 1976.

Wonderful Life, soon to become one of the best-loved American movies of all time. A man is prevented from committing suicide by an elderly angel, who then escorts him back through his life to show him what good he had done. A comedy drama in a fantasy framework, Jimmy Stewart, the star, was the stammering, aw-shucks actor who embodied the small-town values of decency and moral courage. For such a credible embodiment the country seemed to long.

Problems were real and the federal government decided to help American service personnel now taking off their uniforms. In 1944 President Roosevelt had signed the GI Bill (Serviceman's Readjustment Act). With this generous provision of money for books, tuition, and even some living costs, millions of men left the military and went straight to college, usually the first to do so in each of their families.[27] In 1946 men suddenly outnumbered women on American campuses and traditional eighteen-year-old college freshmen found themselves in classes with men of twenty-five or more who had young families and battle experience in far-off places. Ian's father found a faculty position at the YMCA College in Youngstown (later Youngstown State University), then populated by numerous military veterans. He located his family in North Jackson where his children would be reared and attend the nearby North Jackson High School.

The GI Bill both extended and democratized American higher education. Before the Bill, only the elite few went to college. After it, the doors were open to nearly all who were interested. College quickly became the hope, even the expectation of the children and grandchildren of these millions of war veterans. For sixteen years the country had been in crisis, first with economic disaster and then with massive military engagement. Now there was a chance for a new beginning. That beginning included college, housing, and having children. During the 1940s, America's population grew by 19 million, more than twice the growth of the 1930s. The 1950s would move to an even higher level of growth, a virtual "baby boom." In fact, the very large American birth rate between 1946 and 1964 would come to be the "baby boomer" crowd, whose sheer size would have major social and economic effects in the U.S. to the end of the century and beyond.

The years 1946-1950 were awkward years of national readjustment for the victorious United States. One frightening dimension of this new world was inaugurated dramatically on July 16, 1945. This was the day the world

---

[27]One excellent study of this dramatic development is John Norberg, *A Force for Change: The Class of 1950* (West Lafayette, Ind.: Purdue University, 1995).

changed, the day the "Trinity" project oversaw the first detonation of a nuclear device. One observer on the scene in New Mexico reacted with an astonished "O, God!" The issue was ultimate. Hiroshima, Japan, soon would be the first city in human history devastated by such a bomb. What that bomb did on the ground was surprising, awesome, horrifying, humbling. The American children growing up in the peace to follow would be the first to feel the fear that suddenly human existence itself might be obliterated with only minutes' notice. Even so, the young were riding a big wave of change that included many positives. Promise was in the air. College students of the time had survived the great depression as teenagers. They had won the big war as young adults. Now they would try to make the best of the peace in the midst of a new world of rapidly expanding technology and new calls for freedom, all in a setting of heightened expectations. The Jackson-Milton class of 1959 was born in the middle of all this frantic and fearful bustle. By the time they were becoming aware of the world, the mass bloodshed of the war had ended and all of these worldwide adjustments were happening. What impacted them directly, however, was local life in the United States.

BIRTHS OF THE BABY BOOMERS

The "baby boomers" are the generations of Americans born between 1946 and 1964. Fertility rate is the number of births per 1,000 women aged 15 to 44. Source: *Historical Statistics of the United States* (Washington: U.S. Bureau of the Census, 1975), 1:49.

Year	Fertility Rate	Births (Millions)	Year	Fertility Rate	Births (Millions)	Year	Fertility Rate	Births (Millions)
1944	89	2.9	1953	115	4.0	1962	112	4.2
1945	86	2.9	1954	118	4.1	1963	108	4.1
1946	102	3.4	1955	118	4.1	1964	105	4.0
1947	113	3.8	1956	121	4.2	1965	97	3.8
1948	107	3.6	1957	123	4.3	1966	91	3.6
1949	107	3.6	1958	120	4.3	1967	88	3.5
1950	106	3.6	1959	119	4.2	1968	86	3.5
1951	111	3.8	1960	118	4.3			
1952	114	3.9	1961	117	4.3			

TABLE 8

Babies were everywhere. Most Americans focused much of their lives on family, assuming that marriage and children were standard parts of being happy. The average number of children was 3.2 per family. Couples wanted and usually could afford these children. America's gross national product climbed a steep 250 percent between 1945 and 1960. These were good times to be working as parents and fun-loving as kids. At the end of the 1950s in the United States there would be 10 million more youngsters between the ages of 5 and 14 than at the beginning, with some 4 million bicycles produced annually for them to ride. The country was on the move. To sustain the high level of productivity and employment of the war years, it now was becoming necessary for Americans to play harder (with more expensive toys) and consume at a prodigious rate. Most people found themselves up to this exhilarating task.

World War II had been midwife to a social revolution. Surely in the victorious nation, now the major power in the world, there would be major implications for higher education, labor unions, national economics, political activity, and certainly personal and social values. There were, and it all came with a price. David Riesman's widely-read book *The Lonely Crowd* (1950) pictured inner-directed Americans being replaced by new outer-directed corporate types. Being outer-directed seemed a condition demanded by the times. People were inclined to take their social cues from those outside the home and thus they would remain lonely members of the crowd because they rarely came close to themselves. It was a big world on the move. The winds of change seemed to carry the masses along predetermined paths. Sometimes the personal results were quite negative.

Such negative results were immortalized in 1949 by Arthur Miller's drama *Death of a Salesman.* Willy Loman, very lonely in the crowd, was a lower middle-class traveling salesman, a character created by Miller to represent many Americans trying to ignore the realities of their limited private worlds and seeking to sustain themselves by illusions. Loman had tended to accept at face value the highly publicized ideals of blatant optimism and material success. Not personally able to stay up with a very competitive environment of high expectations, he becomes reduced to suicide as his chosen self-destructive way of bettering his family with the insurance money. Willy had become a tragic figure, a quiet failure in the middle of a society loudly boasting of dizzying success. The "alternative to futility"[28] lay with the rarely welcome realization that what really is needed to sustain a true happiness involves more

---

[28]D. Elton Trueblood, *Alternative to Futility* (N. Y.: Harper & Brothers, 1948), 14.

than *things*, no matter how expensive and advanced they are. Without real faith in key intangibles, material goods can become a curse rather than a blessing.

The bomb, the competitive materialism, trying to keep pace with the neighbors, high expectations, and the anxiety that it might not happen for me and mine left many people ragged and isolated. For them, outward war had ceased, only to be replaced by inward turmoil. Where could personal peace be found? The answer that appeared widely was a renewal of inner faith in a God beyond human strife who can bring inner peace. Best-selling books soon included Rabbi Joshua Liebman's *Peace of Mind* (1946), Bishop Fulton Sheen's *Peace of Soul* (1948), Dale Carnegie's *How To Stop Worrying and Start Living* (1948), evangelist Billy Graham's *Peace With God* (1952), and Rev. Norman Vincent Peale's *The Power of Positive Thinking* (1952). And how does one rear children properly in the middle of the postwar world of the 1940s, allowing their individuality, building their self-esteem, but not losing parental control? First published in 1945, Dr. Benjamin Spock's *The Common Sense Book of Baby and Child Care* became the standard guide for the growing multitude of America's parents. He counseled a happy medium, with less restrictive discipline than taught in the past and more overt emotional support of children, with mom not working outside the home, particularly for the crucial first three years of a child's life. Many hard-working Americans, typically with several children and not always mom at home, now lived with some economic anxiety—especially if they were "climbers" in an increasingly asssertive society.

In 1948 the United Auto Workers (UAW) pressed for and got a unique contract provision from General Motors. This contract included an "escalator clause," thought to be the first in any American industry. With World War II over and wartime price controls abolished, inflation was growing and the level of real wages of many American workers was falling through no fault of their own. People with blue collars and growing families wanted some economic stability. They felt they had earned the right to enjoy a peaceful and prosperous America and a good and reasonably secure standard of living for their families. This escalator clause was simply a cost-of-living formula guaranteeing that wages would increase automatically if the Bureau of Labor Statistics reported that the cost-of-living index had risen. On May 25, 1948, the historic labor agreement was struck. It was hailed by *Fortune* magazine as "the treaty of Detroit." Now auto workers, and soon many others, could feel more comfortable planning their economic futures. They were officially recognized as having the right to a secure standard of living protected by an inflation-adjusted income. In the Youngstown, Ohio, area this was very significant since the auto-related steel industry was a major part of the economy and employed so many fathers and mothers of the Jackson-Milton class of 1959. Later the large Lordstown assembly plant of General Motors would be built close to the high school, and several members of the local 1959 graduating class would become long-term employees and be affected directly by subsequent contract issues between workers and the giant company.

A New Social Landscape

World War II seemed a turning point in the nation's quest for greater ethnic and racial equality. The U.S. population in 1945 included 11 million foreign-born people and another 23.5 million with at least one foreign-born parent. Most of these 34.5 million Americans, 25 percent of the total population, were of European descent (see Table 3). The J-M class of 1959 grew up far from a major immigrant entrance city like New York. Nonetheless, included in it were Nancy (maternal grandparents Norweign), John (family Croatian), Dorothy (family Slovac), Maureen (father immigrated from Lebanon when he was fourteen), and Ian (his mother was the first English-speaking generation of Norweign immigrants). German, Scotch-Irish, and English family histories were common. Given this rich diversity of immigrant identity, one might expect high levels of tolerance from those who once had fled persecution themselves. In fact, racism was very much part of American life.

As the war began for the United States at Pearl Harbor, the public's fear focused this racism on a newly hated Asian group, the Japanese. Some Americans thought that Japanese Americans were signaling "Jap" submarines with their laundry hanging on clotheslines and photographing the Golden Gate Bridge in preparation for an Asian assault on San Francisco. In 1942 President Roosevelt ordered all Japanese and Japanese Americans living in California, Oregon, and Washington to be forcibly relocated to internment camps for the duration of the war. Although many of these new "prisoners" were American citizens with few if any ties to Japan and no criminal histories, their constitutional rights were suspended. "The only good Jap is a dead Jap," shouted a congressman from California on the floor of the House of Representatives. Fear mixed with prejudice can generate frightening results quickly, even in the United States. Another executive order of President Roosevelt sought to go in the opposite direction by ending prejudice in the military against African-Americans. Persons of color did serve in large numbers, but usually in segregated units and given inferior assignments.

The Japanese-American relocation center at Amache, Colorado, one of the ten barracks-type cities constructed to be the temporary home of 110,000 Americans of Japanese descent who were "relocated" during World War II.

Changes in the lives of American blacks and women helped to create at least the preconditions for the later emergence of a new social landscape in America. The global war had initiated social change in America "more than almost any event since the Industrial Revolution."[29]

In the Youngstown, Ohio, area there was considerable social strife as volatile economic shifts brought pressure and often dislocation. Frequent discrimination was practiced against the Irish, Italian, and various Eastern European communities that had migrated there over the years. Independence and integrity were values cherished in rhetoric and sometimes challenged in practice. The call for freedom and social equality certainly was beginning to fester in the African-American community. Many Southern blacks had first arrived in the Youngstown, Ohio, area around 1919, the year many of the parents of the high school class of 1959 were being born. Many of these blacks had come as strikebreakers and stayed on to enjoy the lack of Southern laws that threatened lynching if they disturbed the set social order. But there also were limits to what white Youngstowners were prepared to permit. While there were no Jim Crow laws, the public did discriminate in hiring and housing. In the local mills, African Americans tended to be hired "for the hardest, dirtiest, and hottest jobs, the ones that others refused to work."[30] Neighborhoods were effectively segregated by real estate brokers who "protected"

---

[29]William Chafe, *The Unfinished Journey: America Since World War II* (N.Y.: Oxford University Press, 3rd ed., 1995), viii.

[30]Frederick Blue, et al, *Mahoning Memories: A History of Youngstown and Mahoning County* (Virginia Beach, Va.: Donning Co. Publishers, 1995), 109-110.

white housing areas. This was not only the case in the South. Ian vividly recalls that, as a boy in the late 1940s and 1950s, there were segregated water fountains and bathrooms in the local Youngstown Greyhound Bus stations, strictly separate facilities.

As late as 1940, seventy-five percent of all American blacks still lived in the rural South. But in the 1940s, largely because of the rapid mechanization of cotton production and the lure of employment for displaced farmhands, more than two million moved to western and northern industrial areas like Youngstown and Pittsburgh. This massive social migration, one of the more significant demographic shifts in all of American history, would help to bring social change nationwide in the years just ahead. The world war had moved the process along with an increased mixing of races in the military and the avowed goal of defeating the racism and aggression of Nazi Germany and Imperial Japan. What had to be stopped abroad sooner or later would have to be brought into question at home. So world war provided the early spark for the American civil rights movement. It would begin slowly, then emerge dramatically by the 1960s. But already in the 1940s the political scene was shifting in favor of some attention to the awkward reality of racial inequality.

Historic Forbes Field in Pittsburgh was a scene of segregated baseball, being the home of both the Pirates and from 1930 to 1948 the Homestead Grays of the Negro League. Joe Louis, heavyweight boxing champion, won admiring headlines by enlisting in the Army and becoming one of the first black Americans to be featured on a patriotic poster. In 1947 W. E. B. DuBois and other "radical" African-Americans embarrassed the Truman administration by bringing before the newly formed United Nations Commission on Human Rights charges against the American government. In July of 1948 President Truman ordered an end to segregation in the nation's armed forces. Segregation, however, is as much an attitude as it is an issue of mere public policy. Widespread marginalization of people of color persisted in popular culture through the 1940s and beyond. A very popular radio program of the time was "Amos 'n' Andy." While it had its redeeming features, including its intent to be just pure fun, the program still tended to present blacks as unreliable and even hapless people.[31] Another program was that of the radio comedian Jack Benny, with Rochester, his servile Negro valet.

These denigrating stereotypes of African-Americans were usually greeted by largely white audiences as natural, not malicious, and very funny.

---

[31]See Melvin Ely, *The Adventures of Amos 'n' Andy: A Social History of an American Phenomenon* (N.Y.: 1991).

Jackie Robinson broke the color barrier in professional baseball in 1947 as a member of the Brooklyn Dodgers.

Unfortunately, widespread segregation was still practiced widely and legally, even in the churches. Declares black activist Benjamin Mays:

> I believe that throughout my lifetime [b. 1894], the local white church has been society's most conservative and hypocritical institution in the area of White-Negro relations.... The church boasts of its unique origin, maintaining that God, not man, is the source of its existence.... Christian fellowship across racial barriers is so inherent in the very nature of the church that to deny fellowship in God's House, on the basis of race or color, is a profanation of all that the church stands for.... The Negro's song, "Take All the World and Give Me Jesus" was never considered seriously by the white man, even though he may have believed in heaven. He had as much of Jesus as the Negro—and the world besides![32]

An effective addressing of this issue would not come until the 1950s, and even then the solution would be only partial.

The year 1947 was socially pivotal in U.S. history. The world headlines told of the Dead Sea Scrolls being discovered in Wadi Qumran, India and Pakistan becoming separate nations, and the *Kontiki* crossing the Pacific Ocean. Back in the U.S., Jackie Robinson became the first twentieth-century black man to play baseball in the major leagues. The president of the Brooklyn Dodgers, Branch Rickey, knew that there was considerable money and playing talent available if the color line between the Negro leagues and the all-white major leagues could be crossed. He made the first move with Robinson, who then earned recognition as rookie of the year, helped the Dodgers win the National

---

[32]Benjamin E. Mays, *Born To Rebel: An Autobiography* (N.Y.: Charles Scribner's Sons, 1971), 241-242.

League pennant, and literally revolutionized the game of professional base-ball. Less than three months after Robinson's debut, Larry Doby joined the Cleveland Indians as the first African-American in the American League. Richard, Barry, and others from the J-M class of 1959 watched him play in Cleveland. By 1959 every major league team had been racially integrated. In the public eye, integrated baseball had begun to render absurd the traditional contention that the white and black races were incapable of interacting fruit-fully for common ends. Robinson and Doby hardly ended racism in America, but at least after them white Northerners were less likely to accept passively other forms of blatant racial injustice.

If the elimination of gender and racial stereotypes was a slow and often painful, although a persistent process, nothing seemed able to hold back the rapid advance of some new things. Various technologies that had evolved to support the war effort were adapted quickly to exciting new peacetime uses. Prominent among them were fascinating new consumer technologies like television and computers, even though televisions were still owned by rela-tively few families and computers were cumbersome, slow, and not adapted to widespread personal use. But they both now existed, were fast capturing the public imagination, and soon would alter the social landscape dramati-cally. Other rapid advances were being made in the popularity of professional sports and, on the downside, in the widespread fear of communism. So the parents of the high school classes of 1959 were living in a rapidly changing world as their children entered elementary schools in 1946-47. These parents brought with them the depression values of thrift and neighborliness. They also brought the harsh lessons of war and the anxiety to get on with and ahead in life. Do not put dreams off until tomorrow, most Americans now believed, because tomorrow may never come—or may look very different when it gets here. America as a nation can do anything if it focuses its mind and might on the task. Now that the war was over, most citizens saw the task as finding a way to be successful and happy—and not worry too much about things like the obvious dangers to world peace.

Professional sports began emerging as big business with the availability of new television revenues. By 1950 Saint Louis Cardinal star Stan Musial was making $50,000 per year and jockey Eddie Arcaro upwards of $70,000. There was a "white-collar explosion."[33] Emerging rapidly was an altered class struc-ture in America. The nation had been dominated primarily by farmers, then industrial workers after World War I. By 1959, however, a new middle-class

---

[33]Reece McGee, "White-Collar Explosion," *The Nation* (February 7, 1959), 112-115.

of salaried professional, managerial, and technical people comprised almost twenty percent of America's working force. They were manipulating ideas rather than machines and materials.[34] As the class of 1959 was in its sophomore year in 1956, the nation's economy crossed the line from an industrial to a "post-industrial" state, white-collar now outnumbering blue-collar workers for the first time ever.

Communism was being seen as an increasingly frightening menace by mid-century. Russia accomplished a successful test explosion of its own atomic bomb in 1949, putting real fear back into the victorious mentality of post-war America. By 1950 America's National Security Agency had concluded that the world faced a "polarization of power" in which a "slave society" (the Soviet Union) was seeking to triumph over "the free" (especially the United States). The Cold War was on. Again, the soul and even the survival of America appeared at stake. The questions were several and basic. Prosperity at whose cost? Peace at what price? Justice established and maintained in what way? Faith, yes, but faith in what?

In 1946 Dwight Eisenhower, the prominent American military commander soon to be President, said: "Without God there could be no American form of government, nor an American way of life. Recognition of the Supreme Being is the first—and most basic—expression of Americanism." Religious trends in the society seemed to agree, at least on the surface. After a period of decline during the Depression, American churches experienced a revival in the 1940s, especially after the war. About forty-three percent of the public attended church or synagogue before the war; by 1950 some fifty-five percent were actively associated religiously, a figure to explode to about sixty-nine percent by the end of the 1950s. This substantial growth probably came in part from the overwhelming and sobering experience of World War II and the intense anxieties of the Cold War. In part it appeared to be a phenomenon related to the social pressures of new affluence after the war.

Faith expressions tended to be more "liberal." Roman Catholic and Jewish immigrant groups were "blending" more into the general society and losing some of their distinctive edges. The Nazis and the Holocaust in Europe had discredited religious intolerance in the public eye. Interdenominational rivalry gave way to more of a spirit of ecumenical cooperation and tolerance of

---

[34]This trend had been documented earlier by Robert and Helen Lynd in their famous sociological studies of Muncie, Ind., called *Middletown* (1929) and *Middletown in Transition* (1937). They observed a disturbing decline in the culture of the independent citizen, with its traditionally strong biblical and republican elements, in the face of the rise of the managerial business class and its dominant ethos of utilitarian individualism.

Milestones of the Decade

	Best Movie of the Year#	Bestselling Nonfiction Book of the Year	*Time* Magazine's Person of the Year*
1940	*Rebecca*	*I Married Adventure,* Osa Johnson	Winston Churchill, England
1941	*How Green Was My Valley*	*Berlin Diary,* William L. Shirer	Franklin D. Roosevelt, President of the U.S.
1942	*Mrs. Miniver*	*See Here, Private Hargrove,* Marion Hargrove	Joseph Stalin, Stopped Hitler in Russia
1943	*Casablanca*	*Under Cover,* John Roy Carlson	George C. Marshall, Armed the United States
1944	*Going My Way*	*I Never Left Home,* Bob Hope	Dwight D. Eisenhower
1945	*The Lost Weekend*	*Brave Men,* Ernie Pyle	Harry S. Truman, President of the U.S.
1946	*The Best Years of Our Lives*	*The Egg and I,* Betty MacDonald	James F. Byrnes
1947	*Gentleman's Agreement*	*Peace of Mind,* Joshua L. Liebman	George C. Marshall, The Marshall Plan
1948	*Hamlet*	*Crusade In Europe,* Dwight D. Eisenhower	Harry S. Truman, President of the U.S.
1949	*All the King's Men*	*White Collar Zoo,* Clare Barnes, Jr.	Winston Churchill (Man of the Half-Century)

\# Recipient of the Oscar from the Academy of Motion Picture Arts and Sciences.

* A designation on the part of the editors of *Time* of the person, people, or thing that, for better or worse, most significantly influenced the course of world events in the preceding twelve months.

TABLE 9

differences. The human potential for violence and gross evil was so evident that humility and charity seemed called for—especially humility after the development and devastating use of the atomic bomb. With a growth in numbers, tolerance, and liberalism, American religious bodies also were becoming more affluent. Churchgoing became part of the new "suburban" lifestyle.[35] It was accepted as a sure sign of real community, a badge of wholesome conformity to cherished values important for the children who seemingly were now everywhere. On the excessively patriotic side, victory in war had convinced many people that the United States was indeed God's chosen nation. This led easily to a cultural arrogance that could be and sometimes was used to justify American intervention in foreign affairs and to reaffirm the rightness of an extreme anti-communism.

A Cockeyed Optimist

The 1940s were both frightening and exhilarating years. This pivotal decade had seen the horror of the world at war and then the political decisions that reorganized much of the world in the way it would be known for the rest of the century. The harsh military realities of the time were constantly evident, both the fresh memories of World War II and the fresher fears of the Cold War. These were reflected well in the screen classic *Sands of Iwo Jima* starring John Wayne as Sergeant John Stryker.[36] Finally, however, there had come more freedom to sing songs from new musicals like "Oh, What a Beautiful Morning" from *Oklahoma* (1943), "June is Bustin' Out All Over" from *Carousel* (1945) and "Happy Talk" from *South Pacific* (1949).[37] Maybe birth and love now could replace death and hate. Maybe, as Mary Martin sang in *South Pacific,* that glorious musical romance set in the midst of World War II, I'm "A Cockeyed Optimist" and finally I'll meet my man "Some Enchanted Evening." Had the soft glow of humanity's enchanted evening really begun to spread its gentle joy? If so, could it last?

Shifting from music to art, a similar optimism was seen. It was part of the perceived inner meaning of being an American. The country's earliest

---

[35] See chapter three for a fuller description of the development of "suburbs" in American life.

[36] This classic film was nominated for an Academy Award in 1949. While set in World War II, it subtly addressed the war fears common as the 1940s were closing.

[37] In 1948, James Michener won the Pulitzer Prize for fiction with his first book, *Tales of the South Pacific.* This collection of stories, drawn from his experiences as a naval officer during World War II, was brought to the stage and movie screen when Richard Rogers and Oscar Hammerstein turned the book into the hit Broadway music, *South Pacific.* By the time of Michener's death in 1997, he was an American literary icon whose forty-five books, some of epic proportions, often had topped bestseller lists.

colonists in the Northeast—Pilgrims, Puritans, Quakers, "Pennsylvania Dutch"—were fleeing European persecution and corruption (as they saw it) and trying to set up various kinds of religious utopias in the "New World." The utopias were to inform all of personal and community life. In 1912 Russian artist Wassily Kandinsky published his tract *Concerning the Spiritual in Art*. After World War II there arose in America the artistic movement called "Abstract Expressionism" that put American art on the world map and "was to a large extent the product of this deeply implanted instinct for the spiritual and visionary."[38] The terrible war was over. Now it was time to dream, believe, imagine, build anew. The peoples of the world generally acknowledged that the U.S. would be a prime director if not largely in control of the basic course of world history for the second half of the twentieth century.

By almost any standard, the postwar economic power and affluence of the U.S. was amazing, the marvel of the world. In the late 1940s, America possessed forty-two percent of the world's income and accounted for half of the world's manufacturing output. It dominated the international economy like a colossus. To avoid excessive arrogance, however, one must remember that life on the American farm was still hard, one-third of American homes in 1947 still had no running water, most people lived in rented housing, and given groups like African-Americans typically did not share equally in the wealth now available. Richard lived in a farm home in North Jackson that had a hand pump in the kitchen for water and, he recalls humorously, "obviously the outhouse stood like a beacon against the sky." Even so, the late 1940s would later be looked back on nostalgically as really good times in the U.S. In 1949, for instance, three of the bestselling nonfiction books had to do with playing and winning at the card game called Canasta. Leisure time now was available for many Americans. Frank recalls how much his parents enjoyed playing cards at their home in Lake Milton. Now both deceased, he thinks of them in heaven enjoying an endless game and vigorous conversation with dear friends and family.

Was the fulfillment of human dreams for a better world now at hand? Now that peace had come, would it last? Now that new prosperity had come, would it really enrich life and increase social justice? Having achieved the highest standard of living in history, how well would Americans choose to live (quality of life as well as quantity of possessions)? With the largest system of education in the world, for what would the nation educate its growing num-

---

[38]*Time* magazine, special issue titled "American Visions" (Spring 1997), 32.

ber of youth? In what or in whom could people finally put their faith? Americans had relaxed some of their traditional moral standards and religious beliefs; could they preserve themselves from corruption and decadence? Maybe the 1950s would hold the answers. Maybe the shadows of war had passed and the light of lasting peace and real justice lay just ahead. Maybe. The hope seemed to be symbolized well by *Brigadoon*, the Drama Critics' recipient of the Circle Award for the best musical show of 1947. Highlanders were pictured as celebrating a wedding in a mythical Scottish town that appears only for a single day every hundred years. Might such a beautiful day be just ahead for the United States and the whole world with which it now was so interlocked? All hoped it would.

One analyst, however, reflects on an ominous dimension of the boom times after World War II, a trend that would become a social tidal wave by the 1970s. Robert Bork observes that these war years created a sense of national unity very different from the cultural fragmentation to come in following decades. The generations who lived through those depression and then war times of the 1930s and 1940s "were not very susceptible to extreme hedonism, but they raised a generation that was." A new affluence increasingly would come to be coupled with a radical individualism with its "drastic reduction of limits to personal gratification."[39] Is authentic freedom to be defined as the elimination of virtually all social, moral, and religious restraints? The biblical warning too often was failing to be heeded: "You ask and do not receive, because you ask wrongly, in order to spend what you get on your pleasures" (James 4:3).

One thing seemed clear enough. It was a new day in America, a fresh social beginning.[40] Some even were calling it a new time in world history, an "American High," the "Pax Americana." Maybe the perspective of President Franklin D. Roosevelt was right, although soon to be outdated. When he assumed his third term in office in 1941 (just as the high school classes of 1959 were being born and Asia and Europe already were at war), he announced to the nation:

> On each national day of inauguration since 1789, the people have renewed their sense of dedication to the United States. In Washington's day the task of the people was to create and weld together a nation. In

---

[39]Robert Bork, *Slouching Towards Gomorrah: Modern Liberalism and American Decline* (N.Y.: Regan Books, Harper-Collins, 1996), 5, 8.

[40]See William Strauss and Neil Howe, *The Fourth Turning* (N.Y.: Broadway Books, 1997), for a description of these post-war years as the "first turning."

Lincoln's day the task of the people was to preserve that nation from disruption from within. In this day the task of the people is to save that nation and its institutions from disruption from without.[41]

The immediate threat from without was eliminated in 1945. To follow would be a renewed threat of disruption or at least significant erosion from within. In the 1950s and then especially in the 1960s the U.S. would experience increasing wealth, rapid "progress," social strain, the deterioration of much that once was thought traditional and even sacred, and finally internal disruption on a scale not seen since the Civil War a century earlier. The large war on land, sea, and in the air had ceased in 1945; in its place would be new and subtler frontiers of conflict and challenge to the integrity and cohesion of the nation. Would the traditional idealism, faith, pragmatism, and future vision of the American people be adequate to the challenge? The tendency, despite all the possible negatives, was to be a cockeyed optimist.

---

[41]President Franklin D. Roosevelt, third inaugural address to the nation, January 20, 1941.

Taking Time To Reflect

1. In what ways was the decade of the 1940s one of the more momentous decades in the whole history of the world?

2. Is there such a thing as a "just" or "good" war—as World War II typically is viewed by Americans?

3. Why do human governments repeatedly build empires at the expense of other people? Is there something essentially different about the Kingdom of God that seeks to spread its loving reign through Jesus Christ to all corners of the creation?

4. The end of World War II left the United States as a leader of the world, the generally recognized protector of what is good and right. Has this role been played well, or has even this country been empire-building in its own way by use of its wealth and military power?

5. Note again the comments about Arthur Miller's famous drama, *Death of a Salesman*. Do many people in a fast-paced and competitive society like the United States tend to live by illusions and quiet desperation? Is there something in life that is more important than "getting ahead"?

6. On what bases did the victors in World War II seek to build a more just world in which peace could be preserved?

7. What major social shifts in the late 1940s would have long-term implications for life in the United States to the end of the century?

8. In 1946 Elton Trueblood argued that "the only answer to atomic power is moral power." What did he mean? Was he right in the circumstances of the late 1940s? Is he still right at the close of the twentieth century?

9. Late in this chapter, a series of probing questions are posed that involve the relationship between the quality of America's living and believing and its likely success in preserving its integrity as a nation and its effective leadership in world affairs. From the later perspective now available, how has the country done?

Chapter Three

Kids in the Bright Years

1950s

———

Coming home to politics as a 61-year-old novice after 40 years
in the Army, Dwight David Eisenhower nonplused his rivals.
His politics were so vague as to be almost unassailable.
Admitted one frustrated political rival, "It looks like he's
pretty much for home, mother, and heaven."

———

For the Lord of hosts has a day against all that is proud and
lofty, against all that is lifted up and high…. The haughtiness
of people shall be humbled, and the pride of everyone shall be
brought low; and the Lord alone will be exalted on that day.
(Isaiah 2:12, 17)

———

Prior transitions from war to peace were accompanied by painful economic downturns. But the 1950s departed from that tradition as the result of massive federal intervention and the fact that the United States emerged from World War II physically unscathed. The 1950s in the U.S. can be characterized generally as years of economic and technological expansion, political apathy, Cold War anxiety, and a deferring of any real addressing of the nation's significant social problems—racial discrimination in particular. Symbolic was the immensely popular 1935 American musical *Porgy and Bess*. At the end of a hot summer day, a black mother attempts to lull her baby to sleep by singing "Summertime." The baby finally does sleep, but the courtyard of the slum was dangerously awake. In the U.S. of the 1950s, there surely were heat and danger, but it seemed like a long summer evening in which many Americans were pleased for a chance to look the other way and sleep.

A conservative consensus had developed after the nation's enduring of a terrible economic depression and then a world war. It was time for people to catch their breath after all the sacrifices and anxieties. Radical ideologies had been discredited and capitalism now was working wonderfully well. Consumption was king. Memories of war were still relatively close at hand, but the priority was on acquiring the numerous material benefits of peace. Still thinking of itself as a Christian nation, the U.S. of the 1950s respected in principle the warning of Isaiah 2 that danger lies in the path of the proud and haughty. Respect for the biblical tradition, however, impacted very little the national preoccupation with "getting ahead" in what was understandably believed to be the greatest nation on earth. One major peace benefit was the opportunity of millions of Americans to be part of growing and more settled families, with fathers no longer being shipped across the world and put directly in harm's way (except for the Korean conflict in the early part of the decade).

In 1950 there were some 151 million Americans. By 1960 the nation's population would increase at what some thought the alarmingly high rate of nineteen percent. America was "bullish" on babies and had some trouble assimilating the new army of children being born.[1] School enrollments swelled by thirty percent over the decade as the "baby boomers" born after World War II came of school age. Expansion was a keynote of the decade. The nation now was determined to enjoy a range of new technologies that had been developed earlier for wartime use. The innovations soon reached into nearly every American home. Musical recordings became a typical example. In 1950 most records were 78 rpm and were played on raspy, single-speaker sets. By 1960, however, 45 rpm records and long-play albums were being enjoyed on high-quality, low-cost stereophonic sound systems. At the production level, these new technologies tended to be labor-saving and soon would even be labor-replacing in some cases.

Sometimes known as America's "Golden Age," the 1950s needed constant and heavy investment to fuel the rising level of consumer demand. Increasingly "it did not need people except as consumers...[although] for a generation this was not obvious."[2] Before the pain of downward economic

---

[1]From 1950 to 1960, for instance, the number of Girl and Brownie Scouts jumped from 1.8 to 4 million and Little League baseball teams from 766 to 5,700. The "patron saint" to guide the care of these children was Dr. Benjamin Spock, whose book *Common Sense Book of Baby and Child Care* sold about a million copies every year in the fifties.

[2]Eric Hobsbawm, *The Age of Extremes* (N.Y.: Vintage Books, Random House, 1994), 266.

adjustments were sure to come, the fifties was a time to produce, consume, and enjoy. The American economy was growing so fast that the industrial working class remained well employed. The U.S. had reached mid-century in a position of pride and power in the world community. As one historian notes, in the 1950s it seemed clear that this was "God's country."[3]

Typical characterizations of this decade focus on the public's preoccupation with comfort and contentment. It was a time of rapid economic expansion and general social conservatism. There was a resurgence of religious activity, too often the kind uncritically supporting the social status quo. In 1959 the phenomenon of big fins on big automobiles peaked, a ready symbol that it had been a decade of the open road that seemed to lead to a big and wonderful future. The ride was a mixture of fantasy and self-indulgence—and what a ride it was! In 1972 a young drama student was chosen to play a male character of the 1950s in a 7-Up commercial. Although Mandy Patinkin knew little about that decade at the time, he later admitted: "As soon as I put on the black leather jacket, the jeans and the boots, and combed my hair into a greasy ducktail, something happened to me. My shoulders dropped, my head cocked at an angle, and I felt tough and sexy. I felt on top of the world. And then I knew what the '50s were all about."[4]

Ominous, But Upbeat

The decade began awkwardly indeed. By 1950 Russia had military forces far superior to the United States (at least in sheer volume) and appeared out to conquer the world. The real obstacle was America's monopoly on possession of the atomic bomb. That very year, however, President Truman learned that atomic secrets had been leaked to Russia for years. There seemed no choice. The U.S. would have to begin active development of an H-bomb, a super weapon far more destructive than the atomic bombs dropped on Japan. The first was test fired in 1952, totally obliterating a Pacific island with a power previously unknown to humanity. But Russia tested an explosion of its own H-bomb in Siberia the very next year. A frightening arms race was on. For the next four decades this extremely dangerous and expensive race would be a central feature of international life. Military spending in the U.S. rose sharply to $44 billion in 1953, a stunning sixty percent of the federal budget.

Korea long had been a battleground for Russia, China, and Japan, but it was a faraway land little known to most Americans. Following World War II,

---

[3] J. Ronald Oakley, *God's Country: America in the Fifties* (N.Y.: December Books, 1986).

[4] "Back to the '50s," *Newsweek* (October 16, 1972), 82.

A chaplain pray-ing for wounded troops during the Korean conflict.

the Korean peninsula had been occupied by U.S. troops in the south and units of the U.S.S.R. in the north. This division, supposed to be temporary, quickly hardened in the Cold War atmosphere. Suddenly, in June 1950, about 90,000 soldiers from the north stormed into South Korea. Within a day, American war planes arrived from bases in Japan, with the Seventh Fleet and American ground troops not far behind. President Truman assumed that Russia was an active partner in North Korea's aggression—the initial invasion southward was led by 150 Russian-built tanks.[5] He acted decisively and without even consulting with Congress, an important precedent that would become so controversial in the Vietnam war of the next decade. Truman emphasized that this was a "police action" of the United Nations. Many American veterans of World War II, only now getting their domestic lives back together, got the call to active duty once again. The Security Council of the young United Nations (minus the boycotting U.S.S.R.) voted unanimously to send in troops. This would be the first time in history that a world organization would mobilize to stop aggression (although a large majority of the personnel and equipment would be American).

The stakes got even higher when the Chinese became directly involved, devastating many U.N. units with waves of some 360,000 attacking troops. Their alarming advance southward finally was stopped at the 38th parallel along a ridge of mountains later known as Heartbreak Ridge and Pork Chop Hill. General Douglas MacArthur pressed for all-out war on China, even sug-

---

[5]Later it was learned that Soviet pilots had battled American planes over South Korea, masking their identity by wearing Chinese uniforms and using Chinese phrases over the radio.

gesting the seeding of the banks of the Yalu River with radioactive waste. President Truman, who earlier had ordered the dropping of the two atomic bombs on Japan, said no to MacArthur and had to replace him. The president did order an attack on North Korean forces, the first attempt by the U.S. since the onset of the Cold War to go beyond containment to seek the actual destruction of an established communist regime. But Truman wanted no U.S. crossing of the Russian or Chinese borders, determined to avoid a "gigantic bloody trap" of war with China. This restraint finally helped bring a military stalemate. The armistice finally was signed in July 1953, and has permanently divided Korea to this day. Before that signing, however, 34,000 Americans had been killed in action and another 103,000 wounded and missing. South Korean casualties were about 1 million, with North Korean and Chinese an estimated 1.5 million. The final result, a typical irony of war, was that the boundary between North and South Korea had moved only a few dozen miles from where it was before the conflict! The whole affair helped lead in 1952 to the Republican Party retaking control of the White House and Congress. People were weary of conflict, taxes, inflation, and frequent charges of corruption in high places. They tended to blame President Truman, who chose not to run again in the face of it all.

War seemed to keep reappearing in one form or another, especially in Southeast Asia. In 1954, for instance, Ho Chi Minh led Vietnam in a final defeat of the French, who had hoped to reclaim their colonial holdings after the Japanese occupation during World War II. This successful move for independence ended eight years of war that had cost 400,000 lives. Another vestige of European colonial influence was ending. Just beginning was a political situation in Vietnam that would bring chaos to the very streets of the United States in just a few years. Most American high school students in the 1950s had no idea where Vietnam even was! That too would end soon. Meanwhile, members of the J-M class of 1959 walked into Mr. Long's class one day and heard him announce soberly: "Today there is a war on every continent!" He meant the "Cold War" that recognized no geographic borders, but was frightening the whole world. We young men in the class would end the decade with high school diplomas in our hands, draft cards in our wallets, and the fearful thought of being assigned a 1-A status.

The two major adversaries of the Cold War were now poised to "battle" for dominance in this world and in even a race into the space beyond this world, a race having both military and commercial implications of unimagined proportions. The United States, a little complacent in its supposed leadership of the world, was shocked by the U.S.S.R.'s successful launch of Sputnik I in

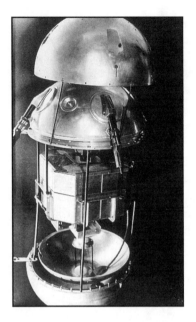

Seen here is Sputnik I, the first Russian satellite to enter space, displayed on a stand shortly before its launching on October 4, 1957.

October 1957, and in 1959 still lagged far behind in the technology for exploring space. Sputnik was humanity's first satellite in space, a technological "Pearl Harbor" that dealt a serious blow to America's belief in its scientific and weapons superiority in the world. A little ball weighing less than 200 pounds was racing around the Earth at 18,000 miles per hour, carrying Russian markings, doing communist business of unknown dimensions, and shaking America's self-confidence. G. Mennen Williams, governor of Michigan, ridiculed the American space effort:

> Oh little Sputnik
> With made-in-Moscow beep,
> You tell the world it's a Commie sky
> And Uncle Sam's asleep.[6]

Public debate in the U.S. soon swirled around the question of whether America's schools were inferior to those in Russia. Federal, state, and local appropriations for public education doubled between 1957 and 1964. During the 1950s the U.S. did more than try to refocus education, especially toward the scientific disciplines. It conducted some 122 atomic and nuclear bomb tests, with the dangers of radioactive fallout still little known (or at least lit-

---

[6]Peter Biskind, *Seeing Is Believing: How Hollywood Taught Us to Stop Worrying and Love the Fifties* (N.Y., 1983), 337.

tle admitted). Even so, the stakes were seen as so high that there was no turning back, whatever the risks. The National Aeronautics and Space Administration (NASA) was created in 1958. Peace was understood to be dependent on having the biggest weapons. By the late 1950s there were a few pacifist protesters opposing this weapons testing and stockpiling, but the general public viewed such protesters as naive dupes of the communists. Even if the public may not have been listening, there now were dissenters to the prevailing definitions of the Cold War itself. Not all of the young were members of the "Silent Generation." The relatively few who were ready to speak out were the first trickle of what soon would be a torrent of social protest. Among their leaders was the unlikely figure of a Trappist monk living in the Abbey of Gethsemani in rural Kentucky since 1941. Thomas Merton had read carefully about Gandhi and was exploring in prayer and print the social implications of the Christian gospel. His fresh voice on behalf of peace and against nuclear weapons brought him considerable public attention, even the accusation that he was being used by the communists.[7]

At least Americans could believe in their beloved President Dwight Eisenhower and in the seemingly infinite capacity of the U.S. to meet any challenge. It was natural that the man who would preside politically over America during most of the 1950s was himself perceived to be quite serene and secure, the nation's ideal grandfather. Eisenhower was nearly everyone's hero. He had mobilized and coordinated one of the greatest military adventures in history, the massive Allied invasion of Europe that brought Hitler to his knees. Now he was trusted to end the stalemate in Korea. First elected to the presidency in 1952 with Richard Nixon sharing the Republican ticket, "Ike" led in a welcome respite from controversy and conflict. Charting a very middle-of-the-road political course, he made a difficult target for critics and was the first Republican since Ulysses Grant (President 1868-1876) to serve two full terms.

The year 1959, Eisenhower's seventh in office, probably had been his best. He was drawing power from being able to say, "I'm not running for anything. I'm only trying to do my very best. . .for America." His best had helped the 1950s to be progressive and prosperous on the surface, while remaining on a war footing just beyond common sight. Eisenhower was a shrewd politician who tended to suppress or at least ignore some profound social problems that shortly after his time would erupt to imperil the stability of the nation itself.

---

[7]For a good biography of Thomas Merton, see Jim Forest, *Living With Wisdom: A Life of Thomas Merton* (Maryknoll, N.Y.: Orbis Books, 1991).

Dwight "Ike" Eisenhower (with his wife Mamie) campaigning by train for the presidency in 1952.

At least for the 1950s, however, home ownership was a new joy for many American families, consumerism was virtually a national lifestyle, and TV ads made it appear that the good life was finally being shared by all. Big tensions were just below the surface and would not stay there much longer; but in the meantime the 1950s were the bright years.

The world's business picture in 1959 was upbeat to say the least. Japan had already managed to rebuild its nation so fast after the war's devastation that it now was making major investments overseas. The worst strike in the history of the American steel industry had burdened the U.S. economy in 1959. Even so, production and consumption soared, with a ten percent increase in retail sales over the previous year. The U.S. economy was showing astounding strength. Production was high and unemployment low. Numerous nations were making clear that they were not interested in "Russian borsch or communal Chinese gruel." Having sampled the potentials of free enterprise, "they are determined to set down to the entire meal. The position of the U.S. was never stronger."[8] One example was the initiative of the country's Big Three automakers. Having for years watched the rising number of small foreign cars on American streets, in 1959 they answered with their own compact models, the Ford Falcon, Chevrolet Corvair, and Chrysler Valiant. Americans responded well and were enjoying longer lives in which to drive. In 1900 life expectancy in the U.S. was about 49 years for whites and 33 for nonwhites. By 1950 these numbers were up to 69 and 60 respectively.

---

[8]*Time* magazine, December 28, 1959, 57.

Increased international trade was essential, and that needed to include the major agricultural and industrial centers that bordered the Great Lakes. In 1954 Canada and the U.S. agreed to build a water system able to handle heavy traffic and large ships that would connect the area to world markets. The St. Lawrence Seaway was opened in 1959, helping large quantities of iron ore, wheat, corn, barley, soybeans, and manufactured goods to leave places like Ohio for distant destinations. The U.S. now had a third seacoast. Ohio had become a center for space research and atomic energy projects. Northeast Ohio was becoming not only the "Crossroads" between Chicago and New York; it was conveniently between the ports of Asia and Europe. As commerce boomed, paradoxes persisted.

On the one hand, the American people were frightened by the "Red Menace" of aggressive communism; on the other hand, they were vigorously pursuing the good life for themselves and their families. A ready symbol of the social schizophrenia was the day after Christmas 1947, in New York City. That day the city experienced the heaviest snowfall ever recorded there. The tinsel of the season was heavily blanketed and city traffic was nearly paralyzed by this unexpected event. So it was with the times in general. Peace and progress were the prominent tinsel of the time; but somehow the ongoing celebration was being blanketed with the fearful chill of the Cold War that hovered over all of life with the possibility that suddenly it would disrupt everything. It hardly helped when Nikita Khrushchev visited the U.S. in 1959, the first leader of the Soviet Union to come to these shores. He was brash and belligerent. American images of a defiant Khrushchev joined with memories of the strategic military significance of Alaska and Hawaii during World War II to help win final approval of their longstanding requests for U.S. statehood. In 1959, weeks after all the high school graduations, they were officially added to the Union as states 49 and 50.

The country was expanding, consolidating its world leadership, and determined to face any and all challenges. The members of the classes of 1959 saw all of President Eisenhower's postwar years in office. They also would live through all of the presidencies for the rest of the century. Soon social revolution would gather speed and the threat of world disaster would rise, fall, and always rise again. The remaining decades of the century would slowly and awkwardly run their course. This class always would be there, somewhere on the stage or at least close by in the wings of national life. Its growing-up years were the 1950s, the decade of really good times for the country. It was a wonderful era in which to mature just before graduating from high school, going off to marriage, college, jobs, or military service, and just before chaos hit the country's city streets and blanketed the TV screens. That would be the 1960s. First:

> The whole world, many Americans seemed to think by 1957, was turning itself over to please the special, God-graced generation—and its children—that had triumphed over depression and fascism, that would sooner or later vanquish Communism, and that was destined to live happily ever after (well, almost) in a fairy tale of health, wealth, and happiness.[9]

Really Good Times

The Jackson-Milton class of 1959 grew up in the midst of these times of relief from war, national self-confidence, and economic and social optimism. They didn't realize it, of course, having nothing to compare it with. Most of these young people were members of families with modest financial resources and limited cultural advantages, although they were rich by world standards of the time. Their parents still carried vivid memories of economic hardship and then war sacrifice. These memories were shared with their children in varying degrees, although the children were now being reared in quite a different world.

The Youngstown, Ohio, area was heavily dependent on the steel industry. It had been one of the economically hardest hit industrial centers in the nation in the 1930s (low demand for steel). This changed in 1940 when huge quantities of war materials were needed quickly. Facilities in the immediate Youngstown area soon were turning out one-tenth of the nation's total steel production. Women flooded the workplace as about 14,000 men from Mahoning County were drafted into the service in a 29-month period beginning in 1940.[10] Upwards of 30,000 young men had left Mahoning County by the fall of 1943 to serve in the armed forces.[11] By contrast with the volatile 1930s and 1940s, however, the 1950s seemed in many ways like the whisper of a quiet summer evening. Hopes were high, times were good, most doors were open. The right people had won the terrible war. Goodness had prevailed and there was expanding affluence across America. Now mighty abroad, the world's major postwar power, and mighty at home with production and consumption booming, the U.S. seemed stable, strong, good,

---

[9]James T. Patterson, *Grand Expectations: The United States, 1945-1974* (N.Y.: Oxford University Press, 1996), 311.

[10]Howard Aley, *A Heritage To Share: The Bicentennial History of Youngstown and Mahoning County, Ohio* (Youngstown: The Bicentennial Commission, 1975), 369-370.

[11]Howard Aley, *The Time of Your Life: The One Hundred Twenty-Fifth Anniversary History of the Mahoning County Agricultural Society* (Canfield Fair, 1846-1971), 30.

almost ideal. Federal funds were fueling an unprecedented era of economic growth—financing for home mortgages, stipends for education, money for major new roadways, and investment in scientific research that was rapidly producing massive economic dividends. Eight of the ten bestselling nonfiction books in 1950 had how-to and self-help emphases. They included *Betty Crocker's Picture Cook Book*, *The Baby*, and *Look Younger, Live Longer* by Gayelord Hauser. People wanted to make everything work well.

The ideal of American society in the 1950s seemed to be "togetherness," particularly a cohesive family unit enhanced by the owning of one's own home. Like the hero in Sloan Wilson's *Man in the Gray Flannel Suit*, the ideal male was a hard striver and the female a devoted nurturer. The TV sitcom *Leave It To Beaver* projected the image of a suburban never-never land where nurturing moms and loving dads related constructively to their well-adjusted although sometimes mischievous children. The divorce rate, having peaked in 1946, dropped and remained remarkably stable in the 1950s. On the typical weekday, the father returned home from work to spend time with wife and kids—often all of them eating a frozen "TV dinner" (first introduced in 1954[12]) and watching television together in the evenings. Some four million of these amazing new video boxes now were being carried into American homes annually.

The nation was still heavily committed to newspapers and magazines as primary means of communication and entertainment. In 1950 the country had 1,772 daily newspapers with an average circulation per issue of 53.8 million. But now people were becoming fascinated with this new medium called television. The number of TV stations skyrocketed from 6 in 1946 to 442 in 1956. The first television station in Cleveland, WEWS-TV, started broadcasting in 1947.[13] Two years after the end of World War II only 7,000 TV sets were sold. By the middle of the 1950s, sixty-six percent of all American homes had sets and bulky and awkwardly obvious antennas rising above their roofs. This dramatic development in family life was to alter social values and patterns significantly. For instance, it brought widely diverse people together for the first time in common cultural experiences. In 1950 only three percent of America's rural homes had a television. By 1960 this figure would leap to eighty percent!

---

[12]The first TV ad in 1953 was for Swanson TV Dinners, said to be a "revolutionary new food trend," a "complete quick-frozen turkey dinner ready to heat and serve."

[13]In 1947, Burr Tillstrom went on the air in Chicago with "Kukla, Fran, and Ollie," one of the better loved children's TV programs of all time. A real communication pioneer, Tillstrom had originated numerous TV broadcasts from the World's Fair in 1939.

Lucille Ball and Desi Arnez in a scene from the long-running comedy, "I Love Lucy."

John and Barry were J-M 1959 classmates who lived in Craig Beach on the western shore of Lake Milton (population 400). They remember their first contact with television around 1950. A local family got a TV set and invited the little neighborhood to their living room to watch a late-evening boxing match (they charged a nominal admission fee to their house, probably to help pay for the set!). Boxers Archie Moore, Sugar Ray Robinson, Rocky Marciano, and Ezzard Charles became household names, as did the wrestler Gorgeous George. What a fascination it all was! On a little higher cultural plane, classmate Richard lived very near the school in North Jackson. There now was a TV in his home and the parents arranged for his whole sixth-grade class to come to the house and watch Dwight Eisenhower be sworn in as President of the United States. Eisenhower was the first presidential candidate to use television in the service of effective politics. It already was serving the news industry. On the first telecast of his *See It Now* program (November 18, 1951), Edward R. Murrow was able to show the public simultaneous pictures of the Brooklyn and Golden Gate Bridges, commenting: "We are impressed by a medium through which a man sitting in his living room has been able for the first time to look at two oceans at once." The times were amazing.

The Texaco Star Theater, featuring the outrageous antics of "Uncle Miltie" (Milton Berle), began pioneering in television in 1948. Berle's salary reached the astounding figure of $11,500 per week in 1950-51.[14] In June of 1955 this popular show was canceled. What had happened? Berle saw the young medi-

---

[14]As of January, 1950, the national minimum wage was raised to 75 cents per hour (amounting to $30 per week for five eight-hour days).

um of television already changing: "The unions were in, costs were mounting, star acts had learned the value of television and were demanding more."[15] Now he was off to California to do the first color series. Times were changing, getting more technical, tantalizing, and tense; but they were still relatively simple. Milton Berle and Jackie Gleason were straightforwardly slapstick and clearly hilarious. Lucille Ball, highlighted for years in the very popular *I Love Lucy* show, was side-splittingly funny. Joining her in providing the public with "clean" and crazy fun was Red Skelton. He was an extremely popular comic whose TV show placed among the Top 10 eight times during its run from 1951 to 1971. As a sentimental clown, he delighted audiences by playing Clem Kadiddlehopper and Freddie the Freeloader.

Television shows like *Father Knows Best* subtly reassured Americans every week that traditional gender roles were still the way to true happiness and stability in the midst of much change. Jackie Gleason played Brooklyn bus driver Ralph Kramden in *The Honeymooners*. The hilarious episodes were about two working-class families scheming to make it big in America (one drove a bus, the other worked in the city sewers). Then there was that wonderful TV series *The Lone Ranger*, that allowed loyal viewing millions to "return to those thrilling days of yesteryear." In those days—days people hoped were real again—bandits were on the loose, but humble righteousness on a white horse always prevailed. ABC-TV aired 221 episodes between 1949 and 1957, with NBC and CBS doing reruns through 1961. The legendary masked man portrayed the triumph of good over evil by righting wrongs and selflessly helping hurting people, always arriving at the trouble just in time and riding away in anonymous humility to the musical thrill of the "William Tell Overture." As seen on TV in the 1950s, most things looked new and wholesome, a world of beauty to be enjoyed and material plenty ready to be consumed.

In the early 1950s Walt Disney was planning the construction of Disneyland in Southern California and its initial advertisement on his new television show. His weekly program began in 1954 and soon launched the near cult following of Davy Crockett. Fess Parker portrayed this frontier character with 40 million Americans watching. Suddenly there was a $100 million market for coonskin caps. The Disney program had different segments patterned after the themes of the coming new park—Adventureland, Frontierland, Fantasyland, and Tomorrowland. The idea of the park came in part from Walt Disney's own boredom when taking his two daughters to the merry-go-

---

[15]Milton Berle, with Haskel Frankel, *Milton Berle: An Autobiography* (N.Y.: Delacorte Press, 1974), 318.

Southern California's Disneyland, on opening day in July 1955.

round in a small amusement park, the Southern California version of the park at Lake Milton, Ohio, enjoyed by so many in the J-M class of 1959. Disney believed in family entertainment, but personally was bored by sitting on a bench eating peanuts while the girls rode. What about a family park where parents and children could have fun together? What about a grand place for family togetherness on the weekend? Cars were now plentiful, gasoline was cheap, and there was a burgeoning highway system in Southern California. The new Disneyland, soon a reality, was symbolic of the times:

> ...the essence of America—a place of warmth and illusion, with nostalgia of the past, complexities of the present, and glimpses of the future. As soon as visitors step through the gate, like Alice stepping through the Looking Glass, they will be entering another world—a small midwestern town at the turn of the century, Grandma's Farm, the palace of Cinderella's Prince Charming, the Old West, outer space.... There was to be no cheap carnival atmosphere—no thrill rides, alcoholic beverages, games of chance, shoddy merchandise, or unfair prices for refreshments.[16]

Disneyland opened to the public in July 1955. A million people visited the park in the first seven weeks and immediately it became the premier tourist attraction for both Americans and foreign visitors. It was a modern mecca of

[16]In *Journal of Popular Culture* (Summer, 1992), 150.

Fess Parker portrayed Davy Crockett on television, and suddenly there was a $100 million market for coonskin caps.

welcome nostalgia, imagination, and innocent fun for the whole family. In many ways, it was a picture of the 1950s.

Teenagers of the time tended to focus their lives around the *Top 10* songs on the radio. Some of the most popular artists were Patti Page, Tony Bennett, Kay Starr, Bing Crosby, Eddie Fisher, Perry Como, Nat King Cole, Rosemary Clooney, and amiable groups like the Ames Brothers and the Andrews Sisters. The popular big band and swing music of the 1940s remained prominent, with most popular songs being "idealistic, sentimental portrayals of a dream world of love and romance, untainted by serious social and personal problems."[17] In 1956 high school students were singing and dancing to Elvis Presley's "Love Me Tender," followed the next year by songs of the Everly Brothers and new teen idols Paul Anka, Pat Boone, and Ricky Nelson. Dean Martin, from Steubenville, Ohio, near Youngstown, first teamed with Jerry Lewis in 1947 to become a leading comedy duo of the 1950s. Martin was the smooth straightman who crooned popular tunes on the side; Jerry was the slapstick partner who usually got a pie in the face instead of the girl.[18] Gene Kelly captured the postwar American mood with his muscular, regular-guy showmanship. His clever and lighthearted dancing was never better than in the beloved 1952 movie *Singing in the Rain*. Another hit song of the time was "Everything's Coming Up Roses." At least in general, that is the way it really seemed to be.

---

[17]Oakley, *God's Country*, 11.

[18]Dean Martin died on Christmas day in 1995, in a way symbolizing the closing of what seemed a more carefree era. See Martin's life story in Nick Tosches, *Dino* (N.Y.: Dell Publishing, 1992).

In the 1950s, automobiles became numerous, large, a carrier of the nation's aggressive and mobile self-image.

The moral tone of popular entertainment remained relatively innocent by later standards. The U.S. of the 1950s still largely resembled the small-town America idealized in the Norman Rockwell paintings featured on the covers of the very popular *Saturday Evening Post* magazine. Wishing to avoid any public offense and thus threat to revenues, in the early years of television husbands and wives were shown sleeping in different beds, the ultimate goal of lovers was a passionate kiss, and subjects like rape and homosexuality were strictly taboo. This would begin to change in 1953 when the first issue of *Playboy* magazine hit the newsstands with its centerfold of Marilyn Monroe. Then the novel *Peyton Place* by Grace Metalious was released in 1956 and became one of the bestsellers of all time. The movie industry began to capitalize on "sexy" books to feed the new public taste and tolerance. It also began—gingerly—to handle related controversial subjects: miscegenation in *Island in the Sun* (1957); homosexuality in *Compulsion* (1958); and abortion in *Blue Denim* (1959). By 1959 the really popular TV shows were dominated by brash, frontier-crossing, good-guy westerns. There was *Gunsmoke*, *Wagon Train*, *Have Gun—Will Travel*, *The Rifleman*, *Maverick*, and *Tales of Wells Fargo*. These were joined by the slapstick comedy of Dean Martin and Jerry Lewis, *The Jackie Gleason Show*, *I Love Lucy*, and *The Red Skelton Show*. The nation was expanding, recovering, conquering, laughing, experimenting—and constantly driving.

Earlier the auto industry had to be converted to war production, with only 84,000 cars produced in the U.S. in 1945 and strict gasoline restrictions on the use of cars for private purposes. But as the class of 1959 was beginning high school in 1955, annual sales of cars had rebounded to 7.9 million. And what cars they were! Many had large V-8 engines, tail fins, and quantities of decorative chrome. Concludes one social historian: "There's something wonderful, disquieting, and, in the end, embarrassing about America's automobiles of the 1950s: the lunkers, the dreamboats, the befinned, bechromed behemoths that lurked in the driveways of several million brand new ranch houses in the suburbs (because they wouldn't fit in the garage!)."[19] These bloated Fords, GMs, and Chryslers were signs of the times, carriers of the image Americans had of themselves. By the end of the 1950s, seventy-seven percent of all American families owned at least one car and there were many new places to take them. Booming now was the expanding motel industry, drive-in movie lots, even banks and restaurants that were opening drive-through service. In 1955 the first McDonalds started selling hamburgers in Des Plaines, Illinois. Even food would now become "fast" and car related.

Times seemed relatively simple and carefree, sometimes boring, but really good, even if life was from paycheck to paycheck for millions of families. We kids in the communities around North Jackson, Ohio, trick-or-treated around the local streets at Halloween with lots of homemade fun and little fear of the dark. Out at Lake Milton, Shirley found the Village Craig Beach a wonderful place to grow up. In the summers she played on the lake and joined classmates Delores and John in operating and maintaining children's rides, a bowling alley, and concession stands in the local amusement park. In the summer many families of the area would go to the nearby Canfield Fair, widely heralded as one of the bigger and best in the whole nation.[20] Its 114th annual convening happened during the summer after the class of 1959 had just graduated from high school. Now some 50,000 cars were coming in and out of this fair's gates each summer. Richard was one member of the J-M class of 1959 for whom the Canfield Fair was an annual highlight of his life. A 4-H member from a North Jackson farming family, as a teenager he would tent on the grounds during the whole fair and show his cattle. The Canfield Fair had grown up with and proudly exhibited the life of the nation ever since its founding in 1846 as the Mahoning County Agricultural Society. In the 1950s the fair featured several firsts, including live television coverage, an air-conditioned exhibit, the General Motors Futurama Show, the Lennon Sisters of the Lawrence Welk Show singing to overflow grandstand crowds, and Gabby Hayes, veteran of many western movies who gave personal autographs to a lineup of an estimated 1,100 youngsters. It was America on parade in Northeast Ohio.

The American population had shifted from surviving the Depression (1930s) to winning the war (1940s) to trying to win the peace (1950s). Every

---

[19]Karal Ann Marling, *As Seen On TV: The Visual Culture of Everyday Life in the 1950s* (Cambridge, Mass.: Harvard University Press, 1994), 129.

[20]Howard Aley, *The Time of Your Life*, 50.

Senator Joseph McCarthy, relentless fighter of communism, shown here displaying a document during his telecast, attacking Governor Adlai Stevenson.

weekday morning beginning in 1952, Dave Garroway hosted the popular *Today Show* on television, ending each day's edition of the news with his right hand raised and his gentle voice offering to the viewing public the sincere benediction, "Peace!" Americans surely hoped so. It was a fast-moving and still very dangerous world.

New Worries, Fresh Hope

Good perspective is as important to possess as difficult to find. Those who track the trends in public events usually try to make overall sense of things. One natural occasion for such stock-taking was the middle of the twentieth century. What event in the year 1949, for example, was judged to hold the potential for having the most lasting effect on the course of human history? The choice appeared to the *Christian Century* magazine to be between the negatives of world events and the emerging positives of new technologies.[21] Without question, despite the big war being over, developments on the world scene were hardly encouraging. In 1949 the communists proclaimed the new People's Republic of China. Mao Tse-tung soon drove the American-backed Chiang Kai-shek from the Asian mainland. In fact, there was rising fear that communist agents had penetrated the very corridors of American government. This suspicion sent an ominous fear across the land.

Senator Joseph McCarthy of Wisconsin raised the general level of anxiety in the United States by "finding" numerous communists among U.S. leaders of government and culture. He announced in Wheeling, West Virginia (near Youngstown, Ohio), in 1950 that he had a list of 205 card-carrying com-

---

[21]"Retrospect," *The Christian Century*, December 28, 1949, 1533.

munists still working for and shaping policies of the U.S. State Department. His rhetoric was harsh indeed. McCarthy insisted that if anyone protested the anti-communist campaign that he was leading, they were "communists and queers," "pinkos" threatening the survival of the nation. Lengthy and tense hearings were watched by millions on television. By the time Congress finally condemned his excessive accusations in late 1954, McCarthy had spread much concern that maybe this powerful nation indeed was being undermined from within as well as from without. Things were just too good in this great nation to be ruined by some communist crazies! True Americanism surely called for staunch patriotism, belief in God, opposition to social agitation, and hatred of the "Reds." Since 1947 there had been numerous accusations and "black lists" of suspected communists involved in Hollywood. After all, a relatively few people in the film industry had enormous influence on the viewing public. Hollywood reacted in part by severely reducing the number of films dealing with serious and controversial subjects, focusing rather on comedies, musicals, westerns, and cops and robbers.

This "cold war" cycle of fear caused the classes of 1959 to learn in elementary school how to "duck and cover" as part of routine school safety drills. Beginning in 1958, and unknown to the American public until 1992, was the construction of a gigantic underground bunker in rural West Virginia, intended to enable the president and Congress to survive and function through and beyond World War III. Marxists had overwhelmed China. The Korean Conflict ended in 1953, but to Americans with fervent memories of V-J Day, it seemed like an almost humiliating stalemate with communist aggression. Closer to home, the social revolutionary Fidel Castro seized power in Cuba in 1959, denouncing that country's economic domination by the United States and starting decades of his rhetorical denouncing and threatening of his great foe only about 90 miles to the north. Castro soon became dependent on the Soviet Union, anxious to support him and move its own military presence into the Western Hemisphere and just outside the southeastern door to the United States.

Maybe two world wars in the twentieth century had in fact solved little or nothing on the world scene. Maybe America was not safe from sudden attack from just off Florida's shores. Maybe international organizations, especially the new United Nations and World Council of Churches,[22] somehow could bring sanity and unity to the fragile and still divided national and church

---

[22]The United Nations was first chartered in 1945, while the World Council of Churches convened its first Assembly at Amsterdam in 1948.

families of the earth. Maybe. Like the famous words of Charles Dickens generations earlier, the 1950s seemed to be the best and the worst of times.[23] The world was a wonderful and still a very volatile place.

George McCague, principal of Newton Falls High School neighboring Jackson-Milton, called 1959 "these perilous and challenging times."[24] On the other hand, technology was a new source of hope. Scientists now could create more than devastating bombs. There now was a polio vaccine and the dreaded small pox disease was beginning to be eradicated worldwide. Hope for a triumph over arthritis was coming from the Mayo Clinic and Henry Wallace had bred a chicken that presumably could triple the world's supply of eggs. The American people were enjoying a prosperity not known by any other people in all of human history. Science had made possible the sudden atomic devastation of two Japanese cities. Could new knowledge and skill also lead to the fulfillment of humanity's highest and holiest dreams? Well, at least holy was premature. Even so...

> It was a good time to be young and get on with family and career: Prices and inflation remained relatively low; and nearly everyone with a decent job could afford to own a home. Even if the specter of Communism lurked on the horizon . . . Americans trusted their leaders to tell them the truth, to make sound decisions, and to keep them out of war.[25]

During the 1950s suburbs grew six times faster than cities. Sometimes they were called the "crabgrass frontier." There was a housing boom for the middle class. Of the 13 million homes constructed in the 1950s, 11 million were on the fringes of city limits. Now seen everywhere was the rapid building of superhighways, station wagons, and computers. All of these would connect the cities, fill the garages, and develop the new gadgets now seemingly desired and affordable for most working people. The 1956 Interstate Highway Act provided for the construction of 41,000 miles of freeways to be built over ten years at an estimated $26 billion. It would be the largest public works project in American history to that time. Already by 1954 a 22-mile section of the new Ohio Turnpike was being opened in the Youngstown area. It was the first link in an emerging highway system to carry traffic unobstructed from New York City to Chicago and beyond. Appropriately, it came close to "the

---

[23]The opening line of the classic *A Tale of Two Cities* by Charles Dickens (1859).

[24]McCague was Principal of Newton Falls High School where several of the 1959 Jackson-Milton class attended their freshman year. The quote is from his message to the NF class of 1959, as in the 1959 edition of that school's annual *(NEFAO)*.

[25]David Halberstam, *The Fifties* (N.Y.: Fawcett Columbine, 1993), x.

Crossroads," North Jackson, a mid-point. This new Turnpike had a cloverleaf entrance/exit not far from the local high school. In the process of land acquisition and construction, it altered the lives of numerous local families, causing some uprooting and financial hardship. One member of the J-M class of 1959 (Ian), for instance, was part of a family forced to relocate its home. Their property lost its road access and became awkwardly land-locked. "Progress" comes at a price.

To fill these big new roads, the auto industry was booming. In the middle 1950s, almost as many cars were being junked each year as were being manufactured. Americans "raced to find the newest models with the largest fins."[26] High employment and rising wages among the growing middle class meant enormous buying power. With only about six percent of the world's population, U.S. citizens now were driving seventy-five percent of all existing cars, consuming nearly half of the world's energy, and producing about half of all manufactured products! During the 1950s Americans were buying five to seven million cars per year. The average American accepted the automobile as a necessary part of life—providing mobility, convenience, status, freedom, and privacy. It also allowed suburban living for those working in the city but no longer wanting be to trapped in its increasing problems. A car was accepted as a key to the good life in the United States. One victim was the American romance with the train. Trains in the U.S. had carried over a billion passengers a year in the early 1920s. Ridership dropped to 488 million passengers in 1950 and went on down to 327 million by 1960. Private cars now were handling much more of the short trips and airlines increasingly accounted for the longer ones.

Americans also purchased some four million boats in the 1950s. Not since the 1920s had so many Americans worshipped at the altar of prosperity and been blessed with considerable leisure time and the money to enjoy it. The whole recreation industry blossomed. Lake Milton, near the high school in North Jackson, was busy in the summers with boaters, water skiers, and swimmers from Youngstown, Akron, Cleveland, Pittsburgh, and elsewhere. Summer vacation cottages were numerous. Various members of the J-M class of 1959 were impacted directly. Jane's father worked at his business of selling and repairing boats and motors. Barry worked at Miller's Marina at Lake Milton to keep the gasoline tanks of the boats full and the water skiers equipped and happy. In 1950 Dorothy's father bought a motel at Lake Milton (a growing by-product of the auto craze) and then in 1959 a golf course on

---

[26]William Chafe, *The Unfinished Journey: America Since World War II* (N.Y.: Oxford University Press, 3rd ed., 1995), 118.

the east shore of Lake Milton. Maureen's father ran a business in the Youngstown area that supplied numerous businesses with vending machines, jukeboxes, and pool tables. The father of Francis was said to be involved heavily in Youngstown with both its many bars and bookies. Sometimes Youngstown was called "Little Chicago" because of the relatively high level of its organized crime and related violence. Some of the notorious families kept large speedboats at a private club on Lake Milton just across a small bay from the Amusement Park (and just a few hundred yards from the homes of

---

Supreme Court of the United States
Brown v. Board of Education (1954)
(excerpts only)

Segregation of white and Negro children in the public schools of a State solely on the basis of race, pursuant to state laws permitting or requiring such segregation, denies to Negro children the equal protection of the laws guaranteed by the Fourteenth Amendment—even though the physical facilities and other "tangible" factors of white and Negro schools may be equal....

The "separate but equal" doctrine adopted in *Plessy v. Ferguson*, 163 U.S. 537 [involving transportation] has no place in the field of public education....

Segregation of white and colored children in public schools has a detrimental effect upon the colored children. The impact is greater when it has the sanction of the law, for the policy of separating the races is usually interpreted as denoting the inferiority of the Negro group. A sense of inferiority affects the motivation of a child to learn. Segregation with the sanction of law, therefore, has a tendency to [retard] the educational and mental development of Negro children and to deprive them of some of the benefits they would receive in a racially integrated school system....

We conclude that, in the field of public education, the doctrine of "separate but equal" has no place. Separate educational facilities are inherently unequal. Therefore, we hold that the plaintiffs and others similarly situated for whom the actions have been brought are, by reason of the segregation complained of, deprived of the equal protection of the laws guaranteed by the Fourteenth Amendment....

TABLE 10

Delores, John, Barry, Charles, and Shirley). Americans were playing more than ever before—and not always gently.

Science was transforming common life. In 1954 a vaccine for dreaded polio was developed by Dr. Jonas Salk at the University of Pittsburgh Medical School. Soon it was being administered to crowds of school children across the nation. Polio epidemics had afflicted over 58,000 in 1952 and 38,000 in the U.S. in 1954 and 1955, but the new program of inoculation lowered the number of new cases to 3,200 in 1960. Beyond polio, eighty percent of the prescription drugs in use in 1956 had been unknown as recently as 1941. In 1953, at Cambridge University in England, several scientists discovered DNA and thus opened the door to revolutionary developments in genetics and medical research in the coming years. By 1959 high school graduates were carrying diplomas in their hands and little radios in our pockets. These radios now were possible because of transistors. The stage was being set for the age of computers.

There indeed were new worries like the Cold War and many reasons for fresh hope. The social progress was clear. With it came a deep irony. The worst imaginable, war, can bring about good not otherwise present. Studs Terkel has called World War II "The Good War."[27] During and after this world conflict, the self-satisfaction of Americans ran high. They knew themselves to be living in the richest, freest, most democratic, in short, the best country in the world. Right and wrong were relatively clear. The enemies abroad were unspeakably evil. There was a high price to be paid, but the nation would and could pay it together. The United States belonged to the good. Americans were a committed community, proud of their country. This was the 1950s, still more the *we* than the coming *me* generation. The positive of *we* is mutual identity and support. The negative is mindless conformity. For instance, the 1956 film *The Invasion of the Body Snatchers* satirized citizens as so robotic that none of them even noticed when they had been taken over by aliens.

Separate and Unequal

National pride and social stability were about to be shaken, however. The good life in the U.S. was not equally available to all citizens. Just as the racially all-white class of 1959 was beginning its high school years in North Jackson, a discrimination-weary African-American community was beginning to find its voice and prick the national conscience. The scene was set after the Civil War a century earlier, when legal segregation of black and white

---

[27]Studs Terkel, *The Good War: An Oral History of World War Two* (N.Y.: Pantheon Books, 1984).

citizens of America began. It was formalized in 1896 when the Supreme Court settled the question of whether forcing black people to use separate facilities was a violation of the Constitutional guarantee of equality. In a celebrated case involving street cars in New Orleans, Louisiana *(Plessy v. Ferguson)*, the Supreme Court ruled that "separate, but equal" facilities did not violate the U.S. Constitution. Now states could and often did pass laws demanding racial segregation in restaurants, public schools, and other aspects of public life.

The pricking of the national conscience about the inherent unfairness of this legalized separation had significant beginnings in the 1950s. The dissatisfactions of African-Americans about their social lot were increased by their watching television and naturally wanting a share of the material prosperity now being dramatized as standard for the white majority. Their pride, visibility, and expectations as a race were enhanced even more by the public achievements of Joe Louis, Jackie Robinson, and Willie Mays, greats of the professional sports world. Further erosion of classic social divisions were arising from the young and their new music. The musical craze of the 1950s was rock 'n' roll. Its racial roots and impact are clear. Arising from black rhythm and blues music, some black groups soon became at least as popular among white audiences as white groups. Black superstars like Chuck Berry, Ray Charles, and Fats Domino commanded huge audiences. Rock 'n' roll carried a message that was becoming a slowly rising tide in the 1950s. It was frequently hedonistic, often about sex, unfettered good times, and freedom from parental control and old social barriers no longer easily tolerated by the young. Increasingly, one of these social barriers was legal segregation of the races.

With the effective participation of African-Americans in the U.S. military during World War II, President Truman's desegregation of the military, and rising demands for more widespread change in the 1950s, the legality of the segregated status quo of much of the society would soon end. In the celebrated case *Brown v. Board of Education* (Topeka, Kansas) in 1954, Thurgood Marshall argued before the Supreme Court that segregation was unfair under the Constitution because it damaged African-Americans psychologically, especially the children. He was heard sympathetically. Probably the most far-reaching court order on civil rights in the twentieth century came on May 17, 1954. By a unanimous opinion written by Chief Justice Earl Warren, the highest court in the U.S. ruled that "separate, but equal" laws were "inherently unequal" and thus ceased to be an acceptable principle on which to base local or state law (see Table 10). Would this dramatic new stance be enforced, espe-

Thurgood Marshall (center), attorney for the NAACP, arrives at the Supreme Court Building with aides to argue a racial segregation case. In 1967, he would be named the first African-American member of the Supreme Court.

cially in the face of some defiant Southern states? Warren received hundreds of letters accusing him and the Court of upsetting God's will, aiding the communist cause, and furthering the "mongrelization" of the white race.[28]

President Eisenhower, previously no political champion of full civil rights for black citizens, nonetheless appreciated the increased support of black voters in his 1956 re-election and certainly respected the binding power of the 1954 Court decision. He would back its implementation, but at first with a take-it-slow approach to federally initiated civil rights reform. Eisenhower was not without sympathy for the goals of desegregation, but he wrote this in his diary (July 24, 1953): "It is my belief that improvement in race relations is one of those things that will be healthy and sound only if it starts locally. I do not believe that prejudices, even palpably unjustified prejudices, will succumb to compulsion."[29] In May 1958, he spoke before a racially all-black audience in Washington and said that "no one is more anxious than I am to see Negroes receive first-class citizenship in this country, but you must be patient." The President was not prepared to provide national leadership for rapid civil rights progress. His expertise and preoccupation were in the international arena and its many Cold War concerns. The last thing he wanted was to incite a domestic crisis with dramatic and controversial reform efforts.

Others were not prepared to be so patient with human prejudice operating legally at the expense of other human beings. It happened first in Montgomery, Alabama, then in Little Rock, Arkansas. Rosa Parks, a black

---

[28]Earl Warren, *The Memoirs of Earl Warren* (Garden City, N.Y.: Doubleday & Co., 1977), 302-303.

[29]Robert Ferrell, ed., *The Eisenhower Diaries* (N.Y.: W. W. Norton & Co., 1981), 246.

woman, was riding home by public transportation in Montgomery. She was very tired after a day's work as a seamstress. When the bus filled, the driver ordered all blacks to the back. She refused to give up her seat to a white man. Rosa was arrested on that first day of December 1955 for breaking a local segregation law by her refusal. The court ordered her to pay $14 in fines and court costs, but that was not the end of it.[30] The city's black community organized to protest such segregation, found an inspiring leader in Martin Luther King, Jr., a local Baptist minister, and conducted a year-long bus boycott with the nation watching on TV. Within a year the U.S. Supreme Court ruled that Montgomery could no longer segregate public buses legally. Parks and King had proven that determined, nonviolent resistance could succeed. Their names now were known around the nation and even the world. So was the justice of their cause.

Then came a confrontation in a public high school. Angry segregationists in Arkansas opposed the court's call to integrate Central High School in Little Rock. Governor Orval Faubus was prepared to order the state's National Guard to physically block the entrance of African-American children who wished to attend. President Eisenhower requested that he comply with federal court orders and not resist desegregation. By September 1957, the situation had turned ugly. The President had no choice but to send federal troops to restore order and escort nine African-American children to school. The black musician Louis Armstrong was about to go on stage on September 19 when he saw on TV the crisis in Little Rock. He was preparing to embark on an international goodwill tour as "Ambassador Satch," the personification of the American Dream. But he was so upset at what he saw that he decided he would not grin and play hypocritically before foreign audiences, pretending that his country was really the land of the free. He snapped at President Eisenhower, whom he called "two-faced," a man with "no guts." Governor Faubus was referred to as an "uneducated plow boy."[31] Such public expressions could have led to lynching in the South and professional suicide in show business.

Despite the federal government's desire to go as slow as possible, this show of national resolve was an important encouragement to the emerging civil rights movement. The federal government, while not wanting to stir

---

[30] Within a few months, bus segregation was declared unconstitutional and buses were officially desegregated in December, 1956. Parks, who lost her job because of the boycott, moved to Detroit and resumed working as a seamstress.

[31] Laurence Bergreen, *Louis Armstrong: An Extravagant Life* (N.Y.: Broadway Books, 1997), 471.

social turmoil and thus reluctant to act, apparently would when necessary. The Supreme Court decision of 1954 was indeed the law of the land, slow and troublesome as its full implementation obviously would be. As implementation finally did come, so did the rapid rise of "white flight" to residences located in racially homogeneous suburbs and the number of private schools that would try to retain their segregated status by avoiding public money. Even so, by 1959 the South seemed to be turning the corner on race relations. Desegregation was initiated in a few school districts. It was becoming clearer that defiance of the law of the land, as now interpreted clearly by the Supreme Court, was futile in the long run.

All of this social turmoil still seemed far from experienced reality, however, if you were living in little communities like Pricetown and Craig Beach and were catching a bus each weekday morning to the not-much-bigger North Jackson, Ohio. Yes, the members of the J-M class of 1959 also had their occasional squabbles on the bus going to and from school, but they were over things far more petty than the racial discrimination that Rosa Parks had just faced in Montgomery, Alabama. In the 1950s it was common in the dominant culture to have at least a stereotypical if not a nasty attitude toward blacks. The parents of numerous members of our class held coarse racial attitudes and routinely used abusive language in reference to African-Americans. Jim's father was vocally prejudiced against people of color, Catholics, and Fundamentalists. Numerous blacks worked for Nancy's father in a steel mill in Youngstown. He thought that most of them were lazy, wanting their checks for just putting in the time. Nancy remembers her father saying that he would give them the hottest jobs at the furnaces in order to sort out the few real workers. His prejudice, according to his daughter, really was against laziness, not skin color as such.

An exception to the rule in the Northeast Ohio of the time was the very modest home of Judy on the east side of Lake Milton. She had a close relationship with Mabel, a "black nanny," who lived close by. Once there was a death in Judy's family and the staff of a funeral home in nearby Newton Falls tried to refuse entrance to Mabel and her husband. Judy's father objected and threatened to stop and move the funeral. The blacks were admitted reluctantly. Shirley recalls one summer day in the late 1950s when a large banner was hung over the entrance to the amusement park at Lake Milton. It read, "Nigger Day," signaling to many hundreds of visiting blacks from Youngstown that for this one day they were welcome to this popular summer playground. They were not admitted into the dance hall, however, and were forbidden to be on the adjacent beach or in the water. There could be playing as long as any social mixing of the races was carefully controlled—and the water was not allowed to get "contaminated"! It was an unpleasant sign of the times. Pressure was mounting, but change would be slow.

Seeds of Change

Whether known or not, seeds of social change were being planted everywhere. Much of the coming change would bring considerable turmoil and dramatic new developments on many fronts; but first there were the many seeds being planted. During the 1950s, for instance, the basic research was done on "the pill," a medical contraceptive development that in a few years would help release a social revolution in American sexual attitudes and practices. In 1951, Harry Hay founded the first gay rights organization in Los Angeles, with a lesbian group emerging in San Francisco in 1955. These were very small groups and their cause gained little public attention until the 1970s. The first case of AIDS was reported in 1959. Such developments, far out of the mainstream of the time, would be large newsmakers in the future. Very much in the social mainstream was the rush for materialistic gain, grabbing for a piece of the good life. Shortly this would feed a mass questioning of the real meaning (if any) of life itself. In 1955 James Baldwin previewed much that lay just ahead. He wrote: "I love America more than any other country in the world, and, exactly for this reason, I insist on the right to criticize her perpetually."[32] The 1960s would witness much social anger, a dramatic civil rights movement that would change the face of America, street marches, radical new life styles, deep suspicion of the established institutions of family, church, and government. But for the J-M class of 1959, the more stable 1950s came first.

The instability was coming quickly, however. On the one hand, the new *Revised Standard Version* of the Bible was the nation's bestselling nonfiction book in 1952, 1953, and 1954. On the other hand, the "post-Christian" era was already being announced in the 1950s. The Judeo-Christian tradition, long the nation's leading religious context for the public's values and vision, had become synonymous in the minds of many people with narrow and irrelevant "religiosity." There was a boom in erecting new church buildings, but a bust in public perception of what was happening inside many of them. Numerous social analyses spoke of a culture-captured faith that no longer was inspiring the ethos of the times as it long had. At least one voice was going outside the church buildings to reach people and call them back to real faith. In the summer of 1957, a Billy Graham Crusade filled Madison Square

---

[32]James Baldwin, *Notes of a Native Son* (Boston, 1955).

Garden in New York City with the biggest "revival" meeting since the Billy Sunday mass meetings much earlier in the century.

Meanwhile, back in the new suburbs there developed higher levels of informality and neighborliness. People tended to spend more time with each other and be socially involved. Cooperation and volunteerism increased and the "service" industry began to grow rapidly. The new rage in American kitchens came from the development of the plastics industry, especially the home-party way of having fun with neighbors and then selling them the newest shapes and sizes of the self-sealing marvel called Tupperware. In fact, commercial preoccupations tended to replace religion for many people. "Blue laws" began to be challenged so that increasingly one could do routine shopping on Sunday. Seeking to counter this "secularizing" trend, in 1954 President Eisenhower signed a law that included "under God" in the nation's Pledge of Allegiance. He commented: "From this day forward, the millions of our schoolchildren will daily proclaim in every city and town, every village and rural schoolhouse, the dedication of our nation and our people to the Almighty." In years soon to come, the issue of prayer in public schools would become highly controversial since new voices would insist that the public should not sponsor or even host overt religious expressions—people of another or of no faith might be exposed and religiously influenced against their wills. But in the 1950s, in village schools like Pricetown, Ohio, where Frank, Richard, Carole, John and others of the 1959 J-M class were still at the elementary level, praying in school and saying "under God" on a daily basis was still a rarely questioned way of public life.

Religious activity enjoyed dramatic growth in the society generally. Louis Seltzer, editor of the *Cleveland Press*, wrote a piece for his paper in 1952 that focused on the need for religion in a material world: "We abound with all of the things that make us comfortable. We are, on the average, rich beyond the dreams of the kings of old.... Yet...something is not there that should be." He touched a nerve. Forty-one newspapers reproduced his editorial. In that same year the new *Revised Standard Version* of the Bible sold 26.5 million copies. By 1956 the phrase "In God We Trust" was being engraved on all U.S. currency. FBI Director J. Edgar Hoover urged Americans to get their children to church. Since communists are anti-God, he concluded that to believe in God is to be a true anti-communist American. Even Hollywood got involved, producing the epic religious movies *Quo Vadis* (1951), *The Robe* (1953), and *The Ten Commandments* (1956).

The Billy Graham Evangelistic Association had been incorporated in 1950 and Graham rose to national and world prominence in the 1950s. The first clergyman to become a television "star" was not Graham, however, but Bishop Fulton J. Sheen whose show *Life Is Worth Living* aired from 1952 to 1957. Probably the most popular religious figure of the time was Norman Vincent Peale. His *Guideposts* magazine had a circulation of 800,000 by the end of the 1950s and his 1952 book *The Power of Positive Thinking* was an enduring bestseller. Commented one critic: "Peale turned God into a friend and business partner, and he transformed religion into a practical faith, into a tool for solving life's problems and for achieving happiness, prosperity, peace of mind, and success, that was often measured in monetary rewards."[33] In 1955 a young pastor from Iowa, Robert Schuller, migrated west to found a new Christian congregation in Garden Grove, California. The property market was booming and a drive-in theater was the only place he could find to begin. Schuller advertised, "Come as you are in the family car." This casual unconventionalism and a guest appearance by Norman Vincent Peale launched a vigorous ministry that by the 1970s would be housed in the dramatic "Crystal Cathedral."[34]

Back in Northeast Ohio, in the immediate vicinity where the J-M class of 1959 was finishing its schooling, two religious figures were joining Schuller in gaining national prominence.[35] Rex Humbard had become a Pentecostal minister in the mid-1940s and was active in a traveling Christian ministry of revival meetings. In 1952, after a successful meeting in Akron, Ohio, Rex and his wife Maude Aimee settled there and founded a congregation in a leased old theater. Television was a rapidly growing medium and Humbard saw its evangelistic potential. After only one year the ministry was feeding its worship services via television to six TV stations in Ohio, Pennsylvania, and West Virginia.[36] By 1956 the 5,000-seat "Cathedral of Tomorrow" was dedicated, the first church in the U.S. specifically designed for radio and television broadcasting of its services (soon the home of over 15,000 worshippers). It was a few miles to the west of North Jackson in Akron, Ohio.

---

[33]Oakley, *God's Country*, 325.

[34]See Robert Schuller, *Move Ahead with Possibility Thinking* (Old Tappan, N.J.: Spire Books, 1967).

[35]In addition to Rex Humbard and Kathryn Kuhlman, a more traditional woman minister was leading the rapid growth of a new congregation in nearby Newton Falls (later it would also televise its services, was the home congregation of Barry [J-M class of 1959], and would be the chosen church home of his classmates Charles and Carole in later years). See Barry Callen, *She Came Preaching: The Life and Ministry of Lillie S. McCutcheon* (Anderson, Ind.: Warner Press, 1992).

[36]For detail, see Rex Humbard, *Put God On Mainstreet: An Autobiography* (Akron: The Cathedral of Tomorrow, 1970).

A few miles to the east and south of North Jackson was much of the dramatic ministry of Kathryn Kuhlman.[37] After an eventful and sometimes troubled ministry that often featured physical healings, she had moved to Pittsburgh in 1947 and began a grueling schedule of "miracle services" in large auditoriums and churches in both Pittsburgh and nearby Youngstown, Ohio. These major public events were attended by thousands of people and sometimes were resisted by some local ministers who judged the lines of people being "slain in the Spirit" at the hands of Kuhlman not to be authentic Christian ministry. Some of these thousands of people seeking help, of course, were drawn away from their home churches to a new loyalty to such spectacular religious events.[38] Kuhlman hosted a radio program from Pittsburgh that aired on 60 stations around the world and between 1966 and 1976 would be featured on television broadcasts taped at CBS Television City in Los Angeles.

By 1959 membership in American churches and synagogues had leaped to 112 million, with ninety-seven percent of the American people declaring that they believed in God. Congregations multiplied to serve the new suburban constituencies and often joined the local school in being a chief vehicle of community togetherness and values. There were unprecedented increases in church membership—from 86.8 million in 1950 to over 114 million in 1960 (see Table 11). President Eisenhower frequently commented on the importance of faith and the close ties between Christianity and Americanism in a country battling godless communism. To be sure, there were sharp critics of all this church growth and political acceptability of believing. Was it really an expression of authentic religious faith? Were religious associations reflecting the ethos of the times by preaching a gospel of comfort and security? Were the churches and synagogues merely more manifestations of marketplace consumerism—pick the one you like best and get out of it whatever you can? Were they emulating the corporate business organizations by becoming subtle instruments for social adjustment in a time of rapid change—if you come, you belong?

---

[37]See her bestseller, *Kathryn Kuhlman, I Believe in Miracles* (Englewood Cliffs, NJ: Prentice-Hall, 1962), and Helen Hosier, *Kathryn Kuhlman: The Life She Led, the Legacy She Left* (Old Tappan, NJ: Fleming Revell, 1976).

[38]Kuhlman, in response to criticism, typically had on the platform with her supporting ministers from various denominations. Frequently invited by her to the meetings were doctors from respected medical schools. They were asked to attend and authenticate apparent physical healings—which she always insisted were the work of the Holy Spirit and not of herself.

The general religious atmosphere of the nation tended to be a mixture of blandness and uniformity. There were even political overtones. FBI director J. Edgar Hoover urged, "Since communists are anti-God, encourage your child to be active in the church." Sunday schools were full, although American men were less inclined to get involved. GIs, now the heads of growing households, often equated religion with mere church-going and a "true believer" with fanaticism. Reinhold Niebuhr, preacher-professor at New York's Union Theological Seminary, lashed out at the "undue complacency and conformity" that he saw as woefully inadequate to address the ills of modern society.[39] Will Herberg complained about the secularization and homogenization of religion in his book titled *Protestant-Catholic-Jew* (1955). These three major faith families had for all practical purposes become functionally equivalent in American life. Americans appeared to be moving away from sharp religious distinctions to a common ground for national identity, one that, Herberg argued, encouraged a deeper commitment to an American way of life based on materialism and consumerism than a vital religious faith. The National Council of Churches was formed in 1950. Its concern for Christian unity was judged by many as furthering the decline of denominational loyalties and thus weakening religious commitments. Its intent, rather, was to weaken the scandal of rampant division and thus strengthen a united Christian witness.

The 1950s was more a priestly than a prophetic time, with people having their felt needs met more than their questionable values challenged. At the end of the decade the movie Elmer Gantry played to packed theaters, dramatizing a hypocritical, silver-tongued, skirt-chasing, boozing evangelist who, unfortunately, became almost as well known to the public as Billy Graham. The society at large was oriented to public order, family stability, conformity, institution building, and a belief in progress; but, throughout this national "high," America "lacked any adult generation focused on inner spiritualism."[40]

The parents of the J-M class of 1959 reflected the historic religious patterns of the nation. Betty's father had been raised by an uncle, a Baptist minister, in a congregation which her mother attended. Betty recalls that in her home

---

[39]One of Niebuhr's classic books is *Moral Man and Immoral Society* (N.Y.: Charles Scribner's Sons, 1932). His thesis was that a sharp distinction must be drawn between the moral and social behavior of individuals and of social groups—national, racial, and economic; and that this distinction justifies and in fact necessitates political policies which a purely individualistic ethic must always find embarrassing.

[40]William Strauss and Neil Howe, *The Fourth Turning: An American Prophecy* (N.Y.: Broadway Books, 1997), 169.

in the years of her growing up, actions like drinking alcoholic beverages and playing cards were frowned on as sins, despite the fact that her parents then were not active religiously. Barry's parents had strong roots in a conservative Methodist tradition and shared the same general outlook on "worldly" living, although his father had been "liberalized" somewhat during his years of military service and was not particularly judgmental of others or opposed to a rare game or drink himself. He smoked much of his adult life, a habit he was not proud of and actively discouraged in his son. Values and attitudes were strong and generally conservative whether or not going to church was now part of life's routine. He did return to his early Christian faith later in his life.

Several families were associated with the First Federated Church in North Jackson, an interdenominational Protestant congregation adjacent to the

MEMBERSHIP OF RELIGIOUS BODIES
IN THE UNITED STATES
(Estimated)

	Total Membership	Christian: Protestant	Christian: Roman Catholic	Jewish
1951	88,676,000	52,162,000	29,242,000	5,500,000
1952	92,277,000	54,230,000	30,253,000	5,500,000
1953	94,843,000	55,837,000	31,476,000	5,500,000
1954	97,483,000	57,124,000	32,403,000	5,500,000
1955	100,163,000	58,449,000	33,397,000	5,500,000
1956	103,225,000	60,149,000	34,564,000	5,500,000
1957	104,190,000	59,824,000	35,847,000	5,500,000
1958	109,558,000	61,505,000	39,510,000	5,500,000
1959	112,227,000	62,544,000	40,871,000	5,500,000
1960	114,449,000	63,669,000	42,105,000	5,367,000

During the decade of the 1950s, a very high percentage of all religious affiliation in the United States was in the Judeo-Christian tradition. All U.S. Presidents have had a personal religious affiliation except Jefferson, Lincoln, and A. Johnson. These affiliations all have been Christian, except the Unitarians J. Adams, J. Q. Adams, Fillmore, and Taft. Only Kennedy has been Roman Catholic. The most frequent affiliation has been Episcopalian. During the 1950s, Truman was Baptist and Eisenhower Presbyterian.

TABLE 11

high school.[41] Richard, for example, at least through grade six never missed Sunday school in this congregation, although his parents rarely attended, especially after he was young. Across the street from the high school was a Roman Catholic parish[42] where other parents of the class were active, including Frank's. The parents of Dallas were "semi-active" in St. Catherine's Roman Catholic parish in Lake Milton, the parish where Jane and her mother were very active (her father had no interest or involvement in anything religious). Neither Frank, Dallas, Jane or virtually any other Roman Catholic in the 1950s was aware that something of major proportions was about to happen worldwide within this very large faith community. In 1958 a new Pope was chosen. Angelo Giuseppe Roncalli was an aging cardinal expected to be merely an interim, "caretaker" pope. Taking the name John XXIII, in 1959 he stunned his church by calling for an ecumenical council, the first to convene in nearly 100 years. In the early 1960s this council, Vatican Council II, would bring a wave of significant "modernization" to the Roman church.

There certainly were those with little or no religious affiliation. The parents of Charles never went to a church in his memory. They were not hostile; religion just had no relationship to their lives. Neither did John's parents have any religious ties. Bill's parents attended the First Federated Church in North Jackson, but usually only for Easter and Christmas services. Most local families had some strong religious roots a generation back, but some had become preoccupied otherwise. Several fathers of the J-M class of 1959 worked long hours in area industries, sometimes to the neglect of their families. Barry's father worked constantly, rarely taking time off except for fishing and hunting trips. He even had his own shop behind the house where he often worked evenings and weekends. He was moral, inventive, dedicated to providing for his family, yet better at it financially than emotionally and spiritually. John's dad was much the same except for his addiction to alcohol and a much wider separation from the lives of his children. Jane's father delivered mail in Youngstown and worked in his Lake Milton business selling and repairing boats and motors. He tended to take good care of his family financially, but

[41]The first "federated" service was held in 1928, combining the efforts of three local Christian fellowships that had been struggling to maintain regular services (Disciples of Christ, United Church of Christ, and Presbyterian).

[42]In 1935 the Cleveland Diocese surveyed the Jackson Township area and located 105 Roman Catholic families, enough to justify a new mission parish. In June 1937, the first mass was offered in the gymnasium of Jackson-Milton High School, with the building across the street purchased in 1941 (the year the members of the class of 1959 were being born).

Elvis Presley (1935-1977), performing in 1956.

not so much emotionally. Overt religious involvement and displays of affection for one's family seemed not to be a common male trait of the time.

A Fragile Stability

The high school classes of 1959 had good years in which to grow up, but they would shortly launch their adult lives in the volatile 1960s. Soon they would have to face the social critique and dire predictions launched by George Orwell in his sobering 1949 novel *Nineteen Eighty-Four*.[43] In a clever and disturbing satire, Orwell created the distorted totalitarian society of Oceania and through it tried to alert the postwar world to the dangers of television, thought control, the big lie, mass hysteria, and the probability that soon "Big Brother" would always be watching, judging, and controlling. The pervasive problem, argued Eric Fromm in 1961, was the evolving nature of modern society itself. Westerners had become "a centralized managerial industrial society, of an essentially bureaucratic nature, and motivated by a materialism which is only slightly mitigated by truly spiritual or religious concerns." The danger was selling out to a totalitarian "Big Brother" and becoming "automatons who will have lost every trace of individuality, of love, of critical thought, and yet who will not be aware of it because of 'double-think.'"[44]

---

[43]George Orwell, *Nineteen Eighty-Four* (N.Y.: New American Library ed., 1961; original ed., 1949). The 1961 edition carries a significant "Afterword" by Eric Fromm. See Fromm's *The Sane Society* (N.Y.: Reinhart & Co, 1955).

[44]Eric Fromm, as in his Afterword to George Orwell's *Nineteen Eighty-Four* (1961 ed.), 266-67.

Milestones of the Decade

	Best Movie of the Year#	Bestselling Nonfiction Book of the Year	*Time* Magazine's Person of the Year*
1950	All About Eve	Betty Crocker's Picture Cook Book	The American Fighting Man (GI Joe)
1951	An American In Paris	Look Younger, Live Longer, Gayelord Hauser	Mohammed Mossadegh, Premier of Iran
1952	The Greatest Show On Earth	The Holy Bible, Revised Standard Version	Elizabeth II, Queen of England
1953	From Here To Eternity	The Holy Bible, Revised Standard Version	Konrad Adenauer, Chancellor, West Germany
1954	On The Waterfront	The Holy Bible, Revised Standard Version	John Foster Dulles, Sec. of State, U.S.A.
1955	Marty	Gift From The Sea, Anne Morrow Lindbergh	Harlow Curtice, President, General Motors
1956	Around the World In Eighty Days	Arthritis And Common Sense, Dan Alexander	Hungarian Freedom Fighters
1957	The Bridge on the River Kwai	Kids Say The Darndest Things, Art Linkletter	Nikita Khrushchev, Premier, Soviet Union
1958	Gigi	Kids Say The Darndest Things, Art Linkletter	Charles de Gaulle, President, France
1959	Ben-Hur	'Twixt Twelve And Twenty, Pat Boone	Dwight D. Eisenhower President, United States

Recipient of the Oscar from the Academy of Motion Picture Arts and Sciences.

* A designation on the part of the editors of *Time* of the person, people, or thing that, for better or worse, most significantly influenced the course of world events in the preceding twelve months.

TABLE 12

Soon there would be a national outburst of individualities, of "love-ins," of public trashings of hated bureaucracies. But the 1950s was a more stable, even if a very transitional time. Rather than challenging a social system that was generally judged to be working rather well, at least in materialistic terms and for those who were part of the dominant culture, the focus of most people was on getting ahead, getting on with life in a country taken for granted as being good and full of opportunity. The stability might have been fragile, but for the most part it remained steady. Young people were mostly "square." Art Linkletter's bestselling book in 1957 and 1958 was titled *Kids Say The Darndest Things!* To rebel tended to mean little more than sneaking cigarettes, driving a car too fast, surprising one's parents with a "flat-top" haircut, or getting "All Shook Up!" with the music and vigorous gyrations of Elvis Presley. The American Dream was defined largely in terms of exercising one's freedom to find a good job, buy a nice home, and enjoy a private piece of the nation's continuing stability and growing prosperity. *Betty Crocker's Picture Cook Book* was the bestselling nonfiction book in 1950, followed by the Bible (the new *Revised Standard Version*) in 1952, 1953, and 1954, clearly reflecting the people's strong interest in homemaking, children, and religion. Politics abroad was far away and hopefully irrelevant; but dinner on the table and the "sock-hop" at the school on Saturday night was where growing-up life really was.

Millions of parents worried openly that the uncontrolled pelvis of Elvis and his intoxicating rock-and-roll music would lead their teenagers to immoral excess and attraction to the new gangs led by ducktailed "hoods" wearing black-leather jackets. Many of the males of all ages, even some criticizing their own children's new preoccupation with Elvis, were themselves fascinated by Marilyn Monroe, the decade's most visible sex symbol. The teenage idols of the time, Elvis Presley, James Dean, and Marlon Brando, were all resisting the traditional values that parents thought World War II had been won to preserve. Instead of a strictly set bedtime for the young, the bestselling musical recording of 1955 was "Rock Around the Clock" by Bill Haley and the Comets. Dean's *Rebel Without a Cause* dramatized the growing alienation of a young generation judging society's prosperity and preoccupation with upward mobility both sterile and destructive. When he was killed in his car in 1955, Dean seemed to pass into the status of enduring legend, a symbol of teenage rebellion for generations to come. Everything he said and did was "cool." Brando in *The Wild Ones* issued a cry for the individual to abandon the self-deception of a consumer culture. From January of 1956 until he was drafted into the Army in March of 1958, Elvis Presley had fourteen consecutive million-seller records. Young people now had their own music.

While Elvis Presley and Jimmy Dean were well-known names to the young, known and better respected by the older generations of the time was the name of Albert Einstein (1879-1955). At least during the first half of the twentieth century, Einstein was the most widely known and celebrated scientist in the world. His theory of relativity, developed especially in the first decade of the century, enabled this rather eccentric theoretical physicist to alter the way humans understood the functioning of the physical universe. He won the Nobel Prize in physics in 1921. As a Jew who decided to flee Nazi Germany prior to the Holocaust, Einstein's final years were spent in the United States. In 1939 he joined a few others in writing to President Roosevelt concerning the possibility of the U.S. developing an atomic bomb, warning that Germany likely was beginning such an ominous venture. Death came to this intensely curious and creative intellectual in 1955, just as members of the J-M class of 1959 were ready to begin their high school years.[45] His great achievements, however, were hardly known or thought of as significant to us as we lived the existence of typical teenagers of the 1950s in the often mundane realities of generally unsophisticated middle America.

Even though students in the 1950s were sometimes called the "silent generation," caught up in little more than status seeking, many were quietly beginning to raise serious questions. They were the modest leading edge of much that lay just ahead. There still was a stable conservatism, a tenacious desire to retain memory and meaning. In 1955, for instance, some 35 million people went to classical music performances, more than twice the year's attendance at major league baseball games. Academy Awards for the best motion picture went to *Around the World in 80 Days* (1956), *The Bridge on the River Kwai* (1957), *Gigi* (1958), and *Ben-Hur* (1959). The conservatism came to the surface musically with the Four Lads and their sentimental ballad called "Moments To Remember" (1955). The gentle nostalgia of this beloved song became a treasured highlight of dances and year-end high school proms across the nation. There really were good moments to remember.

By the graduation day of the high school classes of 1959, the following describes well the American youth of the time:

> In contrast to previous generations, they were more affluent, better educated, talked more openly about sex, had greater mobility through the widespread ownership of automobiles by their parents or themselves, demanded and received more personal freedom, had more conflicts with their parents, and were the subject of more media and

---

[45]For an excellent biography of Einstein, see Abraham Pais, *Subtle Is the Lord* (Oxford, 1982).

parental concern. But they were not yet in rebellion, for although their life-style had departed from the conventions of their elders, their basic ideas and attitudes were still the conservative ones that mirrored the conservatism of the affluent age in which they grew up.[46]

In March 1959, *Time* magazine reported the results of a survey of the 1949 class of Princeton University, data gathered for the tenth-year class reunion. The average member of this class of 1949 was characterized in 1959 as "plump, prosperous. . .is worried about the state of the world, yet comfortably sure of his own place in the sun." The irony was the juxtaposition of comfort and worry. By 1959 prosperity was obvious, but the world was again very dangerous indeed. Two Stanford University seniors reported soberly in 1958: "Each graduating class has been faced with problems it did not create, but we are the first generation to know that our failure will mean the destruction of mankind."[47] The J-M class of 1959 was about to be part of whatever was to be, hopefully not mass destruction. Meanwhile, prosperity had become an alluring opiate of the young. The 1950s was an era of unprecedented economic growth. The number of Americans who thought of themselves as middle class increased dramatically, based heavily on government programs supporting major growth in family housing, highway construction, and higher education.

Around Our High School

This big world and national scene was hardly in the consciousness of most of the members of the Jackson-Milton class of 1959. When Barry occasionally had to hitchhike home from a basketball practice, those six country miles out to Lake Milton seemed like the whole world to him. He and his classmates were far more conscious of John Rayburn, school superintendent (1951-1970), and Mary Lucy Lauban, principal (1953-1965), than they were of the executive and congressional branches of the national government, although there was the senior class trip to Washington, D. C. While in the nation's capital, a handful of these high school seniors joined Shirley in electing the sobering experience of standing in a long line in the Capitol Rotunda to view the body of the Secretary of State, John Foster Dulles. Other class members were not so sober, some too freely ingesting the drug of choice at the time, alcohol. The death of Dulles, so key an administration member, was a blow to President Eisenhower, who was having much-publicized health problems of his own during his second term. But this class

---

[46]Oakley, *God's Country*, 290.
[47]As quoted by William Sloane Coffin, Jr., "Heirs to Disillusion," *The Nation* (May 16, 1959), 449.

hoped to focus more on personal opportunities than on potential national dilemmas.

The world was at peace in the sense of a lack of open international warfare. Unfortunately, school administrators at Jackson-Milton High School sometimes found themselves in sharp conflict with some students—the little wars where most Americans really lived. Mr. Rayburn was thought by some not to like the group of students from the Lake Milton area who first were bused to North Jackson for their sophomore year in 1956. John was one. He and the superintendent had more than one shouting match, once over John's wearing his shirttail outside his pants. This confrontation happened in front of some of John's peers and he responded angrily at this public embarrassment caused by a school official. On graduation day, when Mr. Rayburn handed John his diploma and offered the ceremonial handshake, John shoved the hand aside and told the man where he could go!

In 1956 a young woman just out of college began and ended her teaching career in the same year. She came to Jackson-Milton High with a prim-and-proper elitist attitude and a sincere love for fine literature. Soon feeling uncomfortable with the lack of sophistication and expected academic seriousness of her class, she told them that they were "a bunch of farmers."[48] Some students were offended and decided to get even. For the next few days some of her students came to class with patches on their pants or skirts, straw in their hair, and even a little deliberately planted barn odor. Occasionally they would unscrew classroom light bulbs before her arrival, then, to her confusion and embarrassment, tighten them when she had gone to get janitorial help. For her the whole experience was so disturbing that apparently she had a nervous breakdown and abandoned teaching. While none of the students involved ever meant for that drastic a result, and some of them really were farmers, they had no wish to be treated as stupid "country hicks." Even so, a few were capable of acting like violence was a ready option.

Jim, for instance, now admits to having been "the most rebellious and arrogant student" in the class. He hated authoritarian discipline and recalls being expelled at least three times for clowning around or fighting. One day a classmate, Tom, unintentionally tore Charles's shirt. Charles, a little older, rough-hewn, and not having that many shirts, took offense and began beat-

---

[48]Judy was there and remembers somewhat differently what this teacher actually said. The teacher, she recalls, told the class that "they were essentially a farming community." Many class members took this to be an implied insult and thus retaliated. When the young teacher cried openly the next day in the face of their reacting antics, some class members stopped and were ashamed of their actions.

ing Tom right in the school hallway. Another classmate intervened in this momentarily ugly scene. Such things also were known to happen on the way to or from school. A few students had part-time jobs and even their own cars; most came to school on buses, some from the Lake Milton area riding 45 minutes each way. One day Virginia and Freda began an eye-scratching brawl on the bus, for what reason no one now remembers. Many do remember the bus driver occasionally stopping in the middle of the country and refusing to drive on until a reasonable order prevailed.

Most of the time class members spent their high school years figuring who they were and what should come next. Many like Delores had no expectation of college, little developed academic inclination, and more interest in friends and extra-curricular activities than anything else found at school. Sports was big. John, for example, reports that he hated high school, but loved playing football for Jackson-Milton. Local sports fever was especially high in 1954 when the Cleveland Indians excited Ohio and the nation with one of the great baseball seasons of all time. This team had four pitchers who each won at least twenty games that year and a record number of team wins. It was a hard lesson that summer and fall for the excited young sports fans around North Jackson. They were basking in these many victories when suddenly they had to suffer through this team of destiny losing the World Series to the New York Giants in four straight games. The class of 1959 was learning about life, about the thrill of victory and the agony of defeat.

Better times were ahead, if not for the Indians for a long time, at least for Don Larson. In 1954 he had lost 21 games for Baltimore. Then through a trade he made it to the World Series in 1956 with the New York Yankees. In game two he failed to last two innings; but in game five he came to the mound a second time and proceeded to pitch his way into history. It would be the only perfect game ever pitched in postseason play. Most of us stared at a television set in the Jackson-Milton cafeteria and were inspired to think that, if lowly Larson could rise to such unexpected heights, maybe anything was possible. We lived in an area that competed hard and was used to winning. Jim Brown carried the football 12,312 yards for the Cleveland Browns from 1957 to 1965, a dramatic career. Ohio State University went to the Rose Bowl three times in the 1950s, beating its West Coast rival every time (California in 1950, Southern California in 1955, and Oregon in 1958). Sports was an area in which at least young men were to excel. Parental relationships and academic pursuits, unfortunately, seemed more optional matters to many of the young.

Some in the class, however, were less than inspired. Charles did not have a close relationship with his parents and had little direction of his own. His

Mary Lucy Lauban, principal of the Jackson-Milton High School from 1953 to 1965. Her words in the 1959 yearbook, The Echo: "...go throughout your life collecting and compiling those memories of good deeds which lead to a full, happy and rewarding life...."

approach to high school? "Do the least I could!" He hung with the guys, hitch-hiked frequently, and got into a fight occasionally. Lacking much identity or security from his home, he was academically passive and socially aggressive. "I guess I was trying to prove something," he reported much later. Stan was the same in many ways. His chief goal in high school was "trying to get a diploma, then get out and get a job." "I was rotten, no doubt about it!" Keep in mind that "rotten" then meant things like being a little reckless with a car, sneaking around some school rules, and playing practical jokes on teachers. Stan nailed shut the shop teacher's desk drawer one day and often used the excuse of "working on scenery" for J-M's little drama department as a way of getting out of class. Bill joined Stan in being glad to get out of class at any opportunity. His father, with no college education, had a good job as a fore-man at Republic Steel in Warren and Bill would go to join him as soon as high school was out of the way. In the meantime, he saw school as just "putting in the time." In his senior year he bought his own car, got ticketed for drag rac-ing with classmate Frank, and found Principal Lucy Lauban, to his surprise, supportive when he had to stand before a judge.

There was plenty of sassy individualism in the J-M class of 1959. Once it actually proved constructive. The principal, Lucy Lauban, got a call at school one day saying that a field was on fire and threatening her home. She rushed out in near panic. Stan and about eight of his friends somehow heard what was happening. Without permission to leave school, they jumped into two student cars and were soon at the Lauban's home. They helped end the dan-ger and were rewarded with grateful permission to go home and change their smoked clothes before returning to school where they belonged. Sometimes the individualism was sad and hurtful. Tom's father was older, had been gassed in WW I, and now was a non-abusive alcoholic who collected junk. Tom was ashamed of his family, took the easiest courses he could, and felt inferior. When he could not borrow a decent car to take a date to the homecoming football game his senior year, he got drunk, went to the game that way, got thrown off the football team, and quit school just short of graduation.

While the high school certainly had its academic, cultural, and extracurricular limitations, as did many of the homes from which students came, it also had its share of program diversity and opportunities for the setting and time. Latin was still taught as a foreign language, a holdover from a more classic curriculum. Taking two years of this language helped Barry in his later literary and teaching career. Harry, on the other hand, had musical interest and talent. The 1959 school yearbook, *The Echo*, records him having participated four years in Choir, Rhythmaires, Vocalaires, and Mahoning County Music Festival, and three years in the school's *Fun and Frolics* and on the stage crew. Shirley, with her strong theatrical interests, choreographed all of the staged events during 1957-1959. The stage was next to the basketball floor in the gym, reasonably large and versatile for modestly produced musical and dramatic events. In fact, the gymnasium itself was virtually new in the late 1950s, the envy of many high schools in the area.

Ian, class vice-president, was president of the school's chapter of the National Honor Society (years 3 and 4), vice-president of the Student Council (4), on the Scholarship Team (1, 2, 3), participant in Buckeye Boy's State (3), and, along with classmate Jim, a young pilot with the Civil Air Patrol in Youngstown. There was a modest marching band and a full schedule of football, basketball, baseball, and track events, primarily for male participants. Girls had special activities like various musical groups and being usherettes and cheerleaders. In 1959 Carole was Homecoming Queen and Nancy the May Queen. There were formal-dress dances on these celebration occasions where popular songs like "Tammy" by Debbie Reynolds and "Volare" by Domenico Modungo were heard. Most students loved these school events as social highlights of each year. Others, like Barry, lacked much in the way of dress-up clothes, ready transportation for evening events at the school six miles away, and in a few cases even faced a religiously-based stigma about the moral wholesomeness of dances.

The practical focus of the curriculum was evident with courses in "shop," "commercial," "secretarial," and "home economics." There were several band and choir ensembles, loved by some students, although good settings for others to do their "acting up." Vocal music teacher Florence Kovachik once had a real problem. She had a way of "pounding" on the piano early in the morning. So, as a practical joke before she arrived one day, some of the students actually removed the hammers from inside the upright piano in the classroom—Judy now admits being the one who dropped them out the window and Shirley was one of the several hammer removers. How funny and frightening it was when Mrs. Kovachik's skilled hands landed on the keys, only to hear nothing of music inside! Yes, classes, music, sports, and practical jokes were common. Commonplace also was prayer inside and outside the school. Jesse regularly joined other Roman Catholic students in a released-time program that took them across the street from the school to the local Roman Catholic parish for regular religious instruction on school time.

A few members of the J-M class of 1959 got beyond sports and personal identity issues and managed to focus on taking academics seriously. Richard's parents fully intended college for him (he would be the first in his family), and he did well both in high school sports and in the classroom. Barry wrote a serious essay on the Hungarian Freedom Fighters, based on the daring and idealistic revolt in 1956 that was crushed quickly by the Soviet Union. Principal Lauban liked this writing effort, read it appreciatively to the English class that Richard, Barry, and others were in, and even made an effort to have it considered for national publication. This was the humble beginning of Barry's later literary career—launched in part by the high standards and active encouragement of a teacher. Mrs. Lauban was also a positive influence on Larry. For him, she was a key source of his awakened academic interest and discipline. Their classmate Judy, college bound and academically inclined, would be named salutatorian at the 1959 graduation. But as a junior she had a problem with the same teacher who had encouraged Barry, prepared Richard well for his college experience, and awakened Larry.

Principal Lucy Lauban's teaching field was English, but students knew her best as the strong-willed disciplinarian and sponsor of the local chapter of the National Honor Society. Judy did exceptionally well on some standardized exams in several fields, but chose not to indicate particular interest in pursuing the field of English. Lauban objected, thought Judy was making a mistake or just not cooperating, and apparently (behind the scenes) blocked her induction into NHS. Judy's friends Ian, Richard, Carole, Jeannette, Frank, and Barry were inducted as juniors. Judy, strong-willed herself, was deeply offended. The next year Lauban relented and agreed to Judy's induction as a senior at the ceremony on April 8, 1959. In the "tapping" moment in front of the whole high school, Barry was assigned the honorable task of carrying the Society's treasured symbol, the yellow rose, to Judy, seated with the student body. The arrival of the rose was the public announcement of her acceptance into the Society. Judy refused to accept it. Not knowing all the background of her strong feelings, Barry was confused and embarrassed. Her friend Betty, seated next to her, urged her to accept the induction, late as it was. Finally, he thrust the flower into her hand, almost pleading with her to relieve the awkwardness. Judy slowly rose and walked forward to join the membership—a "giving in" she later would regret.

Judy had two special friends in the class, Betty and another Judy. Their recreation was limited to studying together, enjoying sleepovers, and occasionally—and rather innocently—taunting the teachers in little ways. One day they each decided to come to class wearing shorts, knowing that such "indecency" was not acceptable. Betty's taunting, however, was little more than a mild tease. After all, she now says, "I was an idealist. I wanted to save the world, do something caring and giving." She was a gentle soul, partly why Barry finally got up the nerve to ask her to the senior prom as his "safe" companion.

Jane was active in the school's chorus and bands, concert and marching. But, of course, she could not be in competitive sports. In those years there were none for girls. Young women were supposed to exercise during gym periods and then be satisfied cheering for the boys at formal athletic events. Jane wanted to be a veterinarian because of her love of animals. Her struggle with problems of self-esteem were not helped by one of the teachers at the high school who told her that her hope was in vain. She was not college material, he said. That put-down angered her and built her resolve to stay in the college-prep program. She graduated in 1959 and went on to nearby Kent State University. While her subsequent decision to marry ended her college career early, she surely proved wrong her teacher's discouraging prognosis. Other teachers were more encouraging in their counsel to other students.

Some class members lived relatively isolated early lives in places like the village of Craig Beach on the west side of Lake Milton, the resort area about six miles west of the high school in North Jackson. This beautiful lake was a summer playground for thousands of fun-seekers from nearby cities like Youngstown, Akron, Cleveland, and Pittsburgh.[49] Originally formed by the construction of a dam in 1914-17 in order to create an industrial water reservoir and area flood control, Lake Milton later was used more for recreational purposes. Its size, a maximum of one mile wide and about six miles long, provided much fishing, boating, and lovely shoreline. By the 1930s there was a rather large amusement park and public beach along the western shore, adjoined by the grocery store operated by Betty's parents (a stop for the

---

[49]The population of Craig Beach Village was 198 in 1940, 569 in 1950, and 1,139 in 1960. On weekends in the summers of the late 1950s, thousands of others joined the local residents—primarily to play at the beach and in the adjacent amusement park.

school bus) and just two blocks from Barry's modest home, a winterized summer cottage like most then in Craig Beach. In the hot evenings of summer, he would fall asleep with his window open, listening to the music of the merry-go-round playing down the street.

John, another class member who lived just three blocks from Barry, set pins by hand in the park's bowling alley, tended to swim the summers away at the public beach just behind the park, and ice skated on the big lake in the winters. He loved this place as a kid, idealizing it as a "fairyland." Jane's father ran a business, one of the very few locally except for a gas station or two, three privately owned grocery stores (no chains), a laundromat, and several taverns. He sold and repaired boats and the motors to power them—which meant that Jane was "spoiled," having access to a boat for unrestricted summer pleasure. The family of Judy came from Western Pennsylvania when she was in the fourth grade. One member, an uncle, became a key manager of various activities at the park. The parents of another Judy moved to Craig Beach when she was in the ninth grade. For years they had been coming from Cleveland for summer weekend vacations at Lake Milton and finally had decided to stay, supporting themselves by running the local laundromat (her father was still there running it in 1997). Everybody knew everybody in the small communities of the area. In Barry's home at Craig Beach, the phone number to be cranked by hand was three longs and three shorts (usually several people would quietly answer most any call to check on whether the conversation was interesting enough to warrant extended listening). There was fun and usually a little change in the pocket to spend at Baldwin's Market or Shultz's store, the two places in the village where food and a few other items could be bought.

Betty was a quiet member of the class of 1959. She was a worker, not a joiner. Her future, however, would be so different from this humble place of beginning. Life would bring many surprises. That would be true for many in the class—and not true for some others. At the time of the graduation of this class, the world was at peace (so far as they knew) and there was hope for a job for all. It soon would be time to get more serious about life. Meanwhile, there was lots of fun mixed with the varying stories of private families. For the young there was trouble around on occasion, but in the Jackson-Milton area young people tended to create it themselves—and it had little real consequence beyond the moment. That was a mark of the times.

In the summer months the amusement park and its adjacent beach out at Lake Milton was the gathering point for youth from many neighboring communities. Locals from the Jackson-Milton class sometimes would sit on the guardrail along the beach and taunt carloads of cruising youth. Occasionally the coarse fun took an ugly turn. Charles and classmates John and Frank were hanging around the dance hall at the Craig Beach amusement park one summer evening. Two students from nearby Austintown were there. The J-M guys "mouthed off," trying to prove something by intimidating the out-numbered visitors. This time it backfired. Before the evening was over, several carloads of young Austintowners pulled up and went into action. Charles remembers being beaten badly. He was fortunate that bruises, cuts, and a little humiliation were all that he suffered.

During his sophomore year another Frank in the class was nearly killed. He was on his way to a dance with friends when he lost control of a car on an icy road and soon was being given the last rites by a priest. He did survive and was tutored by classmate Ian in his effort to catch up with lost class work. Ian, active in the Civil Air Patrol, got Frank interested in flying a small aircraft locally. But Frank's time was limited. What there was went into competitive sports and part-time jobs—three paper routes, helping farmers, especially his own parents. They had 25 acres about four miles from the high school, raising their own vegetables and goats, although most of the family income came from his father's job as a steelworker in Youngstown.

That is how it was. There was fun, time for growing up, danger, hope, pranks, learning, and really good friends. Such was the case around this one high school and in thousands of similar settings around the whole country.

Forever in Tomorrowland

The late 1950s had been good years to grow up and go to school. That was about to change for young people and for the country at large. Perhaps the songs Americans were singing reflected the complex national feeling. Some hummed or whistled "All Shook Up!" Some joined Perry Como in singing "Round and Round," while still others, showing a sense of resignation, decided with Doris Day that "Whatever Will Be, Will Be." Some were sobered by the rising again of tyranny in the world, joining the determination of the song "Climb Ev'ry Mountain" from *The Sound of Music* (1959). Significantly, of the two classic musicals released in 1957, most awards went to *The Music Man* over *West Side Story*. Maybe people needed the delightful nostalgia of a duped town in Iowa more than a strong dose of the brutal street life of a major city. The former was traditionally idealized American reality; the latter was increasingly the nation's harsh experience and future.

After all, the decade had been one of paradoxes. It had been a time of optimism in the midst of a gnawing fear of a doomsday bomb. It had been a time of great poverty for some in the midst of unprecedented prosperity for

Photo of the Jackson-Milton High School Class of 1959 in Washington, D.C.

many. There had been much flowery rhetoric about human equality in contrast to the great tyrants of the world; there also was rampant racism and gender discrimination. The 1950s (just before the social revolts of the 1960s) joined the 1920s (just before the Great Depression) as a nostalgic decade of games and growth. The 1920s had been a happy era of prosperity, popular Republican presidents, and zany fads (the Charleston and goldfish swallowing, for instance). The 1950s had been the same, only with hula hoops, Davy Crockett hats, Barbie dolls, and barbecue grills in the backyard. Unlike the 1920s, however, the 1950s were not years to be followed immediately by economic depression, a big bust after a bustling boom—although the 1960s would surely be extremely turbulent in other ways.

The 1950s were years when most people still were proud to be Americans, generally trusted their leaders, and shared a consensus on beliefs and values basic to the nation's life. It was a decade of vigorous growth and change, often seen by later historians as serene and even sterile when compared to the pain and confusion of the decade to follow. The "boomer" kids of the mid-1950s were watching 4.5 hours of television a day, digesting a black-and-white parade of simple plots full of competent parents, smart scientists, and happy endings. There were loyal *Lassie* animals and rambunctious *Dennis the Menace* kids in a middle-class world that loved and supported children. These children developed a "psychology of entitlement" in a time when the mainstream culture was imparting to them a benign worldview. In fact, frequently watching the TV game *Truth or Consequences*, kids were subtly

encouraged to think that truth brings delightful payoffs and any consequences of error are but embarrassing jokes.

The J-M class of 1959 was excited about what it considered its ideal
opportunity, a senior class trip to the nation's capital (see the photo on page
126). Graduation came just as the remarkable decade of the 1950s was winding down. It was an end and a beginning—for the class and the nation. That
year a movie director eliminated Burt Reynolds from an audition process
because, according to this director's poor judgment, Reynolds had no talent
and would have no future in the movie business! That same year the high
school graduating classes were ready to try their wings at adult life. Did they
have what it would take? Would the "bright years" continue for them and the
country? Only time would tell. In the 1950s, the seeds had been sown for dramatic events soon to come. Some of them would be wrenching indeed for the
nation generally and for many of its citizens personally.

During the 1950s many future and rather rosy predictions appeared, like
Fortune's The Fabulous Future: America in 1980 (an anthology of articles by
eleven distinguished Americans on America twenty-five years into the
future). These writers were sure of the continuing further expansion of the
American economy and its technology, all aided by a free enterprise system
that soon would create a near utopian life-style. Numerous forecasters predicted that America's future would be like Disney's Tomorrowland, marked
by "well-mannered youth, a wholesome culture, an end of ideology, an order-
ly conquest of racism and poverty, steady economic progress, plenty of social
discipline, and uncontroversial Korea-like police actions abroad. All these predictions, of course, were wildly mistaken."[50] The peace and prosperity that
prevailed from the mid-1950s (after McCarthy and the Korean War) to the
end of the decade made these years at least seem like a great time to be alive.
They were the "bright" years, wonderful years in which to grow up just
before the classes of 1959 and the nation itself had to learn the harsher realities of what growing up really meant. In the meantime, in 1959 the light
shining on the nation's future's path appeared bright indeed.

---

[50]William Strauss and Neil Howe, *The Fourth Turning: An American Prophecy* (N.Y.:
Broadway Books, 1997), 16.

Taking Time To Reflect

1. How does a society find the right balance between a status quo of almost mindless conformity to accepted social standards and radical citizens of independent conviction who are prepared to call into question the traditional foundations that have held a given society together?

2. This decade saw a large increase in church belonging. How did people like Will Herberg and Reinhold Niebuhr evaluate and even criticize this "religious" growth? Compare the public images of Elmer Gantry and Billy Graham.

3. Recall the historic decision of the U.S. Supreme Court in *Brown v. Board of Education*. Can you understand how many Americans of that time honestly felt that this decision upset God's will, aided the communist cause, and furthered the "mongrelization" of the white race? Where do such attitudes come from? Are there examples of them yet today?

4. What kind of resistance to legally authorized injustice is morally acceptable? Compare resisting aggressive communism in Korea by military force with Martin Luther King, Jr.'s non-violent boycotting in Alabama. Is one acceptable and one not?

5. The "American Dream" for many people in the 1950s was to exercise one's freedom to find a good job, buy a nice home, and enjoy a private piece of the nation's stability and prosperity. Was Eric Fromm right to be concerned when life is "motivated by a materialism which is only slightly mitigated by truly spiritual or religious concerns"?

6. The consistently strong economic growth of the 1950s, with low unemployment (4.5 percent average) and inflation (2.1 percent average), relied heavily on large federal programs like the GI Bill and Federal Aid Highway Act. Is a big and strong federal government essential to the country's well-being? Are citizens "entitled" to numerous benefits from the government? Did a "psychology of entitlement" emerge that would have major consequences for the country's future?

7. Does peace in the world really depend on who has the biggest weapons? Was such an assumed dependence a driving force in the 1950s that dictated where much of the nation's attention, worry, and money went?

8. What was life like in a typical high school in the 1950s? What did people usually do to "get in trouble"? Have things gotten less innocent and more dangerous in today's schools? Why? Has attention to serious academics increased for the average student?

Chapter Four

Parenting in the Glare of Many Fires

1960s

———

Let the word go forth from this time and place...to friend and foe
alike...that the torch has been passed to a new generation of
Americans...born in this century, tempered by war, disciplined by a
hard and bitter peace, proud of our ancient heritage...and unwilling
to witness or permit the slow undoing of those human rights to
which this nation has always been committed...[1]

———

The messianic hope generated by the successful revolution
[Revolutionary War] and nurtured by the defeat of slavery in the
Civil War for long made it possible to overlook or minimize the
extent to which the [U.S.] society failed to achieve its own ideals....
But in the decade of the sixties, for many, not only of the deprived
but of the most privileged, that promise had begun to run out.[2]

———

If the 1940s had launched a new era, an "American High," the 1950s had
been the decade during which that era took firm root and laid the foundation for the next stage in a cultural cycle. The 1960s now would face a consciousness revolution that would raise hard questions and tear at the very fabric of a proud and prosperous nation. One historian characterizes the years

———

[1]John F. Kennedy, Presidential Inaugural Address, January 20, 1961.
[2]Robert Bellah, Phillip Hammond, *Varieties of Civil Religion* (N.Y.: Harper & Row,
1980), 168.

1957 to 1960 as "A Center Holds, More Or Less."[3] The year 1960 was a troubled one around the world—much of the trouble anti-American in tone. No Nobel Peace Prize was awarded that year. A U.S. reconnaissance plane (U-2) piloted by Francis Gary Powers was brought down in Russia in May. Nikita Khrushchev reacted angrily. Then in September both Khrushchev and Fidel Castro of Cuba arrived in New York City for an opening session of the United Nations General Assembly. The tension was so high and security so tight that the area looked like an armed state. The Cold War was in danger of serious overheating. Peace among the super-powers still prevailed, but just barely. Peace in the U.S. society itself would not prevail for much longer. Many of the social ills that had been festering for decades would force their way onto the national agenda. Also, the country would find its way to the moon and into the longest, most controversial, and least successful war in the nation's history. If the 1950s had been dull, the 1960s would be quite a contrast!

John Kennedy was elected in November 1960 to the presidency of the United States in the closest presidential election since 1888. He was the youngest person ever to be elected president and symbolized both strong ties to the nation's past and a desire to move the nation over fresh frontiers. John F. Kennedy was a Roman Catholic, the first ever to be president.[4] He was a hero in World War II and many of the leaders he chose to be closest to him in Washington had been bomber pilots, landed on the beaches of Normandy, suffered in a Japanese prison camp, or had worked in the forerunner of the CIA. Here were people used to winning. Several were university professors equally at home with both intellectuals and industrialists. They formed an aggressive and confident new administration which, with Kennedy at the lead, "expressed an impulse that ran deep in American culture and intellectual life. The opportunity to give it free reign was, for a time, thrilling."[5] By the end of the decade there would be mass disaffection from what had been common understandings of American culture itself. But before the storm of cynicism

---

[3]Title of chapter 14 of James T. Patterson, *Grand Expectations: The United States, 1945-1974* (N.Y.: Oxford University Press, 1996), 407ff.

[4]Kennedy faced and largely defused the political issue of his Catholicism in a speech to the Houston Ministerial Association in 1960. He told the Protestant clergy that "the separation of church and state is absolute" and "no Catholic prelate would tell the President—should he be a Catholic—how to act and no Protestant minister should tell his parishioners for whom to vote."

[5]Charles Morris, *A Time of Passion: America, 1960-1980* (N.Y.: Harper & Row, 1984), 21.

and rebellion arrived, there first came a fresh breeze of warmth and hope. That breeze included elements of young adventure, dignity, elegance in government, and a daring and idealistic aggressiveness full of fresh rhetoric about humanitarian advances. Said the young president in his inaugural address, "the torch has been passed to a new generation of Americans."

For One Brief Shining Moment

The decade of the 1960s began with the highest of hopes. On January 20, 1961, John Kennedy took the oath of office as the youngest man ever to be elected president of the United States. He brought with him the dreams of a new generation. If President Eisenhower had been the comforting grandfather image to the nation in the 1950s, President Kennedy would be the vigorous young-adult image for the 1960s. During his campaign he promised to pioneer a New Frontier that would conquer "uncharted areas of science and space, unsolved problems of peace and war, unconquered pockets of ignorance and prejudice, and unanswered questions of poverty and surplus." Sensing the anxiety created for Americans by the obvious superiority of the Soviet Union in the technology of space exploration, he promised to land a man on the Moon by the end of the 1960s. To America's enemies in the Cold War, he extended this warning: "We shall pay any price, bear any burden...to assure the survival and success of liberty."

Kennedy had written *Profiles in Courage* in 1955 highlighting American leaders who had put the interests of their country above personal gain in times of crisis. This book won the Pulitzer Prize in 1957.[6] Now in 1961 Kennedy would have the chance to be courageous himself. He made the point often that he was the first American president born in the twentieth century. To the young of the country he issued a call to a compelling cause: "Ask not what your country can do for you—ask what you can do for your country." It was a verbal flood of hope in a veritable sea of churning problems. This young president was handsome, charming, and married to Jacqueline who added to the impression of presidential vibrancy and grace. More, however, would be required than political style. In 1958 John Kenneth Galbraith had complained in his book, *The Affluent Society,* that Americans appeared dazzled by the glitz of the biggest economic boom yet. Glitz must not be allowed to distract from very real problems.

---

[6]It now appears that, in fact, John Kennedy was not the principal writer of this volume and, at least on the basis of this one well-known book, should not be acclaimed a distinguished author and intellectual.

An example of the continuing boom appeared dramatically in the immediate area of Jackson-Milton High School in 1966. The giant General Motors Corporation completed construction of a major new automobile assembly plant near Lordstown, just a short distance from the high school. To be assembled there initially by over 7,000 new workers and newly automated procedures was GM's sub-compact Vega. Reportedly, General Motors had chosen this site for the most advanced plant then existing anywhere in the auto industry because the northeast Ohio area offered an attractive work force. Specifically:

> The steel and manufacturing industries in eastern Ohio and western Pennsylvania have been badly depressed by foreign competition; many men had lost their jobs. GM believed that it would thus acquire a work force that would be happy with the relatively high wages and that would do all tasks that were asked. Moreover, GM knew, many workers would be young and inexperienced in auto manufacturing, and thus, unlike the older workers, would not contest the new automated methods or the high speed of production. And here, in mid-America, GM believed, the nation's traditional work ethic would still be alive.[7]

This plant was an economic windfall for the local area. Several members of the local class of 1959, like Dorothy, Charles, and Tom, would work in this plant for the balance of their careers. But social and eventually even economic turmoil were in the wind, turmoil that would shake the nation even in the midst of its significant expansion.

Deep divisions in American society were now closer to the surface. The politically far-right John Birch Society had been formed in 1958 and Barry Goldwater's *The Conscience of a Conservative* was high on the nonfiction best-seller list in 1960. To the political left, opponents of the conservative status quo gained real ground after the economic recession of 1958. In that year a young John F. Kennedy won easy re-election to his Senate seat from Massachusetts and soon would run as the Democratic candidate for the White House in 1960. He would succeed and bring to the presidency a fresh style, a wit and wealth, and a group of Harvard-educated and other intellectuals, all seeming to suggest significant change. In fact, Kennedy ran a centrist campaign that promised to wage the Cold War more vigorously than ever and was not inclined to be aggressive in dealing decisively with pressing civil

---

[7]William Serrin, *The Company and the Union* (N.Y.: Alfred Knopf, 1973), 286. Beyond the nature of the available work force, there were attractive tax incentives offered in the face of some concern being expressed about the quality of the local schools.

President John F. Kennedy and his wife Jacqueline, and their children, John Jr. and Caroline, in front of his father's home on Easter Sunday, 1963.

rights issues. His election lacked any clear public mandate. Would his be the "voice crying in the wilderness" announcing a whole new day for America? At first, it appeared unlikely, although newly hopeful.

John Kennedy reached successfully to the media, quickly becoming the first president to allow his press conferences to be televised live. There were high public expectations of a "New Frontier" and a Kennedy "honeymoon" with a new Democratic Congress. Theodore White soon wrote of the brilliance of Kennedy and his advisers and spoke almost reverently of the "personal hush" that surrounded presidential activity.[8] His elegant wife Jackie reported later that Jack had been sickly as a boy and spent hours reading about King Arthur and the Knights of the Round Table. As President he identified closely with *Camelot*, the Broadway musical by Lerner and Loewe that sentimentalized the days of chivalry and heroism. He especially loved the lines

> Don't let it be forgot,
> that once there was a spot,
> for one brief shining moment
> that was known as Camelot.

---

[8]Theodore White, *The Making of the President, 1960* (N.Y.: Pocket Books, 1961).

Jackie observed that the Kennedy administration was in some ways a Camelot-like experience, "a magic moment in American history, when gallant men danced with beautiful women, when great deeds were done, when artists, writers, and poets met at the White House and the barbarians beyond the walls were held back."[9]

The early years of the 1960s in America were full of hope, energy, prosperity, and the continuing crises in the Cold War. The later years would deal variously with an avalanche of activism on behalf of civil rights for African-Americans, equal rights for women, and a war on poverty declared by President Lyndon Johnson. There would be extreme social suffering from the growing frustrations of a massive American involvement in a land war in Southeast Asia. Many citizens would feel forced to ask questions like: Was America being corrupted by materialism? Was the nation really pursuing an imperialistic foreign policy? What needed reforming in the society at home and how best could the job get done with the least blood in the streets? Whatever had been on hold in the 1950s surely was loose now!

The Jackson-Milton class not only left high school in 1959, but soon left one decade for another that would be very different indeed. Reared in the post-war period of relative social calm, economic expansion, and world peace, most Americans entering the 1960s as young adults were in for a particularly rough ride. In fact, the roughness often came from the acted-out consciences of the young themselves. Betty now reflects on those years just after high school. The social turmoil affected us all. While in high school, we were protected from most of the society's deep ills, a characteristic of the 1950s. The society was good in general; but then came graduation. Soon we were shocked, offended, frightened, forced to experience some new reality and take some new responsibility. A question forced its way forward. While trying to launch families and careers, how does one be responsible when the legitimacy of the traditional structures of social responsibility are themselves being brought into question?

These volatile years of the 1960s would bring a social upheaval greater than anything seen in the United States since the Civil War of the 1860s. Back then it was Abraham Lincoln who came to represent the needed liberation of some of the country's citizens from slavery and a holding together of the Union. A century later it would be the fresh image projected by John F. Kennedy. He challenged the nation in his Inaugural Address in January 1961:

---

[9]*Life* magazine, December 6, 1963.

Now the trumpet summons us again...not as a call to bear arms, though arms we need...not as a call to battle...though embattled we are...but a call to bear the burden of a long twilight struggle...a struggle against the common enemies of man: tyranny, poverty, disease, and war itself.... And so, my fellow Americans, ask not what your country can do for you...ask what you can do for your country.

What a decade to begin rearing children! Judy, for instance, was four years away from her graduation when she and David had their first child. Others were to join this family in '64, '68, and '69. Classmates Frank and Carol married in 1960 and had their three children in '60, '61, and '69. Classmates Judy and Jesse married in 1962 and had their two daughters in '63 and '66. Harry married outside the class in 1963 and their two children came in '64 and '66. Tom's marriage was in 1961 and the four children came in '61, '64, '68, and '70. A few members of this 1959 class, like classmates Charles and Carole, did not marry until 1964 and did not have their daughters until '72 and '74. Another Judy suffered the loss of her father before high school graduation. Right after she got her diploma, Judy returned to Pennsylvania, her family roots, to take a job in a store. Soon she found her way to Virginia for better employment, met and married Larry in 1964 and they had three children between 1965 and 1969. Mac did not marry until 1969, with his children being born in '71 and '72. One classmate, Marjorie, never married. The typical experience of this class was marrying soon after high school and having children from the early 1960s to the early 1970s. These were the years during which much laughing and crying started coming from the masses of the nation's adults, with the reasons far beyond the joys of new marriages and the crying of many newborns. It was a time of national turmoil and soul-searching, of breaking out and holding on, of snapping old bonds and reaching for new ideals.

The wild and unpredictable decade of the 1960s was symbolized well by the accident that Judy suffered in the middle of the decade when she had two small children. Walking on a city street in Warren, Ohio, she was struck by the car of a speeding teenage driver and was forced to spend eight difficult months in a hospital with the constant threat of never walking again. Much of the decade of the 1960s seemed just like that. It began optimistically, with energy and new vision; it ended with much grief, cynicism, and fear that the nation might lose its footing permanently. Failed idealism easily hardens into hostility.

Another symbol of the times was one of the more dramatic finishes to a baseball World Series game ever played. The Pittsburgh Pirates were playing in the 1960 fall classic, their first appearance in the Series since 1927. As expected, they were threatened with elimination by the mighty bats of the perennial winners, the New York Yankees. But the Pirates managed to survive to the seventh and decisive game after being beaten 16-3, 10-0, and 12-0. The scene was set. Bill Mazeroski, scrappy little Pirate second baseman, led off the bottom of the ninth with the score tied 9-9. It seemed like the whole world was watching breathlessly. The second pitch from Yankee Ralph Terry disappeared over the wall in left field, touching off pandemonium in Pittsburgh's Forbes Field and around the nation. The lowly Pirates had risen from the depths to claim their equality with the establishment Yankees. It was a signal of the times just ahead—the disinherited claiming their rights from an entrenched national establishment. Shortly Dick Gregory would announce: "Baseball is very big with my people [blacks]. It figures. It's the only time we can get to shake a bat at a white man without starting a riot!"[10]

That line from *Camelot* seemed to say it well: "for one brief shining moment." Those first years of the 1960s were brief and bright, an afterglow of the 1950s now newly energized and magnified by the mystique of John and Jackie Kennedy.[11] The national economy was booming. Even Bill Mazeroski could hit a key home run. True, African-Americans and other minorities in the culture soon would be shaking more than baseball bats in the faces of mainstream society. But first, hopes were high and the world of higher education was expanding rapidly. The baby boomer generation was coming of age and beginning to flood onto the nation's campuses.

High Hopes and Higher Education

Just before the troubled Vietnam era in America and the social chaos it would help to bring, the J-M class of 1959 tried to get itself established in life. Some did this by going off to college, even though most parents of this class had no college experience themselves (the few exceptions included Ian's parents who both were college teachers in Youngstown and Jim's father who was an industrial engineer with a masters degree). Going on to college was by now an increasingly common parental expectation of many high school graduates, a phenomenon spurred greatly by the GI Bill that first introduced college-going to so many American families after World War II. Before World War II, approximately 160,000 Americans graduated from college each year. By 1950

---

[10]Dick Gregory, *From the Back of the Bus* (1962).
[11]This may well have been a positive mystique magnified in the public perception well beyond what reality justified. See Seymour M. Hersh, *The Dark Side of Camelot* (Boston: Little, Brown, & Co., 1997).

the figure had risen to 500,000, with war veterans in 1949 accounting for forty percent of all college enrollments.

The 1960s felt the full effect of the postwar baby boom and numerous technological advances. Now the country was experiencing the urgent need for a more highly trained workforce. In 1960 the United States was the first society in the history of the world to have more college students than farmers. By 1969 the number of college students in the U.S. would be triple that of farmers. Machines could work the land; the "information age" would soon come to dominate, causing a high percentage of workers to dig in data and not the soil. Development of the integrated circuit in the 1960s revolutionized electronics and certainly the rapidly growing field of computer science. Larry's father had been a leader in military applications of electronics during World War II. At the end of the century, Larry and also his son Lance would be carrying on this tradition through the dramatic technical advances of the decades to follow the 1960s.

The collegiate options for the J-M graduates of 1959 included both newer public institutions and much older church-related private institutions. They were Ohio State University in Columbus and, closer to home, either Youngstown College, Kent State University, Mount Union College, or Geneva College.[12] The school in Youngstown was an excellent example of the typical evolution of schools of higher education in American urban centers. It was a YMCA school from 1888 to 1944, a private college from 1944-1967, and then a state university.[13] Engineering and business naturally were strong curricular emphases in this industrial center. Kent State University, located some miles west of Lake Milton, began in 1910 as a "normal" college, with its principal goal being the preparation of teachers for Ohio's public schools. Its mission became more diverse and comprehensive in 1935 when it became Kent State University. In 1955 there were about 6,000 students; in 1970 there would be over 21,000.[14] Such dramatic growth was a sign of the times. Geneva College, associated with the Reformed Presbyterian Church, was founded in

---

[12]The State of Ohio is a national leader in the field of higher education. In the 1990s there would be 156 colleges and universities in the state, with combined annual enrollments of more than a half-million students.

[13]See Alvin Skardon, *Steel Valley University: The Origin of Youngstown State* (N.Y.: Youngstown State University, 1983).

[14]See William Hildebrand and others, eds., *A Book of Memories: Kent State University, 1910-1992* (Kent, Ohio: Kent State University Press, 1993), 105. It was on May 4, 1970, that national attention was fixed in horror on the campus of Kent State when four students protesting the Vietnam War were shot by Ohio national guardsmen. See chapter five.

1848 in Northwood, Ohio, served as a station on the Underground Railroad during the post-Civil War period, and moved across the state line to Beaver Falls, Pennsylvania, in 1880. Mount Union College began about the same time as Geneva, was chartered in 1858 by the State of Ohio, and then was fully related to the Pittsburgh Annual Conference of the Methodist Episcopal Church in 1864.

There were some in the class like Carole who did not consider going to college—it was not even an option in her thinking. She and Charles, a classmate, were soon to marry and settle down locally for their full adult lives. The adults in John's life had no college experience. So, since he did not even like high school, he thought only of military service and a job. Nancy had been in high school primarily for social reasons, dreaming of attending beauty school afterwards. She loved her high school experience, except for its more serious academic aspects like having to memorize classic passages from Shakespeare's *Macbeth* in Lucy Lauban's class. Her beauty-school dream was fulfilled in Youngstown right after graduation—and she then worked in that business for 27 years. Later she would be a cook in the North Jackson restaurant that in 1994 would host the thirty-fifth year reunion of her own high school class.

Mac dreamed of training for a medical career, but high school bored him academically, there was no financial support from his family, work after high school was not dependable in the first years, and government help for veterans became no option when he failed his physical and was rejected by the military. Frank had thought about college, was good at math, and had a chance to go to nearby Mount Union College on a scholarship. But he was afraid that staying so near home might mean that eventually he would wind up working in the steel industry and on the farm like his dad—and he wanted a change from breathing smoke, picking vegetables, and milking goats. So he went directly from high school graduation to St. Louis to live with relatives, leaving steel and farming far behind. Frank started out as a mailboy in a commercial printing firm "out west" where his uncle was a printer. College was not in the picture. Larry did not include college in his plans either, but he had a father skilled in electronics who inspired him to pursue the same field in the military. There were others, however, who went off to the wider world of more formalized "higher" learning.

For those who went on to college, the experience varied widely in its impact on their lives. Ian's parents both taught at Youngstown College, so he just went there with them, an easy and almost automatic decision that later would lead to graduate schools and a long career in higher education. Richard went to Mount Union College, the first in his family to go to college. He prepared for teaching, but after graduation married his high school classmate Delores and entered a successful career in retail sales. His college classmates included Bill, also from Jackson-Milton High School (soon to be killed by a sniper in Vietnam) and a daughter of Desmond Tutu, an Anglican priest from South Africa who in 1984 would be awarded the Nobel Peace Prize in recognition of heroism shown in using peaceful methods to resist apartheid (South Africa's system of racial separatism and discrimination). Richard was privileged to meet Rev. Tutu and hear him speak on the Ohio campus. Several young women went on to college. Betty and Judy were good friends. Neither had been far away from their high school until they left together to become students at Ohio State University in Columbus, about three hours away by car. Betty, gentle by nature, surely was not one to create chaos in the streets. She felt deeply, however, about what she later would judge the injustice and pure waste of America's long and painful involvement in Vietnam. Leaving home to prepare to be a nurse, she soon met and later married a young man from India. His ethnicity and Hindu religion represented quite another world from the all-white and generally Christian culture of the North Jackson area. Betty found him attractive and his commitments compatible with her own religious and ethical instincts, which no longer were directed by the strict beliefs of her fundamentalistic Christian upbringing.

Betty's roommate at Ohio State was her close friend Judy. Judy dreamed of becoming a veterinarian, so college had always been her plan, even though her parents had no college background themselves. The traditionalism of the time made it difficult for a woman to prepare for this profession that usually had been reserved for men. But Judy was assertive (also a growing characteristic of the times) and broke the gender barrier with her obvious gifts and determination. Even so, she did not complete the program because of a personal choice. Soon her boyfriend was drafted into the military and they decided to get married. Two babies came along, one in 1963 and another the next year. She decided not to finish her schooling, putting top priority on her children's rearing. "It was a shame that I didn't go on with school," she reflected much later, "but I don't regret my decision at all. I'm probably happier this way than if I'd gone on." Later, Judy's daughter did become a veterinarian.

Barry left for college straight from high school, even though his parents also had no college experience. He was fortunate to have an aunt working at Geneva College only one hour away in Beaver Falls, Pennsylvania (the area of his family's origin before World War II). He lived with her and thrived academically in this Reformed Presbyterian environment, quite different from his Church of God upbringing in Newton Falls, Ohio.[15] For him, college made all the difference. By 1963 he had completed undergraduate preparation for teaching American history in high school, but decided to continue his education, eventually leading to three different graduate schools and becoming an ordained minister, a college professor, and a higher education administrator. His wife, whom he met at Geneva and who joined him as a Geneva graduate (elementary education) in 1963, taught a fifth-grade class in Indiana to make possible his first years of graduate school. When their son was born in 1967, Barry's wife, like Judy, ended her teaching career to put top priority on being a full-time mother, something neither of them ever regretted.

Nursing was a popular aspiration for young women in 1959. Judy dreamed of being a nurse, but it turned out not to be practical. Her father, a welder in Newton Falls, had a heart attack, had no insurance, went on public assistance, then died in September 1958, just as she was beginning her senior year. Gone was her hope of college, even though a gift from her future mother-in-law allowed later preparation as a practical nurse. Shirley wanted to be a healer of the world's hurts and immediately after high school went with Judy from the class to a school for practical nurses in Youngstown. For Shirley there would be a long career in the nursing field. Soon, for example, while still in Youngstown, she would be one of the first nurses trained to work with radioactive material that then was beginning to be used for cancer treatment. Another Judy in the class also lost her father before graduation and did not consider attending college.

Colleges and universities were becoming crowded and pressed hard by growing public expectations of them. The president of the Indiana campus where Barry first prepared for ministry and later was to teach for over three decades said of the 1959-60 time: "Colleges which are either unable or unwilling to change, modify, and face the new day with courage and imagination will be left behind like the village gas station deserted beneath the new interstate highway."[16] By the end of the decade, campuses everywhere were scram-

---

[15]Later I would publish extensively, in part exploring and preserving with appreciation this church heritage of my youth. See, for instance, *Contours of a Cause: The Theological Vision of the Church of God Movement* (Anderson University School of Theology, 1995) and my biography of my home pastor in nearby Newton Falls titled *She Came Preaching: The Life and Ministry of Lillie S. McCutcheon* (Anderson, Ind.: Warner Press, 1992).

[16]Robert Reardon, as quoted in Barry Callen, *Guide of Soul and Mind: The Story of Anderson University* (Anderson, Ind: Anderson University and Warner Press, 1992), 239.

Opposition to U.S. involvement in the Vietnam War brought violence to the streets of America. As an act of defiance, some young men burned their draft cards in public.

bling to determine what changes were appropriate and tolerable. By then many of them had become lighting rods for student protest of traditional social authority structures on and off campus. On numerous campuses the anger might focus on almost any campus policy that was thought archaic and restrictive of a student's own individualistic rights. The unsettledness also was very much about the war that would drag on in East Asia across and beyond the decade. Thousands of college students were sure that the United States had no business killing and being killed in Vietnam or bombing in Cambodia. No longer were many of them willing to keep their strong opinions to themselves. Many centers of higher education became hotbeds of social protest.

Putting on the Country's Uniform

By the late 1960s it would become almost fashionable among the more angry and assertive of the young in the United States to resist the military, even burn one's own draft card in public. The anti-military attitudes and actions of a young man named Bill Clinton would become a national campaign issue in the 1990s. But back in 1959, it surely was different for most young adults. There was fear of the Cold War among young adults, not yet the widespread disgust with a foreign war (Vietnam) that was soon to come. Patriotism still ran high, a lingering aftermath of World War II.

The Cold War with the Soviet Union was constantly featured in the press as the 1960s opened. A dramatic example of a sharply divided world was the awkward status of West Berlin, Germany. To the East German government, dominated by the Soviets, it was an embarrassing symbol of post-war freedom and material prosperity. Approximately 2.3 million East Germans had fled to the West by 1958. Then in 1961 the departing flood was stopped when a huge wall was built to block the exodus. It was one hundred miles long and encircled all of West Berlin except for the heavily guarded Checkpoint Charlie. What a symbol of defiance and desperation in the face of a government that was so hated that it had to barricade its own citizens to keep them from escaping their own country!

Most classmates who had graduated from Jackson-Milton in 1959 were aware that the world was divided and dangerous, that freedom has its price and citizens have their duty. John had not gotten along with his father or his school superintendent, so after high school he was "a survivor, a loner." Even though he had lots of trouble with parental and school authorities, when it came to his country he was generally trusting and patriotic. If the country called, it had its reasons and he would go. It did call, but by then John already was married and was exempted from service. Frank was not drafted because he married early and already had children when the big call-ups came. Ian did not serve in the military as such, but during and after high school he was very active in the Civil Air Patrol, a quasi-military organization that put him in uniform and took him to various Air Force bases. Others were not involved in the military for various reasons.

Barry was a student in college, was granted a student 4-S deferment, then went on to complete his education for Christian ministry with a 4-D exemption. Richard and other male college students also had 4-S deferments. Eight out of ten men of draft age in the U.S. entered the military during the World War II years, while about forty percent served during the Vietnam years. A total of 11.7 million Americans served during the ten years of heavy American involvement in this East-Asian war, 2.1 million of whom actually went to Vietnam and 1.6 million of whom saw combat. About 250,000 women served in the armed forces during the Vietnam era, although only a handful were killed in military action in Vietnam. Betty was an "anti-military" person, but in a few years she would have a son who caused her great anxiety when he had to parachute into Honduras as part of an American military mission. Fortunately, he escaped the bullets aimed his way and did not need to kill to complete his assigned duty.

Many of the young men from the J-M class of 1959 did serve in the armed forces. John served in the Navy from 1959 to 1962. Spending much time in the Caribbean, a real military hot-spot at the time, he nonetheless did not have to face actual combat. James had been in the Civil Air Patrol in Youngstown during high school and then served in the Navy from 1959 to 1963 as an aviation electrician. Based in Georgia and Florida and never going to sea, once he and his unit did have their bags packed and were on the ready for what was feared could be World War III—the Cuban missile crisis. Larry spent seven years in the Army right out of high school, moving into advanced electronics related to missiles. When he completed his service in 1966, his family moved to Arizona to find employment in civilian electronics.

Jesse also was nearly involved in a Cuban-related military crisis. His father, a welder at U.S. Steel in Youngstown, had hoped that his son could become an electrical engineer. So Jesse went to Youngstown College for one year, quickly discovering that college was not for him. He joined the Navy in 1960 and served as a radioman aboard an aircraft carrier patrolling the U.S. east coast on anti-submarine duty. His ship, the U.S.S. *Champlain*, was picked initially to go as a key part of the secret force to invade Cuba (Bay of Pigs), but it was given an alternate assignment at the last minute. The ship instead became privileged to be the vessel to pick up the Mercury spacecraft containing Alan Shephard, Jr., America's first man in space. Jesse would never forget May 5, 1961, that day of scientific triumph for America. He stood on deck and watched that *Freedom 7* capsule drift down to the sea surface and then be gently brought aboard.

Mike also was conventionally patriotic, typical of the J-M class of 1959. The world was dangerous and he would serve willingly as called on. His call came from the Navy and he served from 1960 to 1964. Part of this time was spent on an American ballistic missile submarine, lying hidden in the watery depths of the Atlantic with its massive destructive power aimed at the Soviet Union and always ready to shoot. Mike was a pointman of America's defense, joined by Francis who served as a submariner until 1968, sometimes going on very long and secret underwater voyages. While Mike and Francis lurked below, Dallas sailed about the world on the water's surface, serving on a giant floating war machine, the aircraft carrier U.S.S. *Constellation*. They were joined in the Navy by Tom and others from the same high school class, with Jerry staying on for a full military career and then becoming a senior analyst for a firm contracting with the Department of Defense.

Other men of the class served on land. Right after graduation, Harry had no job and decided to join the Army. He served for three years and was stationed part of the time in Korea as a forward observer watching the North Koreans and participating in "war games." He left the military in 1962 just before one of his classmates was entering. Stan was drafted in November

Milestones of the Decade

	Best Movie of the Year#	*Best-selling Nonfiction Book of the Year*	*Time Magazine's Person of the Year**
1960	*The Apartment*	*Folk Medicine,* D. C. Jarvis	U.S. Scientists
1961	*West Side Story*	*The New English Bible, The New Testament*	John F. Kennedy President, United States
1962	*Lawrence of Arabia*	*Calories Don't Count,* Dr. Herman Taller	Pope John XXIII
1963	*Tom Jones*	*Happiness Is A Puppy*	Martin Luther King, Jr.
1964	*My Fair Lady*	*Four Days,* American Heritage	Lyndon B. Johnson President, United States
1965	*The Sound of Music*	*How To Be A Jewish Mother,* Dan Greenburg	General Westmoreland
1966	*A Man For All Seasons*	*How To Avoid Probate,* Norman F. Dacey	25 & Under
1967	*In the Heat of the Night*	*Death of a President,* William Manchester	Lyndon B. Johnson President, United States
1968	*Oliver!*	*Better Homes and Gardens New Cook Book*	Anders, Borman, Lovell Astronauts
1969	*Midnight Cowboy*	*American Heritage Dictionary of the English Language*	Middle Americans

Recipient of the Oscar from the Academy of Motion Picture Arts and Sciences.

* A designation on the part of the editors of *Time* of the person, people, or thing that, for better or worse, most significantly influenced the course of world events in the preceding twelve months.

TABLE 13

1963, on the very day President Kennedy was shot to death in Dallas! After advanced infantry training, he was shipped to Vietnam and spent two very eventful weeks in that troubled place. His unit immediately went into action, trying to relieve beleaguered forces about to run out of ammunition. Then it happened. Both of Stan's eardrums were ruptured as an artillery round exploded very near his foxhole. Ironically, and this war was full of ironies, the artillery was American, enemy-intended but misdirected. American deaths from "friendly fire" are estimated to have been as high as twenty percent of all American casualties. Stan made it back to a hospital in the States close to Thanksgiving 1965, with his purple heart and general attitude still in tact. "I'm an American and I'll defend my country when called on. The government leaders thought we should be in Vietnam, so I trusted them and did my duty." Classmate Tom agreed. "At the time, I thought that if the government said we needed to be there, then we did." But an increasing number of young people were becoming less trustful, even rebellious.

Dramatically Changing Times

One big show first came to the stage of musical theaters in the 1964-65 season and soon was a beloved classic. Set in the Russian village of Anatevka and focusing on the fortunes of a beleaguered Jewish family, "papa" Tevye, played by Zero Mostel, sang out his mournful determination: "And how do we keep our balance? That I can tell you in a word—tradition!" The production was *Fiddler on the Roof*. Hope somehow managed to hang on as the times were changing dramatically, seemingly for the worse on all fronts. Emphasized were the severe problems of precious family bonds being strained and ancient religious loyalties questioned by the young, all against a backdrop of a rapidly disintegrating social order. It surely was a fitting portrayal of how the 1960s were beginning to be experienced by many people in America. Shortly the nation would be watching *Man of LaMancha*, a musical version of Cervantes' *Don Quixote*. According to Quixote, "the wild winds of fortune will carry me onward, Oh whithersoever they blow." He confesses to a baffled girl that his real mission in life is "To dream the impossible dream...To reach the unreachable star." Here was another reflection of the times. In the 1960s people in America were hoping that good sense would prevail, that the best would emerge from all the confusion. Many times, however, such hope seemed only an idealistic dream.

In the late 1950s, Principal Mary Lucy Lauban had warned Jackson-Milton graduates: "You are entering an era in your life which will be a totally new experience and adventure. You face the uncertainties of a changing world, a world full of new concepts and ideas." She hoped that those were young people who could "act and react quickly to the fortunes of the time."[17] The need to find out about readiness to be good actors and reactors came quickly—and to an extent that not even Principal Lauban foresaw. The dramatic change did not come all at once, of course, and many in the class of 1959 hardly noticed it at first. But major change surely did come as the 1960s wore on. Granted, the decade continued the economic growth of the 1950s. The millions of "boomers," the young born after World War II, were maturing, had higher expectations, and were not burdened by any personal memories of the Depression of the 1930s or the great war of the 1940s. The number of people in the U.S. aged 15 to 24 increased from 24 million in 1960 to 35.3 million in 1970, a jump of forty-seven percent. The nation's colleges and universities were expanding rapidly, often populated by the idealistic and restless who believed that the knowledge and resources were now available to create a progressive society like none other in human history. What they believed possible they expected, even demanded for themselves.

The young increasingly tended to believe that they had "rights" to new levels of "self-actualization." The government, so they thought, should be expected to guarantee an enlarged range of social "entitlements," and be held strictly responsible if it did not. This expectation was heightened by President Lyndon Johnson who departed from his inaugural ball in January 1965, instructing his aides, "Don't stay up late. There's work to be done. We're on our way to the Great Society."[18] His aggressive legislative programs soon to follow would seek to guarantee several government entitlements, accelerating the rights-consciousness of people. Liberal policy makers seemed sure that the federal government could engineer political solutions to social and economic problems. A booming economy in the mid-1960s encouraged the belief that the nation could afford major and expensive policy initiatives. What was underestimated were the deep divisions of race, region, and gender that still persisted. The liberal faith of LBJ in the 1964-1965 period, while attractive and well-meaning, faced serious trouble ahead. At home, as the economy peaked in 1967-1968, African-Americans also had heightened expectations—and they now had new legal protections of the civil rights legislation of 1964 and 1965. They, Hispanic, and Native Americans were

---

[17]Quotation from Principal Lauban's message to the graduating class of Jackson-Milton High School, as in the school annual of 1958.

[18]Allen Matusow, *The Unraveling of America: A History of Liberalism in the 1960s* (N.Y.: 1964), 153.

increasingly self-consciousness and turning to direct action to achieve their rights in actual fact as well as in passed legislation.

Sir Winston Churchill, symbol of stubborn British resistance to Nazi terror during World War II, died in 1965.[19] It seemed that somehow with him went the era of U.S. pride in country. The good years of the 1950s were yielding to years of "cut loose and let it all hang out." The enemy no longer was the Axis powers abroad; the enemy was at home, the "establishment," tradition, and restrictive old-fashioned values. The young questioned sharply any thoughtless faith or patriotism that did not lead to obvious justice in the streets. They pointed fingers at a consumptive greed and military inclination that they saw as threatening the qualities of truly human life and even the physical environment that sustained it. Increasingly the new generation (or at least those young who were acting unconventionally and thus gained the attention of the public media) were widely perceived as considering all of these as mainstream attitudes and actions no longer tolerable. If the 1950s was a relatively calm sea, big and angry waves were now beginning to roll.

The decade of the 1960s began with the market success of ominous-sounding books like *Catch-22* (1961), *Silent Spring* (1962), and *The Fire Next Time* (1963). Joseph Heller's novel *Catch-22* probably was up to that time the strongest repudiation of modern "civilization" to come out of World War II. Using grotesque comedy, Heller confronted what he saw as the humbug, hypocrisy, cruelty, and sheer stupidity of mass society and the flagrant disregard for human life. He belabored fools who manage war. Rachel Carson's *Silent Spring* was a devastating attack on human carelessness and greed that had flooded America's countryside with dangerous chemicals in alarming quantities. James Baldwin's *The Fire Next Time* argued that citizens who were racially black or white needed each other if America was to remain one nation. He pled for a larger truth than the racial-separation call of the Black Muslims. We Americans, he declared, need to hear and respond constructively before the fire of racial conflict is allowed to destroy the very fabric of the society. The emancipation of slaves generations earlier was still an unfinished and dangerous business of American society. Is there a way out of the stupidity of war, the self-destruction of our human living space, and the potential disruption of the social stability of the nation? If the nation's goals were peace and prosperity, the necessarily related issue of justice was now crying for attention.

---

[19]In 1949 Churchill was named by *Time* magazine as "Man of the Half-Century."

The issues soon got very visible. Cassius Clay, born in Louisville, Kentucky, in 1942, was very much a contemporary of the J-M class of 1959. Having won the light heavyweight boxing title at the 1960 Olympic Games, he turned professional and grew arrogant. He seemed to make good his claim to being "The Greatest" when he upset Sonny Liston in 1964 and became world heavyweight boxing champion. That same year, having joined the Black Muslims, he assumed the name Muhammad Ali. In 1967 he refused to be inducted into the United States Army on the grounds that he was a Muslim minister and a conscientious objector. As the national crisis over the Vietnam war and racial tensions deepened, Ali publicly dramatized the nation's identity crisis and the open defiance by many of the government itself. The same turmoil and transition was happening in the international arenas of the United Nations and the Roman Catholic Church.

In 1965 the United Nations was twenty years old, about the age of the earlier League of Nations at the time of its de facto demise in 1939. Now the UN also was in trouble. The basic problem? No country would give up enough of its sovereignty to permit the UN to undertake decisive action when that country's perceived self-interest was on the line. Times had moved from "hot" to "cold" war. It was truly frightening, even if the heat had been turned down. While the U.S. society was becoming more troubled at home, the world scene likewise seemed to be worsening. No organizational mechanism appeared adequate to preserve the fragile peace. A prime example had come in 1962 when the Cuban missile crisis actually brought the world to the brink of nuclear war.

Fidel Castro was heading a communist police state right on America's doorstep. In 1961 the world soon learned that the young President Kennedy had given a reluctant go-ahead for anti-Castro refugee commandos to invade and liberate Cuba. But the "Bay of Pigs" invasion was a fiasco from the start. One of the world's two superpowers had failed to eliminate a significant problem just off its own seacoast. So the other superpower hurried into the circumstance seeking its own advantage. By 1962 Kennedy learned that the Soviets were installing ballistic missiles in Cuba, missiles that could be fitted with nuclear warheads and reach far into the mainland of the United States. The president ordered a naval blockade around Cuba, openly challenging the Russians and potentially precipitating all-out nuclear war. There were some tense and very frightening days while the world watched to see who would back down first—or if someone would strike a first blow that could end human civilizations! Richard, then a student at Mount Union College in Alliance, Ohio, remembers well these fateful days. On this Ohio campus "time seemed to stand still as people really feared that World War III and the rapid end of the world could be at hand." Khrushchev sweat and pondered in Moscow. Soviet freighters, confronted by the U.S. Navy, stopped dead in the water. Who would blink first? Following some urgent negotiating out of the public eye, Khrushchev promised to remove the missiles from Cuba. Civilization would go on—at least for now.[20]

Even the Roman Catholic Church, epitome of institutionalized Christianity, felt dramatic and unsettling new winds blowing. It was confronting the modern world and had to back down from some of its traditional beliefs and practices. Pope John XXIII, elevated to the papacy in 1958, soon announced that he would convene that church's twenty-first ecumenical council. Called Vatican II and convening from 1962 to 1965, it would remain within the mainstream of Catholic orthodoxy. This Council, nonetheless, clearly changed a series of old attitudes and emphases of the Roman Church. For centuries, formal Catholic piety had centered on the mystery of the Mass, celebrated by priests who stood with their backs to the people and spoke the Latin language. Now the priests would turn around and speak in contemporary language—robbing the ancient rite of its mystique for some Catholics and bringing it to life for many others. The Council set forth a less arrogant and more conciliatory tone toward non-Catholics. Protestants now were to be known as "separated brethren" rather than heretics. Even non-Christian religions were said to have the right to exist and conduct worship as adherents saw fit, within the framework of proper morality. Many compared President Kennedy and Pope John, both responsible for encouraging the blowing of some fresh winds of needed change in a new time.[21]

Invited to visit the Protestant church Richard attended in North Jackson, Ohio, a Catholic friend said he would come if he could be assured of being allowed to pray his own prayer when the pastor prayed. Richard's response: "Wow! Do only Catholics think they know how to speak to God?" Barry saw what seemed the same subtle arrogance at work. The old couple living across the street from his home at Craig Beach were good family friends. Although staunch Roman Catholics, they expressed openly their questioning of the

---

[20]In 1989 much new information became public that clarified some of the political pressures and military options behind this dangerous confrontation of the world's two superpowers. See Pierre Salinger, *John F. Kennedy: Commander In Chief* (N.Y.: Penguin Studio, 1997), 113-128.

[21]For biographies of these remarkable men, see Richard Reeves, *President Kennedy: Profile of Power* (N.Y.: Simon & Schuster, 1993) and Lawrence Elliott, *I Will Be Called John: A Biography of Pope John XXIII* (N.Y.: Reader's Digest Press, 1973).

local priest's announcement to his parishioners that it now would be considered a sin to even watch on television the young evangelist, Billy Graham. Then, in the fall of 1959, Barry became a college freshman at Geneva College, a Protestant campus in Pennsylvania. This school had both mandatory chapel attendance for students, often religious services, and many Roman Catholic students from the local industrial city of Beaver Falls. How strange it was to observe so many of his new friends sitting in chapel with their faces buried in books and newspapers, even when their president or dean was addressing the student body. Their parish priests reportedly had ordered them to be voluntarily deaf and blind in chapel so that they could remain faithful Catholics.

These restrictive positions of some local priests, however, would soften considerably during the 1960s. Pope John became a symbol of reformation in the church. Some Christians were going much farther. Suddenly the public became aware that at least a few academic leaders with a Christian identification were announcing that *God is dead!* In October, 1965, the *New York Times* and *Time* magazine reported on the "frontier" work of radical Protestant theologians Thomas Altizer,[22] Paul VanBuren, and William Hamilton. Had humanity reached the peak of its arrogance? At least it seemed clear that modern societies like the United States increasingly were trying to function without the apparent need for some explanation and enablement of life that transcends the human. Such arrogance would only lead to more disillusionment. An Oscar-winning movie in 1967, *The Graduate*, featured a young man (Dustin Hoffman) who felt disconnected from traditional values and the materialistic adults of the older generation. Like James Dean in *Rebel Without a Cause* twelve years earlier, the storyline was of young Americans who felt cut off from conventional American civilization. Such a feeling leads to many kinds of actions, including an openness to things radically new.

Cultural symbols sometimes are surprising and reflective of an era. Joining President Kennedy and Pope John as key social symbols in the 1960s was a strange-looking little car. It came to represent for millions the new mood of simplicity, efficiency, and vigorous individualism. Germany may have lost World War II, but by the 1960s its little "people's car," the Volkswagen, was winning the American public. By 1970 nearly 15,000,000 of the "Bugs" or "Beetles" had puttered off the main assembly line in Wolfsburg, Germany, and found their way to American streets. It was a little vehicle as dependable as a

---

[22]Thomas Altizer, *The Gospel of Christian Atheism* (Philadelphia: Westminster Press, 1966).

One of the social symbols of the 1960s was the Volkswagen. By 1970, nearly 15,000,000 of the "Bugs" or "Beetles" had rolled off the German assembly line and found their way to American streets.

crowbar and relatively cheap to buy and operate. The secret of its success in America, beyond being cheap and dependable, was that it was an honest car, pretending to be nothing other than what it was, a simple piece of unadulterated transportation. It and the times were one in many ways.

Joining the automotive Beetle was a musical "rock" group known as the Beatles. This group of four long-haired young men originated in England and soon helped light a match that ignited a cultural firestorm in the U.S. These four Liverpool-born young musicians formed their group in 1960, had long hair, hypnotic music, and a counter-cultural tone. They reflected a new mystical awareness that featured a radical freedom from past convention and symbolized the personal rebellion and search for identity of many adolescents and young adults of the 1960s. The Beatles were innovative, sometimes integrating electronic techniques and the sounds of the Indian sitar. Dominating popular youth culture across the 1960s, they broke up in 1970 and in 1980 suffered the loss of member John Lennon, who was murdered. Their concerts often were frenzied "happenings" that cultural conservatives viewed with disgust. For example, Daniel Bell was appalled by young people who, he judged, were trying to "transfer a liberal life-style into a world of immediate gratification and exhibitionist display." Their "counterculture" in fact "produced little culture, and it countered nothing."[23]

A major event in the film industry in 1959 signaled much that was coming. The Supreme Court voided a New York law against "immorality" and thus released to the public the film *Lady Chatterley's Lover*. The First Amendment to the U.S. Constitution was interpreted to mean that a state could not prohibit films that made sexual immorality, perversion, or lewdness seem to be proper behavior. People now could speak and view freely,

---

[23]Daniel Bell, *The Cultural Contradictions of Capitalism* (N.Y.: 1976), 81.

The Beatles, rehearsing for their appearance on the Ed Sullivan Show in New York in February 1964.

quite apart from what the public traditionally thought of as right and wrong. The lid was about to come off and out would spew a bewildering mass of experimentation and incivility, sexual explicitness, anger, and social turmoil. One new technical advance only added more fuel to this growing social fire. The "Pill" for birth control came into common use in the 1960s. While it certainly increased a woman's ability to regulate her own reproductive life, it also raised major new moral dilemmas. Did its use directly encourage a wave of more "liberal" and socially destructive patterns of sexual behavior? Did its use violate the will of God, as the Roman Catholic Church insisted? Was it the needed answer to the world's serious problem of overpopulation? Was science introducing the positives of careful family planning or a wave of sexual anarchy?[24]

Whatever the answers to these pressing questions, things hardly would hold still much longer. In 1962 folk-singer Bob Dylan wrote "The Times They Are a-Changin'." The next year he composed "Blowin' in the Wind." The version of this song recorded by the group Peter, Paul, and Mary became extremely popular, the first protest song ever to make the Hit Parade. Change surely was in the wind.

---

[24]In the face of the AIDS epidemic to come later, it has been said: "Sexual activity used to be regulated by the fear of birth; now it is controlled by the fear of death."

Rights For All

As late as 1965 there still was some stability and glory in the society. In professional basketball, for instance, Red Auerbach's Boston Celtics won the championship for the seventh straight year, with the team's Bill Russell, an African-American, honored as the league's most valuable player for the fourth time in five years. Why point out the race of a successful athlete? Because race was one of the major magnet issues now bringing big, overdue, and often very painful change to American society. The courts played a key role in defining the issues and launching change. In May 1954, just as the J-M class of 1959 was being readied for high school, the Supreme Court of the United States reversed the *Plessy v. Ferguson* decision of 1896 with its "separate but equal" doctrine. Now the court held unanimously that segregation in public education was a denial of equal protection of the law. The Court directed the lower courts to admit "Negroes" to public schools on a racially nondiscriminatory basis "with all deliberate speed." Some states grudgingly complied, some did not.

In January 1956, the Alabama Senate passed a "nullification" resolution, and the next month the Virginia legislature adopted an "interposition" resolution asserting the right of the state to "interpose its sovereignty" against the decision of the high court. Nineteen U.S. senators and eighty-one representatives issued a "Southern Manifesto" in March declaring their intent to use "all lawful means" to reverse the desegregation decision. If the Civil War of the 1860s had been fought largely over the slavery issue, it seemed now that the old wounds were coming open again in the 1960s. Spearheading the drive for desegregation was the National Association for the Advancement of Colored People (NAACP) with a membership of some 310,000 in 1956. In December of that year, while most high school students at North Jackson were arriving daily in big yellow buses, Rosa Parks, a 43-year-old seamstress, refused to relinquish her seat on a city bus to a white man in Montgomery, Alabama. The issue of race could no longer be ignored by the nation's white majority. The issue simmered in the 1950s; it boiled in the 1960s.

Now there was significant new civil rights legislation at the federal level and finally some real attempts at enforcement by President John Kennedy, his brother and U.S. Attorney General Robert Kennedy, and others. The myth of JFK pictures him as inspiring an epoch of heroism and sacrifice. While true in part, when this picture includes his being the father of activism and racial reform in the 1960s, it tends to grant more than the record shows. In fact, John Kennedy was a follower who only reluctantly joined the forces of change and protest. Especially in 1961-1962, John and Robert Kennedy moved cautiously on civil rights, keeping politically pragmatic eyes on the public pulse. The president worried about losing the key support of strong Southerners in Congress, and he even appointed four ardently segregationist men to federal district judgeships in the Deep South. He feared that racial unrest at home would damage the nation's image abroad and hurt foreign policy, something about which he cared passionately. Therefore, it was thought better not to press prematurely the issue from the federal level. The strategy that emerged was politically sensitive and conservative: "The Justice Department pursued its litigation. The president provided his words of encouragement. But there would be no legislation. No affront to cultural sensibilities. No social upheaval."[25]

The president and his close associates shared the consensus of the 1950s that "there were no major structural problems in the country, and that the United States was well on its way to being a complete society."[26] But a growing number of others no longer shared this optimistic vision of the social establishment. In 1962 Helen Gurley Brown wrote *Sex and the Single Girl*, a manifesto of female sexual liberation, soon to be joined in 1964 by Betty Friedan's *The Feminine Mystique*, a best-selling expression of the latent frustration said to be felt by millions of stereotyped housewives. The civil rights struggle in Birmingham, Alabama, in 1963 included television highlights of police dogs lunging at defenseless Negro women. This publicity worried President Kennedy politically and made him feel "sick" morally. It helped to convince him that the nation leading the Free World could no longer trample on the rights of its own people like that. He would now support actively an emerging civil rights bill in Congress and urge its implementation— hopefully without violence. Kennedy spoke of the moral issue facing the nation: "If an American, because his skin is black, cannot enjoy the full and free life which all of us want…then who among us would be content with the counsels of patience and delay?" His hope for a peaceful addressing of the problem ended that very night. Medgar Evers, a field secretary for the NAACP, was shot in the back as he returned home to Jackson, Mississippi, becoming an instant martyr to a mushrooming cause.

Then in the election of 1964, with JFK tragically off the scene because of his shocking assassination in 1963 (see page 163), President Lyndon Johnson

---

[25]Charles Morris, *A Time of Passion*, 57.

[26]William Chafe, *The Unfinished Journey: America Since World War II* (N.Y.: Oxford University Press, 1986, 1991, 1995), 177. Kennedy did form the Commission on the Status of Women in 1961 and then in 1963 signed the Equal Pay Act guaranteeing (in intent at least) that women should receive pay equal to that of men performing the same work.

thrashed conservative Republican Barry Goldwater—who had hoped to dismantle dozens of federal domestic programs. Aware of the major problem of poverty in the society among black and white citizens,[27] President Johnson soon announced his "war on poverty," designed to achieve the "Great Society." In his next four years more significant social legislation would be passed than had been seen since Franklin Roosevelt's moves to end the Great Depression in the 1930s. The 1960s witnessed the biggest splurge in domestic spending in the nation's history. Said President Johnson of his own strategy after the Kennedy assassination: "I had to take the dead man's program and turn it into a martyr's cause. That way Kennedy would live on forever, and so would I."[28]

Theoretically at least, these new laws, sacrifices, and bold social initiatives, taken together, represented the greatest advance for the American "Negro" (a word of respect in the 1960s) since President Lincoln issued the Emancipation Proclamation which freed the nation's slaves a century earlier. Theoretically, that is. Mass nonviolent protests and even out-of-control urban riots on behalf of increased civil rights for black citizens would continue to fill many city streets; but there was a strong, sympathetic, and complex man in the White House. Said Time magazine in naming Lyndon Johnson 1964's "Man of the Year": "In him, the conservatism of the self-made Texas businessman and the liberalism of the poverty-haunted New Deal politician pulse like an alternating current."[29]

Thousands of idealistic youth were beginning to put their lives on the line in the name of human justice. The enemy was perceived by many of them to be a selfish and segregated society reluctant to change. President Johnson certainly was both progressive and aggressive in his social policies. Unfortunately, he would "lose his way in the twisted labyrinth of the Vietnam War."[30] This war would bring the most severe division in American society since the Civil War. The irony was shattering. While forging ahead on behalf of civil rights for all citizens at home, the U.S. found itself in a war 9,000 miles away in

---

[27]This awareness had been influenced by Michael Harrington's 1962 book *The Other America*. It argued convincingly that, while most Americans had been celebrating their rising affluence during the postwar era, more than 40 million Americans were mired in a "culture of poverty," hidden from view and passed on from one generation to the next. Kennedy had read this book and asked his advisers to suggest a plan of attack. Johnson would carry the attack in a bold way.

[28]As quoted by Chafe, op. cit., 229-30.

[29]*Time* (January 1, 1965), 23.

[30]Edmund Harvey, Jr., ed., *Our Glorious Century* (Pleasantville, N.Y.: Readers Digest Association, 1994), 315.

which much of the world, and many in America, saw the U.S. as a colonialist aggressor supporting a totalitarian regime. President Kennedy's call for sacrifice "to assure the survival and success of liberty" was being replaced in the streets by chants of "Hey, hey, LBJ, how many kids will you kill today?" Draft resisters angry about U.S. involvement in Vietnam were featured on the evening news yelling "Hell, no! We won't go!" Some of them defied the government by burning their draft cards in front of television cameras. They may have been a small minority of all young people, but they were very vocal and, thanks to television, very visible.

These surely were turbulent times. Martin Luther King, Jr., came to Birmingham, Alabama, in 1963 just as several members of the J-M class of 1959 were graduating from various colleges. He orchestrated a large-scale, nonviolent campaign of sit-ins, marches, and economic boycotting of white businesses. When the black protesters were met with police dogs, fire hoses, and church bombings, the sympathy of the nation and more active support from the federal government were gained for the plight of America's oppressed black minority. African-Americans across the South were inspired by the rightness of the cause and filled with new hope, making easier the organizing of the well-publicized "March on Washington." There in the nation's capital, on August 28, 1963, Martin Luther King delivered his memorable "I Have a Dream" speech to some 200,000 massed near the Lincoln Memorial. King announced dramatically that he dreamed that "one day, on the red hills of Georgia, sons of former slaves and the sons of former slave owners will be able to sit down together at the table of brotherhood." He hoped for his own children that they would not be judged "by the color of their skin, but by the content of their character." If that happened, he concluded as the whole nation watched on television, then would come the glorious day when all Americans, regardless of race or religion, could "join hands and sing in the words of the old Negro spiritual: 'Free at last. Free at last. Thank God Almighty, we are free at last!'"[31]

Here was a defining moment in American history. That great day of King's dream would not come quickly or easily. Just days after the March on Washington, four young black girls were killed by dynamite hurled through a window of the Sixteenth Street Baptist Church in Birmingham, Alabama. King persisted, leading a five-day, fifty-four-mile march from Selma to Montgomery, Alabama, in March 1965. Stokely Carmichael, who chaired

---

[31]For a good biography, see James Haskins, *I Have a Dream: The Life and Words of Martin Luther King, Jr.* (Brookfield, Conn.: Millbrook Press, 1992).

Martin Luther King, Jr., during the August 1963 March on Washington, D.C., where he delivered his memorable "I Have A Dream" speech.

the Student Non-Violent Coordinating Committee (SNCC), popularized the slogan "Black Power" in 1966. Racial riots broke out in numerous "ghettoes" of America's large cities, including many now outside the South. There was the Watts area of Los Angeles (Aug. 1965), where 28 blacks died and $200 million in damage was done, and Detroit (July 1967) where 40 died, 2,000 were injured, and 5,000 were left homeless by looting and burning that was stopped only by 4,700 paratroopers dispatched by the President of the United States. Obviously the stability of the nation was at risk.

How would urgently needed social change finally be brought about? Two models emerged in the 1960s. One was symbolized by a famous 1964 photograph in which a scowling Cassius Clay looked condescendingly down at the limp body of the unconscious Sonny Liston. Clay had bragged that he would capture the heavyweight boxing title—and now he had. Use your mouth for sure, and your fists to the extent necessary. Here was a frightening symbol of a growing attitude among many people open to the option of violence. Tens of thousands now were reading or at least hearing about the new *Autobiography of Malcolm X*. This book followed Malcolm's volatile personal journey from the cross of Jesus to the crescent of Islam. It was put together by his friend Alex Haley before Malcolm's own assassination. Violence appeared an attractive option for grasping however possible what was judged a higher level of social justice.

The other option was very different, and more effective in the long run. A key public figure of the 1960s was the young Baptist preacher, Martin Luther King, Jr. In 1964, at age 35, he received the Nobel Peace Prize, the youngest

LETTER FROM THE BIRMINGHAM JAIL
Martin Luther King, Jr., April 1963

While imprisoned in Birmingham, Alabama, for eight days for partici-pating in a civil rights march, Martin Luther King, Jr. wrote to eight white Alabama religious leaders who were urging blacks to withdraw support from King and the other civil rights activists. His response defends the need for and appropriateness of the nonviolent movement for civil rights, directing readers to the best in the American dream and to the most sacred values in the nation's Judaeo-Christian heritage. He argued that all great political questions are fundamentally moral questions to which religious leaders must speak with courage. He wrote, in part:

We know through painful experience that freedom is never voluntarily given by the oppressor; it must be demanded by the oppressed.... One has not only a legal but a moral responsibility to obey just laws. Conversely, one has a moral responsibility to disobey unjust laws.... How does one determine whether a law is just or unjust? A just law is a man-made code that squares with the moral law or the law of God.... Hence segregation is not only politically, economically, and sociologically unsound, it is morally wrong and sinful.... Thus it is that I can urge men to obey the 1954 decision of the Supreme Court, for it is morally right; and I can urge them to disobey segregation ordinances, for they are morally wrong....

In no sense do I advocate evading or defying the law, as would the rabid segregationist. That would lead to anarchy. One who breaks an unjust law must do so openly, lovingly, and with a willingness to accept the penalty. I submit that an individual who breaks a law that conscience tells him is unjust, and who willingly accepts the penalty of imprisonment in order to arouse the conscience of the community over its injustice, is in reality expressing the highest respect for law....

Was not Jesus an extremist for love: "Love your enemies, bless them that curse you, do good to them that hate you, and pray for them which despitefully use you, and persecute you." Was not Amos an extremist for justice: "Let justice roll down like waters and righteousness like an ever-flowing stream."... Was not Martin Luther an extremist: "Here I stand; I cannot do otherwise, so help me God."... And Abraham Lincoln: "This nation cannot survive half slave and half free."... So the question is not whether we will be extremists, but what kind of extremists we will be. Will we be extremists for hate or for love? Will we be extremists for the preservation of injustice or for the extension of justice?...

Yours for the cause of Peace and Brotherhood,
Martin Luther King, Jr.

TABLE 14

recipient ever. In his acceptance speech he said that this award is "a profound recognition that nonviolence is the answer to the crucial political and moral questions of our time—the need for man to overcome oppression and violence without resorting to violence and oppression." He admired the earlier model of Mahatma Gandhi of India. King actively taught the way of Jesus Christ—and soon would join Jesus in being executed for his noble efforts! Others soon became involved. Hispanic-American Cesar Chavez became a nationally recognized symbol of ethnic pride and economic justice. His daring leadership of the 1968 boycott of California grape growers affected the buying practices and attitudes of many mainstream Americans nationwide.

King was assassinated in Memphis, Tennessee, in 1968 while he was supporting striking municipal sanitation workers. Was this the last hope for nonviolence, final proof that it would know only failure in a society apparently bent on violence? King's sudden and senseless death set off a wave of new riots in 130 cities in twenty-nine states and virtually assured congressional passage of the 1968 Civil Rights Act providing for the selling and buying of housing free of the factor of racial bias. King had told his followers: "I just want to do God's will. And He's allowed me to go to the mountain. And I've looked over, and I've seen the Promised Land. I may not get there with you. But I want you to know tonight that we as a people will get to the Promised Land." Through peaceful means, King had helped to bring revolutionary change. He had elevated the human spirit and heightened hope. Later the United States government would officially honor what King represented by declaring his birthday a perpetual federal holiday.

Many smaller communities in America were troubled by all this social turmoil, known mostly to them by the constant media reporting. Even when not immediately affected by the violence, virtually no one was untouched by the hard questions and moral pain. No "Negroes" were part of the J-M class of 1959, and there were only a few living in the feeder neighborhoods or worshipping in the area churches. But it surely was different in nearby Youngstown and Warren where many of the fathers of the class worked. A large influx of African-Americans from the South had begun when immigration from Europe was cut off after World War I. This continued through the 1950s. By 1960 nearly twenty percent of Youngstown's municipal area was racially black. This social reality reached westward from the city to Jackson and Milton townships in at least two ways. Those from this more rural area who were employed in Youngstown or nearby Warren often had their negative stereotypes of blacks fed by their contacting only a laboring class of recent immigrant workers.

Judy's father had been running a small laundromat in Craig Beach since 1954. The amusement park and adjacent public beach were the local highlights of social life during the summer. In fact, they were all there was except for three family-owned grocery stores (two belonging to Betty's parents), the fire hall, two taverns, two gas stations, and a skating rink and small golf course (bought by Dorothy's father in 1959) located on the lake's eastern side. Something changed in the 1960s, however. Why? According to Judy's dad, there had been an accidental death on the park's big wooden roller coaster some years earlier. Added now was the park owner's new practice in the late 1950s of contracting to have "colored" weekends during some weeks of the summer. This had encouraged many hundreds of African-Americans to flood the little (white) village with its park and nearby baseball field, bent on having a good time on hot days. When concern arose among local residents about potential trouble from "those people," parents like Judy's stopped allowing their teenagers to roam the park just for fun. Soon the park closed, never to reopen.

It seems crude and unforgivable now, but in the 1950s and 1960s the attitudes of many of the Beach's villagers echoed that of Barry's grandmother. Her porch looked out on the local baseball diamond where John, Charles, and he often used their free time to throw and hit a ball. Barry recalls her observing with dismay that a number of blacks (her words were much less complimentary) had invaded the place and were having their own game, practically in her front yard. Their very presence made her nervous. The cultural gap was wide. Richard was candid in highlighting the challenge for him and millions of other Americans. His high school (Jackson-Milton) in the 1950s had no African-American students. His college (Mount Union) had only a handful in his four years as a student. In fact, the large corporation for which he would work for over thirty years would bring him into very little multi-racial contact, especially at the management levels. Did that leave him a "bigot"? Probably so, he later admitted of himself. That is not something about which one should brag; it is just a simple fact arising largely from one's social experience.

Having been active since at least the 1930s, the wooden structures of the Craig Beach Amusement Park had grown old and even dangerous. Something had to change. Likewise, the prejudicial racial attitudes and actions of so many Americans were antiquated and hardly tolerable in the new sensitivities of the 1960s. The process of dismantling the park in 1965 was relatively quick and easy. The process of ending racial discrimination in the larger society would not be nearly as quick or painless. For a society filled with prejudice, more than a few buildings had to come down. For instance, John admitted that in the 1960s he privately appreciated the justice of the civil rights movement, but he was not ready to "withstand the establishment." This common reluctance was an obstacle to change. Somehow it would have to come down. Ian had wanted to go to the South and express his moral indignation (idealism) by joining the marchers against injustice. He had the heart to go, but reflected later that somehow he just lacked "the decisional tools" and just never got there.[32] Was there something in the local culture of the Midwest that obstructed prophetic and sacrificial moral action? Maybe, but change would come.

Carl B. Stokes was elected mayor of nearby Cleveland in 1967, the first African-American mayor of any major U.S. city. It was becoming clearer that the self-righteousness of the North (maligning racially "backward" Southerners and trying to ignore its own racial prejudice) would somehow have to be addressed. Benjamin Mays, an outstanding black leader in the South, ended his 1971 autobiography with this:

> President John F. Kennedy could predict that in ten years we would place a man on the moon, and his prophecy came true. President Nixon asserted that we could fly to Mars in ten years or more. If we can set a timetable to get to the moon and to Mars—and meet it—God knows we can set a timetable to build a more just society. It's a matter of national will and commitment. It is also a matter of individual responsibility. If these things are not done, I predict that there will be terrifying days ahead in the "land of the free and the home of the brave."[33]

Is Anything Nailed Down?

Everything that once seemed securely nailed down now appeared to be coming loose. Children entering the first grade in 1933 went through their high school years knowing only one president for the entire time they were in grades one through twelve. Children starting grade one in 1960 would suffer a parade of five presidents in thirteen years, including seeing on television the brutal assassinations of at least three nationally beloved public figures. For

---

[32]Many young people from the North did go South. One was Jonathan Daniels, a seminary student from the Episcopal Divinity School in Massachusetts. Witnessing for the civil rights of all citizens, he was shot to death in Alabama in August 1965. A garden of memory at the Abbey of Gethsemani in Kentucky now honors his sacrifice.

[33]Benjamin Mays, *Born To Rebel: An Autobiography* (N.Y.: Charles Scribner's Sons, 1971), 321.

people not living at the time, it is hard to convey how shocking was the nation's experience at the sudden and tragic loss it suffered in 1963. Members of the J-M class of 1959 were very much there and, like most Americans of the time, they tend to still remember their exact locations when the awful news first reached them.

Judy had journeyed to San Antonio, Texas, to join husband David for the exciting occasion of the completing of his military service. On November 21, 1963, David again became a civilian and the couple drove through Dallas on their way home to Ohio. They cleared the city just before President John Kennedy was to arrive, not knowing, of course, how close they came to touching one of the horrors of recent history. Frank came even closer to the awful event. He had accepted his J-M diploma in 1959 and immediately hit the road on his wandering way somewhere west. Running out of money in Dallas, Texas, he settled there for a time as a free-lance printer. Taking a coffee break with his buddy on Friday, November 22, 1963, they decided to go outside to watch the President drive by. The shooting that shook the world happened right in front of them! Was anything sacred or safe anymore? Ian was walking on the campus of Youngstown College and heard the "Star Spangled Banner" and other patriotic music being played continuously on car radios. Asking someone why this was happening, he learned that JFK had been pronounced dead in Texas and the local radio stations were airing nothing but somber patriotic music.

Barry's wife was teaching a fifth-grade class in a small Indiana town to help him through a nearby graduate school in preparation for Christian ministry. A mischievous little girl in her class was sneaking some listening time on a little radio (with earphones placed to her head as unnoticably as possible). Suddenly she approached the teacher with the shocking news. "The President's been shot!" At first she was scolded for the radio and the unlikely story; but she insisted. Within minutes the whole world would know that it really was the truth. Dorothy was working on an assembly line not far from the Jackson-Milton High School when the awful news came. Carole heard the news while working in a beauty shop in Canfield, Ohio. Richard, a senior at Mount Union College, was doing his student teaching at Alliance High School. He still recalls how ominously quiet were the usually noisy halls as the students moved between classes. Maureen was living in a rural setting near the high school where her daily awareness was far from turbulent social issues on the national scene. Even so, she was "devastated" on hearing of the death of JFK and decades later would still get "chills" when she thought about it. For her, Kennedy had been a symbol of goodness and hope. Few

Americans would ever forget that minute when they first heard the shocking word about the violent death of a beloved president. Tom was standing by the driveway at the farm near North Jackson, Ohio, when his wife came out and told him the news. He could not believe it. "Surely this had not happened in the United States!"

John Fitzgerald Kennedy had been elected president of the United States in 1960 in a close race that was the first political event noticed and taken seriously by many in the high school classes of 1959. The youngest man ever elected to this high office (only 43), he embodied a new era. His good looks, youthful energy, and reforming rhetoric inspired a new national vision. It was a welcome vision in stark contrast to half a century of isolationism, depression, and war. Launching the Peace Corps in 1961 was an extension of this vigorous, frontier-crossing president who challenged a new generation to ask not "What your country can do for you?" but "What you can do for your country?" Even though the Soviet Union called the Peace Corps a "super-spy organization," it was seeking to embody the idealism of unselfish service to underdeveloped countries. It enjoyed some notable success. On the other hand, the Soviet Union was right at least in assuming that Kennedy also was very focused on the crisis of the Cold War and was equally active in developing special forces to block the Soviet Union's proclaimed support for wars of national liberation all over the globe. In this context, even the Peace Corps was, in part, designed to win the hearts of developing countries and thus save them from the clutches of communism.

How typical of the turbulent 1960s that the idealist should meet a tragic fate, that the man inspiring a youth corps for peace should fall victim himself to senseless violence. The date of November 22, 1963, lives in infamy for America. President Kennedy arrived in Dallas that day with an eye toward the 1964 election. He hoped that this time the Democrats could win this key state of Texas that they had lost in 1960. But the country was about to lose more than it could comprehend. It was the end of any sense of national innocence that may have been left over from the euphoria of winning the great war of the 1940s and leading the way in saving the world from tyranny. Tragedy now stalked America's very heartland and threatened to break the nation's heart.

The day was sunsplashed and balmy—unfortunately. The president decided to ride in an open limousine without benefit of the usual protective bubble. As the presidential motorcade passed the Texas School Book Depository building, gunshots suddenly rang out and the president reached for his throat with clenched fists. His life would end shortly. Something bright and seemingly irreplaceable had been ripped out of the nation's heart. A man named Lee Harvey Oswald would be apprehended nearby, apparently the gunman.[34] It was as if hell had broken loose. Vice-President Lyndon Johnson took the oath of office in an airplane, the cramped quarters of Air Force One. The grief-stricken Jacqueline Kennedy stood by his side, a new widow now staring into the unknowns of her own future and that of her country. The whole nation was in shock. Maybe Rap Brown was right. "Violence is as American as cherry pie."[35] Only two days later, as Oswald was being transferred to the city jail with the whole nation watching by television, Jack Ruby, a local nightclub owner, stepped out of a crowd and shot Oswald to death at point-blank range, screaming at him, "You killed my president, you rat!"

Almost 100 years earlier the murdered Abraham Lincoln had lain in the East Room of the White House, victim of an assassin. Now it was the beloved John Kennedy. He was the first president to be assassinated in more than 60 years, beyond the memory of most then living. Americans believed that such things did not happen in the United States. They watched through their tears as television stations covered the state funeral, moved by the sight of a riderless horse following a caisson on which the casket was carried. The bagpipers of the British Army's "Black Watch" regiment played at Queen Elizabeth's command. The Panama Canal was closed. Chicago's Loop area was deserted; the nation's public transportation system stopped in grieving respect. When the J-M class of 1959 had visited Washington, D. C. in 1959 on its senior trip, Secretary of State John Foster Dulles was lying in state, a victim of cancer. But President Kennedy's funeral was much more than that. This was a national sadness overlaid with shock, disbelief, even near panic about what was happening to the country itself.

In 1964, five of the ten best-selling nonfiction books in the United States were about John Kennedy.[36] The next year Billy Graham's *World Aflame* was high on the list. The nation was grieving, remembering, worrying. According

---

[34]In 1959, when members of the J-M class of that year were marrying or going to college or the military, Oswald already had dropped out of high school and was being discharged from the U.S. Marines at his own request. He then defected to the U.S.S.R., only to be denied citizenship there, possibly because of his history of being emotionally disturbed.

[35]Hubert (H. Rap) Brown, *Die, Nigger, Die*, 1969.

[36]They were: *Four Days* (American Heritage); *Profiles in Courage* (JFK, memorial edition); *A Day in the Life of President Kennedy* (Jim Bishop); *The Kennedy Wit* (Bill Adler); and *The John F. Kennedys* (Mark Shaw). Added in 1965 were two more, *A Thousand Days* (Arthur Schlesinger, Jr.) and *Kennedy* (Theodore Sorensen). The bestseller in 1967 was *Death of a President* (William Manchester).

Lyndon Johnson taking the presidential oath of office, with Jacqueline Kennedy standing by his side.

to historian Jules Witcover: "…the young president's sudden death led columnist Mary McGrory to remark to fellow Irishman Daniel Patrick Moynihan, then the Assistant Secretary of Labor, that 'we'll never laugh again.' To which Moynihan replied: 'We'll laugh again. It's just that we'll never be young again.'"[37] Members of the J-M class of 1959, now young adults, joined the nation in not being quite so young anymore.

Unfortunately, the violence did not stop with the presidential assassination. Robert Kennedy, the president's brother who had been appointed United States Attorney General in 1961, proved to be aggressive in enforcing civil rights legislation in reluctant southern states. Then, as a senator from New York during the years 1964-68, he was a vigorous voice for constructive social change. He emerged as an attractive presidential candidate. He and Martin Luther King, Jr., had become national symbols of vision and courage on behalf of justice for all the nation's citizens. Then, again shockingly, they each fell victim to an assassin's bullet, King in Memphis in April 1968, and Kennedy two months later in Los Angeles while campaigning for the presidency. Our best were being ripped from the nation one at a time.[38] There was rioting in Youngstown, Ohio. Shirley was then an emergency room nurse and

---

[37]Jules Witcover, *The Year the Dream Died: Revisiting 1968 in America* (N.Y.: Warner Books, 1997), xi.

[38]Adding to the string of 1968 disasters was the sudden loss under mysterious circumstances of the U.S.S. *Scorpion* (SSN 589) on May 24. When it exploded, this at-sea American nuclear submarine likely was engaged in a dangerous maneuver with a Soviet vessel seeking to shadow an American Polaris submarine. If so, the event was one of the more serious incidents of the entire Cold War. See Dan Van der Vat, *Stealth At Sea: The History of the Submarine* (Boston: Houghton Mifflin, 1995), 334-335.

found herself in the middle of the pain brought in off the streets. What she saw was not pretty. She did what she could, observing later that people of any skin color bleed and die just the same. Was rationality gone? Could democracy survive such a wave of violence? Is a gun the final answer to profound human problems? These questions lurked in hearts everywhere and often burst out of their mouths in frustration and fear.

The violence was by no means limited to the United States or caused only by American racial attitudes or political hatreds. President Kennedy had begun America's military involvement in Vietnam. Within days after Kennedy's assassination, President Johnson had moved to make this war his own. He announced to Henry Cabot Lodge, "I'm not going to be the president who saw Southeast Asia go the way China went." Johnson followed the tendency of the 1950s to see the world defined largely by the Cold War. Rather than viewing various movements around the world as efforts to be free of Western colonialism, he saw them as part of the worldwide communist conspiracy. Like the proud Texan he was, he would draw whatever guns were necessary to be sure that right prevailed. To keep the communists from winning in the Vietnam region, therefore, Johnson supervised a process that saw the number of American troops in Vietnam increase from 16,000 to 500,000. His presidency would be marked by two wars, one on poverty at home and one against the communists in Vietnam, with the tragic irony that "waging one ensured the defeat of the other."[39]

John Kennedy in his inauguration address had laid out a challenge for a renewed America of domestic equality and international peace, leadership, and service. He knew that such a task would not be finished soon, but he had said, "Let us begin." Then Lyndon Johnson, in his first major speech as president, played off this challenge with his own "Let us continue." While he and Congress surely did continue, expanding Kennedy's "New Frontier" to the quest for a "Great Society," unfortunately every dollar diverted to Vietnam took away from what Johnson hoped to accomplish at home. What he thought was a high moral stance abroad became widely perceived, even at home, as arrogant American militarism against the poor of another nation. The television-viewing American public wallowed nightly in gross images of devastation and human carnage. The political "doves" had seen enough and demanded a negotiated settlement. The "hawks" insisted that the government in Washington was getting too many Americans killed and should just end

---

[39]Chafe, *The Unfinished Journey*, 273.

the thing with overwhelming force like President Truman had done with the two big bombs over Japan in 1945.

Many Americans now reflect back on America's massive involvement in the Vietnam War and still are not sure whether it was a mistake to have even been there in the first place. They tend to be more sure, however, that it certainly was a mistake to be involved and not have fought to win (doing whatever was necessary). Jane was an outspoken critic of America's involvement in Vietnam. She thought the U.S. never should have gotten tangled in it in the first place. In the 1960s, however, she was hardly prepared to disrupt society at home over the issue. Many others of her generation became more aggressive, going well beyond speaking out. Social revolt surfaced in more and more ways. Jane's classmate John became a marijuana smoker as part of his search for personal identity. Young Americans often were now seeing hypocrisy and inhuman selfishness in the country's power structures and war commitments. Many of them decided to strike out in a very different direction, some constructive, some bizarre.

Was Vietnam the source or merely the trigger of the student radicalism that shook the nation in the late 1960s and early 1970s? Why would so many young people come to the harsh judgment, beyond their opposition to the U.S. involvement in Vietnam, that the U.S. itself was deeply immoral? Why would the brightest, best-educated, most affluent members of the baby-boomer generation actively express disrespect and even hatred toward the very culture that had lavished multiple privileges on them? One answer they often gave was that, in their view, the country was unacceptably racist, sexist, authoritarian, and imperialistic.[40] Their rhetoric certainly was steeped in moral idealisms. Other contributing factors, however, surely were the facts that the baby boomers had the leisure and affluence to be politically active, that their numbers in higher education had doubled to almost ten million during the 1960s (congregating them together in settings where they had few adult responsibilities and many "leftist" professors), and that this generation had been reared with a daily belief of their own importance and a deep conviction of their inherent right to social entitlements, including the right to be free of authoritarian parents and governments. Even so, for many of the young, the moral idealism was very real. Ian now looks back and offers this generous analysis: "The 1960s was the decade without Uncle Sam. He represented what needed cleansing. Western civilization gave itself a chance at a new start."

---

[40]A vigorous leader in inspiring the student radicalism was an organization called Students for a Democratic Society (SDS).

There was, to be sure, the escapist and even criminal elements of student protest. The 1960s soon reeled from Timothy Leary's "turn on, tune in, drop out!" philosophy for a generation of youth who had numerous members discovering new psychedelic drugs, subscribing to or just sneaking glances at the new *Playboy* magazine,[41] and even burning their draft cards in public. The popular musical *Hair* celebrated the joys of youthful rebellion and portrayed the promise of a brighter future, an "Age of Aquarius" free of war and social strife. This rock musical featured frontal nudity of female actors who were paid extra for disrobing. The Haight-Ashbury district of San Francisco attracted thousands of "flower children" who tended to be rootless, jobless, and peaceful young people seeking the enlightenment of some free-form existence. The Grateful Dead became a musical voice of this peace-and-love generation. Scenes of "hippie" life culminated in 1967 with the "summer of love" (just before the "winter" of approaching despair). Soon many of these seekers for utopia became sick, hungry, and even fearful. The hippie ideals of love, peace, and the rejection of materialism suffered from fragile faith foundations. Could it be that a person's latest "high" is all the reality there is? Maybe the moment and only the moment is everything after all. It seemed and soon became clear that these cut-loose, self-oriented idealists "could survive the real world for only a brief moment."[42]

Once such young people were true believers in the political process of liberal reform. Shortly, however, most of them who survived at all became cynical and increasingly alienated from their own nation. Their energy shifted to either "dropping out" altogether or trying to revolutionize the country's central values and structures through direct action. Disenchantment, protest, and non-conformity slowly took hold in large segments of the society. Widespread social change was in the wind. Civil rights marches, once a means of peaceful protest when led by Martin Luther King, Jr., by 1966 had espoused "black power" and sometimes employed violent means. Dangerous new drugs now were on the streets and sometimes violent demonstrations were breaking out on prominent college campuses. There was near chaos in Chicago when the Democratic Convention convened there in 1968. The Cuban missile crisis (October 1962), the Six-Day Arab-Israel war (June,

---

[41]Beginning in 1960, this magazine added to its explicit photos of nude women an "Adviser" column giving guidance to readers seeking new and more imaginative ways of practicing sex. At the end of the decade an estimated 20 percent of adult American men were in regular contact with this publication.

[42]Harvey, op. cit., 339.

1967), and the ongoing Vietnam War were some of the dizzying agonies of the time.

Barry was scheduled to be in the Middle East in 1967 on an archaeological trip with his new colleagues from Anderson College (University) in Indiana where he now was a junior faculty member (a long way from Craig Beach where he had lived until high school graduation in 1959 with rare access to a library, let alone a collegiate environment). Delayed because of the war, this Indiana group of religious academics did go in the summer of 1968 and saw firsthand the large new refugee camps of Palestinians in Jordan and Lebanon. Barry returned to the United States and, with his wife and infant son, moved to Hyde Park in Chicago to begin work on a doctorate in a seminary across the street from the intellectually famed University of Chicago. Even this sophisticated university neighborhood was experiencing the unsettling effects of aggressive social disobedience. Some said that "disorderly" conduct could not be tolerated; others said there was no choice but to resist evil forcefully if justice ever were to come. In this latter group was Rev. Jesse Jackson, born in 1941 with the J-M class of 1959 and associated with the same graduate school in Chicago that Barry now was attending in the late 1960s. In 1967 Martin Luther King made Jackson head of Operation Breadbasket, an organized attempt to pressure employers to hire black workers. Ordained a Baptist minister in 1968, Jackson organized Operation PUSH (People United to Save Humanity) in 1971. His vigorous African-American voice would be heard across the country for decades to come.

Within the first hour of residence in their third-floor apartment, Barry's young family was frightened by the sounds of what seemed like distant explosions. Rushing to the back porch overlooking an alley and looking northward toward downtown Chicago, it became obvious that the sounds were fireworks. The celebration was for Hubert Humphrey who had just been nominated as the presidential candidate of the Democratic Party. Grant Park along Lake Michigan shortly became a virtual battleground that seemed like an urban civil war. The campus of the University of Chicago, just a few blocks from their apartment, was seized by rebellious students and then surrounded by Mayor Richard Daley's police. The siege was on, as it was on other campuses. Many of the idealistic young were crying out for more social justice and radical political change. Right-wing politicians like Governor George Wallace of Alabama were demanding the use of more force to maintain law and order in the nation. Most Americans fell somewhere between these extremes. They were anxious, perplexed, hopeful, very unsure, often afraid.

The presidential election of 1968 was surely the most eventful and painful in the nation's history. It started with President Johnson stunning the nation by announcing that he would not seek reelection. The man in the White House is both the chief repository of the nation's highest aspirations and the supreme scapegoat for its frustrations. Johnson had apparently had enough of what he saw as the scapegoating. Vice-President Hubert Humphrey threw his hat into the political ring. Soon George McGovern did the same. Both were led in the polls by Robert Kennedy, who then was shot to death on June 6 by an Arab nationalist bitterly opposed to his support of Israel. The Democratic National Convention in Chicago was marked by chaos in the streets. Richard Nixon got the Republican nod, although he was bothered by the far-right independent candidacy of George Wallace, who himself was shot by a would-be assassin and put in a wheelchair. The country was

> ...on the verge of a national nervous breakdown.... If in the past American political divisions had been primarily based on region and class and ethnicity, a new ingredient had now been added, profound generational differences.... Those who had suffered through the Depression and fought in World War II and who tended to accept the word of the existing leadership were on one side; their children, raised in a more affluent and more iconoclastic age, were on the other.[43]

Nixon's strong call for "law and order" helped his presidential campaign in 1968 and his narrow defeat of Humphrey in the election. Social idealism and political reform can be good; but the public now was saying with increasing volume, so is a stable and safe society!

Mainstream Americans were growing tired of dissent that was marked by violence. Would conventional patriotism survive? Was social sanity nearly gone? Could President Nixon settle things back down? Hardly, except on the surface. Most members of the J-M class of 1959 were "mainstream" Americans. Dallas, for example, had served more than four years in the Navy, had gotten out before the big action in Vietnam, and soon was convinced that the street protesters in the U.S. were irresponsible for the most part and "letting the country down." He had become a policeman in Dayton, Ohio, and soon faced from the "establishment" side some rioting in Dayton. What he recalls seeing were some people honestly crusading for civil rights and numerous others just looting in an orgy of greed. Bill, a classmate of Dallas, reflected clearly the confusion of the times. He was sensitive about social issues, but not a public protester. He was not sure if the country should

---

[43]David Halberstam in his Foreword to Jules Witcover, *The Year the Dream Died*, ix.

be fighting in Vietnam, but hated to see the U.S. government not finish successfully what it started and had paid so much for. If he had been called to go and fight in Vietnam, he would have at least considered fleeing to Canada instead (as many did to avoid the draft)—although he probably would have stayed and served in spite of his inner conflict.

Little seemed nailed down. It was a difficult time for everyone. Blame for the mass social protests in the late 1960s was often placed by parents and the media on communists, drugs, rock musicians, college professors, and infectiously charismatic figures like the presumably psychotic and murderous Charles Manson. It was hard for mainstream society to face squarely the deep alienation of many of its own children who were open to these many influences. To recognize and affirm the alienation would have been to accept the harsh judgments on the older generation and on the basic institutions of the society. Naturally, most members of the established culture were not prepared to do such a thing.

Faith, But Faith In What?

The floodgates of change were open in the society, change of all kinds. New vaccines against long dreaded diseases came along and certainly were welcome; but other new things were less welcomed by traditional Americans. A popular expression of "the new morality" was the book *Situation Ethics* by Joseph Fletcher.[44] Maybe what is right is not to be defined by any enduring set of absolutes, but only by the circumstances of the moment and the principle of love. Maybe the shackles of all legalistic moralities should be relaxed or eliminated altogether.[45] The 1960s also was the time when practicing religion in public school settings was legally curtailed. Any kind of religious devotional exercises was removed by the Supreme Court decisions in *Engel v. Vitale* (1962) and *Abington Township School District v. Schempp* (1963). The 1960s was the leading edge of what has come to be called the "postmodernist" era. A chief characteristic of this "deconstructionist" time was establishing the lack of

> ...a broadly accepted worldview that connected technology, politics, and religion. Instead, the world witnessed the flourishing of disparate

---

[44]Joseph Fletcher, *Situation Ethics: The New Morality* (Philadelphia: Westminster Press, 1966).

[45]This trend was countered in 1968 when Pope Paul VI issued *Humanae Vitae*, reaffirming the traditional Roman Catholic prohibition of birth control devices or medications. There was a cry of protest from many Catholics to this reaffirmation, especially in the U.S. But the Pope insisted on holding the line. He had set his church on a collision course with the "modern" world.

ecological, feminist, and liberationist spiritualities, of mystical, shaman-ist, and occultist paths, of resurgent fundamentalisms and religious nationalisms.[46]

Rolling Stone magazine first appeared in 1967 and soon tended to speak for a rebelling generation. Uninhibited personal expression among the young now seemed to be everywhere, and often was infused with a new rush of social idealism. Some of the young did just "drop out." Many others marched for human rights, spoke out against capitalistic excesses, joined President Kennedy's Peace Corps, and were pleased by President Johnson's declared war on poverty and his "Great Society" programs. "Relevance" was now the pop-ular cry of the young. School curricula responded. Mini courses and a cafe-teria of elective offerings came on stream. Literary classics like *Ivanhoe, Silas Marner,* and *A Tale of Two Cities* found themselves competing for student attention with *Catcher in the Rye* (1951) and *Lord of the Flies* (1954). It was a new and very difficult time. What was so relevant about these now-popu-lar novels from the 1950s? They appealed to the questioning and rebellion of the young. J. D. Salinger's *Catcher* proved extremely popular. It was about a teenager soon to be dropped from school who chooses to spend three days and nights in New York City. What he saw, suffered, and said provided a dis-turbing collage of vulgar words and ugly images of phoniness and corruption in the adult world.

Some 400,000 of the more "liberated" young massed in rural New York in August 1969 for the Woodstock Rock Festival, an outdoor orgy of loud music, booze, sex, and idealistic social protest. It was a place of irony, the rare display of a tantalizing mixture of the ridiculous and the admirable—often demanding in humanly destructive ways the rapid return of the truly human. It was the culminating event of the wave of "countercultural" activities of the 1960s, an anti-authoritarian mass of young people happily listening to a non-stop rock concert, much of the time in the rain and mud. To a still largely conservative American population that had sacrificed much in World War II and Korea to preserve the safety of democracy around the world, it seemed that responsible freedom was being unraveled by a tide of self-seek-ing and highly irresponsible youth. Rather than being interested in the more traditional and nostalgic musicals like *Hello, Dolly!* (1964), this human sea of "flower children" at Woodstock listened, sang, drank, and danced to the protesting idealisms of Joan Baez; Blood, Sweat and Tears; Arlo Guthrie; Jimi Hendrix; and others.

---

[46]Robert Ellwood, *The Sixties: Spiritual Awakening* (New Brunswick, N.J.: Rutgers University Press, 1994), 331.

The Woodstock event came to symbolize an era of free-loving, drug-tak-ing "hippie" youth that would end shortly with some harsh realities, includ-ing the drug-related deaths of rockers Jimi Hendrix and Janis Joplin and the shooting of several student protesters at Kent State University—all within one year of Woodstock. One extreme seems to stimulate the other. Richard Nixon won the presidential election in 1968 by a very slim margin over Democrat Hubert Humphrey (with the reactionary George Wallace of Alabama receiv-ing 10,000,000 votes). Nixon had no mandate, unless it was to dismantle things that Lyndon Johnson had erected. Conservative backlash was now a reality. One historian reports the growing disillusionment:

> Lyndon Johnson's decision not to run for a second term sounded the knell for the rationalist era that had been ushered in just eight years before. All of his and John Kennedy's proud new policy initiatives lay in shattered wreckage.... America had lost its postwar illusion of omnipotence. John Kennedy had suggested that America lacked mere-ly the will to achieve global greatness. The expenditure of $100 billion in Vietnam and the loss of 50,000 American lives, if nothing else, demonstrated resolve. But the enterprise was a failure; the result was only corrosive doubt and disillusionment. Kennedy and Johnson had told the country that it did not know the limits of its greatness. Now it did, and they were crushingly small, and it had still to plumb the depths of its weakness.[47]

William Golding's *Lord of the Flies*, very popular among college students after its 1959 appearance in paperback and then its being made into a movie in 1963, was no prettier than Salinger's *Catcher in the Rye*. It attempted to trace the defects of human nature and the supposed dependence of society on the ethical nature of the individual. Political systems are critiqued sharply in the dramatically pictured struggle between civilization and barbarism. This novel symbolized how a new generation was coming to see things in the United States. The J-M class of 1959 was in the middle of this time of social strain, even chaos at times, although in general they were less cynical than the more radical of the young, having had positive social experiences in the 1940s and 1950s. By sharp contrast, the 1960s, full of cries for justice in the midst of prosperity for many, was a brash, escapist, angry, venturesome, vio-lent, frontier-crossing decade, quite a time for the 1959 J-M class members to begin their families and careers!

Perspective is important. In some urban streets, intellectual circles, and government offices, and certainly on all television screens, not much seemed

---

[47]Charles Morris, *A Time of Passion*, 104-105.

Hare Krishna devotees on the city streets in Philadelphia.

sacred or secure anymore. The 1960s surely were turbulent years. On the other hand, there was a "silent majority" in the land who still were close to their traditional cultural and religious roots and values, who were not protesting in the streets but rather were either confused, fearful, and/or embarrassed by all that they were hearing but never seeing except on television—an assassinated president, riots in the cities of the nation, human carnage in Vietnam, and apparently out-of-control teenagers. A deep shadow seemed to have fallen. Would light come again to a troubled society losing faith in itself and bolting all traditional faith structures?

Actually, faith of various kinds was newly alive in some quarters, but it was hardly new faith in the U.S. itself or in the traditional establishments of classic faith communities. It has been argued that the "hippie" counterculture of the 1960s changed America more than its ambiguous politics.[48] Various Asian spiritualities now were being considered by many people as the way to opt out of social status seeking and the whole dehumanizing apparatus of a highly industrialized and socially decadent society. Especially popular was TM (Transcendental Meditation). Thus:

> To external achievement it posed inner experience; to the exploitation of nature, harmony with nature; to impersonal organization, an intense relation to a guru. Mahayana Buddhism, particularly in the form of Zen, provided the most pervasive religious influence on the

---

[48]See Timothy Miller, *The Hippies and American Values: The Utopian Ethics of the Counterculture*, 1965-1970 (1991).

counterculture; but elements from Taoism, Hinduism, and Sufism were also influential. What drug experiences, interpreted in oriental religious terms...meditation experiences...showed was the illusoriness of worldly striving.[49]

Thomas Merton, widely read Christian monk living in a Kentucky monastery, sought to rejoin faith and action, prayer and political protest, love and readiness to build bridges of dialogue and understanding. He encouraged activists like the priests Philip and Daniel Berrigan in public protests against the Vietnam War. A special concern of Merton's in the 1960s was the gulf between Christianity in the West and the great spiritual traditions of the East. While opposing the U.S. military involvement in Vietnam, Merton traveled in 1968 to ancient spiritual centers in India and Thailand. His accidental death in Thailand yielded an ironic symbol of the way the world then was. The body of this monk, dedicated to peace, was flown home in the bay of a U.S. Strategic Air Command bomber along with American soldiers recently killed in Vietnam. Merton's brothers at the Gethsemani monastery buried him beside the church with the grave marked only with the standard little white cross reading "Father Louis."[50] Rain turning to snow fell on the crowd of monks as the funeral service ended with the reading of these words that conclude Merton's own autobiography:

> But you shall taste the true solitude of my anguish and my poverty and I shall lead you into the high places of my joy and you shall die in Me and find all things in My mercy which has created you for this end and brought you...to the Cistercian Abbey of the poor men who labor in Gethsemani that you may become the brother of God and learn to know the Christ of the burnt men.[51]

There it was, a picture of the 1960s. The era, among other things, was one of anguish, death, sacrifice, and the search for an inner solitude that could provide a vision reaching beyond the turmoil of the times. Some were searching for an inner peace, a joy and harmony in relating to God, other human beings, and the natural environment in humble and mystic ways instead of in pride, power, and prosperity through establishment religious means. The

---

[49]Bellah and Hammond, 176.

[50]Barry, J-M class of 1959, chose across the 1980s and 1990s to journey annually to this monastery for personal spiritual retreats.

[51]The widely read autobiography of Thomas Merton is titled *The Seven Storey Mountain* (Harcourt Brace).

God to whom many were seeking to relate in new ways was frequently getting redefined:

> So the new religious imagination conceived of a church or temple that was egalitarian, concerned with subjectivity, driven by feeling rather than highly consistent doctrine; and it imagined a God who himself enjoyed rich subjectivity and was not very legalistic. This God was apparently also easy with pluralism, well aware that Americans are not likely ever to be very much alike in religion. That Sixties God is pretty much the God that has been worshipped ever since in this corner of the world, whether by liberals or conservatives, Catholics, Protestants, or Jews.[52]

In some contrast, however, there arose the "Jesus Movement" of young people disillusioned by the failure of various activisms and now aware that drugs and free sex provide no permanent "high" and can be very dangerous. They turned rather to conservative and emotional Christian faith. Still countercultural (long hair, outlandish clothes, youth jargon minus the profanity, and general disdain for the established churches), they accepted Jesus in warm personal relationships and witnessed actively, if sometimes unconventionally. Parallel to this was the "Pentecostal" resurgence that sought fresh power in Christian faith by reclaiming special "gifts of the Spirit" like speaking in "tongues." At first shunned by the established churches, this movement soon would influence all Christian traditions.

Most prominent in the 1960s among established Christian churches, especially in their academic and headquarters circles, was the concern for reestablishing a sense of the faith's relevance to pressing social issues. German theologian Dietrich Bonhoeffer had been imprisoned in Germany for his anti-Nazi activities and then executed in prison just before the camp was liberated by American troops. He coined phrases like "religionless Christianity" and "man has come of age." God's purpose is to liberate human beings from sin and suffering. Jesus was said to be the "man for others," soon a slogan for an American Christianity that tried hard to hit the streets for Jesus on behalf of real justice. To be "religionless," Christians were told they must stop separating the sacred and secular realms of life.[53] Here were highly visible keynotes of the faith as it sought to be faithful in the turbulent 1960s.

---

[52]Robert Ellwood, 335.

[53]For an overview of the work of Dietrich Bonhoeffer, see Stanley Grenz and Roger Olson, *20th-Century Theology: God and the World in a Transitional Age* (InterVarsity Press, 1992), chapter five.

Earth finally was put in dramatic perspective when viewed from the moon. Humans live on a very small, beautiful, fragile planet.

By the Light of the Moon

The 1960s was certainly a decade of affluence, with the average American's real income increasing fifty percent over 1950 and the country's high standard of living remaining the envy of the world. But the later years of the decade suffered the loss of national innocence, pride, and cohesion. There was a darkening cast to how life was being viewed, symbolized frighteningly in 1965 by a massive stoppage of electrical power that suddenly blacked out most of the Northeastern states and part of Canada. This darkening was expressed clearly in popular culture by the Rolling Stones' demonic song "Sympathy for the Devil." Mick Jagger, assuming the persona of Lucifer, would mock his listeners as he recounted musically the disasters of history—the crucifixion of Jesus, the Russian revolution, the Nazi blitzkrieg, the Kennedy assassinations. He was right, at least in part. There surely was much of the demonic being perceived—many of the young seeing it in the country's military-industrial establishment and the stunned establishment often seeing it in the rebellious and unrealistic young.[54] It was a dramatic, angry, and confusing time. There was a mass disaffection from the common understandings of U.S. culture, a serious erosion of the common sensing of the inherent legitimacy of the basic American institutions of public life.

Some of the spirit of these difficult years is seen in the first Super Bowl and in the first human foot ever to be set on a land surface not of this earth. In 1967 the American sports public witnessed the staging of the first "Super

---

[54]See Marshall Berman, "Sympathy for the Devil: Faust, the '60s, and the Tragedy of Development," *American Review* (January 1974).

Bowl." After years of competing for the best players, the National and American Football Leagues faced each other for a head-to-head championship. But it was not until Super Bowl III in 1969 that either the NFL or the public took the AFL very seriously. In his last year at Geneva College, Barry was a student teacher in Beaver Falls, Pa. One of his American history students, Joe Namath, had a golden right arm. On occasion Barry would watch his student quarterback the local football team on Friday nights. Joe obviously was a gifted athlete, soon found his way to the University of Alabama, and then into the AFL with the New York Jets. The lowly Jets, now quarterbacked by "Broadway" Joe Namath, were big underdogs against the powerful Baltimore Colts in Super Bowl III. Many thought that Namath could beat the Colts about as easily as a man could actually walk on the moon. Well, Joe brashly bragged in advance that the Jets would win. The year was 1969. The Jets pulled off a dramatic victory. The win exemplified the common attitude of players and fans of professional athletics in the 1960s. Vince Lombardi put it bluntly: "Winning is not everything; it is the only thing."

Whether in professional sports, in civil rights for African-Americans, or in the race in the United States to beat the Soviet Union to the moon), the mad dash to win was often painful and exhausting. The softer and lighter side of life always prevailed just beyond the media spotlight. For instance, best-selling nonfiction books of the 1960s were not all about rockets, bombs, and riots (see Table 13). People obviously still cared deeply about the Bible, cooking, money, health, and simple humor. Cartoonist Charles Schulz's first book, *Happiness Is a Warm Puppy*, made the nonfiction bestseller list in 1962 and headed the list in 1963—with the second bestseller that year being his *Security Is a Thumb and a Blanket*, to be joined in 1964 by *I Need All the Friends I Can Get* (number two) and *Christmas Is Together-Time* (number five).[55]

Beyond the inner-space issues of faith, security, humor, and how to live practically, it was outer space that had captured the imagination of the American public and its scientists in the 1960s. Helping greatly was a television program that premiered in September 1966. It was an outer-space version of *Wagon Train* set on a starship operating three-hundred years in the future. At first this program was not expected to succeed commercially. *Star Trek*, however, soon proved durable and over the coming decades would rise above nearly any other television show ever aired. For a nation embroiled in Vietnam and mired in a Cold War, creator Gene Roddenberry wanted

---

[55]I would become casually acquainted with Charles Schulz in the 1970s and 1980s through Schulz's relationship with the Church of God (Anderson, Ind.) and Anderson University in Indiana where I was a professor and dean.

Americans to see the light of a coming day when bloodshed and prejudice would be banished from the Earth and even challenged in the cosmos. He cast the starship's crew with multiethnic characters that included an African-American woman who carried major responsibility. This was social commentary wrapped in science fiction, the fearless crew of the U.S.S. *Enterprise* going where no one had gone before—with fascinating techno-gadgetry and reassuringly benevolent intent.

Stepping back into the reality of Earth in the 1960s, space was "the last frontier," the one already being explored and maybe exploited by the Soviet Union for other than benevolent purposes. Like Namath's bold claim, although the Soviet Union started first in the 1950s, the United States had determined to catch up and would win. President Kennedy had promised such an American success by the end of the decade. It was a difficult and costly process ($33 billion during the 1960s), including the tragic deaths of three astronauts in a flash fire in their command module while still on its launching pad (January 1967). But during the Christmas week of 1968 three other Americans (Borman, Lovell, and Anders) successfully journeyed to the moon and sent back to earth stunning photographs of itself. It was a triumphant climax to a deeply troubled year in the United States. Christmas traditionally celebrates the birth of Jesus Christ, hope of the world. Now three American "wise men," overwhelmed by what lay before them, staged a Christmas eve telecast during which they took turns solemnly reading to the world the first ten verses of Genesis: "In the beginning, God created the heaven and earth...."

Space was the "last frontier." Americans were the first humans to be present on any body in space other than Earth by engaging in direct exploration of the Moon's surface.

What hope for humanity was being born here? Poets spoke of a new birthing. The human race now had glimpsed more than another new colony or continent; it finally had seen a new age that could reshape humanity's self-understanding and destiny. Archibald MacLeish wrote: "to see ourselves as riders on the earth together, brothers on that bright loveliness in the eternal cold—brothers who know now they are truly brothers." Then in July 1969, it finally happened. The Eagle touched down on the moon and an American actually set his foot on a body other than Earth. As Neil Armstrong's foot contacted the moon's surface for the first time, he said to the world: "That's one small step for a man, one giant leap for mankind." Then an elated President Richard Nixon added: "For one priceless moment in the whole history of man, all the people of this earth are truly one." Most Americans and fascinated citizens of many other nations celebrated simultaneously the stunning scientific accomplishment of the lunar landing because it was a victory "purely accomplished: in Vietnam, in the carious slums, in the polluted environment, no clear victories seemed possible any longer."[56]

The opportunity had never existed before. Looking back from space at the beautiful blue ball called Earth was an experience that offered humanity a whole new perspective on reality itself. This little globe floating quietly in space appeared as one peaceful place with no disruptive national boundaries or human distinctions. Could this fascinating and reconciling view of the Earth from space ever become a functioning reality back where people really lived? One could hope and pray. American poet Archibald MacLeish wrote of the moon after that first landing:

> Before the first men tasted time, we thought of you. You were a wonder to us, unattainable.... Now our hands have touched you in your depth of night.

Modern society was seeking new light in the vast darkness of space. By learning more about what is "out there," could humans gain more self-understanding back on Earth? From the vast silence of space, could people find the key to peace for the noisy and ugly conflicts on this little blue marble that was their common home? From the depths of the distant darkness, could there be some source of new light?

In 1969 Hollywood released *Easy Rider*, a memorable treatment of the hippie counterculture of the time. The film made antiheroes and martyrs out of asocial drifters. As the public watched, it was tempted to wonder whether the

---

[56]*Time* magazine, January 5, 1970, 12.

decade of the 1970s would bring more realistic and hopeful approaches to the justice, solidarity, and stability so urgently needed in American society. In fact, the next decade would bring these—in its own awkward and generally unsatisfying ways. There was a "silent majority" who cherished older and well-entrenched social and spiritual values in contrast to what they viewed as the "liberal" excesses of the 1960s. The consensus center of the nation's values and ideals that had held relatively firm in the 1950s "cracked in the 1960s, exposing a glaring, often unapologetic polarization that seemed astonishing to contemporaries."[57] There soon would be a scramble to regroup and reassert social controls, with some success and much failure.

"Middle America" would seek to reclaim its more traditional culture.[58] The events of 1968 had shattered Kennedy's vision and then Johnson's dream. A conservatism that only four years earlier had been emphatically rejected in the presidential candidacy of Republican Barry Goldwater now started to take root across the nation. Richard Nixon in Washington was to be the key political instrument. The central question now often posed was: "This is the greatest country in the world. Why are people trying to tear it down?" Coming into vogue was a backlash against black militancy, white intellectuals, and long-haired young radicals. The "middle" of America was farther left of center politically and socially than it had been in the 1940s and 1950s, but patience was virtually gone for people like Black Panther leaders Eldridge Cleaver and Bobby Seale. Already idealized were John and Robert Kennedy. They were seen as having had an idealism about a good, just, and rational America, an America of strength, togetherness, prosperity, and respect.

Could such a patriotic idealism soon come again? "Of course the ideal 'Republic' dreamed by the founders [of the U.S.] never existed in actuality," Sydney Mead reminds us. "It was a vision, an artist-people's creative idea that imbued them with the energy to strive—and with considerable success—to incarnate it in actuality."[59] The striving would go on, but soon in more conservative and rarely more successful ways.

---

[57]Patterson, *Grand Expectations*, 457.

[58]*Time* magazine named as its 1969 "Person of the Year" the whole class of people it identified as "Middle Americans" (issue of January 5, 1970).

[59]Sydney Mead, "American History as a Tragic Drama," *Journal of Religion*, 52 (October 1972), 60.

Taking Time To Reflect

1. The administration of President John Kennedy is said to have believed that there were no major "structural problems" in the U.S. of the early 1960s and that the country was on its way to being "a complete society." Was this judgment correct? What would it take to be a "complete society"?

2. Patriotism, love for and pride in one's country, is one thing. Another is covering over its problems at the expense of real justice. How can there be both pride and needed self-criticism in a modern society?

3. In a free society, does every citizen have a moral responsibility to disobey unjust laws—as did Martin Luther King, Jr.? Is there some dependable standard for determining what is unjust? Did King's non-violent approach to public protest work effectively for increased social justice in the 1960s?

4. Situation ethics argues that there are few if any fixed moral standards, only decisions to be made in light of current circumstances. Is that the case? On what basis does a person or a whole society determine what is really good and right?

5. Is it true, as claimed frequently, that the God typically worshipped in the United States since the 1960s is focused on human subjectivity, not overly concerned with precise doctrines, and generally comfortable with "pluralism" in religious beliefs and practices?

6. As Dietrich Bonhoeffer taught so influentially, should Christians stop separating the sacred and secular realms of life, thus including vigorous effort to liberate people from both sin and social injustice? Does spiritual-experience-oriented conservative Christianity work against social justice by default? What is "religionless" Christianity?

7. The United Nations was proving unable to preserve world peace, in part because member nations could not be forced to act constructively against their wills for the good of the larger community of nations. Is there some better way for nations to work cooperatively to solve international crises?

8. Real frontiers have become fewer and fewer in the twentieth century. What impact did the "last frontier" of space have on the imagination and politics of the U.S. in the 1960s? What does the biblical book of Genesis have to do with science and outer space?

Chapter Five

Deaths in Search of Dawns

1970s

———

The Roman gods were amplified humanity, not divinity.... All
their gods put together could not give them a sufficient base for
life, morals, values, and final decisions. These gods depended
on the society which had made them, and when this society
collapsed the gods tumbled with it.[1]

———

You have set our iniquities before you, our secret sins in the
light of your countenance. (Psalm 90:8)

———

The 1970s in many ways seemed like a non-decade. These were transitional years in which the defining trends of the 1960s played themselves out
(especially before President Nixon's resignation in 1974) and the trends of the
coming 1980s were being prefaced. Peter Carroll's excellent history of the
United States in the 1970s, titled *It Seemed Like Nothing Happened*,[2] deliberately announces the central irony. What was in the 1970s can be viewed as
having less of its own identity than what went just before and was to come
just after. While the 1970s certainly was not merely a time characterized by

———

[1]Francis Schaeffer, *How Should We Then Live?: The Rise and Decline of Western
Thought and Culture* (Old Tappan, N.J.: Fleming Revell, 1976), 21.
[2]Peter Carroll, *It Seemed Like Nothing Happened: America in the 1970s* (New
Brunswick: Rutgers University Press, 1982, rev. 1990). Carroll argues that the Richard
Nixon administration started this false designation of the 1970s, trying to keep in the pre-
Nixon 1960s the "times of great agony—the agonies of war, of inflation, of rapidly rising
crime. . .and of anger and frustration that led finally to violence and the worst civil disorder in a century" (State of the Union Address in 1972). In fact, the 1970s had its full
share of the same.

the culture of inertia, passivity, and retrenchment, it appears to have been largely that. Its elusive reality is a maddening mixture, both a reflection of the recent past and an emerging sample of what was soon to come.

The decade's opening year, 1970, was referred to by one editorialist as "A Time of In-Betweenity." Before the year began, the mass media was filled with hopes for the 1970s. There was an eagerness to leave behind what some were calling that "slum of a decade," the 1960s. But 1970 turned out to be an in-between ambiguity—as would the whole decade to follow. The Cambodia-Kent State series of tragic events climaxed the first six months, a last gasp of the 1960s that produced devastating backlash and soon scattered most student protesters away from the political process. The release of Charles Reich's book *The Greening of America* was a throw-back to the 1960s. It was outlandishly optimistic about how the youth culture would bring about a happy new day for America. Both pessimism and optimism surfaced in these 1970 events. Could the young mature beyond an unfettered idealism that the public would no longer tolerate? Could the not-so-young avoid slamming the door to innocence, creativity, and compassion? The action now was in between these options, as the decade was in between John Kennedy and Ronald Reagan.

A Sandwiched Decade

So much seemed to be happening in the 1970s, but was the country really going anywhere except backwards? From the larger perspective of the nation's high expectations for the good life, expanding ever since World War II, much seemed to die in the 1970s—or at least fall on unwelcome hard times. Where could one find the light of a fresh dawn in the face of a series of painful societal reversals? What, in the final analysis, constitutes the "good life"? One thing would become freshly clear. The "gods" of governmental programs and personalities are fragile and fleeting indeed. Their sins in secret have a way of becoming all too public. Therefore, "out of the shattered hopes of the sixties there emerged a cynical privatism, a narrowing of sympathy and concern to the smallest possible circle," a pulling back and tightening up that for many people was "truly frightening."[3] For many others, it was about time. The so-called "silent majority" was determined to regain control of a society it felt had been wallowing in permissiveness, anarchy, and tyranny by the minority.

Sandwiched awkwardly between the revolutionary 1960s and the expan-

---

[3]Robert Bellah, Phillip Hammond, *Varieties of Civil Religion* (N.Y.: Harper & Row, 1980), 177.

sive new "Gilded Age" of the 1980s, the 1970s featured this confusing cultural paradox:

> Feminism, drugs, progressive education, busing, pornography, exotic religions, paranoia, welfare, ethnic politics, long hair, blue jeans, platform shoes, and amphetamines lingered from the 1960s. Conservatism, cowboys, televangelists, flag-waving, energy saving, rising cost of living, teen moms, pickup trucks, overseas investments, Sun Belt shift, cocaine, sound bites, and acid rain anticipated the 1980s.[4]

The U.S. would be profoundly shaken, but determined to stand fast nonetheless. There would be a marked inward turn in the American mind and spirit. Something of these years that contrasted with the recent past of the 1960s is seen in two presidential statements to the American people. In 1961 John Kennedy had said that Americans would "pay any price, bear any burden, meet any hardship, support any friend, oppose any foe to assure the survival and the success of liberty." In 1971 Richard Nixon said that "Americans cannot—and will not—conceive all the plans, design all the programs, execute all the decisions, and undertake all the defenses of the free nations of the world."

American society in the 1960s had been like the turmoil of human adolescence. While many members of the J-M class of 1959 were dealing with career building and young children in their homes, the nation had been trying to find its way into some kind of fresh adulthood amid youthful idealisms and fitful mood swings. The 1960s had been full of the exuberance and sometimes out-of-control actions of protest and change. Something was trying to be recognized and taken seriously—often with failed experimentation and considerable pain in the process. What kind of growing-up world would follow? Much like adolescent children who become young adults, the 1970s would remain turbulent, but with a surprising return to many aspects of the earlier status quo of the 1950s. In the earlier Eisenhower era, however, there had been a general respect for government. The 1970s would suffer a Republican president, Richard Nixon, resigning the high office in disgrace and later a Democratic president getting elected largely because of the growing distaste of Americans for their own government. Carter, the "peanut farmer" from Georgia, lacked acquaintance with official Washington, an anti-qualification that appealed to a Washington-weary public and then later would become a negative in his ability to function effectively in office.

The 1970s in many ways was a decade of American disillusionment squeezed between the optimistic and inspiring presidential personalities of

---

[4]Victor Bondi, ed., *American Decades: 1970-1979* (Detroit: Gale Research, a Manly Book, 1995), vii.

John Kennedy (1960s) and Ronald Reagan (1980s). There was a tendency to look back nostalgically to the 1950s and see only "bright" and relatively innocent growing up times of young Americans like the J-M class of 1959. In the grand sweep of American history, the 1950s had been one of the more bland decades ever. The television show *Happy Days* now idealized this earlier mischievous but harmless teenage culture. By 1974 the country was ready for the emergence of a new storyteller spinning tales of the glories and humor of simpler places and times. His name turned out to be Garrison Keillor and his new radio program, only a risky experiment at first but soon to become an American classic, was *A Prairie Home Companion*. While the setting of Keillor's many beloved stories over the coming years was the fictional Lake Wobegon located somewhere in the conservative Lutheran culture of small-town Minnesota, it just as well could have been Ohio's Lake Milton of the 1950s that was so real to Judy, John, Shirley, Charles, Delores, Frank, and Betty. Another member of the J-M class of 1959, Ian, knew especially well the Keillor-type culture through the Wisconsin heritage of his own mother.

In the years 1970 through 1976, the famous Tussaud's Wax Museum in London, England, handed out questionnaires asking visitors to name the people in history whom they most admired. Only three names were in the top five highlighted each of these years—Joan of Arc, Winston Churchill, and John F. Kennedy (Jesus made some but not all of the lists). These were judged by this public sample to be the people who had best led and given new hope in times of crisis. But violent deaths had come to John Kennedy, Bobby Kennedy, and Martin Luther King, Jr. Who was left to admire and follow? The decade of the 1970s would very much need great people to admire. However, most Americans would be disappointed with their new choices. A fresh pessimism over intractable economic woes would highlight anti-heroes like D. B. Cooper who jumped out of a highjacked Boeing 727 over southern Washington on November 24, 1971, with thousands of stolen dollars. The weather was bad, he eluded three trailing Air Force planes, and was never seen again. Who was stealing what—and would they ever be caught? Had "big government" idealisms died very expensive deaths? The catching-up time had come. It was sometimes called the end of liberalism and was illustrated dramatically in 1975 when New York City ran out of money and defaulted on its huge debts. Faced with rising public demands and scarcity of resources, New York's experience was a "disaster of excess," a fiscal collapse symbolizing "the exhaustion of the great liberal impulse that had inspired public policy for forty years."[5]

---

[5]Charles Morris, *A Time of Passion: America, 1960-1980* (N.Y.: Harper & Row, 1984), 180.

In 1972 the president of a mid-western college announced his hope that "the turbulent 1960s, with their rebellious, impatient, tuned-in, turned-on, tell-it-like-it-is, revolutionary approach to the world" was over.[6] It was and it wasn't. What increasingly was over for sure was the American experience of seemingly unlimited postwar abundance and optimism. Now would come a new pessimism and real limits beyond popular ignoring. America and the industrialized Western world generally had been living in a golden age of economic expansion ever since World War II. Beginning in the early 1970s, however, times of economic and social crisis returned. The great global boom decades of the 1950s and 1960s yielded an era of worldwide difficulty. The "gods" of big money, high position, and military might suffered harsh defeats. The typical societal "gods" turned out to be only amplified humanity after all. Citizens increasingly were aware of the contemporary meaning of Psalm 90:8—"You have set our iniquities before you, our secret sins in the light of your countenance."

The 1970s were years in which there were frequent deaths of social idealisms and active and often experimental searches for new dawns of faith, hope, and social stability. One question addressed frequently by Americans who were open to the supposed insights of biblical "prophecy" was whether the coming dawn would be a return of social progress or a dramatic arrival of dire "tribulation" prior to the return of Jesus Christ to initiate the end of time itself. The best-selling nonfiction book of the decade was Hal Lindsey's *The Late Great Planet Earth*.[7] This publishing phenomenon showed how deep were the feelings of the nation's Christian fundamentalists and other social conservatives concerned and even alarmed about the trends of the times. Lindsey drew on a very predictive view of biblical prophecy and saw a nuclear apocalypse soon to the caused by an anti-Christ, followed shortly by the return of Jesus Christ.[8]

---

[6]Robert H. Reardon, quoted in Barry L. Callen, *Guide of Soul and Mind: The Story of Anderson University* (Anderson, Ind.: Anderson University and Warner Press, 1992), 278. Barry, J-M class of 1959, was now a faculty member on this Indiana campus.

[7]Hal Lindsey, *The Late Great Planet Earth* (Grand Rapids: Zondervan, 1970). By the 1990s the sales of this author's work would total some 28 million!

[8]For a different view of biblical prophecy and contemporary times, see Barry Callen, *Faithful in the Meantime: A Biblical View of Last Things and Present Responsibilities* (Nappanee, Ind.: Evangel Publishing House, 1997). This book directs attention to present responsibilities in light of future hope rather than speculating about a whole scheme of presumed knowledge about God's future, speculation that often detracts from engaging the present redemptively as God's called agents.

Jeffrey Miller (later known as Lama Surya Das) represents another 1970s' way of dealing with dying idealisms of the young and the continuing search for a way forward to some kind of meaning and hope. A young Jew from New York, he had been a radical youth activist in the 1960s. He had marched on Washington, got teargassed for his anti-war demonstration near the Pentagon, and later was rained on at the Woodstock Festival in 1969. He also was touched personally by the 1970 killings at Kent State (see page 193)—it could well have been him, and it was both the girlfriend of his best friend and another young man from Long Island with his same name! Miller, having spent the summer of 1969 working in a Manhattan law firm, learned that he "was not cut out to be one of the Gray Flannel fifties men, vying ceaselessly for a better berth on the Titanic.... The concept of fighting for peace seemed a contradiction in terms." Kent State had helped him to want to "gentle myself and find a non-violent way to contribute to a more harmonious and sane world."[9] The path taken was a journey to the ancient East and the traditional teachings of Tibetan Buddhism. A series of such quests and options would become virtual fads in the American 1970s.

A key stimulant to the popular presence of such quests and fads was the near apocalyptic mood of the times. Is there no more to life than the endless and finally self-defeating grasping for material goods? Was history itself winding down and heading toward its end? Would God tolerate much more? Was President Richard Nixon right in assailing his political enemies as purveyors of "violence, lawlessness, and permissiveness"? The early years of the decade watched him protecting what he called the "silent majority" of patriotic Americans from the dangerous clutches of liberals and leftists who were accused of wielding excessive power in the press and on too many college and university campuses. If, as is commonly assumed, Nixon was a "self-pitying, humorless, confrontational, and deeply suspicious public official,"[10] he fit well in a decade itself characterized by these same very unpleasant adjectives.

The Chaos Recedes and Rises

The years 1961 to 1974 have been referred to aptly as "as arrow's arc of idealism." The grand arrow was "launched with John Kennedy's presidential inauguration in 1961, soaring through the Summer of Love in 1967, plummeting after the Kent State massacre in 1970, plunging into the post-

---

[9]Lama Surya Das, *Awakening The Buddha Within: Tibetan Wisdom for the Western World* (N.Y.: Broadway Books, Bantam Doubleday Dell, 1997), 6.

[10]James Patterson, *Grand Expectations: The United States, 1945-1974* (N.Y.: Oxford University Press, 1996), 742.

Watergate muck in 1974."[11] The social idealism and even revolutionary romanticism seen in the decade of the 1960s melted for many Americans into a pool of profound disappointment. President Nixon cut back on public welfare programs and even the churches lost the luster they recently had put on aggressive social ministries of their own. In the nation's colleges, the hot passion of social revolution cooled down to a spirit of fun and games. The trend was to catch one's breath, pull back into relative passivism, focus on oneself, even "drop out" in frustration and disgust. Idealism's arc had run its course and hit the hard ground by 1974.

Politics at the end of the 1960s brought (or reflected) a real turning point in the direction of American life. Just as the suspicion and isolationistic McCarthyism effectively stopped for a time much of the building momentum for social change that had emerged in the wake of World War II, the political agony of the politics of 1968 saw a cresting of the forces for change that had been building since the late 1950s. Following their cresting came their polarization, even their marginalization, a process of decline that would last throughout the 1970s. In 1968 the antiwar candidacies of Robert Kennedy and Eugene McCarthy seemed a last chance for disaffected critics of America to make the difference they thought so crucial. When that election was over, however, McCarthy had lost, Robert Kennedy was dead, and the "old order" somehow had survived and even triumphed. Many Americans were glad that the society had not fallen apart as they had feared in the late 1960s. Many others despaired that their dream of a society free of war, injustice, and poverty now might not be possible in their lifetimes. The new fact was that the social activists who had energized American politics since the late 1950s were now out and the politics of the right had assumed control. Richard Nixon was mobilizing the "forgotten" Americans around the issues of patriotism, alarm about crime, and traditional middle-class values.

The administration of President Richard Nixon assumed office in 1969 with the professed intention of "bringing us together." But a combination of misdirected leadership, double-digit inflation, and a cluster of high-level scandals soon would undermine his ability to achieve this lofty-sounding goal. Nixon insisted in his first inaugural address (Jan. 1969) that Americans "cannot learn from one another until they stop shouting at one another." Unfortunately, there still was shouting—and shooting—to come. When reelected in 1972, Nixon restated in his second inaugural (Jan. 1973) what he had first announced in 1969 as the Nixon doctrine: "The time has passed

---

[11] *Life* magazine, July, 1996, 46.

when America will make every other nation's conflicts our own, or presume to tell the people of other nations how to manage their own affairs." After all, the U.S. was having difficulty managing some of its own affairs.

Vietnam protesters charged that this Nixon doctrine was just meaningless Washington rhetoric from another public official. Muhammad Ali, Mr. Boxing of the 1970s, was the one high-profile athlete that was politically outspoken in the style of the 1960s. Loudly denouncing the Vietnam War, he questioned the disproportionate number of ghetto blacks carrying the burden of the fighting, preached a Black Muslim message of revolutionary change in black communities, and still maintained an extraordinary popularity that cut across racial lines.[12] Fortunately, however, that divisive war in Southeast Asia finally was concluding (basically an exhausted pull-out by the U.S.). Maybe something really would change. It would, but the change was largely negative. The Cold and Vietnam Wars had badly overextended U.S. resources and nearly crippled U.S. economic competitiveness with nations like Japan and Germany. The defeat in Vietnam (although characterized by some as a choice of the U.S. to depart with honor) was forcing many Americans to recognize national limits in a nation used to limitless horizons. Such a recognition greatly weakened an historical assumption typically held by Americans since at least the 1840s, namely the belief that the U.S. is God's chosen nation destined to teach the rest of the world how a government should operate by and for the people.

During the 1970s there finally came some subsiding of the social chaos, wild experimentation, and often frustrated idealism of the American society of the 1960s. The golden age of the dramatic expansion of U.S. higher education ended. After twenty-eight consecutive years of growth, two years of decline in college enrollments took place in 1975 and 1976. Students now were more cynical, detached, and self-absorbed than their older brothers and sisters. College courses in yoga, Zen, and transcendental meditation proliferated. The jangling noise of protesters muted into more of a series of gentle jerks on the unsure path of personal hungering, striving, and occasionally despairing. The return of relative social quiet, however, would bring its own problems. Outrageous public actions often were replaced by orgies of personal indulgence and political embarrassment in high places. What could not

---

[12]In the Summer Olympic Games in Atlanta, Georgia, in 1996, Ali would be the popular choice of the person to light the Olympic flame to initiate the games. His popularity had endured. Part of Ali's mystique in the 1990s was his courage in the face of an obvious physical disability.

Commercial expansion soon came to include large shopping malls. Designed for convenience, they became symbols of an affluent society dedicated to consumption.

be cleansed by idealistic rhetoric maybe could be overwhelmed or at least ignored by conspicuous public consumption or dangerous stunts like those of Evel Knievel, an Elvis-bedecked motorcycle stuntman who would fly over anything for money and publicity—including Idaho's Snake River Canyon. As Americans played and consumed, they slowly came to appreciate Ralph Nader who symbolized a new consumer protection movement of the 1970s that distrusted industrial self-oversight and government regulatory agencies. Let the consumer beware!

Protection or not, there certainly was a continuing trend toward large-scale consumerism. Commercial expansion was prominent in the area of Jackson-Milton High School in Ohio. In 1970 the Southern Park Mall was completed at Boardman by Edward DeBartolo, foremost plaza builder in the nation. It ranked among the first and finest anywhere, 1.3 million square feet of luxurious opportunities to spend and indulge. It was a sign of the times. Barry's mother, for example, lived in Craig Beach where nothing could be bought except groceries and common household supplies. For her, a trip to Boardman was the highlight of the month. Rarely would this family venture into downtown Youngstown for any reason, although the father went to the nearby mills for work most days of the week; but often they would travel just as far to the free parking and wide array of shopping delights all gathered together in the new suburban mall.

Especially for middle-class families, however, growing economic realities were pressing harder and harder against the desire to expand and consume.

By 1970, ninety-seven percent of American households owned a TV set, sixty-one percent a color TV, and eighty-four percent at least had one car. But from the mid-seventies on, taxes and prices began to grow faster than income. From 1973 to 1979, family income grew by fifty-two percent, while the average price of a new single-family home jumped 105 percent ($30,500 to $62,400). The rising cost of a college education forged way ahead of income growth. In 1950, consumer debt had accounted for only thirty-seven percent of after-tax income. By 1978 it had risen to a dramatic eighty-three percent! Most people could no longer maintain the standard of living to which they had grown accustomed. A general mood of pessimism and even foreboding had replaced the traditional American optimism.

President Nixon turned around John Kennedy's famous call for patriotism that had launched the Peace Corps in the 1960s. Now the call was: "Let each of us ask, not just what will government do for me, but what I can do for myself." Nixon also said in his second inaugural address to the nation: "Let us again learn to debate our differences with civility and decency, and let each of us reach out for that precious quality government cannot provide—a new level of respect for the rights of one another."[13] This ideal, comforting at least in its rhetoric, was to be tested to the limit. "Rights" was now a widely coveted commodity; respect, however, would soon be harder than ever to find.

Peace With Dishonor

The decade of the 1970s opened with pain, anger, and death. Somehow it was the inevitable aftermath of the tortured late years of the 1960s. Generally speaking, America's many years in Vietnam had mixed rather awkwardly the complex issues of military strategy abroad and political pragmatism at home. Jesse recalls it all as being political. "If we did need to be in Vietnam, at least our military should have been allowed to do a military job. I feel badly that so many young Americans had to serve and often die under rules of limited engagement." Many Americans agreed with Jesse. In the early years of American involvement, however, most did not. The *Washington Post* and the *New York Times* supported the war policy at least through 1966. After President Johnson's decisive escalation of American involvement in 1965, polls showed that about seventy percent of Americans thought well of what apparently had to be done. But the 1968 Tet Offensive raised the stakes to a near breaking point.

---

[13]As reported in *Time* magazine (January 29, 1973), 8.

A trigger for dramatic protest and often violence on many of the nation's large urban campuses was President Nixon's April 30, 1970, approval of an American invasion of Cambodia. By then there were numerous angry and outspoken youth who thought that their nation's involvement in Vietnam was now an unjustified exercise in military arrogance and an unnecessary infringement on their own life and liberty. Nixon had devised a policy that he hoped would meet the political requirements of finally getting American soldiers home while being able to declare that the U.S. had won the Vietnam War. This president had no intention of being the first in this country's history to have lost a war. He decided to "go for broke" by sending American forces into Cambodia to destroy the central headquarters of the North Vietnamese army operating from there against South Vietnam. "If when the chips are down," Nixon declared to the nation, "the U.S. acts like a pitiful helpless giant, the forces of totalitarianism will threaten free nations and free institutions throughout the world." Knowing that his action would bring some angry reaction, he added: "I would rather be a one-term president and do what I believe is right than be a two-term president at the cost of seeing America become a second-rate power and to see the nation accept the first defeat in its proud 190 year history." The driving issues seemed to be pride, power, and insecurity.

There followed the expected trouble on more than two hundred campuses, resulting in millions of dollars of damage and hundreds of hours of disturbing television footage. The worst happened in Northeast Ohio near the North Jackson High School. In the city of Kent, Ohio, and on the campus of Kent State University trouble began on Friday, May 1, 1970. By Sunday there were tanks at campus entrances. Governor James Rhodes held a press conference at the city's main fire station, reacting to recent street violence and denouncing the student demonstrators as "worse than the Brown-shirts and the Communist elements and also the Night Riders and Vigilantes...the worst type of people that we harbor in America."[14] Suddenly on May 4 there were four dead students at Kent State University, just a few miles from the high school in North Jackson.[15] Very seldom has the U.S. military been used against its own citizens; this was a sad exception. Exactly who was to blame

---

[14]Quoted in William Hildebrand, et al, eds., *A Book of Memories: Kent State University, 1910-1992* (Kent State University Press, 1993), 166. Included in this book are pages of dramatic photos.

[15]See William Gordon, *Four Dead In Ohio* (Laguna Hills, CA: North Ridge Books, 1995), and James Michener, *Kent State: What Happened and Why* (New York: Random House, 1971).

The tragic confrontation on the campus of Kent State University in Northeast Ohio, on May 4, 1970. Four students were killed in a confrontation with the Ohio National Guard.

never has been determined officially. Years of investigation and court proceedings led to no one ever being held accountable.

If not the why of these deaths, at least the what of the event is shockingly clear. About 115 members of G Troop of the Ohio National Guard, on campus in full riot gear and fully armed, faced about 2,000 student "demonstrators," some apparently bused in from elsewhere. The troops moved forward, intending to clear the crowd and take control of a turbulent campus scene. Then it happened. The armed men were tense, thought they heard shots, and began firing on a crowd of students in a parking lot area. Thirteen seconds later four students were dead or dying, nine others were wounded, one paralyzed for life. Soon the whole university was closed until further notice. All classrooms and dormitories were chained shut. Analyses of this event are numerous and differ significantly from each other. Robert Bork, for instance, has detailed the student protests and violence on this campus during the two previous years and especially the two days prior to the shootings.[16] He points

---

[16]Robert Bork, *Slouching Towards Gomorrah: Modern Liberalism and American Decline*. (N.Y.: Regan Books, Harper-Collins, 1996), 44-46.

out that a grand jury exonerated the Guardsmen, insisting that they fired in legitimate fear of their lives. The later Scranton Commission determined that "the actions of some students were violent and criminal...[and] the indiscriminate firing of rifles into a crowd of students and the deaths that followed were unnecessary, unwarranted, and inexcusable." Bork is not one of many who view the actively protesting students as having been admirable idealists, agreeing instead with the grand jury that a large part of the blame belonged to the university administration that progressively had surrendered control of the university to radical students and faculty.

At least three members of the J-M class of 1959 were touched directly. Dorothy's sister was a Kent State student at the time, although not personally involved in the incident—most students, of course, were not. Mac was living in a house in Kent with five other young men for convenience to his work. He came home on the fateful day to face the police and military closing the campus and the town with an alarming show of force. What did he think of the Kent State events, reflecting back many years later? America's involvement in Vietnam was "garbage," he observed, so some opposition to it was justified. But throwing stones at armed guardsmen was not justified. Coupling that excessive student action to the fact that the local guardsmen were undertrained and overly impulsive in difficult circumstances proved to be the formula for unnecessary tragedy. Tom, a J-M classmate of Dorothy and Mac, concluded that the deaths were sad, but sometimes how the rebellious wind up, especially when there are outside instigators and drug use. Another Tom in the class now judges that live ammunition should not have been used. The whole thing "just got out of hand." He worked with a Kent State student who was present on the campus when the shootings happened. According to that man, anyone on campus could easily have stayed away from the trouble. Those involved really wanted to be involved, at least in acts of defiance. They should not have been so belligerent and taunting, so inviting of violent response.

In furious sympathy with the dead, protesting students erupted in anger on numerous campuses around the nation. Eleven days after the Kent State shootings, Mississippi highway patrolmen riddled a dormitory at Jackson State College. Two black students were killed. A white grand jury investigated this bloody incident, absolved what appeared to many to have been trigger-happy police, and warned students to expect more of the same if there was any more civil disobedience. A poll taken shortly after the Kent State killings showed that most Americans, while sickened by the whole thing, were wholeheartedly supportive of the action of the Ohio National Guard. Some journalists wondered whether a decision had been made at the national level that student demonstrations across the nation had gone too far and that an example had to be made. Did these four dead students in Northeast Ohio represent the most popular murders ever committed in the United States, as one recent writer judges?[17] Anger was on every hand. Student protesters seeking an end to the Vietnam War and the political system that created it now viewed May 4 as a symbol of despair. Many townspeople in Kent blamed the faculty and administration of the university for tolerating, probably even supporting the violent protests that had upset their city's life. Maybe never before had the gap between "town and gown" been so wide. Whoever was really at fault, a numbed nation was being forced to look at its own soul—and it saw evil at work.

Reality, so common wisdom says, is what is *perceived* to be reality. Those who were angry, outspoken, and radically experimental in their lifestyles surely were getting major media attention, and thus were widely perceived to be the growing national reality. But, as presented in the book *The Real Majority* (a favorite in the Nixon White House):

> To know that the lady in Dayton is afraid to walk the streets alone at night, to know that she has a mixed view about blacks and civil rights because before moving to the suburbs she lived in a neighborhood that became all black, to know that her brother-in-law is a policeman, to know that she does not have the money to move again if her new neighborhood deteriorates, to know that she is deeply distressed because her son goes to a community college where LSD has been found on campus—to know all this is the beginning of contemporary political wisdom.[18]

In fact, most Americans felt badly about racial discrimination in the past, were not really bigots, but also did not wish to be blamed for the sins of others in the past and were exasperated with the severe social tensions that had accompanied the civil rights movement. Dallas had become a career police officer in Dayton, Ohio, after his military experience. He saw his share of racial tension firsthand, some of it expressions of idealism on behalf of justice and some just violence and even looting as expressions of personal greed. Naturally the white majority was frustrated, frightened, and losing patience.

---

[17]Gordon, *Four Dead In Ohio.*

[18]Richard Scammon and Ben Wattenberg, *The Real Majority* (N.Y.: Coward-McCann, 1970), 71.

Although hardly funny, national life seemed full of irony and sometimes a comedy of errors. As Vice-President Spiro Agnew teed off at the Bob Hope Desert Classic in 1971, the gallery ran for cover. His drive ricocheted off a man and his wife. Agnew cringed, approached the crowd accompanied by Secret Service agents, offered his apologies, returned to the tee, only to scatter the crowd with another wild shot. Was this kind of event blown out of proportion by the media? Agnew certainly was a harsh critic of the mass media and protesters against the Vietnam War, and he ardently defended conservative social values. If the media was under scrutiny, so were political figures. Were national politicians out to get the public? Were they to be trusted? Maybe so, and apparently not. Unfortunately for Agnew and the nation, in 1973 he found it necessary to resign the vice-presidency after pleading no contest to bribery and extortion charges coming from his time as governor of Maryland. He was the first vice-president in the nation's history to be forced out of office by legal troubles. Nixon named House GOP leader Gerald Ford of Michigan as Agnew's replacement. This was only a prelude to more torment soon to come to national politics.

International pride and success were judged crucial for political survival, so somehow President Nixon needed to come up with successful foreign initiatives. Otherwise he would not have the respect of the nation as a presidential statesperson. Without that respect he was unlikely to be re-elected in 1972. Nixon managed the task by visiting China in 1972, a major media triumph for a traditional fighter of all communists. Equally significant was the brokering of a new spirit of détente between the U.S. and the Soviet Union that culminated in a 1972 Moscow summit and a Strategic Arms Limitation Treaty (SALT). These initiatives helped sweep Nixon into a second term.[19] He won a landslide victory in his quest for a second term, defeating George McGovern after candidate Edward Kennedy had driven off a bridge in Massachusetts, resulting in the death of a woman passenger in suspicious circumstances,[20] George Wallace had been put in a wheelchair by the rifle

---

[19]George McGovern, U.S. Senator from South Dakota (1962-1980), campaigned on a liberal reform platform, calling for an end of the U.S. involvement in the Vietnam War. He had been a special assistant to President John Kennedy and director of the Food for Peace program. His running mate in 1972 was Sargent Shriver, former director of the Peace Corps. Despite such strong identification of this ticket with aspects of the Kennedy legacy, times had changed and the Nixon-Agnew ticket triumphed.

[20]This accident happened on July 19, 1969, only hours before America landed its men on the moon, the dream and promise of Edward's deceased brother, President John Kennedy. Edward Kennedy's aspirations for the presidency were badly damaged by this suspicious event, but Massachusetts would continue him in the U.S. Senate for decades to come.

bullet of a deranged young man in Maryland,[21] and Edmund Muskie from
Maine had humiliated himself in public by overreacting to a false rumor
about his wife. The Democratic Party was in shambles; political luck was
smiling on Richard Nixon. When inaugurated for a second term in 1973,
Nixon looked like he might be securing his place as one of the truly great
presidents. He had won every state except Massachusetts and the District of
Columbia. The Vietnam nightmare would soon be over, presumably without
an obviously humiliating defeat (Nixon had managed to convey to the public an image of himself as peacemaker). The Cold War showed signs of some
warming. China now seemed almost an American ally. The economy was
booming. Nixon's popularity ratings were consistently higher than John
Kennedy's ever were.

President Nixon, freed for fresh action with the election now over, maneu-
vered in Southeast Asia, both bombing and peacemaking. A cease-fire finally was signed in Paris in January 1973, although killing in Vietnam would go
on. In the eighteen years of American involvement, the nation expended
$150 billion, suffered 58,000 Americans killed, 300,000 wounded, 2,500
declared missing, with hundreds of thousands making it home safely, only to
feel rejected by a society they had risked their lives to represent. What a contrast with the veterans of World War II who came home to wild cheers, huge
parades, and generous GI benefits. On V-J Day in 1945, Times Square in New
York had been mobbed in a wild display of pure joy. In 1973 it was deserted.
The Vietnam "peace" was an empty reality and the veterans who survived
were an almost scorned crowd at home. This would fester into resentment for
many men and women who often had physical and now psychological war-
related battles to face at home.

Shirley met Vietnam veterans in VA hospitals who were openly ashamed
of their involvement in the war, spoke of American atrocities, and felt bitter
and confused about their rejection by the very American people they had
sought or been forced to serve. Judy, Shirley's classmate, had a cousin whose
foot had been badly damaged by a landmine in the very Vietnamese village

---

[21]George Wallace has been called the most influential loser in American politics. Four-
time Alabama governor and four times an unsuccessful presidential candidate, he was a
central figure in the launching of the conservative political movement that put Ronald
Reagan in the White House in 1980 and finally gave Newt Gingrich and the Republicans
control of the Congress in 1994. In the 1960s and 1970s, Wallace championed and vigorously encouraged the conservative reaction of millions of Americans that has come to
be known as white backlash, silent majority, alienated voter. See Dan Carter, *The Politics
of Rage: George Wallace, The Origins of the New Conservatism, and the Transformation of
American Politics* (N.Y.: Simon & Schuster, 1995).

where he had lovingly taught the people to be self-sufficient farmers. How ironic and frustrating, a symbol of the whole American operation in Vietnam. Shirley recalls twin boys from Lake Milton, Ohio, killed in Vietnam within a day of each other. Nearly every town in the United States had its own sad stories of pain and grief. The whole ordeal would haunt America for many years to come. One of the more emotional of all sites in Washington, D. C., today is the great black wall, the Vietnam Memorial, that has engraved on it the names of all Americans lost in Vietnam. It is a place to remember, mourn, and maybe heal.

Without the U.S. military presence, South Vietnam soon would fall to the North and a destabilized Cambodia would suffer mass killing of its own citizens on an almost unimaginable scale (an estimated two million people in three years by the Khmer Rouge). After all of the years of U.S. rhetoric and military action, what American policymakers had feared from the beginning actually happened. Communism and chaos prevailed. One lesson America learned was the danger of large-scale military intervention abroad—a hard lesson after believing itself to be nearly invincible in light of its total victory in the "good war" of the 1940s. Politicians and military leaders now became wary of "quagmires" like the one that swallowed so much of humanity in Southeast Asia. Like its Vietnam veterans, the U.S. would suffer a depression of spirit and pride that would be very slow to heal. President Nixon, despite all, called the result "peace with honor." An untarnished image was so important to the president, ironic indeed since very soon his public image would be virtually destroyed.

So much had happened in Vietnam, so little had been gained, and something precious had been lost in America. A failed war effort of such magnitude threatened central elements of the country's self-understanding, namely:

> America's belief in the invincibility of its military power (Could anyone really believe that America might be defeated by a ragtag guerrilla army from Hanoi?); the trust that Americans had in their government (Could anyone really believe that America would fight an "unnecessary" war?); the morality of American actions (Could anyone really believe that American forces would engage in systematic poisoning of the Vietnamese countryside or the massacre of innocent civilians?). By the end of the Vietnam War, many Americans *did* begin to believe the hitherto unbelievable about themselves and their nation.[22]

---

[22]Ronald A. Wells, *History: Through the Eyes of Faith* (Christian College Coalition, Harper SanFrancisco, 1989), 8.

Clearly, democracy was not easily transferable to Third World regions that lacked any historical experience with "liberal" values and representative government. Being a superpower did not mean automatic success in international ventures.

The darkness of death was everywhere and the light of reason, integrity, and real peace seemed a distant dawn. In fact, integrity was about to become a major issue with President Nixon himself. Nixon's personal insecurity had led him to authorize a campaign of secret subversion against his Democratic opponents during the 1972 campaign. The details were almost petty, the script for a made-for-television movie. The results shook the nation. Just four months before election day in 1972, five burglars were caught by Washington police as they broke into Democratic National Headquarters at the Watergate Hotel, apparently trying to steal campaign secrets. Soon this bizarre circumstance would lead to the greatest constitutional crisis the country had faced since the Civil War.

Watergate is a hotel, but in American myth it soon became the symbol of a near national disaster that erupted out of nasty presidential politics. President Nixon got reduced in the public eye to "Tricky Dicky" when White House officials, finally forced to testify, revealed that illegal proceedings had occurred in the Oval Office itself and that there were audio tapes of the incriminating conversations. Nixon fought the call for access to the tapes. Finally he was forced by the Supreme Court to release some of them, one with Nixon saying: "I want you all to stonewall it, let them plead the Fifth Amendment, cover up, or anything else." The "smoking gun" was the audio tape of Nixon's recorded order on June 23, 1972, for the CIA to stop the FBI from investigating the Watergate break-in.

The American public was appalled at these unguarded glimpses of a profane, conspiratorial chief executive. Impeachment talk got serious in Congress. Even Republican leaders called for a presidential resignation, now seeing no alternative. Summarizes one historian:

> Within months [after his great 1972 election victory] he was a hunted man, crashing in breathless flight through the underbrush of Watergate revelations—burglaries, wiretaps, bribery, misuse of power—his enemies in full cry, tendrils of his own lies and deceptions coiling about his feet, until the hounds were upon him and he fell. The pursuit lasted about a year and a half, during which time Nixon gradually ceased to function as President, leaving the country rudderless....[23]

---

[23]Charles Morris, *A Time of Passion* (N.Y.: Harper & Row, 1984), 151.

President Richard
Nixon giving his
farewell address to
members of his staff
and cabinet in the East
Room of the White
House. At his left, his
son-in-law, David
Eisenhower.

Filmmaker George Lucas began work on the film *Star Wars* (1977 release) during the height of the Watergate scandal, imagining his work in part as a dramatic polemic against the corruption of the Nixon administration. Indeed, Nixon himself was Lucas' initial inspiration for the insecure and repressive Emperor whose imperial storm troopers enforced a totalitarian nightmare.[24] This movie was a sensational box-office success, a triumph of special effects that made inter-planetary warfare, strange creatures, and hyperspace-jumping at least a celluloid reality. It was an imaginative technological dramatization of what had just been all too real back on Earth.

Richard Nixon was the first president since Andrew Johnson in 1868 to face a serious threat of impeachment. He chose to spare himself and the nation that painful humiliation by announcing his historic resignation from the presidency of the United States on August 8, 1974, the first sitting president ever to do so. It probably is fair, whatever his own guilt, to also see Nixon as the needed scapegoat for the sins of the nation. On April 30, 1974, Senator Mark Hatfield had received a courtesy voice vote for his "Proclamation for a National Day of Humiliation, Fasting and Prayer." He used the model of Abraham Lincoln in the crisis of 1863, relying on 2 Chronicles 7:14. "If my people, who are called by my name, will humble themselves and pray and seek my face and turn from their wicked ways, then will I hear from heaven and will forgive their sin and heal their land."

Candor and Conservatism

Coming on the heels of the Vietnam War, the Watergate affair only deepened an already substantial public cynicism toward government. Said one

---

[24]David Meyer, "Star Wars, *Star Wars*, and American Political Culture," *Journal of Popular Culture* (Fall, 1992), 100.

bumper sticker of the day: "Don't vote. It only encourages them." Members of the J-M class of 1959 are probably typical of working-class Americans. While a few members like Ian and Richard say they have not grown more cynical about government, many join Judy, Jane, Michael, Dallas, and John in reporting considerable cynicism. Except for the occasional school board term (e.g., Ian) or role as a union officer (e.g., Charles), this class generally has not chosen to run for elective offices. Most have voted regularly, especially in presidential elections. The political innocence, however, is gone. Charles recalls that "we were brought up to believe in government, but I don't believe in it now." He and Frank, both career men in large industrial plants in Northeast Ohio, agree that "companies and unions have changed so that greed now controls." Bill adds a religious element: "God will stop blessing this nation because of all the corruption."

In the 1970s many Americans even began to doubt a now longstanding faith that science and technology really work together for the betterment of the human condition. For instance, with the discovery of major toxic waste sites such as New York's Love Canal and the frightening nuclear accident at Three Mile Island in Pennsylvania, it had begun to appear that the merits of "growth" and "progress" might now be outweighed by their significant dangers. The brutality of the war technologies employed in Vietnam and the continuing threat of nuclear annihilation just added to the growing impression that, on balance, "advancement" in science and technology was hardly an inevitable positive, especially given the apparently pervasive "retardation" (sinfulness?) of the people who too often use such new tools for the wrong reasons or in the wrong ways.

Following Richard Nixon in the presidency was his vice-president, Gerald Ford, who declared immediately that "our long national nightmare is over." The nation very much wanted to believe him. Two critical issues, however, were very divisive. What should be done about the tens of thousands of young men who had evaded the draft in political protest during the Vietnam years, either living "underground" in the U.S. or leaving the country? And what should be done about Richard Nixon himself? Should he be allowed to be prosecuted—surely an ugly prospect for Nixon and the nation that could drag on for years? President Ford sought a flexible approach that he hoped could be healing for the nation. He offered an earned re-entry plan for draft evaders requiring a term of public service. Relatively few took advantage of this offer, a plan thought much too generous by offended war veterans. Many liberals scoffed at the plan as hypocrisy when Ford proceeded in September 1974 to grant a full pardon to Richard Nixon. They judged Nixon more guilty of injuring the nation than any draft evader. This pardon dropped Ford's public popularity from seventy-one to forty-nine percent in one week, the largest single drop in polling history, and probably cost Ford the 1976 election, which he lost to Washington outsider Jimmy Carter. Carter would proceed to grant an unconditional pardon to all who had peacefully resisted the draft during the Vietnam War. It was an attempt to close the books on an ugly era in American history.

Ironically, Richard Nixon finally, although in an unintentional way, had succeeded in his 1968 promise to "bring us together again." Americans were together at least in their resolve that he leave office! People from all walks of life had joined to save the federal government from the control of personal whim and to defend it as a government of laws. It had been a long and difficult national ordeal. More and more Americans were losing faith in the ability of the nation to move on to a better future.[25] The high hopes that had driven the society since 1945 had somehow stumbled. Optimism and idealism were now rare attitudes in a chastened nation. Faith in the opportunity for upward mobility for one's children, so central to the classic American dream, weakened. The near-fantastic expectations about the "good life" that followed World War II now faded as the national economy and sense of moral dignity declined, especially after 1974.

By the mid-1970s there was much to lament in national life. Something to celebrate would be timely, a welcome relief. That something came along as a rare and wonderful happening on July 4, 1976. It was the nation's two-hundredth birthday. It was like when each of the world wars had ended or when Neil Armstrong and Buzz Aldrin stepped out onto the surface of the moon for the first time in human history. Americans all over the country again smiled the same smile, cheered the same cheer, were together at the same time in feelings of natural pride and hope. The magnificent parade of tall ships passing by the Statue of Liberty in New York Harbor was framed by a stunning display of fireworks and an incomparable rendition of the "Star Spangled Banner" by vocalist Sandi Patti, Barry's personal friend. In those glorious moments, despite all the country's differences and even despair, there was an unstoppable rush of positive emotion at the sheer privilege, despite everything, of just being an American. It was a magnificent national birthday party.

---

[25]See Daniel Yankelovich, *New Rules: Searching for Self-Fulfillment in a World Turned Upside Down* (New York, 1981), 181-184.

Within all the national turmoil and occasional exuberance, grassroots America was adjusting, evaluating, sometimes reeling, clearly aging.[26] There emerged the "Gray Panthers" who successfully encouraged Congress to pass laws to end age discrimination. Americans were adapting to some social changes, and holding tenaciously to some traditions that in their view still yielded personal hope and social stability. Whatever President Nixon's abuses of power, he did succeed in mobilizing a conservative majority and in blocking any meaningful protest from the left. In fact, protest began coming from those on the right who were lamenting the deterioration of traditional standards of American society.

Pornography, for example, was big business in the early 1970s. Annual sales of "dirty paperbacks" topped $200 million and receipts from hard-core movies was estimated at $800 million per year. Outraged Americans began fighting back. A New York criminal court challenged the notorious 1973 film *Deep Throat* and banned further showings because it was judged "indisputably and irredeemably obscene." In 1973 the U.S. Supreme Court ruled that local and not national standards must prevail in future pornography decisions. This was hailed as a victory for "anti-smut" groups and resulted in the closing of many "adult" bookstores. But people "in the business" decried the Court's decision as censorship and a violation of the Constitutional right to free speech. Numerous Americans insisted that they had the "right" to do as they pleased, even if the general public viewed their actions as an outright degrading of humanity.

If free speech was an area of heated debate, the nation's economy was threatening to become a disaster zone. Although household incomes increased, real wages began falling in the early 1970s when the economy first soured. This trend would continue into the 1990s. Even the big three auto makers—General Motors, Ford, and Chrysler—were at the mercy of changes in the world oil market and consumer preferences at home. The future of this giant industry now seemed to be in Japan, not Detroit. By the end of the 1970s, Chrysler had to be propped up by money from the federal government. Energy shortages and a declining competitive position in relation to foreign manufacturers dampened public optimism generally. Given Vietnam and Watergate, trust in the judgment and fairness of politicians was very low. In 1945 the interest being paid on the national debt was $3.8 billion a year.

---

[26]By 1970 life expectancy in the U.S. had risen to 69.5 years for white men and 77.2 years for white women. Across the decade those in the American population over 65 increased twenty percent and twelve million people joined the American Association of Retired Persons (AARP).

By 1970 that figure had risen to nearly $20 billion and would soar to $60 billion by decade's end. Unemployment joined the negative trend, rising from 3.2 to 6.7 million Americans across the 1970s. There was an inflationary spiral. U.S. trade showed a plus $2.7 billion in 1970 and a minus of $27.6 billion in 1979.

There were many signs of a deterioration of the very fabric of American society. Social problems were as great as ever, but now there was less of a common social bonding and a decreased national will to address the problems creatively. People were escaping inward and were all too ready to let problems outside themselves and their families just rot where they lay. "Do your own thing," once a countercultural slogan, was subtly becoming a mainstream creed. The age of idealism was edging into the age of apathy and indulgence. There was, however, some resistance to change. Probably no small city in America has been studied as much as Muncie, Indiana. It is identified only as "Middletown" in the famous series of sociological studies and publications in the 1920s and 1930s, and again in the 1970s and 1980s. These studies showed that there surely had been much social change over the decades in this typical midwestern city. But by 1979 the most recent research findings were surprising on several fronts.

The amount of change in Middletown (Muncie) was less than expected in several areas. Although technological modernization was obvious and rapidly moving ahead, many basic social values had remained remarkably stable— in spite of the 1960s.[27] In typical middle America, mobility had increased, but there still was high value being placed on family solidarity. There was actually a smaller generation gap than had been found in the 1920s. A majority of high school students still regarded the Bible as a "sufficient guide to all the problems of modern life." What there was more of was active religious faith, although it was being practiced with a new level of tolerance. Residents of Muncie in the late 1970s, in contrast to the 1920s, were less conscious of denominational lines, more eager to attend church, and less judgmental of those who choose not to attend. The supernatural remained a meaningful reality for the large majority, although many now were less clear about the sole authority of the Bible or whether Christianity was the single true religion.[28] Traditional values and attitudes rooted in the Christian tradition also

---

[27]See Theodore Caplow and Howard Bahr, *Public Opinion Quarterly* 43 (Spring 1979), 1-17. Two major publications of the Middletown III studies were *Middletown Families* (1982) and *All Faithful People* (1983).

[28]Dwight Hoover, *Middletown Revisited* (Muncie, Ind.: Ball State University, monograph #34, 1990), 28-29.

were being compromised more readily. An enduring legacy of the "liberation" movements of the 1960s became evident in the 1970s. The longstanding American belief in self-denial and the Protestant work ethic seemed to be replaced widely by the new rules of self-fulfillment, immediate gratification, and personal rights and freedom.[29]

The 1970s was the me-generation decade. Self-absorption was now common, often destructive. If the baby boomers in rebellion during the 1960s could not change the world, they could at least focus on changing themselves. They put on running shoes, got American Express cards, and wandered in a disco wasteland in search of financial, physical, and spiritual fulfillment. A sharp contrast was evident. On the one hand, there was a clear resurgence of conservative Christianity, some of which was now politically aggressive (for instance, the "Moral Majority" of Rev. Jerry Falwell). On the other hand:

> Even the best educated and most secular classes merely substituted one set of religious rituals for another—jogging and mantras for conventional prayer; the obsessive tracking of success in "relationships" instead of a balance sheet of good and bad deeds; encounter sessions rather than religious retreats; the miracles of EST in place of the cures at Lourdes.[30]

On the positive side, the new sense of personal freedom in the society found many women and African Americans forcing open previously locked doors that had kept them in "their place." But welfare rolls mushroomed and the number of divorces skyrocketed.[31] "Hippies" now were being absorbed into the social mainstream. Some of them still searched actively for personal fulfillment and turned to conventional religion. Many others looked in very unconventional places. Now there were "Jesus Freaks," tongues-speaking pentecostals, the fresh presence in the West of Eastern faiths—and something more sinister, cults. Occasionally, community-hungry people would grant full control of their lives to a fanatic religious leader, usually with tragic results. Soon there were professional "deprogrammers" seeking to save young people from the dehumanization of brainwashing. Now the public was very aware of Hare Krishna, originating in India, and the "Moonies" collecting money in

---

[29]In his studies of the changing American character, Daniel Yankelovich found a major shift from the "ethic of self-denial" to the "ethic of self-fulfillment" (*New Rules: Searching for Self-Fulfillment in a World Turned Upside Down*, New York, Random House, 1981, 4-5).

[30]Morris, *A Time of Passion*, 226-227.

[31]The rate of divorce per 1,000 people moved from 2.2 in 1960 to 5.2 by 1980, more than a doubling.

airports and parking lots for the Unification Church and its self-identified messiah, Sun Myung Moon from South Korea. On one truly tragic day in November 1978, 913 followers of Jim Jones and his People's Temple Church committed mass suicide in Jonestown, Guyana, a "colony" this cult leader had leased as the "Promised Land."

There was an obvious hunger for belief. Much that was believed was like the fast-food culture—bland, no problems, relatively cheap, bringing immediate satisfaction whatever the long-term implications. But the hunger and surprising new religious commitments were real enough. Studs Terkel put it this way:

> Though William Jennings Bryan may have suffered humiliation at the "monkey trial" in 1924, his admonition—study the "Rock of Ages," not the age of rocks—sways astonishing millions today [1988], particularly the young, citified as well as rural.[32]

Millions of Americans were evaluating the competing values of traditionally white, Christian America and those of the radical 1960s by watching weekly for nine years (1971-1980) a television program called *All In The Family*. Here was heavy social and political satire done as a comedy series and set in a presumably typical middle-class home. Archie Bunker, the man of the house, was often crude and overbearing in relating to his seemingly naive and infinitely patient wife Edith. He was a disturbing mirror to the real fathers in millions of homes. Archie was brash, arrogant, lovable and loyal, yet terribly prejudiced and narrow on many subjects. His grossly stereotypical judgments brought constant laughter (helping the viewing audience look at itself and maybe even laugh at itself). Much of the drama in this fictional TV household came when the daughter, Gloria, married a young social activist left over from the 1960s and the couple moved into the Bunker home. Now previously off-limit subjects for TV became matters of open conversation in this home—and in many of the homes of the nation.[33]

While Archie was mechanical and not able to be in touch with and express his feelings of love (so typical of the males of the times), he surely got emotional when confronted with the social radicalism of Mike, his son-in-law whom he insisted on calling "Meathead" since supposedly he was dead from

---

[32]Studs Terkel, *The Great Divide* (N.Y.: Avon Books, 1988), 15.
[33]Episodes were built around subjects like pregnancy, atheism, racism, gender equality, male dominance, female menopause, rape, gun control, and draft dodgers. "Meathead" often precipitated the issue and Archie reacted with shock and disgust at views he considered wholly unacceptable in the eyes of "real Americans."

*Archie Bunker and his son-in-law, "Meathead," in the popular television series, **All In The Family**.*

the neck up. While painful and funny fireworks usually followed, this strange household was trying to talk openly about the previously unspeakable, trying to facilitate increased understanding and appreciation between the clashing values of two very different generations. What, after all, is the "true American way"? Archie at least acted like he was sure that he knew, often quoting from the Bible with outrageous manipulations of its text to support his already set opinions. He was rude and crude, loved and hated, a helpful mirror by which the culture could reflect on itself. When the American society looked at itself it saw frustration, previously unacknowledged racism, and fresh resistance to "big government" running private lives. The host of government programs developed in the 1960s to eliminate poverty, expand welfare, and improve education (the "Good Society" of Lyndon Johnson) were generating a backlash that kept gathering strength across the 1970s. Assistance to nonwhites now seemed inherently unfair to struggling whites; school busing programs seemed to threaten the fragile social cohesion of established neighborhoods.

Maybe even more popular during the same period than *All In The Family* was *M*A*S*H* (aired 1972-1983), a bawdy and bloody anti-war TV comedy. The scene was a mobile surgical hospital that treated wounded GIs behind the lines during the Korean War of the 1950s (although the viewing audience just as easily thought of it as Vietnam in the 1960s and 1970s). The cast of odd characters included Alan Alda as the outrageously free-spirited Hawkeye Pierce and Loretta Swit as Major Margaret "Hot Lips" Houlihan. Here was an opportunity for a war-weary nation to process its feelings in a non-divisive way. These skilled and usually beleaguered American surgeons and nurses regularly visited the country's living rooms to hilariously highlight the absurdity and futility of war. They maintained their sense of humor as a way of keeping their own sanity. The country needed some good laughs in the face of rugged reality. The final episode of *M*A*S*H* lasted two and a half hours and was seen by an estimated 125 million emotional viewers.

If people are shaped by the stories they tell and choose to make their own, then millions of Americans were changed at least somewhat for the better in 1977. Called *Roots* and adapted from a bestselling book by Alex Haley, this intensely dramatic novel for television froze the attention of tens of millions as it ran for twelve hours spread over eight consecutive nights in January 1977. Here was a serialized story of one black family that began in 1750 with white slave traders abducting the teenage Kunta Kinte in Africa and hauling him to the United States for sale. From a plantation in Virginia through his family's succeeding generations, the public watched a parade of brutality, escape attempts, hateful scenes, and tender moments. The series ended in Tennessee where Tom, a free man and great-grandson of Kunta Kinte, was trying to provide a better life for his family. Was this family saga a significant part of the American past, unpleasant but important to retell? Apparently so. Would its lessons help to reshape a still racist society? Hopefully.

From a very different cultural setting, could remembering a near ideal family from the mountains of Virginia in the 1930s and 1940s help recover wholesome family life in the troubled 1970s? Many hoped so or at least just enjoyed the nostalgic experience of the popular TV series, *The Waltons*. In this country home were the loving, hardworking parents, several children, bound-

John Amos and Madge Sinclair in the 1977 television mini-series, **Roots.** *This epic story of the many generations of one family highlighted the long injustice suffered by African-Americans.*

Milestones of the Decade

	Best Movie of the Year#	Bestselling Nonfiction Book of the Year	*Time* Magazine's Person of the Year*
1970	*Patton*	*Everything You Wanted To Know About Sex But Were Afraid to Ask,* David Reuben, M.D.	Willy Brandt
1971	*The French Connection*	*The Sensuous Man,* M. Lyle Stuart	Richard Nixon President of the U.S.
1972	*The Godfather*	*The Living Bible,* Kenneth Taylor	Richard Nixon and Henry Kissinger
1973	*The Sting*	*The Living Bible,* Kenneth Taylor	John Sirica
1974	*The Godfather, Part II*	*The Total Woman,* Marabel Morgan	King Faisal
1975	*One Flew Over a Cuckoo's Nest*	*Angels: God's Secret Agents,* Billy Graham	Women of the Year
1976	*Rocky*	*Your Eroneous Zones,* Dr. Wayne W. Dyer	Jimmy Carter President of the U.S.
1977	*Annie Hall*	*All Things Wise & Wonderful,* James Herriot	Anwar Sadat
1978	*The Deer Hunter*	*Mommie Dearest,* Christina Crawford	Deng Xiaoping
1979	*Kramer vs. Kramer*	*Aunt Erma's Cope Book,* Erma Bombeck	Ayatollah Khomeini

\# Recipient of the Oscar from the Academy of Motion Picture Arts and Sciences.

* A designation on the part of the editors of *Time* of the person, people, or thing that, for better or worse, most significantly influenced the course of world events in the preceding twelve months.

TABLE 15

less love and patience, the paternal grandparents, and deep roots in the land, extended family, and network of dependable if sometimes eccentric neighbors. Close-to-the-earth humor and nostalgia was also obvious in the success of James Herriot's *All Things Wise and Wonderful*, best-selling nonfiction book in 1977 about a British veterinarian in the 1930s and 1940s. Related episodes were dramatized in a popular TV series called *All Creatures Great and Small*.

The Giant Slumps, Conservatives Multiply

The Nobel Peace Prize for 1979 was given to Mother Teresa of Calcutta, India, founder of the Missionaries of Charity. She in turn gave the $200,000 award to the poorest of the poor, explaining in her acceptance speech: "The prize is the recognition of the poor world. Jesus said, 'I am hungry, I am naked, I am homeless.' By serving the poor, I am serving him." Her attitude was reflected somewhat in the best musical recording of 1975, "Love Will Keep Us Together" by The Captain and Tennille.[34] Unfortunately, Mother Teresa contrasted sharply with the times, especially with the grand expansion of wealth in the United States since World War II. But even that wealth was now coming into some question. Probably the greatest shift of the 1970s was the halt to the climb in economic growth experienced since the late 1940s. The annual inflation rate began to rise from its three percent level in 1967 to twelve percent in 1974, and it remained in double digits for most of the 1970s. The Dow-Jones average of major industrial stocks fell in value by 36 percent between 1968 and 1970, the sharpest drop since World War II. Productivity declined. U.S. imports exceeded exports for the first time since 1893. The international marketplace was getting very competitive. Americans became frustrated, even bewildered by events that shattered their usual sense of direction and control.

Ever since World War II the United States had thought of itself as the world's dominant super power and super economy, the exporter to the world of the superior values of capitalism and democracy. But now the Arab (OPEC) oil embargo that began in 1973 confirmed the extent to which Americans no longer controlled even their own economic life. Home owners had to turn down thermostats, wear heavy sweaters, and sometimes wait for hours in long lines at gas stations. The 55-mile-per-hour speed limit on highways was first imposed by the federal government in 1974 to save

---

[34]As judged by the National Academy of Recording Arts and Sciences with the granting of its annual Grammy award.

energy and lives. Also that year, construction crews began laying the $8 billion trans-Alaska pipeline to increase the flow of domestic oil. Behind all this was a frightening new question: Was America losing control of her own destiny?

The U.S. was consuming 30 percent of the world's available energy and importing at least one-third of the oil it was using. As one official in the Nixon administration had pictured America's growing dilemma, "Popeye is running out of spinach." Americans began buying cheaper, fuel-efficient cars made abroad. Domestic automakers had to cut production. By 1975 the nation was in its worst economic slump since the Great Depression of the 1930s. Some called the period 1974-1975 the "Great Recession." Wage and price controls ended in April, 1974. In that one year consumer prices rose 11 percent and wholesale prices 18.8 percent. Such alarming increases forced the Federal Reserve to clamp down hard on the money supply, driving interest rates upward to 11 percent, the highest to that point in the twentieth century. Unemployment in 1975 reached 8.5 percent, the highest since before World War II. Americans, stunned and frustrated, were turning to the many escapes of self-preoccupation—singles' bars, encounter groups, pop psychology, TM (transcendental meditation), and exotic religious cults. The "human potential" movement promised its followers a souped-up psyche free of obstacles to pleasure and success. It was the "Me Decade" with the human self solidly placed at the center.

Turning inward, of course, was in large part a reaction to the outwardly souring circumstances of the society itself. The economic boom of the 1950s and 1960s had begun yielding to negative trends, creating failed small businesses, abandoned family farms, and talk of a new "Rust Belt." Unfortunately for the rosy memories of the J-M class of 1959, this wave of industrial deterioration and shutdowns had no more obvious representative than Youngstown, Ohio. Some public analysts had begun calling this proud steel-producing center the country's biggest ghost town.[35] Carl Sandburg, in his *Smoke and Steel*, earlier had announced poetically the heart of the traditional reality in this region of the country:

> So fire runs in, runs out, runs somewhere
>   else again,
> And the bar of steel is a gun, a wheel, a
>   nail, a shovel,
> A rudder under the sea, a steering-gear in
>   the sky;

---

[35]Studs Terkel, *The Great Divide*, 11.

> And always dark in the heart and through it,
>   smoke and the blood of man.
> Pittsburgh, Youngstown, Gary—they make their
>   steel with men.

But what had been the traditional industrial backbone of the United States now was falling on hard times. A particularly bad day in September 1977 became known around Youngstown, Ohio, as "Black Monday." The steel industry by then was in decline nationally. Control of many large manufacturing companies had passed from local people to "outsiders." Politicians usually had chosen to ignore the inevitable and the labor unions seemed powerless. Then it happened. On September 19 the Lykes Corporation announced that it would close most of the Campbell Works of the Youngstown Sheet and Tube Company. Within weeks some 4,100 local workers permanently lost their really good jobs.[36] During the period of 1977 to 1979, the three largest steel mills in the Youngstown area were shut down, eliminating over 10,000 primary jobs.[37]

James, for example, was one member of the J-M class of 1959 who in 1979 lost his excellent job in Youngstown as a structural ironworker. The auto industry was struggling with rising employee benefit costs and the significant incursion into the American market of well-built and low-priced foreign cars. The population of Mahoning County (including the city of Youngstown) dropped from 303,400 in 1970 to 264,800 by 1990. Harry moved his family to Florida in 1979 where there were in-laws and more employment independence. He would drive a small delivery truck in the Orlando area and at least be his own man. The percentage of the Youngstown population living below the poverty level was 14.2 in 1970 and 18.2 in 1980 (with Ohio's overall percentages 10.0 and 10.3 respectively). Youngstown now suffered the image of being a cradle of organized crime. Once known as "the Steel Valley," a mighty marvel of manufacturing, the *Los Angeles Times* (April 25, 1983) now said of Youngstown: "The great ruins of a powerful industry stand abandoned and rotting in the Mahoning River Valley, an industrial Stonehenge." Nearby Cleveland was a major urban area that also experienced economic and population decline across the decade. It had been shocked and embarrassed in 1969 when oil from industrial dumping caught

---

[36]See Terry Buss and F. Stevens *Redburn, Shutdown at Youngstown* (Albany: State University of New York Press, 1983).

[37]Staughton Lynd, *The Fight Against Shutdowns: Youngstown's Steel Mill Closings* (San Pedro: Singlejack Books, 1982). The 1980 census of the city of Youngstown reported about 115,000 residents, some 45,000 of whom were members of minority groups.

fire in the Cuyahoga River, damaged two bridges, and forced major cleanup efforts. The city was forced to default on some of its financial obligations in 1978, the first major city to do so since the Depression of the 1930s.

Fortunately, some better times would come. For instance, Cleveland would launch a lake front renovation project in 1985 and its famed Cleveland Clinic and Cleveland Orchestra would continue as two of the better medical and musical institutions in the nation. In the greater Youngstown-Warren area (about 500,000 inhabitants), General Motors had chosen some years earlier to locate the new and expensive automobile assembly plant in nearby Lordstown, only a few miles from the Jackson-Milton High School. It employed several members of the J-M class of 1959 for the balance of their working careers. But that did not help the difficult experience of thousands in the late 1970s. Daniel Yankelovich recalled watching an NBC News special in January 1979 entitled "The American Family: An Endangered Species?"[38] Featured were the unusual (a lesbian couple with five children from previous heterosexual marriages, a young woman later to die when cult leader Jim Jones would lead more than nine hundred of his "family" to mass suicide, etc.). But Yankelovich's attention was drawn to a traditionally married couple in their thirties who were living in a trailer in Youngstown, Ohio. The husband was now an unemployed steelworker from Youngstown Sheet and Tube. He reported that he had benefits to cover family necessities, but insisted that he did not like accepting money for which he had not worked ("it's like taking it out of someone else's pocket"). He was devastated that he could not work with dignity to provide for and protect his family—what he assumed every man should do. His wife said she wanted to stay home with the children where she judged that she belonged, instead of losing contact with the children and humiliating the husband by going into the workplace herself. Marriage and raising a family was "my whole life."

This struggling Ohio family was hardly as exotic as the nontraditional "families" paraded on the program. It was included in the program because it might be an endangered species representing a set of family values and structures quickly becoming only a holdover from what once was the near universal American pattern. For good or ill, much was changing. The change in the social roles of men and women was obvious in the best-selling nonfiction book of 1971, *The Sensuous Man* by M. Lyle Stuart, and then in 1974 *The Total Woman* by Marabel Morgan. Two other bestselling books bracketed the decade of the 1970s and illustrate the dramatic shift in the nation's

---

[38]As reported in Daniel Yankelovich, *New Rules: Searching for Self-Fulfillment in a World Turned Upside Down* (N.Y.: Random House, 1981), 106-109.

cultural mood and its wide range of reactions to transformations in family and personal life. They were Charles Reich's *The Greening of America* (1970) and Christopher Lasch's *The Culture of Narcissism* (1979). Each author was a critic of American society and supplied catchwords that crystallized for many readers the hopes and fears of the 1970s. Reich looked hopefully to the future, celebrated personal liberation and what he saw as the coming peaceful overthrow of the prevailing social order in favor of a new consciousness of endless freeing and becoming. Lasch lamented the loss of the patriarchal, self-denying American past and denounced the recent social changes as evidence of moral decay and impending cultural collapse.

Reich saw the student and youth counterculture of the late 1960s as the leading edge of a coming revolution in human consciousness. He rejected the "plastic" world of corporate and suburban America, along with the "rationality" that too often was ravishing nature and had unleashed war in Vietnam. A higher plane of civilized life was spreading rapidly, he judged, promising "a higher reason, a more human community. . .a renewed relationship of man to himself, to other men, to nature, and to the land."[39] By sharp contrast, later in the decade President Jimmy Carter lamented the emptiness of life for so many and the common worship of self-indulgence. He recommended that his staff read Lasch's *The Culture of Narcissism*. Lasch spoke of a narcissistic personality that was the product of a decadent social order, late capitalism, and a family that had been undermined by that deteriorating system of structures and values. The narcissistic self must depend on the vicarious warmth of others. Fearing dependence, it never can escape its own inner emptiness. Such supposedly is what had become of American culture. The new fads of jogging, health foods, and encounter groups were judged signs of despair in people who had no hope of improving their lives in any of the ways that matter. For Reich, liberated selves were about to redeem American society. For Lasch, narcissistic selves were in the process of destroying it. Needed was a revival of what would again orient people to traditional values and beliefs.

When President Carter ran for the presidency in 1976, a feature of his campaign was emphasis on the significance of serious religious faith. Carter, an acknowledged "born again" Christian, raised the public visibility of "conservative" religion. *Newsweek* called 1976 "the year of the evangelicals."[40] A

---

[39]As quoted in Arlene Skolnick, *Embattled Paradise: The American Family in an Age of Uncertainty* (N.Y.: BasicBooks, HarperCollins, 1991), 134.

[40]"Born Again," *Newsweek* (Oct. 25, 1976), 68-78.

FREEDOM OF RELIGION AND FOR ABORTION
Select Decisions of the United States Supreme Court

The United States traditionally has emphasized the separation of church and state. The First Amendment to the U.S. Constitution contains two references to religion: the "establishment" clause, which forbids laws respecting the establishment of religion, and the "free exercise" clause, which forbids laws prohibiting the free exercise of religion. Generally, dissemination of religious beliefs, observance of religious practices, and equality of religions are protected. Various Supreme Court decisions have applied these general principles in specific and controversial circumstances. Examples follow. Included is the 1973 decision on abortion, vigorously opposed by many Americans on religious grounds.

Engel v. Vitale, 1962. The use in public schools of a prayer prepared by the state board of education violates the Establishment Clause of the first Amendment to the Constitution. The prayer in question, prepared by the New York State Board of Regents for voluntary use in its school districts, read: "Almighty God, we acknowledge our dependence upon Thee, and we beg Thy blessings upon us, our parents, our teachers and our country." Controversial ever since as a decision of the Court seemingly hostile to religion, the Court argued rather that the union of church and state leads to the degradation and destruction of both, and often religious persecution of those in the minority. [A poll in the mid-1990s estimated that 69 percent of Americans favored a constitutional amendment that would make prayer legal in public schools.]

Wisconsin v. Yoder, 1972. A state must make provisions in its mandatory education laws for students whose religious beliefs prevent them from attending secondary school.

Tilton v. Richardson, 1971; *Hunt v. McNair*, 1973; *Roemer v. Board of Public Works of Maryland*, 1976. Federal funds may be provided under specified restrictions for the construction of colleges, including church-related institutions, because of the high degree of academic freedom provided. Annual grants also are valid if they are not used directly to further religious purposes.

Bob Jones University v. United States, 1983. No aid or tax exemption may be given by a state to an educational institution that discriminates on the basis of race.

Roe v. Wade, 1973. Upheld is the right of a mother to decide, in consultation with her doctor, whether or not to have an abortion. There are, however, "compelling points" at which the state's "compelling interest" permits it to undertake regulation of abortions. The state has a compelling interest in protecting the health of the pregnant woman and the potentiality of human life. Each grows in substantiality as the woman approaches term and, at a point during pregnancy, each becomes "compelling." [In 1972, before abortion was legal, there were about 587,000 reported abortions in the U.S. In 1980 there were 1,297,606.]

TABLE 16

major feature of the 1970s certainly was the resurgence of conservative Christianity. One way to assess the religious temper of the 1960s and 1970s is to compare the seminary students, those in Christian-related graduate schools actively preparing for ministerial vocations. In the 1960s there was high interest in social issues and the intent to join the action in the name of Christian compassion. The established church tended to be seen as part of the problem, causing unusual interest in abandoning loyalty to the church as such and pursuing non-congregational ministries through councils of churches, inner city projects, and even secular agencies. Becoming the standard local pastor seemed almost a sellout to irrelevancy. In the 1970s, however, this changed. Students preparing for ministerial careers were more conservative theologically, less focused on social action, had greater involvement in personal piety (prayer groups, Bible study, etc.), and again had real appreciation for the local church. Conservative seminaries experienced a population explosion during the decade. Barry was Dean of such a seminary from 1973-1983 and saw it grow from 65 to 188 graduate students.[41]

Dean Kelley, in his widely quoted book *Why Conservative Churches Are Growing*,[42] concluded in part that churches grow if they are strict in their demands on members and provide them with real structural meaning for their lives. Such churches tend to give certain answers in an uncertain world. One fresh interdenominational vehicle for conveying such answers was Marion "Pat" Robertson whose popular Family Channel began broadcasting on TV in 1977 as an alternative to what was perceived as unacceptable levels of violence and immorality on the standard networks. Robertson had purchased a bankrupt television station in Virginia in 1959 and then founded what would become the highly successful Christian Broadcasting Network (CBN). The flagship program was *The 700 Club* (syndicated nationally in 1972 and still on the air today). By 1979 this program reportedly had 7,000 volunteer prayer counselors working 24-hours-a-day and receiving one million prayer requests in 1977 alone. Regent University was founded in 1975 as CBN University in Virginia Beach, Virginia, to offer professional education to Christians in law, business, communications, and public policy. Joining other leaders like Rev. Jerry Falwell, Robertson intended that the Christian

---

[41]The school was Anderson University School of Theology in Anderson, Indiana (associated with the Church of God, Anderson). For a history of this university which details such growth, see Barry Callen, *Guide of Soul and Mind: The Story of Anderson University* (Anderson, Ind.: Anderson University and Warner Press, 1992).

[42]Dean Kelley, *Why Conservative Churches Are Growing* (N.Y.: Harper & Row, 1972, rev. ed. 1977).

community make a difference in American society. Supportive and also widely influential by the 1970s after its founding in 1956 was the significant magazine *Christianity Today*.

A large segment of the public was ready for a reintroduction of the supernatural into their lives. Billy Graham's book *Angels: God's Secret Agents*,[43] for instance, became the bestselling nonfiction book of 1975 in the United States. The entertainment media exhibited a fascination with demons in films such as *Rosemary's Baby* and the several *Exorcist* presentations. "Evangelical" Christianity was very visible to the public by decade's end and increasingly was bothered by the concern that government had and would further try to regulate its institutions and social standards (see Table 16 for select decisions of the Supreme Court and the Appendix for a critique). President Nixon, while not personally professing "born again" Christianity, clearly had courted the favor of evangelicals. When he fell into political disgrace, Jimmy Carter came along. An openly committed evangelical, he nonetheless failed while president to impact public policy with his personal religious commitments. Hope finally would turn to another, Ronald Reagan, a champion of conservative relationships and causes. An important question persisted. How separated should church and state be? Was the Supreme Court right in arguing (*Engel v. Vitale*) that mixing church and state tends to degrade both and often leads to religious persecution? Surely authentic faith has relevance for the larger culture; but in the 1970s had the U.S. culture, in all its fascination with the supernatural, become antagonistic to strongly-held faith that sought to express itself politically? It seemed so to many believers.

Frontiers and Frustrations

Frontiers were quite apparent, especially in the area of technological advances. In 1967 South African doctor Christiaan Barnard had performed the world's first successful heart transplant. It was only the beginning. Marcian Hoff (b. 1937) was hired by a new company, Intel, to work with a group of engineers designing silicon chips to fit inside a handheld calculator. The result altered society itself. What they combined on a fingernail-size chip included the functions of a calculator and the logic unit of a mainframe computer. They had created the microprocessor. In 1971 Intel ran an ad in *Electronic News* to announce the breakthrough and ask for help in discovering its potential uses. Soon such chips would be commonplace and doing an amazing range of things. In 1975 alone, the National Aeronautics and Space Administration spent $2.4 billion on research and development.

---

[43]Billy Graham, *Angels: God's Secret Agents* (Garden City, N.Y.: Doubleday, 1975).

Maybe the nation, feeling frustrated and even dirty about Vietnam, could at least do something to clean up the sad state of the environment itself. Ever since Rachel Carson's warning in 1962 (*Silent Spring*), people had worried more and more about the unsightly and dangerous status of much they were seeing, eating, and breathing. This was hardly President Nixon's personal passion, but he was savvy enough not to swim hard against this growing tide of reform. In January 1970, the National Environmental Policy Act set up the Environmental Protection Agency and new federal standards for clean air and water. By April the nation was staging its first "Earth Day" with numerous Pro-Earth speeches and cleanup efforts involving some 10 million schoolchildren. The toxic-waste crisis that forced the permanent evacuation of 1,000 families from New York's Love Canal residential community (1978) highlighted the magnitude of the danger to the general public. An accident at the Three Mile Island nuclear power plant in Pennsylvania (March 1979) prompted some 100,000 citizens to flee their homes. Was "civilization" beginning to kill itself? Worst of all, the world's population had nearly doubled since the beginning of the century (now more than 3 billion people) and was threatening to double again by the year 2000. Could the planet survive such a crush of hungry bodies? What were the alternatives?

A Frenchman named Jacques Cousteau was entertaining and enlightening TV audiences worldwide with his fascinating films of the worlds beneath the oceans and seas—and the urgent need to care for the planet. After he led a 1972 voyage to Antarctica, millions for the first time saw the extraordinary beauty of sculptured ice formations under the sea. In 1977 the "Cousteau Odyssey" series premiered on PBS. Cousteau wanted to teach the world to save itself. In his 1975 album *Windsong*, John Denver[44] dedicated one song to Cousteau and all who served on his good ship, the *Calypso*. Following are the lyrics of one verse and the chorus:

> To sail on a dream on a crystal clear ocean,
> To ride on the crest of the wild raging storm,
> To work in the service of life and the living
> In search of the answers to questions unknown,
> To be part of the movement and part of the growing,
> Part of beginning to understand.

---

[44]John Denver gained millions of devoted fans with his optimistic and nostalgic music during the struggling 1970s. His first big hit was "Take Me Home, Country Roads" (1971), followed by "Rocky Mountain High," "Thank God I'm a Country Boy," and "Sunshine on My Shoulder." He was killed in 1997 in a private plane accident.

Aye, Calypso
The places you've been to,
The things that you've shown us,
The stories you tell.
Aye, Calypso,
I sing to your spirit,
The men who have served you
So long and so well.

Two members of the J-M class of 1959 represent key dimensions of the environmental crisis. One man was and still is a quiet activist on behalf of the well-being of the earth and its living systems. Ian engaged in post-high-school years of academic study and extensive field work in Wyoming, New Zealand, and British Columbia, then settled in 1970 in a faculty position at the University of Vermont. There he shared his time between the academics of botany and the practical aspects of environmental assessment projects in New England and consultations for the National Park Service. His family's private lifestyle was back to nature, close to the earth, respectful of the delicate balance of the systems of life, centered in close family life. The other man was and still is a pollution victim personally. Richard's first years out of high school were spent in the military, mostly in Europe. Back home in Northeast Ohio in 1963, he married and began a truck-driving career. Then it happened. In 1976, when he was only 37 years old, he was transporting toxic chemicals, was involved in a spill, and came into direct contact with some hazardous waste. His health deteriorated rapidly. Doctors and hospitals became frequent experiences as Richard's nerves and emotions suffered. By 1977 he had been diagnosed officially as having a degenerative disease and was terminated from his work and put on lifelong disability. He always would insist that the problem really rooted in his exposure to the spilled chemicals. Humans and their environment clearly were at risk, although responsibility was rarely taken by anyone.

If moral and environmental decay were not enough, another danger to life and property now was all too evident. Could modern societies survive terrorism, another increasing problem that had become frightening and frustrating indeed? As a political/military weapon, terrorism had been successful in Vietnam and now surfaced dramatically and tragically during the 1973 Olympic Games in Munich, West Germany. Palestinian terrorists massacred eleven Israeli athletes in their residence at the Olympic Village. How ironic that this Twentieth Olympiad, billed as the "Games of Joy," also saw Jewish-American swimmer Mark Spitz win seven gold medals. Was the Holocaust of the 1940s over or not? When, if ever, does perceived social injustice warrant indiscriminate violence? This politically motivated massacre seemed more proof that the 1970s was something of a non-decade. In some ways it was a throwback to the horrors of the early 1940s and even to a fresh awareness of the economic struggles of the 1930s. In other ways it was a time of fresh hope that the 1970s was none of these bad memories. It was a time when the present both feared a return of the negatives of the past and longed for a brand new future modeled on a nostalgia for the 1950s. Some of the longing was driven by religious fervor and would become frightening in its own right.

This frightening fervor became painfully the case in Iran toward the end of the 1970s. The powerful Shah of Iran, enjoying the support of the United States, oversaw increasingly violent repression of his outspoken and activistic opponents, even while he was seeking a fresh world image as one responding positively to the civil rights concerns of America's new president, Jimmy Carter. President Carter said in his inaugural address in January, 1977: "Our moral sense dictates a clear preference for those societies which share with us an abiding respect for individual human rights." While intended as fresh commitment to the frontier of high morality, millions of Iranians saw its implementation in their country as a frustration of social justice—and an affront to the Islamic faith. Individual freedom and justice are defined differently in varying religious contexts. A previously exiled religious leader, the Ayatollah Khomeini, took over Iran in February 1979. In October the deposed Shah was granted refuge in New York City, proving to the mass of Iranians that the United States supported all of the injustice that he represented to them. Two million angry Iranians demonstrated in Teheran on November 1, shouting "Death to America!" Three days later the U.S. embassy in Teheran was stormed and fifty-two Americans were taken and remained publicly humiliated and mistreated hostages for 444 frustrating days, while their captors demanded the Shah's return for trial.

President Carter's outstanding presidential success, at least in international affairs, was to wring from Israel and Egypt an historic peace agreement signed dramatically at Camp David in 1979. Otherwise, there is justification for the sad generalization that "intelligence, goodwill, and simple decency were not enough for a successful presidency."[45] Carter was the third succes-

---

[45]Morris, *A Time of Passion*, 211. Once out of office, however, the Carters became respected, even beloved humanitarians. Beginning in the mid-1980s, they helped build low-income housing for the poor as part of the nonprofit organization Habitat for Humanity. Jimmy Carter also traveled extensively throughout various developing countries, helping as a private citizen to monitor elections, establish relief efforts, and conduct peace negotiations.

sive Democratic president to have come to an abrupt end. Kennedy fell to an assassin. Johnson felt forced by negative circumstances to not run again in 1968—a shocking announcement to the public at the time. Carter's failure to rescue the American hostages in Iran effectively ended his chance to be re-elected in 1980. His damaged presidential credibility helped lead to Ronald Reagan's landslide presidential victory.

Anger over life-and-death issues was very evident in more places than Munich and Teheran. On January 22, 1973, the headlines told of the death of America's thirty-sixth president, Lyndon Johnson. With little success, he had waged two painful wars while in office in the 1960s, the one against poverty in the U.S. and the other the disastrous one against Vietnam. At the very time of his death there also was announced a Supreme Court decision which unleashed a new legal circumstance that millions of Americans would come to view as even worse than a few ugly murders in Munich, social chaos and failed foreign policy in Iran and Vietnam, or even continuing poverty. In its Roe v. Wade decision, the U.S. Supreme Court struck down the states' restrictions on a woman's legal ability to have aborted an unwanted fetus, at least in the first trimester of pregnancy. "A fetus," read the 7-2 majority opinion, "is not a person under the Constitution and thus has no legal right to life." Judged of primary consideration were the rights of choice and privacy of the pregnant woman.[46] The general rise of "rights" consciousness in the culture, the physical danger often involved in "back alley" abortions, and the potential tragedy of uncontrolled population growth had joined to shift the Court's opinion toward a more accepting view of abortions. In 1969, seventy-four percent of American women believed that premarital sex is wrong; four years later, only fifty-three percent did. In 1965, twenty-six percent of Americans opposed abortion—even when the pregnancy was a significant risk to the woman's health. Only a few years later this had dropped dramatically to eight percent.[47]

---

[46]For a critical response to this Supreme Court decision, see Pat Robertson, *America's Dates With Destiny* (Nashville: Thomas Nelson, 1986), chap. 19. For a detailed history of the abortion issue published twenty-five years after *Roe v. Wade*, see James Risen and Judy Thomas, *Wrath of Angels: The American Abortion War* (N.Y.: BasicBooks, 1998). By 1998 the abortion issue was more complicated and controversial than ever, with fresh debate over "partial birth" abortions and the new potential of human cloning. In the face of dramatic technological developments, many now feared a science that functions in a near moral vacuum that seems to defy national consensus.

[47]See Rosalind Rosenberg, *Divided Lives: American Women in the Twentieth Century* (N.Y.: 1992), 201. Officially, women have been allowed to join the U.S. armed forces in some roles since 1901. Only in 1973, however, when the all-volunteer military was launched and under pressure from the women's movement, did the services actively begin to recruit women. In 1976 the U. S. military academies were opened to women.

Pro-life and pro-choice demonstrators meet on a sidewalk in Illinois. The issue of abortion has been a hotly-debated legal and moral issue since the 1970s.

The official view of many Christian bodies, however, had not changed. The National Council of Catholic Bishops, for instance, issued a pastoral letter warning Roman Catholics that anyone undergoing or performing an abortion placed themselves in a state of excommunication from that church. Is abortion the right of reproductive choice or outright murder on a massive scale? Is a fetus only a bit of vegetating matter or, as Cardinal Cooke put it, are we engaged in "slaughter of the innocent unborn?" A human fetus was said not to be a "person." In only a few years after this decision approximately three out of ten pregnancies in the U.S. would end in abortion, and abortion would be the most common surgical procedure for women of childbearing age. It also would be one of the more divisive of all social issues in the U.S. to the end of the century.[48] Is such a practice, so heavily used for a range of reasons, an obvious sign of the society's moral fabric maturing or coming apart?[49]

---

[48]For a vigorous 1997 statement of concern, see the Appendix.

[49]More precisely, the Court ruled that there exists an inherent right of privacy which prohibits state interference in the medical relation between a woman and her physician.

Members of the J-M class of 1959 reflect both sides of the national debate on the morality of abortion. Betty and many others insist that it is a woman's right. Maurene would not do it herself, but is sure that others should have a choice, although it should be done early if it is to be done. Nancy had suffered three miscarriages before having her first son. While she is pro-choice, doing it early in pregnancy is the only legitimate option—"those 'near birth' abortions are murder!" Many men in the class were pro-life in orientation. While Charles could not justify abortion morally, he admitted that it is almost better than unwanted and abused children. Stan insisted that women do not have a right to end the life of another (the fetus being "another") and he is angry that people can use his tax money to do it. Jim is very direct in his anti-abortion view. "The Nazis would be proud of us! More babies are slaughtered in the U.S. than died in the Holocaust." With less fiery rhetoric, Mac simply admits that he does not like the very subject of abortion; even so, it is someone else's choice and not his business. Human life is only when "it's out and crying."

Two other subjects were also becoming centers of public concern and debate. What about the social acceptability of "sexual preference" and tobacco advertising? Considered a sin and crime in Western religious and legal traditions, the homosexual form of "sexual preference" was officially categorized as a mental illness. In 1968 the category was liberalized slightly by the American Psychiatric Association to a "non-psychotic mental disorder." The Gay Rights movement kept growing, more institutional barriers fell, and social acceptance—or least tolerance—grew. Then in 1973 the APA abandoned its traditional view of homosexuality as pathological. The next year the National Organization for Women reversed its traditional disdain of lesbians and endorsed gay rights. This "sexual preference" now had joined "pro-choice" abortion as part of the "do your own thing" environment. Was this yet another frontier rightly being crossed in the name of justice or merely another frustration of public decency and morality arising from comprehensive self-centeredness?

The freedom to advertise cigarettes wherever and however was becoming morally questionable. There was increasing scientific evidence arising across the 1960s that there were serious health hazards associated with smoking. In April, 1970, Congress passed the Public Health Cigarette Smoking Act disallowing all cigarette advertising on television and radio (although the industry continued a massive advertising program in other media). One of the more popular ad campaigns of the early 1970s saw Virginia Slims cigarettes targeting newly "liberated" women. Thinner than usual cigarettes were shown with slender and self-assertive female models. The caption read, "You've Come a Long Way, Baby." Was the new advertising restriction a positive frontier crossed for the sake of public health or an unjust frustration of a legal big business in the United States? This debate would rage for the rest of the century, with the scientific evidence mounting even higher and the tobacco industry continuing to claim until 1997 that it meant little or nothing. Several members of the J-M class of 1959 have been chain smokers across their adult lives, having grown up in an environment where smoking was common. At least one class member, Jesse, would have open heart surgery in the 1990s and attribute a large part of his heart problem to decades of smoking. Only then did he "kick the habit." Millions were trying to join him.

Around such volatile issues, especially abortion, a "New Right" formed in the 1970s. While millions of Americans "dropped out" of politics because of disillusionment with both major parties, millions of others were galvanized into action because of their outrage at what seemed to them the excesses of the 1960s and a "humanistic" assault on the most basic values and institutions of society—the family, church, patriotism, and sexual morality. They became aggressive in opposition to public policies of affirmative action, busing for racial balance, feminism, legally sanctioned abortions, abolition of prayer in public schools, and permissiveness toward pornography and sexual freedom. This New Right frequently drew on the thought of Christian fundamentalists like Tim LaHaye who identified "humanism" as America's great enemy. Dedicating his 1980 book *The Battle for the Mind*[50] to Dr. Francis Schaeffer, LaHaye sharply criticized the modern "religion" of humanism that he said taught nation-destroying atheism, evolution, amorality, and a socialist world order. Reporting that humanists now controlled the U.S., he called on Christians to be alert, run for public office, and carefully screen all candidates receiving their votes.

George Wallace, four-term governor of Alabama who four times failed to gain the White House for himself, has been called the alchemist of the new social conservatism that reshaped American politics in the 1970s and 1980s. His genius

> …lay in his ability to link traditional conservatism to an earthy language that voiced powerful cultural beliefs and symbols with a much broader appeal to millions of Americans: the sanctity of the traditional family, the centrality of overt religious beliefs, the importance of hard work and self-restraint, the celebration of the autonomy of the local community. On the flickering television screen and in giant political

---

[50]Tim LaHaye, *The Battle for the Mind* (Old Tappan, N.J.: Fleming Revell, 1980).

rallies, he evoked images of a nation in crisis, a country in which thugs roamed the streets with impunity, antiwar demonstrators embraced the hated Communist Vietcong, and brazen youth flaunted their taste for "dirty" books and movies. And while America disintegrated, cowardly politicians, bureaucrats, and distant federal judges capitulated to these loathsome forces.[51]

By 1979 a decade-long attempt to pass an equal-rights-for-women amendment to the U.S. Constitution finally failed for lack of enough state ratifications (judged by numerous conservative Christians and others as a victory against radical feminism).

Meanwhile, issues of church and state became the frequent focus of public debate (see Table 16). Since 1959 the *Journal of Church and State* had been a vehicle for serious scholarship in this volatile arena, sometimes called "the greatest subject in the history of the West." Typically in question was the complex task of determining what the nation's founders believed and intended about the role of religion in public life. The First Amendment to the U.S. Constitution says that "Congress shall make no law respecting an establishment of religion, or prohibiting the free exercise thereof...." Two streams of interpretation of this amendment have been obvious. Separationists believe that the founders intended to separate church and state by depriving the state of its power to either aid or hinder religion. Accomodationists believe that the state retains at least limited power to be able constitutionally to advance religion as a moral good.

Probably the public's greatest concern about the nation's young was the widespread and dangerous use of illegal drugs. The counterculture had taken an anti-social, self-destructive, even a pathological turn. In the 1960s young people often experimented, especially with psilocybin mushrooms, mescaline, and LSD, frequently as part of a broader search for intense spirituality and meaning in life. But in the 1970s drug users increasingly were turning to amphetamines, cocaine, opiates, and heroin, rejecting meaning altogether, reflecting a deep dispiritedness, and resorting to crime to support the awful result. Addicts replaced hippies. On the religious front, there was some decline during the 1970s in the popularity among the searching young of the "New Religions" that had flourished in the late 1960s and early 1970s. The youth culture became smaller, with less leisure to experiment in more economically difficult times. The mass suicide at Jonestown, Guyana, made "People's Temple" a term with which to stigmatize cults generally.

---

[51]Dan Carter, *The Politics of Rage*, 12.

In fact, as the new religions were already turning old, an old religion was experiencing genuine newness. Millions of Americans were returning to a very traditional Christian faith as apparently the only real anchor in the terrible storms of the day. Now some 50 million Americans confessed a "born again" experience of life transformation through faith in Jesus Christ. Very prominent public leaders openly associated with this type of Christian faith, including Senator Mark Hatfield, former President Nixon aide Charles Colson,[52] and Presidents Gerald Ford and Jimmy Carter. The number of Christian television ministries was growing rapidly, in part by taking advantage of the burgeoning new medium of cable television. Pat Robertson's Christian Broadcasting Network (CBN) was the largest. Many born-again Christians, Catholic Pentecostals, and Hasidic Jews embraced enthusiastic (often "charismatic") new forms of the old faith, forms that provided intense experiences of personal transformation and committed community that were attractive especially to the young.[53] The best-known Christian organization seeking to involve believers in the political process was the Moral Majority formed in 1979 by Rev. Jerry Falwell. He had been inspired by Francis Schaeffer, about whom it has been said:

> Perhaps no intellectual save C. S. Lewis affected the thinking of evangelicals more profoundly; perhaps no leader of the period save Billy Graham left a deeper stamp on the movement as a whole. Together the Schaeffers gave currency to the idea of intentional Christian community, prodded evangelicals out of their cultural ghetto, inspired an army of evangelicals to become serious scholars, encouraged women who chose roles as mothers and homemakers, mentored the leaders of the New Christian Right, and solidified popular evangelical opposition to abortion.[54]

The frontiers of life in the U.S. society of the 1970s were a maddening mixture of the exhilarating, frightening, and fulfilling. It was a time of fascinating technological advances, frightening environmental concerns and terrorist outbreaks, confusing hard drugs, mass abortions, and sex-preference rights, and a collage of disillusionment and fresh faith. It was both the follow-through and the death of the 1960s. It seemed like little really got done in the midst of so much that was happening.

---

[52]Charles Colson, *Born Again* (Old Tappan, N.J.: Chosen Books, Revell, 1976).

[53]The best-selling nonfiction book in 1972 and 1973 was *The Living Bible*, a contemporary translation by Kenneth Taylor. In 1975 it was *Angels* by Billy Graham.

[54]Michael Hamilton, "The Dissatisfaction of Francis Schaeffer," *Christianity Today* (March 3, 1997), 22.

Life Is Not Forever

Presidents Nixon, Ford, and Carter all promised to continue the high American standard of living known since World War II, but only if Americans accepted certain compromises forced by a changing world. Something had died in America. Less American arrogance about its supreme in the world was now necessary; so was some tightening of belts at home. Constant economic expansion and massive government assistance programs were fading realities. Nonetheless, Americans resisted these presumed necessities and finally found in Ronald Reagan someone who gave the clear impression that he would not allow America to bend or back up in the face of anything or anyone. This fresh patriotic conservatism of the late 1970s reasserted traditional assumptions regardless of contemporary realities. It would be a way of life in the coming 1980s.

In the summer of 1980, just before Ronald Reagan was first elected president, Jimmy Carter was the nation's benevolent but beleaguered political leader. Americans were held hostage in Iran, a true national embarrassment. The United States had not permitted its athletes to participate in the Moscow Olympics, a political boycott objecting to policies of the Soviet Union. The American economy was paralyzed and public morale had sunk to its lowest level since the Great Depression of the 1930s. Something was dead and needed a dramatic resurrection. The darkness was becoming oppressive. Where should people look for a dawn?

Recall that elite class of 1965 from Palisades High School in California, the class that had made the cover of *Time* magazine.[55] They had their first reunion in 1975. Having enjoyed every cultural and financial advantage and still under thirty years old, they learned that an amazing eleven percent of the class now had an arrest record, most on drug or political charges. Eighteen individuals already had a history of psychiatric hospitalization. The reunion itself quickly deteriorated into the haze of the familiar pungent order of marijuana, with a half-dozen classmates openly snorting cocaine near the bar. At one point the master of ceremonies had to shout to win a moment of silence in honor of the five people from the class who had died since high school. This was the same class judged to have unlimited possibilities. But it was not working out that way. As one of their former teachers said, the years 1965-1975 were "the saddest years of the century."[56]

---

[55]*Time*, January 29, 1965.

[56]As quoted in Michael Medved and David Wallechinsky, *What Really Happened to the Class of '65?* (N.Y.: Random House, 1976), 285.

What happens to "radical" youth who hit the world's harsh realities? Some are lost in self-destructive and socially disruptive behavior. Others adapt and change. Elvis Presley, pioneer of rock-and-roll music, died in 1977. While the idol of the young in the 1950s and to become a social icon in the 1990s with the widely heralded issuance of a U.S. postage stamp bearing his image, during the 1970s Presley had faced personal difficulties, including a long-term drug dependency. He had retreated from public appearances and was rarely seen outside his Memphis mansion, known ironically as Graceland. His death, a subject of some controversy, was officially attributed to heart failure, a likely result of his chronic overuse of prescription barbiturates. Presley's quiet personal ordeal symbolized the larger societal struggle. In the 1970s the American mainstream had to adapt and change. It embraced some aspects of the earlier counterculture; in turn, the counterculture tended to join the mainstream. Many student radicals of the 1960s became college professors; feminists became politicians; antiwar protesters became stock-brokers. At the decade's end, with a decided political shift to the right, American culture and lifestyle was a strange mix of counterculture innova-tion and capitalistic consumerism. The innovation would be a constant tar-get of the conservative leaders of the 1980s. The consumerism would be a national way of life.

Most members of the J-M class of 1959 were not living in the fast lane like the class of 1965 from Palisades. Was the J-M class representative of what Richard Nixon had thought of as America's "silent majority"? In general, clearly yes. Most still lived in "middle America," worked hard, were conven-tionally patriotic, and were very family oriented. Betty and Ian, however, were obvious exceptions in varying ways. Each was attuned to academic commu-nities, was environmentally sensitive, and had been impacted deeply by mul-ticultural experiences not then typical of the Midwest. This class gathered for its first reunion in May 1977. Twenty-two members sent ahead brief bio-graphical sketches of their lives in the first eighteen years after high school. Here are a few samples:

> Thomas had joined the Navy and from his home port of San Diego had sailed the Caribbean and Mediterranean. In 1962 he went to work at Packard Electric in Warren, just a few miles from the J-M high school. Starting as an apprentice tool and die maker, he became a jour-neyman in 1969 and by 1977 owned his own welding and tool com-pany. He had two children and lived in nearby Leavittsburg.

> Betty had married a man of Indian descent, had three children, was a nursing graduate of Ohio State University, had started an Indian

Cultural School for Indian children in Columbus, and was partner in an Indian import shop.

William had gone to work at Packard Electric in Warren and had remained employed there the entire eighteen years. He had three children and lived at Lake Milton.

Jane married within a year out of high school to a machine repairman at General Motors, was a nurse, mother of three, and still lived in the immediate vicinity of the high school.

Richard was married to Delores, a classmate. They had two children, had lived in Dayton, Ohio, and Pittsburgh, Pennsylvania, and now for three years had been in Grand Rapids, Michigan, where Richard was area sales manager for a large firm.

Ian was living a rustic life in rural Vermont with Mary and one son. Having completed an extensive period of academic preparation (Youngstown State, University of Wyoming, study in New Zealand, and then a completed Ph.D. in Canada), he now was employed by the University of Vermont's Botany Department and Environmental Program and consulted with the National Park Service.

Lucille married right out of high school, had four children, still lived near the high school, and was active in the Girl Scouts, 4-H, church, and the Ladies Auxiliary of the Fire Department.

James had spent four years in the Navy, then married, had two sons, and was an ironworker with United States Steel in Youngstown. Having become an active Christian, he now hoped to become a minister.

Marjorie was still single, had worked in Boardman for several years, and now was head of her department at a small manufacturing firm in nearby Canfield.

William had three children, had worked for all these years at Republic Steel in Warren, doing some farming on the side.

Like the decade of the 1970s generally, this class, young as it was (36 years for most), already had known some hard times. Beyond the education, military service, careers, and children, there had been the sobering experiences of life-threatening health crises and even death. Judy was first diagnosed with multiple sclerosis in 1977. Frank, for example, although a diabetic, was having no particular symptoms of any other problems. Suddenly in 1978 he found himself in the Cleveland Clinic receiving five bypasses in an open heart procedure not yet that common. In that first reunion in 1977, the gathered J-M group stood in silence at one point to recognize reverently the loss of two of its members. The first was Jeannette in 1972 and then Charles in 1974. Each had died suddenly, both with young children, one by her own hand, apparently in response to marital unfaithfulness, and the other with a heart attack after a vigorous softball game. While most of the parents of the class members would not die until the late 1980s and the 1990s, there already were painful exceptions. For instance, Judy's father died in 1958 (even before she had graduated from high school), Ian's father died in 1962, Bill's in 1972, the fathers of Marjorie and Nancy in 1973, Barry's parents in 1974 and 1979, and John's father in 1976. The generations were moving on, usually the men first.

Death of sorts also came in relational forms with other endings. Jerry retired in 1979 from a 20-year career in the Navy. By then some of his 1959 J-M classmates had experienced painful marriage disruptions. Ian endured a divorce in 1972 after a very short-lived marriage. Dallas endured a "nasty" divorce in 1974 and would settle for a congenial common-law relationship the next time. Shirley and another classmate, Charles, married right out of high school, had three daughters, and for their first years lived at Craig Beach on beautiful Lake Milton. But Charles had employment problems and the family finally relocated to Florida in 1972. Soon, after more than two decades of marriage, divorce had ended this relationship and Charles, soon remarried, would wind up living in Hawaii, largely cut off from his previous life. What happens to personal faith in such a circumstance? Shirley, still a nurse in Florida, worked on some Sundays and finally got out of the habit of church-going. But her faith in God actually grew in her marriage travail. "I am very religious," she reports now, "but my church is out in the woods. I don't need a building to put it in." For many religious believers in America, the structures of their various traditional beliefs had crumbled and they had retreated inward.

On the political scene, the end of the 1970s was the end of an era. In 1978 cancer was stealing away the life of Hubert Humphrey who for thirty years, including four unsuccessful tries for the presidency, had been the "liberal" from Minnesota who believed fervently in the ability of government to alleviate social misery. But forty-five years after the inauguration of Franklin Delano Roosevelt, the nation as a whole no longer shared this vision of an effective and magnanimous federal government. Insisted the director of the National Association of Neighborhoods, "there's a new recognition that the country's not going to be saved by experts and bureaucrats. It's going to be saved by some moral vision and some moral hope coming from the grassroots and the neighborhoods."[57] People were looking for practical ways to get beyond their cynicism and feeling of powerlessness. Christina Crawford did it by trying to "tell it all" in the bestselling *Mommie Dearest* in 1978. Here was a morbidly disturbing personal saga of the adopted daughter of famous movie actress Joan Crawford. On a lighter note, Erma Bombeck released 1979's bestselling *Aunt Erma's Cope Book* satirizing self-help advocates with a "be yourself" philosophy and the therapy of laughter in tough times. The times were tough. Following the near calamity at Three Mile Island earlier in the year, Ralph Nader told a gathering of over a hundred thousand in Washington in May, 1979:

> The history of the nuclear power industry is replete with cover-ups, deceptions, outright lies, error, negligence, arrogance, greed, innumerable unresolved safety questions, and a cost-plus accounting that taxes our citizens as consumers and tax-payers. There has to be a better, safer way to heat water."

There also had to be a better way for a nation to face its problems and live out its destiny.

In October 1979, a crowd gathered to honor the memory and heritage of John F. Kennedy by dedicating a magnificent library just built at Columbia Point, overlooking the waters of Boston harbor. Senator Edward Kennedy said that "we can recall those years of grace, that time of hope. The spark still glows. The journey never ends. The dream shall never die." But President Jimmy Carter shared a more bleak diagnosis. The world of 1980 "is as different from what it was in 1960 as the world of 1960 was from that of 1940.... We have a keener appreciation of limits now, the limits of government, limits on the use of military power abroad, the limits of manipulation without harm to ourselves [of] a delicate and balanced natural environment." Then he added: "We face centrifugal forces in our society and in our political system—forces of regionalism, forces of ethnicity, of narrow economic interest, of single issue politics [that] are testing the resiliency of American pluralism and of our ability to govern."

Carter earlier had made the following observation while on the campaign trail during the country's bicentennial year (1976): "One of the real problems in this country these days is the lack of roots, the mobile society …the absence of anything that lasts in people's lives." Not even centuries-old dreams seemed enduring any more. In 1975 a Viking spaceship used complex new scientific instruments to learn that apparently there was no life on Mars

---

[57]As quoted in Peter Carroll, *It Seemed Like Nothing Happened*, 318.

after all. What about life back on Earth? Faith in many of its classic foundations had faltered. The nation remained haunted by the dark shadows of Vietnam. There still were numerous American families with "MIA" members (missing in action, unaccounted for). How can people work through grief when the line separating life and death no longer can be found for sure. As the 1980s approached, there were many griefs in quest of resolution, many deaths in search of dawns, many pessimisms in search of fresh faith.

Taking To Reflect

1. In the 1970s there was a conservative reaction to the social radicalism of the late 1960s, just as many in the Depression 1930s were highly critical of the economic and social excesses of the 1920s. How can people gain a fair perspective on the past, not coloring it heavily by their current fears, disillusionments, and assumptions? Do we remember history or create it?

2. How "free" is free in a free society like the United States? The Supreme Court on the one hand has allowed a wide range of liberty in what many citizens judge society-polluting indecency and the danger to unborn life of a woman's now-established "right" to end a pregnancy. On the other hand, it has insisted on a narrow range of liberty on religious devotion and practice in public schools.

3. Was the ending of the Vietnam War a military defeat for the U.S.? Did it at least join with growing economic problems to question the traditional American assumption that the U.S. is God's chosen nation destined to protect and teach the rest of the world how a nation should behave?

4. Some argue that the "popularity" of religious faith fluctuates with the times, and that the 1970s naturally was a good time for conservative faith communities. Is the level of serious commitment to religious belief largely a byproduct of social circumstances?

5. What about that basic tenet of modern secular nations that says science, technology, and education will work together to yield a dramatic betterment of the human condition? Is there such a thing as the religion of "humanism"? What lesson was to be learned from the events at Love Canal and Three Mile Island?

6. There appears to be a perennial hunger for belief in something (Someone) that gives meaning to life. What was so attractive about tragic cult movements like the one of Jim Jones that led to a mass suicide? What distinguishes a "cult" from a more standard faith community?

7. Was the U.S. losing control of its own destiny in the 1970s? The OPEC oil embargo, for instance, made clear that the great American economy was now very much part of an international economy. Was "Popeye running out of spinach"? Was there a socialistic one-world-order conspiracy?

8. When, if ever, does injustice justify indiscriminate violence such as the bombing of cities or terrorism at an Olympic Games (1973)? Is the aborting of an unwanted pregnancy when there is no health risk to the mother legally justified violence?

Chapter Six

Looking Everywhere For New Light

1980s

———

Ronald Reagan described his presidential role this way—
to rescue America, restore confidence, and sweep away all the doubters.

———

If the foundations are destroyed,
what can the righteous do? (Psalm 11:3)

———

Hopes were not high among Americans as the 1970s closed and people tried to look ahead. One survey reported that the number of Americans who believed that the nation had entered an era of enduring shortages had increased from forty percent in the middle of the 1970s to sixty-two percent by that decade's end. Responses to a Gallup poll of the time showed that seventy-two percent of the public agreed with the statements that "we are fast coming to a turning point in our history" and "the land of plenty is becoming the land of want."[1] Moving to the 1980s apparently was going to be an uncomfortable chore. Concludes historian Eric Hobsbawm: "The history of the twenty years after 1973 is that of a world which lost its bearings and slid into instability and crisis. And yet, until the 1980s it was not clear how irretrievably the foundations of the Golden Age had crumbled."[2] Americans could not see, of course, that even more change was coming than a downward economic turn in U.S. history. Who, for instance, would have thought in the

———

[1]As reported by Peter Carroll, *It Seemed Like Nothing Happened: America in the 1970s* (New Brunswick: Rutgers University Press, 1982, 1990), 340.

[2]Eric Hobsbawm, *The Age of Extremes: A History of the World, 1914-1991* (N.Y.: Vintage Books, Random House, 1994, 1996), 403.

Cold War frenzy of 1979 that within ten years the great U.S. foe, the mighty
and feared Soviet Union, would disintegrate into a series of loosely connected countries? What a decade it would be!

Ironically, there was in the United States a reality of abundance existing in
the face of growing public cynicism about political and economic affairs
and a widening separation between the rich and poor. The social rebellion of
the 1960s did not end with the withdrawal of the United States from Vietnam
or the great catharsis of the Watergate crisis that brought down President
Nixon. In fact, "the children of Aquarius merely shaved their beards, traded
in their ragged jeans and baggy dresses for three-piece suits, and marched off
into the workplace toting their revolutionary new view of the world."[3] The
"anti-institutional shouts that had originated in the pot-laced dronings of
Haight-Ashbury hippies could be heard in the free-market chatter of Wall
Street brokers and Main Street merchants."[4] In the 1980s, even the rich U.S.
cities found themselves having to get accustomed to the sight of beggars on
the streets and homeless people sheltered in doorways and sleeping in card-
board boxes (unless they had been removed from public visibility by the
police). Even so, this was the announcement made by President Reagan in his
State of the Union message on January 15, 1984: "It's morning in America.
America is back, standing tall, looking to the eighties with courage, confidence, and hope." Summarized Walter Russell Mead:

> Many millions of people, themselves caught up in the toils of the
> urban and suburban economy, attribute their alienation to the destruc-
> tion of an imagined past. As they wander from Kmart to Pizza Hut, they
> look back to the good old days on Walton's Mountain, where God was
> in heaven and Mom was in the kitchen, when families were happy,
> when all towns were small and all folks were good. [Jimmy] Carter
> briefly captured their interest by evoking their love for this nonexistent
> past, but [Ronald] Reagan stole their hearts by pledging to restore it.[5]

---

[3]Charles Colson and Jack Eckerd, *Why America Doesn't Work* (Dallas: Word Publishing, 1991), 52.

[4]William Strauss and Neil Howe, *The Fourth Turning: An American Prophecy* (N.Y.:
Broadway Books, 1997), 199. Robert Bork offers this judgment: The 1960s was "a malig-
nant decade that, after a fifteen-year remission, returned in the 1980s to metastasize more
devastatingly throughout our culture than it had in the Sixties, not with tumult but quietly, in the moral and political assumptions of those who now control and guide our
major cultural institutions. The Sixties radicals are still with us, but now they do not par-
alyze the universities; they run the universities" (*Slouching Towards Gomorrah*, 53).

[5]Walter Russell Mead, *Mortal Splendor: The American Empire in Transition*, as quoted by Arlene Skolnick, *Embattled Paradise: The American Family in an Age of Uncertainty*
(N.Y.: BasicBooks, HarperCollins, 1991), 125.

The Prime Directive

The international preface to the decade of the 1980s was menacing. President Jimmy Carter had become more aggressive in foreign affairs when in November 1979, revolutionaries in Iran seized the American embassy in Teheran, grabbed numerous hostages, and openly paraded them before television cameras, mocking the power of the U.S. The American public was outraged and increasingly frustrated as months would pass with no resolution. The president endorsed new military expenditures that helped reheat the Cold War. Anticipating the need for some military action, especially after the Soviet invasion of Afghanistan in December 1979, Carter warned that "not every instance of the firm application of the power of the United States is a potential Vietnam." After all, he added, the country now faced "the most serious threat to world peace since the Second World War."

In January 1980, seeking to assert world leadership, the White House had appealed to American allies to boycott the Olympic Games scheduled for Moscow in July 1980. After all, how can the world engage in friendly competition in the service of peace when it is engaged in deliberately dangerous and unrelenting confrontation and outrageous abuse of innocent humans? Moscow should not be dignified by being host to such an admirable world event. The U.S. athletes did not go to the Games. Embarrassingly, the European allies ignored Carter's boycott call, allowing his political opponent in the 1980 presidential election, Ronald Reagan, to scold that "our allies are losing confidence in us and our adversaries no longer respect us." Elect me, he was saying to the public, and you will not have to put up any longer with this national impotence. Carter's public approval rating dropped dramatically. There was a rising conservative tide. A former movie actor known by his macho cowboy scenes on the big screen soon would be in the nation's presidential saddle.

More was at stake than shifting American politics. It now was believed by numerous analysts that a whole intellectual and spiritual era in human history was standing awkwardly on its last feeble legs. The "modern" age was in definite decay and what was to follow, soon to be called the "postmodern," was only beginning to take some shape. Considerable tearing down of the modernist "Enlightenment" consensus was under way (see Table 17). The vision guiding this major shift was the basic set of assumptions on which people in the West have lived in recent centuries. These assumptions were no longer self-evident and were being abandoned by increasing numbers of people, leaving the difficult task of somehow getting it all together again on some other base.

DYING "MODERNIST" ASSUMPTIONS

Many of the underlying social assumptions of twentieth-century America have been rooted in the intellectual history known as the "Enlightenment" that began in the late seventeenth and eighteenth centuries in Europe.

Negatively, the Enlightenment's tendency has been to reject the rule of dogma and special revelation that gives religious establishments and feudal hierarchies their strict and unquestionable authority. It has featured a willingness in principle to dispense with external, including divine authority if that is where scientific evidence and human logic and experience leads. Thus, the concept of a Creator of the universe could be relegated to that of a remote caretaker of things or even be viewed as only a theoretical and maybe irrelevant possibility.

Positively, the Enlightenment has sought the rule of human reason and the freeing of humans for an unfettered intellectual quest for new knowledge and self-determination. This quest may or may not lead to the justification of a religious perspective on life and reality. Presumably it would lead to human betterment through an evolutionary process. The keys to social progress are thought to be information, education, and the freedom for informed self-determination.

Given this perspective, soon dominant in the West was the rise of the scientific method and its systematic search for and authentication of what can be shown to be "true." This Enlightenment tradition seeks to discern, understand, catalog, and hopefully master and utilize information for human good. In the United States, Thomas Jefferson (1743-1826) was influenced deeply by the Enlightenment. Through him and others, so were the founding concepts of the nation itself.

In the 1980s it was becoming clearer that reality appears more complex than the rigid categories of human rationality. Intellectual know-how and gathering mountains of "data" had not delivered the good life for most of humanity. Massive infusions of federal money had not solved festering social problems in the U.S. Progress toward true justice and peace obviously are not the inevitable outcomes of rational thinking and living. The concept of "sin" (some inherent evil) began to be taken more seriously, even outside traditional religious circles.

Is it turning out that the era which was to bring new light ("Enlightenment") has only extended or even deepened the darkness? Has it really been little more than a grand but finally pretentious experiment in human idealism and arrogance? What is the alternative?

TABLE 17

Astute observers found disturbingly applicable the old assertion of Matthew Arnold that we are "wandering between two worlds, one dead, the other powerless to be born."[6] The in-between time is destabilizing, disturbing, even dangerous. Human beings need meaningful communities and coherent cultures in order to function in truly human ways. What is a "culture"? Two realities are required simultaneously: (1) some structure of relationships and enterprises needs to exist; and (2) within that structure, causing it to cohere as a viable culture, must be a common set of meanings, values, and goals which are shared significantly by at least most participants. Some of the basic building blocks of Western culture were cracking in the 1980s. Much would change. Much effort would be expended to deny the cracks and seek a revitalization of previous times. The American structure was both shifting and seeking to remain essentially stable.

The 1980s, another awkward and transitional decade, certainly got off to a jolting start in the scenic Northwest. In March 1980, the beautiful Mount St. Helens came alive after 123 years of volcanic inactivity. A 4.2 magnitude earthquake rumbled beneath it. Within a week the first steam-explosion blasted a 250-foot-wide crater through the volcano's ice cap. Two months and many smaller earthquakes later there was a "bulge" pushed outward 450 feet that was a mile long. Finally, on May 18, the whole top of the mountain blew off.[7] In many ways the whole American culture seemed to be acting the same way. Large-scale philosophic and cultural shifts began to be very evident in the 1980s, bulges with frightening potential. Several social assumptions once thought forever sacred fell on hard times. The United States tried to take a fresh grip on a new future, partly by trying to stand tall again and grasping for recovered aspects of the "good years" of the country that got lost in the turbulent 1960s and 1970s.

Being between two worlds, yesterday and tomorrow, the 1980s in the U.S. would be newly exhilarating and very expensive in many ways. The exhilaration was symbolized by the two international experiences Barry had. The Billy Graham Association convened the Congress on World Evangelization in Lausanne, Switzerland, in 1974. It was a major gathering of Christians from around the world, marking especially the emergence of Third World evangelical movements. The church movement within which Barry ministers

---

[6]Matthew Arnold, "Stanzas from the Grand Chartreuse" (1855).

[7]Ironically, this eruption covered much of the forested area in which, nearly ten years earlier, Dan Cooper is thought to have landed with $200,000 of ransom money after the only successful skyjacking in U.S. history. Since he has never been found, this eruption only added to Cooper's legendary status.

sent him as a North American delegate, and then in 1980 staged its own centennial celebration on the campus of Anderson University in Indiana (where
he then was dean and professor). Church representatives from many nations
of the world were present for this week of celebrating the church's past and
reaching for a vision of its future. The American contingent of the church was
having to reassess its new role in a growing and maturing network of associated national churches from all over the world. In the 1980s, the United
States in general was reaching for a similarly fresh grasp on what was good in
its past so that it too could celebrate again—but in a world very different than
in earlier decades. The whole planet now was a "global village."

The economic side of the difference was especially clear in the industrial
area of Northeast Ohio and neighboring Western Pennsylvania. Plant closings
in the Youngstown area had been traumatic in the late 1970s. Now came a
recession in the early 1980s and another wave of closings in the nearby
Pittsburgh area. It seemed like a "swift decapitation of an entire industry built
over the course of a century."[8] In the difficulty of all this demise, however,
there emerged in Pittsburgh an extraordinary episode in American urban history. There soon was a substantial renaissance. It was marked by a widespread
commitment of the city's public and private leaders to largely abandon its
industrial past and forge a new economic and cultural identity. This involved
relegating the area's steel-centered, heavy industry legacy mostly to the care
of historians and evolving in its place a strategy of modernization encom-
passing economic diversification (with an emphasis on professional services), nurture of the advanced technology and research sectors, a reduced
but streamlined, more efficient, and more competitive manufacturing component, and a new awareness of the direct economic benefits of cultural
vitality and heightened quality of life and their role in enhancing the community's image as a place to live and do business. The nearby city of
Cleveland, Ohio, was actively about a similar task.

In American politics, the 1980s was the decade of Ronald Reagan. As governor of California he had gained the reputation of having reduced taxes and
intrusive government. His conservative rhetoric played well with a growing
population of older Americans, many of whom were moving to the "Sunbelt"
states of the South and West where hostility to "big government" was endem-
ic. He had stood firm against the "Consciousness Revolution" of the 1960s,
himself symbolizing in California the primacy of the establishment culture.
Now Reagan re-emerged to symbolize "the defeat of that Establishment and

---

[8]Roy Lubove, *Twentieth-Century Pittsburgh: The Post-Steel Era, Vol. 2* (University of
Pittsburgh Press, 1996), 7.

The 1984 election saw the first serious African-American candidate for president of the United States—Jesse Jackson, shown here speaking at the Sept. 19, 1981 Solidarity Day in Washington, D.C.

the primacy of the self." To use the terminology of Strauss and Howe, the nation's historical cycle was shifting through a "third turning" to a period of "culture wars."[9]

Somehow in 1980 it did not matter to the public that he already was sixty-nine years old and had not held public office since his retirement from the governorship of California in 1974. Reagan was first elected president of the United States by a landslide in 1980—489 electoral votes to Jimmy Carter's 49.[10] The U.S. Senate also was recaptured by the Republicans for the first time since 1953. It was the biggest defeat suffered by an incumbent American president since Herbert Hoover lost in 1932. Even the youngest voters (aged eighteen to twenty-four) gave Reagan sixty percent of their votes. They were hardly clones of the campus radicals and anti-war protesters of almost two decades earlier. Although the New Right led by Rev. Jerry Falwell claimed credit, the Reagan landslide probably was more a vote against an inflation rate then at a stunning twelve percent, interest rates at fifteen percent, unemployment touching eight million Americans, and the sheer frustration of an apparently impotent President Carter who still could do nothing about the fifty-three American hostages still in Iranian captivity.

Reagan would be re-elected by an even bigger margin in 1984 and then would be succeeded in 1989 by his faithful vice-president, George Bush. The 1984 presidential election saw the vigorous attempt of Jesse Jackson to gain the Democratic nomination, the first serious African-American ever to do so.

---

[9]William Strauss and Neil Howe, *The Fourth Turning: An American Prophecy* (N.Y.: Broadway Books, 1997), 201.

[10]Only 53 percent of eligible voters cast ballots in the 1980 election. In countries like Germany and France, voter participation was near 85 percent in the 1970s.

*Geraldine A.
Ferraro, first
woman candi-
date for vice
president,
addresses a
rally in
Hartford,
Conn., August
1984.*

He did succeed in bringing to the polls more black voters and highlighting that the nation was still divided too much by race, gender, and class barriers. Winning the Democratic nomination was Walter Mondale who chose a woman, Geraldine Ferraro, to run as the vice-presidential candidate—also a first. The 1988 presidential campaign included the Republican candidacy of Rev. Pat Robertson, prominent religious broadcaster. He had some impressive credentials and spoke forthrightly about moral issues the nation should address. Although he insisted that he had no intent of imposing his strong Christian views on anyone, most voters did not find him enough of a mainstream politician and he dropped out of the race. It was Ronald Reagan's decade. He symbolized the nation's desired self-image at the time. The country was suffering deeply after the defeat in Vietnam, the disgrace of Watergate, and the disintegration of the economy in the 1970s. Most American voters apparently wanted limits on the growth of government at home, a more assertive foreign policy, and a greater honoring of traditional moral values in the institution's of the nation. They saw in Mr. Reagan real hope in all these regards.

The man in the White House for the 1980s, the "great communicator," projected straight talk and fresh hope.[11] He refuted the thesis so common in popular histories written in the 1970s and 1980s that pictured recent American history as the sad tale of decline in which a once proud nation had betrayed

---

[11]Reagan was known as "the Gipper," referring to George Gipp, a legendary Notre Dame football star that he once played in *Knute Rockne—All American*. Later, as a movie actor turned politician, he had stage presence and a gift for one-liners, often borrowed from old movie scripts.

its ideals, lost a war, and allowed its economy to crumble.[12] More compatible with Ronald Reagan would be the 1990 history by Michael Barone, *Our Country: The Shaping of America from Roosevelt to Reagan*.[13] Barone would seek to demolish the prevailing mood of cynicism and apathy by showing instead that the great American political and economic systems had worked and were continuing to work. Reagan insisted that it was time to quit belittling and bemoaning and get on with the greatness that still was the United States.

If Richard Nixon had undermined the luster of the U.S. presidency, Reagan's attention to pomp and circumstance, rhetoric and style, would work to restore it. America was again to be viewed as a shining city set on a hill for all the world to see and imitate. The renewal of a sense of pride and progress started immediately with Iran deciding to release its American hostages and Reagan deciding to stage an extravagant inauguration festival designed to uplift the national spirit and launch "an era of national renewal." The change of administrations provided a unique moment for patriotic splendor—yellow ribbons wrapped around the old apple tree to welcome the hostages home, the Stars and Stripes rippling in the wind, brass bands in parades featuring full military regalia. President Reagan announced that big government was the problem, not the solution to the nation's problems. The country seemed ready for "News from Lake Wobegon," a popular feature on Garrison Keillor's rustic and nostalgic radio program *A Prairie Home Companion*. Lake Wobegon was being projected by a skilled and humorous storyteller as America's mythic little town where "all the men are strong, all the women good looking, and all the children are above average." Could that kindly place with such strong traditional roots, meaningful relatedness, and love of even the mundane of life be the U.S. again?

Reagan's first inaugural address evoked the spirit of Franklin Roosevelt's first inaugural by focusing on "an economic affliction of great proportions" and issuing the call for a "new beginning." He had the can-do optimism of the 1940s and an almost fevered anti-communist rhetoric not heard since the 1950s. The Soviet Union was called "the evil empire." This rhetoric encouraged a new rush of patriotism and a very large arms buildup. The president called for a new crusade to "take government off the backs of the great people of this country, and turn you loose again to do the things that I know you

---

[12]See, e.g., William Manchester, *The Glory and the Dream: A Narrative History of America 1932-1972* (Boston: Little, Brown, 1974).
[13]New York: The Free Press, Macmillan, 1990.

can do so well, because you did them and made this country great." Reagan "cultivated an image akin to that of a Western hero riding into town to restore peace, order, and prosperity…. The Reagan persona was well suited to a decade in which many Americans valued style and image over sub-

PAINFUL ECONOMIC REALITIES

	Total Car Sales in the U.S.	Total Sales of Cars Made in the U.S. by American Companies
1978	11.3 million	9.3 million
1979	10.7 million	8.3 million
1980	9.0 million	6.6 million
1981	8.5 million	6.2 million
1982	8.0 million	5.8 million

	GNP* $ Billions	Percent Change from Previous Year
1978	3,021	
1979	3,106	+3
1980	3,132	+1
1981	3,175	+1
1982	3,115	-2
1983	3,231	+4
1984	3,446	+7

*In constant 1982 dollars. U.S. Dept. of Commerce, Bureau of the Census, *Statistical Abstract of the United States: 1987* (Washington: GPO, 1987), 418, and *Statistical Abstract, 1985,* 432.

In Japan, unemployment was less than three percent throughout the 1980s, with inflation very low. During the decade Japan achieved about $400 billion in trade surpluses, reaching a standard of living exceeding the U.S. (measured by the gross national product per capita). A promise of lifetime employment and a culture of consensus created consistently smooth labor relations. Japan's brand of teamwork pushed it into an economic league of its own. In the 1940s, the U.S. had thoroughly defeated Japan militarily. In the 1980s, it was Japan's turn economically.

TABLE 18

stance and worshipped wealth and success."[14] There surely was a lot of glitz, and with it increasing social ironies. They included the awkward contrasts between the glitz and a gathering gloom among the newly homeless, pride in a massive health care system and the increasing number of AIDS victims, and all those dispossessed people trying to survive among the country's numerous possessors of so many "things."

The "prime directive" featured on the very popular *Star Trek* television series involved the principle of non-interference. An officer of Star Fleet, when contacting a previously unknown planet that apparently was making "normal progress toward a technological civilization," was to avoid all disturbance of that planet's social development. The prime directive back in Earth's America in the 1980s centered in a similar politically triumphant and socially conservative agenda. This agenda was the undoing of the liberal consensus that had prevailed since the 1930s and had reached its highpoint in President Lyndon Johnson's "Great Society" of the 1960s. The new thesis was: "Government is not the answer to our problems; government *is* the problem." Like *Star Trek*'s prime directive, the point now was to avoid government interference in life at home—although the federal government could and should rebuild a massive military to interfere with communism abroad wherever possible. "Reaganomics" insisted that the country's problems came from governmental intrusions into the marketplace and excessive taxes that reduced incentives to work, save, and invest.

The path to progress was understood to lay in avoiding federal bureaucracy and regulation and allowing business and industry to do what they should, freely produce a mountain of goods for a mass-consumption society. Presumably, when each pursues self-interest, the good of the whole will be served best. The profits of the rich will "trickle down" to all others. In many ways symbolic of the decade under Ronald Reagan, was the 1985 nonfiction bestseller *Iacocca: An Autobiography*.[15] Here is the story of Lee Iacocca's showdown with Henry Ford, his move to the troubled Chrysler Corporation, and its dramatic turnaround. He became something of an economic folk hero as he led a big company out of near desperation, told about his brand of effective management style, and openly championed hard work and "the values that made this country great."

In the 1980s there was an attempt to return to the 1950s for models of the better life. Back then the United States was master of the world. This nostal-

---

[14]Victor Bondi, ed., *American Decades: 1980-1989* (Detroit: Gale Research, a Manly Book, 1996), 47.

[15]Lee Iacocca, with William Novak, *Iacocca: An Autobiography* (Bantam Books, 1984).

gic backward call found an appreciative audience among the baby boomer generation who grew up in the 1950s and 1960s, now had real resources of their own, and were determined to enjoy good times again. The vision for America now being refurbished featured the "old-fashioned" values of patriotism, religion, hard work, self-reliance, and family togetherness.[16] These were to combine into the only way to eradicate the nation's social woes, sagging economy, and tattered reputation abroad. Particularly hard hit by unemployment in the early 1980s were the auto-producing centers in Michigan, Indiana, and Ohio. For many years the Big Three auto makers and the United Auto Workers had been the symbols of the success of big organizations in American economic life. Now it was the Japanese who had responded more quickly to the emerging world economy and the desire of Americans for cars that were affordable, smaller, well-built, and easy to maintain (see Table 18). It was a threatening situation for American workers with big salary and benefit packages, a determination not to slide downward in living standard, and jobs now in jeopardy. "Buy American!" now appeared as an urgent message on automobile bumpers and in television advertising.

In the face of other problems being posed by the modern world, fresh conservatism was being heard from the Vatican in Rome. With the installation in 1978 of Pope John Paul II came a clear message to Roman Catholics worldwide. There would be no ordination of female priests, no permission to use contraceptives or abortion, and no remarriages in the church after divorce. These restrictions brought a clash with many American Catholics who did not agree and were no longer hesitant to speak out. The U.S. culture was becoming more pluralistic and it was more difficult than ever for many churchgoers to listen to the traditional power structures of the churches as though they were the last word that had come directly from God. With increases in wealth, education, and technology, many people now listened more to their own opinions and consciences than to established authorities speaking politically from Washington or religiously from Rome. Hans Küng, read widely around the world, was well aware that "we reform-minded Catholic theologians find that nowadays...the official Church sometimes blows a harsh wind in our faces." Even so, he judged that the closing of the 1980s was a good time to keep hope alive.

Precisely at a time when everywhere in the world a deep longing for peace has broken through, where in a power system like the East bloc

---

[16]Note the 1989 best-selling nonfiction book by Robert Fulghum, *All I Really Need To Know I Learned In Kindergarten* (Villard Books, 1988). The lessons included sharing, playing fair, not hitting people, cleaning up your own mess, not taking what is not yours, saying you're sorry, taking a nap every afternoon, etc.

The Vietnam Veterans Memorial in Washington, D.C., a sobering symbol of the high human cost of war.

a fully unexpected awareness of political freedom, human rights, democracy, and pluralism has dawned, and a general renewal is on the way…the Church should proceed with its own internal reforms, which had such a hopeful beginning in the Second Vatican Council (1962-1965).[17]

A powerful new Americanism was captured in Lee Greenwood's immensely popular song "God Bless the USA" which he sang at the 1984 Republican National Convention. In June of that year President Reagan visited Normandy, France, to commemorate the 40th anniversary of the American and Allied troops that had rushed from sea and air onto those beaches in 1944 as a massive and costly first step on the road to liberating Western Europe from Hitler and the Nazis. Reagan was remembering movingly an historic episode when Americans were together, noble, sacrificing, proud, and victorious. But fresher war memories needed healing more than remembering for many Americans. Reagan had called the Vietnam War "a noble cause" in 1980. Then in 1982 the Vietnam Veterans Memorial was dedicated in the nation's capital. Maybe this awful wound in the nation's memory and pride finally could be healed and gotten past.[18] The impressive memorial attracted more

---

[17]Hans Küng, *Reforming the Church Today: Keeping Hope Alive* (N.Y.: Crossroad, 1990). Küng was speaking at the end of the 1980s, just after the dramatic tearing down of the Berlin Wall, the ugly symbol of the Cold War, and as the Soviet Union was on the verge of disintegration.

[18]The immensely popular television comedy sitcom *M*A*S*H*, set in Korea rather than Vietnam, had brought outlandish humor to the tragic reality of land war in Southeast Asia. Its final episode was broadcast in 1983 with a stunning 77 percent of the national viewing audience tuned in. Called "Goodbye, Farewell and Amen," the series star Alan Alda said it was a time of saying "goodbye to each other and the experience." Hopefully the same was true for the nation and its long Vietnam nightmare.

than 5 million emotional visitors in its first two years. Controversy remained, however. In 1986, for instance, the movie *Platoon* won four Academy Awards with its unflinching portrayal of the war that raised profound moral questions about the exercise of American power in Southeast Asia.

What actually happened in the American economy during the 1980s? The country turned out to be in less bad shape than it looked to most Americans in 1981-82. Reports one historian: "Underneath surface difficulties, the American economy and American military power remained massive and strong. In the 1980s Americans found that their country was stronger and more resilient than most of them had thought."[19] The real estate market boomed, with many developments funded by "junk bonds" that would go sour and spell economic trouble in the years ahead. Dollars flowed freely in everything from flea-market trivia to pornography. For instance, Bill got started in collecting and selling baseball cards in the early 1980s. From 1985 to 1992 he and his family set up at trade shows from in large cities from Michigan to Florida and made enough money to build a new home in Ohio.

During the 1980s, an industry much more sinister than baseball cards expanded rapidly. The advent of adult movies on videocassette and cable television and the huge growth in telephone sex "services" shifted the consumption of porn from seedy movie theaters and bookstores into America's homes. Millions of Americans were ready buyers, and others were morally outraged. No wonder an estimated 500,000 people gathered in Washington, D. C., on April 29, 1980, under the banner "Washington for Jesus." They were looking for a spiritual revival in the nation that would again sustain traditional morality. At one point, Ben Kinchlow, co-host of the Christian Broadcasting Network, asked the crowd to point their hands toward the Capital Building that houses the Senate and House of Representatives. They did in dramatic fashion, and he prayed: "Loose our nation's capital, all our leaders, and let the power of God flow into that nation, and let this day mark a day of return to the principles of God!" A culture "war" was on.

"Hype" became a public art form in politics, business, sports, and films. Entrepreneur capitalists like Donald Trump and Ivan Boesky became national celebrities. Boesky assured the business-school graduates at a University of California, Berkeley, commencement: "Greed is all right.... You can be greedy and still feel good about yourself." Status symbols of the new elite included expensive foreign cars and cellular telephones. Cinema focused on money in

---

[19]Michael Barone, *Our Country: The Shaping of America from Roosevelt to Reagan* (N.Y.: The Free Press, Macmillan, 1990), 611.

Wall Street (1987), *Working Girl* (1987), and *Fatal Attraction* (1988). Was the whole wave of self-indulgence really a fatal attraction that would come to haunt the 1990s? Early indications pointed that way. In fact, reality itself was becoming something of a room filled with advertising mirrors. People were getting lost in media-manufactured perceptions and ploys. Had consumer hype and commercialism gone mad? Advertising, packaging, and design clearly were affecting the average individual's "spin" or "take" on virtually everything. Having surveyed "the politics of style" in the U.S. of 1988, Stuart Ewen concluded:

> Our own experiences are of little consequence, unless they are substantiated and validated by the world of style. In the midst of such charades, the chasm between surface and reality widens; we experience a growing sense of disorientation.... The way out of this confusion is difficult to imagine.... There must be a reconciliation of image and meaning, a reinvigoration of a politics of substance. Only then will people be able to ensure that the imagery of pleasure is joined to the experience of pleasure; that seductive images of the "good life" are rooted in the principles and practices of a human community; and that images of freedom, satisfaction, and social resistance are meaningfully engaged with the resources and real options available to us in the world we inhabit.[20]

Mass advertising reigned, buying flourished, and big tax cuts did come in the 1980s, but the Democratic Congress refused to reduce social spending as much as the president wanted. The tax cuts failed to generate enough new revenue to offset Reagan's major increases in defense spending.[21] Consequently, the federal deficit grew at an alarming rate. The economy suffered a significant recession in the 1981-83 period. While it recovered impressively, there finally came "Black Monday," a big day of financial reckoning on Wall Street in October 1987. This key industrial index lost some $560 billion worth of the value of its securities. There was a tidal wave of selling reminiscent of the 1929 crash. The mood went from boom to gloom. Suddenly the Reagan revolution looked more like a bust. Said one financier, it was "the nearest thing to a meltdown that I ever want to see." But the president and the economy survived. He was called "Teflon" because nothing bad seemed to

---

[20]Stuart Ewen, *All Consuming Images: The Politics of Style in Contemporary Culture* (N.Y.: BasicBooks, 1988), 271.

[21]Critics called President Reagan's vision of an anti-missile weapons system in space "Star Wars," judging it fanciful, expensive, even impossible.

stick to him, not even the assassination attempt that he endured very early in his presidency.[22]

The Iran-Contra affair, which threatened to be another Watergate undoing of a president in 1985-86, also soiled but did not submerge Reagan. It had become known that, contrary to existing law, the U.S. had secretly sold arms to Iran and then a White House staffer, Oliver North, had diverted the money to the Nicaraguan "Contra" fighters who were resisting the leftist Sandinista government. Apparently the sale to Iran had been initiated at the suggestion of Israel, with the goals of bettering relations with Iran and obtaining the release of American hostages held in Lebanon by pro-Iranian terrorists. North skillfully defended his actions and gained considerable public sympathy. The president may have known about this illegal sale and then diversion of funds, but it was never proven and he continued to govern. The Tower Commission in 1987 did blame Reagan at least for his apparently irresponsible lack of control over the National Security Council.

On the international scene, American money, arms, and even direct military assistance were provided to regimes said to be fighting communists. The U.S. Marines were sent to Lebanon to assist with Middle-East peacekeeping—with tragic loss of life from a terrorist bombing in October 1983 (241 U.S. Marines killed). Two days later the little island nation of Grenada was invaded by three thousand U.S. Marines to topple a new Marxist regime. Several Caribbean nations participated in token ways and were said to have originally invited the U.S. military involvement. The Socialist government of Grenada had allowed Cuba and the Soviet Union to introduce military equipment and build an airfield. President Reagan said that the U.S. was acting to protect the safety of about 1,000 Americans on Grenada; in addition, he surely judged that the very shores of the United States could be endangered if the growing circumstance on Grenada was not stopped. The U.S. paid a price. Eighteen American soldiers were killed in the process and the U.S. had to veto a resolution of the United Nations Security Council condemning the invasion. The U.N. General Assembly voted 108 to 9 (27 abstentions) to "deeply

---

[22]On March 30, 1981, returning to his car after giving a routine speech at the Washington Hilton, President Reagan was shot by John Hinckley, Jr., who fantasized that his dramatic deed would impress a particular movie actress with whom he was infatuated. The life-threatening seriousness of the President's injury was not known by the public at first. But this seventy-year-old man was strong, fortunate, and returned to the White House on April 11, having survived what in 1963 had been so tragic in the case of John Kennedy. In 1982, Hinckley was judged "not guilty" of this attempt on the president's life "by reason of insanity," raising a public outcry about the nation's "softness on criminals."

deplore" the invasion, calling it a "flagrant violation of international law." The American public was generally supportive of the strong action of a popular president, and even international opinion softened when the Cuban/Soviet military build-up on the island became apparent.

Terrorism, however, proved harder to handle and more easily gained international sympathy and support. On December 21, 1988, Pan Am flight 103 had just left London on its way to New York when, at 31,000 feet over Lockerbie, Scotland, it exploded, killing 259 people on the plane and another 11 on the ground. Soon the investigation evidence pointed to a bomb, presumably planted on the plane by two men from Libya. That nation refused to surrender them for trial in the United Kingdom or the United States, leading the United Nations Security Council to place strict sanctions on the country—sanctions which are still in effect years later.

Although a key goal of Ronald Reagan had been to reassert America's prominence in the world, the nation's mounting financial problems were a troublesome issue worldwide. Further, in 1989 *Time* magazine passed by Ronald Reagan and instead named the Soviet Union's Mikhail Gorbachev "Man of the Decade." Reagan had been an ardent opponent of communists everywhere; but it was Gorbachev who helped directly to encourage the collapse from within of the "evil empire" of Reagan's rhetoric (see below). George Bush, Reagan's two-term vice-president, defeated Democrat Michael Dukakis in the presidential election of 1988 by carrying forty of the fifty states. Through Bush, the Reagan decade would proceed to the end of the 1980s and beyond.

Mixing Nostalgia, Escapism, and Faith

Weary of the pervasive pessimism of the 1970s, Americans in the 1980s, especially the newly affluent baby boomers, wanted to enjoy themselves again. The economy improved early into the decade and money really began to flow in 1984. The film industry focused on big-budget adventure spectacles designed like giant thrill rides that provide pure escapist fun. In 1985 Madonna's *Material Girl* video showed the starlet swathed in mink and fluttering greenbacks. Tom Wolfe's best-selling novel *The Bonfire of the Vanities* (1987) centered on a yuppie[23] financier who imagined himself "Master of the Universe" while he was going broke on $1 million a year.

---

[23]A "Yuppie" was a young, urban professional, the symbol of living affluently in "the fast lane." A ready symbol was Jerry Rubin, onetime radical activist against the Vietnam War who began working on Wall Street in the late 1970s. Millions of the radicals of the 1960s were growing more pro-establishment by the 1980s. Financial power and economic security were coming to be seen as good goals after all.

The youth culture began being impacted by the appearance in 1982 of a new cable television network called MTV (music television). It featured video clips to accompany popular songs. Many of these clips either were or bordered on being vulgar, tasteless, and/or violent—delighting teenagers and often offending their parents. While the youth watched MTV, parents (especially the men) often were glued to televised college and professional sports events that were becoming very big business, largely through expanding television contracts. In 1982 television revenue provided $14 million a year per team in the National Football League. By 1990 the per-team annual payout was $26 million. In 1988 CBS agreed to pay $1.1 billion to televise four years of professional baseball. While ABC paid a mere $25 million to televise the 1976 Summer Olympics from Montreal, NBC would pay $401 million for the right to broadcast the 1992 Summer Games from Barcelona. Economics were threatening to overcome sport. The sad shift was symbolized by this comment from Oakland Raiders managing partner Al Davis: "Just win, baby." Winning is what sells television advertising, keeps viewers in front of their sets, and enables the paying of huge salaries to the players. Such was the 1980s.

Television also served science and religion in new ways. A scientist, Carl Sagan, hosted a popular TV series called *Cosmos*, followed by his 1980 best-selling nonfiction book by the same name. He was an able and enthusiastic scientist with personality who initiated tens of millions of American viewers into his perspective on the wonders of space and the deepest questions about the origin and nature of the universe. Sagan was joined later in the decade by Stephen Hawking whose *A Brief History of Time* was the nonfiction bestseller of 1988. Again, a highly respected scientist was reflecting on "the great problem of being—its source, nature, and destiny or (to put it in physical terms) the origin, evolution, and fate of our universe." Obviously, the reading public had real interest in such reflections. Who are we humans in the now-known vastness of space? What really is our origin and destiny? Given the now common "modernist" assumption that the proper role of science is to explain the world without recourse to the divine, some readers were made uncomfortable when Hawking mentioned a "creator" on various occasions in his book.

Several Christian "celebrities" began using television effectively, and they were not uncomfortable at all with a "Creator" hypothesis. Some insisted that true believers could overcome by faith the recently troubled economy and the still despairing society. Believing in Jesus presumably can make one "healthy, wealthy, and wise," they often preached and unfortunately modeled to excess.

Such flamboyant success was portrayed to large television audiences, especially by Tammy and Jim Bakker. Jim, former leader of the *PTL* ("Praise the Lord") program, was sentenced in 1989 to 45 years in prison and fined $500,000 for fraud and conspiracy convictions.[24] Another TV evangelist, Jimmy Swaggart, denounced the moral permissiveness of the society, only to stumble in his own moral failures. Very large audiences watched regularly as Robert Schuller's *Hour of Power* originated from a "glass cathedral" in California. A less flamboyant and more politically inclined conservative television commentator and fundamentalist preacher was Marion "Pat" Robertson, host of TV's the *700 Club*. He would leave his TV ministry briefly to seek the presidency of the United States in the 1988 election. Television "surfing" was becoming one of America's favorite leisure-time activities. Many new channels now were available, and religious evangelists were not all that was being shopped for by the public.

The Christmas season came to symbolize the society's material preoccupation. When remembrance of the birth of the lowly Jesus approached, the country's annual shopping frenzy was let loose. In 1990 Americans spent some $39 billion on Christmas gifts. Clearly Christmas had been transformed from a hallowed celebration of the servant Christ to an orgy of consumer goods purchased to fulfill nearly every wish. The real action had moved from the church to the marketplace, with Christmas now an American festival of abundance and indulgence. In only a five-year period across the middle of the 1980s, the 91 million U.S. households bought 105 million color television sets, 88 million cars and light trucks, 63 million VCRs, and 62 million microwave ovens. It was the biggest spending spree since the one that followed the end of World War II. While stuck in traffic, riding in an airplane, or sitting in a restaurant, people now were commonly seen with cellular telephones held to their ears. Common also were medical CAT scans and recreational "virtual reality" experiences (computer assisted, of course). Shopping malls expanded and other buying options appeared. Mail-order outlets, telemarketing, and home computer services started bringing buying

---

[24]Jim Bakker released his book *I Was Wrong* (Nashville: Thomas Nelson) in 1996. In 1989 he had been convicted on 24 counts of defrauding the public, specifically 114,000 of his followers, by selling them $1,000 lifetime "partnerships," lodging rights at Heritage USA religious theme park in South Carolina. He had oversold the lodging units and used some of the funds to pay PTL operating expenses and support a lavish personal lifestyle. His 45-year sentence was later reduced as excessive and then he was paroled in 1994. In the book, he renounced his earlier preaching of a gospel of prosperity for believers and reported that he also was wrong about this awful era of his life being the end of his ministry. God plans productive futures even amid terrible mistakes.

right to the homes of busy Americans. The home-shopping industry grew in sales from about $1 million in 1982 to $1.4 billion by 1989. "Plastic" money (credit cards) helped fuel the explosion of consumer debt during the decade.

Some observers criticized this frantic marketplace activity as irresponsible overconsumption.[25] Disposability was clearly now the golden goose that was promoting markets always hungry for more, different, better, and new. It seemed like throw-away products satisfied something in the modern temperament. The pace of change was dizzying and exhilarating, causing John Rader Platt of the University of Chicago to conclude:

> The needs of man, if life is to survive, are usually said to be four— air, water, food, and, in the severe climates, protection. But it is becoming clear today that the human organism has another absolute necessity.... This fifth need is the need for novelty—the need, throughout our waking life, for continuous variety in the external stimulation of our eyes, ears, sense organs, and all our nervous network.[26]

Was the consumption of ever-new disposables feeding primordial human hungers, or were the hungers themselves created by a marketplace itself hungry for constant consumers? The country was having a huge party and leaving the bill for future generations. President Reagan could take credit for curbing inflation and expanding economic activity, but at the expense of a huge federal deficit and an alarming trade imbalance with other nations. The United States shifted from the largest creditor nation in 1980 to the largest debtor nation by 1986! The federal deficit, $90 billion in 1982, soared to $283 billion in 1986. Half of the new jobs being created paid wages below the poverty line for a family of four. The society was pressing fast toward two tiers of citizens, those doing quite well indeed and the rest just trying to survive.

Even so, the splurge continued. The nation's founders in the 1700s tended to see luxury as a vice associated with decadence and colonial rule. Now, however, it seemed that Americans were being taught to love luxury, to think of it as a reward for success (For instance, in the 1980s the economic policies of Ronald Reagan were sometimes blamed for creating an overinflated art market with spiraling prices and egos. Freshly fueled by technological advances, the prime symbol of expensive social status, soon to be judged a "necessity," was the flood into homes and workplaces of the computer. In late 1982 more than 1,000 computer companies gathered in the Las Vegas Convention Center to show off their floppy discs, disc drives, joy sticks, and

---

[25]See, for instance, Benjamin Friedman, *Day of Reckoning* (N.Y.: Random House, 1988).

[26]John Rader Platt, "The Fifth Need of Man," *Horizon 1* (July 1959), 106.

modems to a mob of about 50,000 buyers, middlemen, and technology buffs. Children now were routinely learning the meaning of bit, byte, ram, ROM, CPU, and software. The long American love affair with the automobile and television set were being challenged by a giddy new passion for the little box with amazing abilities to produce fun and profit and encourage learning. These "toys" were expensive, but becoming more useful and alluring by the week. Already in 1980 Alvin Tofler had portrayed the coming 21st century as a time in which the computer revolution would have canceled out a fundamental change brought by the Industrial Revolution—centralization and standardization of work in factories, offices, and assembly lines.[27] Whole new options already were emerging.

Naturally there would emerge a counter-cultural movement among some of the young. In the 1980s it was "heavy metal" music. Bands like Motley Crue and AC/DC became popular, featuring very loud electronic guitars, a thumping bass, and almost deafening percussion. Denounced often as socially and spiritually destructive of basic American values because of its shocking language and almost cultic preoccupation with the darker side of life, one interpreter was more generous: "Its main selling points are that adults find it unlistenable, preachers call it blasphemous, and Tipper Gore blushes reading the lyrics…. For all the anthemic raunch, horror-show make-up, and well-planted whispers of Satanism, heavy metal's only discernible message is party hearty."[28] Without the obnoxious cover of glaring sight and sound, "party hearty" is really what many mainstream adults were doing in their more socially acceptable ways.

One example was the 1984 Summer Olympics hosted by the United States in Los Angeles. Even though more than a dozen communist countries stayed away in political protest, for the U.S. these Games were a dramatic success in almost every way. Peter Ueberroth became *Time* magazine's "Man of the Year" for 1984 because of his skilled organizational leadership in planning the Games. The Olympics torch was carried across the country, fueling mass involvement and growing pride. Americans saw themselves proudly and confidently running away from the gloom, gas shortages, recessions, dishonest presidents, and frustrated impotence abroad, carrying high the light of a better day. They were running into a new future of extravagant national pride and optimistic assertion not seen in a generation. "Go for it!" was the official cheer of 1984. The Games, including their great media hype, were a

---

[27]Alvin Tofler, *The Third Wave* (N.Y.: Morrow, 1980).
[28]David Handelman, in *Rolling Stone* magazine (August 11, 1987), 36.

ringing success, with the U.S. capturing 83 gold medals and feeling good about itself again. In fact, "the whole country in the middle 1980s seemed at peace with itself—proud of its strengths, accepting of its diversity and tolerant even of those once regarded as deviants, yet more restrained and tradition-minded in its personal life."[29]

Another counterculture movement was intended to help millions feel good about themselves by being "religious" in a presumably "modern" and timely way. This movement, known popularly as "New Age," broke into the American mainstream in the mid-1980s, especially in 1987 when actress Shirley MacLaine brought her own story of New Age reincarnation to television in a mini-series. Key supporters of this movement were baby boomers, many of whom had left traditional churches but still felt the need for some kind of self-transforming faith and community. Here seemed to be a way to experience hope after giving up on more conventional faith. What was so appealing in New Age was at least its nonthreatening rituals of meditation and yoga that could be practiced on commuter trains and in high-rise offices for focus and relaxation, its reassuring message of self-love, its mystical music that often drew on Christian vocabulary without the restrictions and responsibilities of a Christian worldview, its permission to be an individual in a world of dehumanizing corporate giants, and its seeming political relevance in the face of the rule of Reaganism. Many of its diverse adherents issued a new call to end nationalism, oppose nuclear weapons, and expand environmental awareness. In fact, this "faith" option offered the supposed opportunity to again become one with oneself, one's neighbors, and one's physical and spiritual environment.[30]

Featuring belief in reincarnation, communication with the dead, spiritual healing, out-of-body experiences, even astrology for the highly educated (!), New Agers were drinking deeply (although often unknowingly) of Eastern religious traditions, particularly Buddhism and its predecessor, Hinduism. In the breakneck pace and rank materialism of the 1980s, many people embraced New Age as a spiritual therapy that they hoped would relieve stress and provide some inner peace. Participants typically spoke in subjective and pleasure-oriented terms: "The Maharishi is really *cool*." "Transcendental Meditation gives me a natural high." "The Rev. Moon makes me

---

[29]Michael Barone, 1990, 654.

[30]One Christian critic of the New Age movement speaks of it as a new irrationalism. Noting that "postmodernism" assumes that there is no objective truth, it has "opened up a Pandora's box of New Age religions, syncretism, and moral chaos" (Gene Veith, Jr., *Postmodern Times*, Wheaton, Ill.: Crossway Books, 1994, 192-193).

feel really good about myself." Obviously this modern spirituality was reacting to humanly deadening aspects of modern times in the Western world. It was a celebration of the self, a reaching for relational depth in contrast to what many were experiencing as a mechanical mass society.[31]

The opposite of the syncretistic New Age movement was a conservative turn among key leaders of the 15-million member Southern Baptist Convention, the largest Protestant denomination in the country. With the election in 1981 of Bailey Smith as SBC president, there emerged a new era that tried to make belief in an "inerrant" Bible the litmus test of Christian orthodoxy. With this fundamentalistic religious resurgence came much mixing of faith and political activity among Christians through organizations like the Moral Majority of Rev. Jerry Falwell. This would lead to conflicting public images and, when coupled with the poor ethical examples of a few very visible television evangelists, a falling credibility of religious leaders in the public eye. The 1980s saw widely publicized scandals related to televangelists like Jim Bakker and Jimmy Swaggart. A Gallup poll in 1987[32] showed clearly that these two were less favorably received then than a few years before—and so were others like Jerry Falwell, Pat Robertson, Robert Schuller, and Rex Humbard. Only Billy Graham was unaffected. Compared to a similar study in 1980, far fewer of those surveyed in 1987 were inclined to believe that such televangelists really cared about people, were honest, had a special relationship with God, and could be trusted with money sent in response to their frequent appeals.

In the J-M class of 1959, for example, Mac became upset about his son attending a fundamentalist Bible college, while classmate Jim's proudest moment of life would be having two children graduate together from a conservative Christian university. Jim has a strong belief in God and is active in a church; Mac does not believe in organized religion, although he admits that there may be something like the "Force" in *Star Wars*. Numerous class members had drifted away from the church roots of their childhoods, now calling themselves still strong believers in God, just non-joiners. A few by their middle fifties were clearly non-traditional believers for the historic Jewish-Christian setting of the United States. Betty had shifted from Christian (Baptist) to Hindu identity through marriage, and John, now a mental health counselor and massage therapist in the Youngstown, Ohio, was searching for relatedness to the "universal spirit," an inclusive search through comparative

---

[31]For an excellent study, see Paul Heelas, *The New Age Movement* (Cambridge, Mass.: Blackwell Publishers, 1996).

[32]Gallup Report 259, *Religion in America* (Princeton, N.J., April 1987), 57-58.

Milestones of the Decade

	Best Movie of the Year#	Bestselling Nonfiction Book of the Year	Time Magazine's Person of the Year*
1980	Ordinary People	Cosmos, Carl Sagan	Ronald Reagan, President of U.S.
1981	Chariots of Fire	A Light in the Attic, Shel Silverstein	Lech Walesa, Union Organizer in Poland
1982	Gandhi	Jane Fonda's Workout Book, Jane Fonda	The Computer, "Machine" of the Year
1983	Terms of Endearment	In Search of Excellence, T. Peters, R. Waterman, Jr.	Ronald Reagan and Yuri Andropov, leaders of confronting superpowers
1984	Amadeus	Loving Each Other, Leo Buscaglia	Peter Ueberroth, Summer Olympics in L.A.
1985	Out of Africa	Iacocca: An Autobiography, Lee Iacocca	Deng Xiaoping, China
1986	Platoon	Fatherhood, Bill Cosby	Corazon Aquino, Philippines
1987	The Last Emperor	Spycatcher, Peter Wright	Mikhail Gorbachev, Soviet Union
1988	Rain Man	A Brief History of Time, Stephen Hawking	Earth, "Planet" of the Year
1989	Driving Miss Daisy	All I Really Need to Know I Learned in Kindergarten, Robert Fulghum	Mikhail Gorbachev, "Man of the Decade"

Recipient of the Oscar from the Academy of Motion Picture Arts and Sciences.

* A designation on the part of the editors of Time of the person, people, or thing that, for better or worse, most significantly influenced the course of world events in the preceding twelve months.

TABLE 19

religions and body-mind therapies. Michael was reading with appreciation certain Native American philosophers.

One of the Tom's in the class had fallen away from faith because of the way the world is. To him, religions are "just for show" and evolution makes more sense than creation (his children, however, are baptized Catholics, with a son quite devoted). A few others had a much stronger Christian identification in their fifties than in earlier life. For example, Stan "got saved" and now is very active in a Baptist church not far from his high school. Another Tom is active in the same congregation as Stan and believes strongly in the full authority of the King James Version of the Bible. Jim, an angry and rebellious young man when in high school, was now witnessing joyfully in the Youngstown area as a pentecostal and fundamental Christian. Barry is a Christian minister and university professor of Christian Studies, more devoted to his faith than he was in childhood.

The best-selling *Resident Aliens* sought a fresh way of conceiving religious life in terms both traditionally Christian and based on the assumption that the church now must function at odds with an un-Christian United States. A way was projected that offered potential for Christians to regain their vitality and capacity to nourish hungry souls and stand effectively against the illusions, pretensions, and eroding values of the world of the 1980s. This way was not primarily getting true believers to be politically active, said to be a sure path to being corrupted and silenced by the dominant secular culture. Rather:

> We argue that the political task of Christians is to be the church rather than to transform the world…. The church doesn't have a social strategy, the church *is* a social strategy…. We would like a church that again asserts that God, not nations, rules the world, that the boundaries of God's kingdom transcend those of Caesar, and that the main political task of the church is the formation of people who see clearly the cost of discipleship and are willing to pay the price…. The church exists today as resident aliens, an adventurous colony in a society of unbelief.[33]

A prominent religious historian insists that the passing of "Christian America" is a blessing as well as a tragedy. On the positive side:

> So long as Protestants in the States and in English Canada or Catholics in Quebec thought that the land belonged to them, the temptation to view themselves as gods—to live by sight instead of faith—was

---

[33]Stanley Hauerwas and William Willimon, *Resident Aliens: Life in the Christian Colony* (Nashville: Abingdon Press, 1989), 38, 43, 48-49.

nearly irresistible. But now, with these Christian establishments most-ly a memory, there are blessings to count as well as vanishing monu-ments to mourn. Now Catholic, Orthodox, and the full spectrum of Protestants might learn from each other as fellow-believers instead of fearing each other as antagonists with turf to protect. Freed from the burden of American messianism, churches may find it possible to con-centrate more on the Source of Life than on the American Way of Life.[34]

Dying Social Assumptions

In all of this searching, spending, shifting, believing, and disbelieving, several widely treasured social assumptions of the United States were being brought into sharp question. Little would remain the same. Like Europeans in a prior generation, events now were causing many Americans to question the inevitability of social progress and the role of the U.S. as the leader of renewal in the world, almost a given since World War II. Summarizes one his-torian:

> Indeed, by the late 1980s, a consensus had emerged across the ide-ological spectrum that "something" had gone wrong. Writers on the left (Christopher Lasch), the right, especially the Christian right (Francis Schaeffer), and from the academic center (Robert Bellah) agreed that America was adrift. There seemed to be no clear pattern to events that people would call progressive, and there seemed to be a great deal that threatened stability. Moreover, America had seen itself as a nation of "doers," but now other forces impinged and threatened independence of action. Now they were being done-to rather than doing.[35]

Appearing in 1985 was a major study of American society, possibly the best since David Riesman's *The Lonely Crowd* classic of the 1950s. This new *Habits of the Heart* probed the mix of traits apparently functioning at the core of the American character in the 1980s. Focusing not on the economic losers of the industrial closings, but on the "winners," those at least on the surface appear-ing to be living the "American Dream," a troubling condition emerged. Those doing well financially were nonetheless struggling "spiritually." The authors concluded that Americans, often restricted to a vocabulary of fierce individ-ualism, had largely lost the ability to make adequate moral sense of their own lives. They often faced the dilemma of finding a way to relate the haunting

---

[34]Mark Noll, *A History of Christianity in the United States and Canada* (Grand Rapids: William B. Eerdmans, 1992), 552.

[35]Ronald Wells, *History Through the Eyes of Faith* (HarperSanFrancisco, 1989), 223-224.

aloneness of their aggressive self-seeking to their urgently felt need for the experience of being in a real community where mutual commitment prevails. The common fact found by this study was that few Americans had found "a life devoted to 'personal ambition and consumerism' satisfactory, and most are seeking in one way or another to transcend the limitations of a self-centered life."[36] For most of those people studied, lost was the biblical ideal of self-in-society under the sovereignty of God—and the vacuum thus created was unfulfilling at best.

The disturbing movie *The Big Chill* (1983) pictured well the inner vacuum and quiet tragedy of the 1980s and yet today. Seven college housemates from the 1960s had drifted apart and each had experienced in their separate ways the coldness of the "real" world. Each had entered adulthood as nonconformists and, ironically, most now belonged to one establishment or another. They had been calmed into complacency by material success in their thirties. Stunned by the death of a dear friend of theirs (unexplained suicide), they reunited for the funeral and a few nostalgic days together. They quickly sensed their own mortality and their loss of innocence and idealism. Each reached awkwardly to reestablish an old bond, to grasp some meaning, to fulfill some fantasy, before they separated again, probably forever. The film's feeling is one of quiet desperation, tragic confusion, a sad lostness.

It wasn't until the 1980s that the "me" generation of the 1960s realized the long-term folly of attempting happiness through unfettered liberty. Those who had spent so long defining themselves as *not* their parents now had an identity crisis of their own. Further, they now had children who were beginning to inherit some of the results of earlier extremes of their parents. For instance: "Our high divorce rate, our drug excesses, our preoccupation with material goods…we had all the fun, they [the children] got the hangover; the busted families, the shopping malls, the AIDS virus."[37] This new virus certainly led to more monogamy and condom use. Probably for economic reasons mainly, people also were getting married at a later age. In 1970 the median age at which women first married was 20.8 years; by 1993 it had risen to 24.5 years, with men at 26.5. Whenever they did marry, there now were basic questions being raised and old assumptions challenged. Is "free sex"

---

[36]Robert Bellah, et. al., *Habits of the Heart: Individualism and Commitment in American Life* (Regents of the University of California, 1985, reprint, Harper & Row), 290.

[37]*Life* magazine, July, 1996, 12. The bestselling nonfiction book of 1986 was *Fatherhood* by comedian-educator Bill Cosby (Doubleday). Charming and amusing, Cosby attempted to highlight what it takes to be a good father in a culture full of troubled families and negative moral forces.

really free? Could people really spend and play their way to happiness? What is a "family" and is there anything sacred about it? Were there really the "good old days" to which frustrated people now could and should return? Is economic security a thing of the past for most families and the nation itself?

One social assumption dying rapidly was a legacy of the 1960s. "Free sex" turned out to be not really free after all. By the mid-1980s the general nature and cause of a deadly new virus was known. This virus rendered one's immune system largely inoperable and opportunistic infections likely. AIDS quickly became part of the public's vocabulary and daily dread. It was transmitted through bodily fluids, especially blood and semen. This explained why most victims in the early 1980s were homosexuals and intravenous drug users who shared needles. Much of mainstream America had limited sympathy for those whose "deviant" lifestyles caused them to deserve their unfortunate fates. Patrick Buchanan, conservative spokesman who served as White House director of communications, referring to what initially was viewed as the "gay disease," said that homosexuals had "declared war on nature, and now nature is extracting an awful retribution."

Numerous religious commentators even saw this new scourge as divine judgment on the promiscuous lifestyles that had been leading Americans astray since at least the 1960s. Most citizens could afford to be indifferent if not judgmental since they saw themselves and those they loved in no danger. Sexual abstinence and/or monogamous relationships gained renewed respect, if only for self-protection. Condoms and free needles began to be given away free in some high schools and public centers, creating much controversy. Do such giveaways encourage their related activities or only protect those who would have participated regardless? The AIDS death of Rock Hudson in 1985 and then Liberace in 1987 began a long list of infected celebrities that really caught the public's attention. The problem was spreading to heterosexuals and scientific research of causes and possible treatments accelerated. By the end of the decade, some ten million people worldwide had become infected. Known deaths in the U.S. from AIDS rose from none before 1981 to an alarming 36,000 in 1992 alone.

Schools tried to help with sex education programs. While this was controversial enough, a more central question was troubling the country's educational system. Did Americans as a nation still believe anything together on which they could build a viable educational curriculum? The bestselling nonfiction work of 1987 was Allan Bloom's *The Closing of the American Mind*. He characterized the young of the time as a barbaric lot reflecting an American society that had lost its way. The central problem was said to be that "openness [radical relativism]... is the great insight of our times." Such openness, always claiming to be generous and wise, now had become the biggest danger to society itself. Barely tolerated was the "true believer" in anything— other than the rightness of unfettered tolerance of whatever does not directly threaten public safety. The aim, instead of seeking what is right, had become "not to think you are right at all."[38] What one finds acceptable for oneself never should be thought of as necessarily right for anyone else.

If every educational system has a moral goal that informs its curriculum, a certain kind of human being and society thought ideal, what is left of education if there are no commonly shared goals, no common vision of the public good other than all people being a law unto themselves? If freedom is to be the only absolute, then the traditional motive for education, the search for and enabling the good life, is bankrupt. The souls of the young have become impoverished. The basis for a meaningful society is nearly gone. We seem left only with the overwhelming dominance of material ambition. Television tends to hold people by a sheer succession of sensations, one being as good as another if it distracts and entertains adequately.

Another assumption of popular American culture obviously now in jeopardy was the traditional belief that the family is a sacred unit of society and is to be defined as a husband, wife, and their children. *The Cosby Show* (1984-1992) was a refreshing television exception to the seeming collapse of morality and even civility. It reminded older viewers of the enormously popular television sitcom *Father Knows Best* in the 1950s and 1960s, except that now the actors were African-Americans, the wife was a career woman— sometimes *mother* knew best, sexual matters could be spoken of openly, and the setting had moved from a small town to an urban townhouse. Still portrayed, however, was the image of a "normal" nuclear family.[39] Dorothy, Maureen, and Tom, all from the J-M class of 1959, each went through divorces in the 1980s after having been married for twenty-three years. When interviewed in 1996, each had remained single and spoke with conviction about the country's urgent need to recover stable families for today's children. Said Maureen, for instance: "Parenting requires a mother at home. If you are going to have children, stay home and rear them. Life involves some real commitments." The pain was real and loss of the ideal was recognized.

---

[38]Allan Bloom, *The Closing of the American Mind* (N.Y.: Simon and Schuster, 1987), 26-27.

[39]See June and Timothy Frazer, "Father Knows Best and The Cosby Show: Nostalgia and the Sitcom Tradition," *Journal of Popular Culture* (Winter, 1993), 163-172.

More typical, unfortunately, than this call for commitment, civility, and "normality" were the influential television sitcoms *Roseanne* and *Dallas*. The blue-collar family comedy *Roseanne* featured kids who weren't perky Bradys or impish Cleavers. They smoked, swore, took drugs, and engaged in sexual activity almost at will. Their parents often were cynical, rude, crude, and unfaithful. Then there was *Dallas*. This extraordinarily popular adult TV soap opera aired on CBS from 1978 to 1991. It regularly attracted viewing audiences of 30-40 million Americans and also was watched by millions more outside the United States. Weekly episodes of *Dallas* usually centered on the Ewing family, modern Texans who wallowed in big money, oil, greed, betrayal, sex, and power. Larry Hagman played J. R., the conniving, unscrupulous, unfaithful eldest son. Given the recession of the late 1970s and early 1980s, maybe people with no extra cash enjoyed staying home and being entertained by rich and obnoxious characters. The final episode of the 1979-80 season saw J. R. mysteriously shot. A summer of media hype about "who shot J. R." was resolved on November 21, 1980, when eighty percent of all TV viewers tuned into *Dallas*, some 350 million people in 57 countries! They all wanted to learn the identity of the fictional killer of this fictional character.

The environment was one of media hype, special effects enabled by new technologies, and pure nostalgia. Numerous old images and ideas got recycled. The dollar bottom-line and blockbuster mentality of Hollywood was a boon to the special-effects industry, with some big box-office movies apparently only excuses to show off computerized technology or to merchandise toys. Steven Spielberg and George Lucas were responsible for producing and/or directing six of the top ten moneymakers of the decade. The nostalgia was very evident in the pop songs of aging baby boomers like Bruce Springsteen ("My Hometown," 1985, and "Glory Days," 1985), George Harrison ("All Those Years Ago," 1981), and the Grateful Dead ("Touch of Grey," 1987). The 1960s were being idealized and the shallowness and emptiness of the 1980s was being lamented. With it all, Reagan-inspired nostalgia and a new taste for elegance and style made old-time crooners Frank Sinatra, Dean Martin, and Tony Bennett popular again.

One more classic American assumption weakening during this decade was the economic superiority of the United States. The country, for all its rhetoric and lavish spending, was experiencing larger and larger trade imbalances and was trying to face the fact that it had lost the Vietnam War and no longer was the most prosperous country in the world. Assured economic well-being was a fragile and fleeting ideal for numerous Americans—right in the middle of all the flowing money. Bill had gone to work right out of high school in 1959. The job was in the big steel plant in Warren where his father had excellent, well-paying, and long-term employment. The arrangement for this 18-year-old was that 30 years of employment would lead to retirement with a good pension beginning at age 48. But by the late 1970s the rules had changed. Bill now would have to work until age 65 for what previously had been available at 48. Worse yet, there was no guarantee that the job itself would last that long. So he began looking south for an option. His father had idealized warm-weather Florida, but had died before he could act on his dream. Bill determined not to wait too long. In 1979, he and his wife bought a small structure situated in a little orange grove that was crying for attention. Life would be simpler, more austere, but at least stable. They wanted to "get out of the rat race up North."

Menace of Global Anarchy

The instability in the U.S. was tied to global realities. Something happened on April 26, 1986—a major accident at reactor number four of the Chernobyl nuclear power facility in the northern Ukraine. Big explosions sent radioactive material 36,000 feet into the air. It was a total core meltdown that burned for nine days. Radiation levels nearly twenty percent above normal were soon being recorded as far away as Sweden, with slight elevations even measurable in North America. More than 335,000 people in the Soviet Union were displaced from their homes, with at least 125,000 dead by 1995. Nearby cities were abandoned long-term and cleanup was estimated at $360 billion. Later the reactor itself was encased in a concrete sarcophagus, a drastic but necessary feat of engineering, and a tourist company started booking tours of Chernobyl. This was a little taste of what had worried people ever since that first atomic blast in 1945. Similar events easily could create global anarchy in a matter of hours.

Unfortunately, it nearly happened again, with potentially worse results. In October 1986, an aging Soviet submarine, loaded with nuclear missiles capable of massive destruction, was patrolling menacingly just off the East Coast of the United States. Something went wrong. The K-219 soon would plunge into the depths, crippled and lost. She came within minutes of a nuclear meltdown at sea. If her reactors had exploded, the radiation that would have released into the Gulf Stream would have dwarfed the Chernobyl disaster. An on-board explosion had disabled a missile and forced open a silo hatch to the open sea. A trailing U.S. submarine feared the worst, that a missile had been launched at the U.S. It prepared to do its job—quickly kill the enemy attacker. But it became clear that K-219 had not launched World War III, but was

A giant volcanic eruption blew the entire top off of Mount St. Helens in 1980, spewing ash over much of the American Northwest. It was a dramatic symbol of a fragile and sometimes frightening world.

fighting for its life. It would lose, but at least war and environmental disaster were avoided.[40]

If the dangerous rhetoric, saber-rattling, and alarming accidents related to the Cold War were not enough, two other menaces of global proportions threatened widespread disaster during the decade of the 1980s. One was severe environmental neglect and the other the rise of dangerous fundamentalisms. In 1980 Mount St. Helens blew off its top, killing 57 people and spewing volcanic ash over a vast area of the American Northwest. Then in 1983 scientists studying the stratosphere over the South Pole were shocked to find sharp decreases in ozone, a gas that helps shield the earth from damaging ultraviolet radiation. Little can be done about volcanic eruptions, but many excesses of modern life could be curbed to help with the pollution and even destruction of the atmosphere in which humans exist. The very place of human existence was under daily attack by human lifestyle excesses. The usual "Man of the Year" award of *Time* magazine went in 1988 to the Earth, "Planet of the Year." Something had to be done to protect the little home of humanity in the vastness of space. Sprawling Mexico City was being called an "urban apocalypse" because its crushingly large population often was covered by a fog of pollution that made flying into it like descending into a mist of

---

[40]For the whole story of this frightening incident, see Peter Huchthausen, et al, *Hostile Waters* (N.Y.: St. Martin's Press, 1997).

human excrement. Then the world shuddered in March 1989, when a super-tanker, the *Exxon Valdez*, ran aground and leaked eleven million gallons of crude oil into Prince Edward Sound, Alaska, one of the world's richest wildlife areas. It was an ecological disaster that wind and tides soon had covering about 600 square miles. Could life itself survive human greed and carelessness?

With the well-being of the Earth itself in question, the political relationships among its diverse peoples greatly added to the problem. Several countries in the 1980s were experiencing the collapse of their structural and spiritual cohesion, breaking down into tribes, clans, death squads, terrorist movements, and rabid self-interest groups. The borders of several nations no longer were holding. Many of them had been assigned by the victorious powers after World War II, often without adequate regard to tribal and religious rivalries and hatreds existing for centuries. One tragic example of the results would be Yugoslavia. The Winter Olympic Games of 1984 were staged in the beautiful area around the city of Sarajevo. In only a few years, however, that region would disintegrate into ugly warfare among its ethnic peoples, drawing the U.S. and several European nations into necessary and costly peacekeeping efforts.

A few years earlier were the tragic examples of Iran and Lebanon. The Ayatollah Khomeini, then living in exile in Paris, called for a *jihad* or "holy war" in Iran against the Shah, his followers, and his Western supporter, the United States. His goal was the eradication of the monarchy, the end of all foreign domination, and the establishment of a strict Islamic republic. Soon it all happened. This 77-year-old religious-political leader returned to Iran in 1979 and unleashed a fury of religious fanaticism. Thousands were executed for "crimes against God," young girls were flogged in the streets for wearing lipstick, and boys as young as ten began to be sent to be soldier "martyrs" against neighboring Iraq, a hated "secular" Islamic state. The United States embassy in Tehran was stormed in November 1979, and fifty-three U.S. citizens became hostages, setting off an international crisis that deeply affected the presidency of Jimmy Carter. By the 1980s there were several such revolutions around the world, each seeking a return to the "purity" of an idealized past or future. In Cambodia an estimated three of seven million residents were brutally murdered. There was the "Shining Light" movement in Peru; certain Sikhs in India who assassinated Prime Minister Indira Gandhi in 1984, demanding their own state; and Islamic "fundamentalists" who killed Egyptian President Anwar Sadat in 1981 because he had dared to make peace with Israel. There were more than two million refugees in the world in 1959,

"World Refugee Year." By 1984 there were ten million refugees receiving international assistance. The world had become a mobile and volatile place.

Lebanon, a small paradise of a country in the Middle East, began to disintegrate into warring factions in the mid-1970s. By the 1980s it had become a hellish turmoil with its latest hatreds imploding the country. Christians and Muslims killed each other with a ferocity not seen since the Crusades. "Palestinians" became an identifiable group, with many of them forced into refugee camps. Syria and Israel had become involved and finally the world community sought a peacekeeping role. But on October 23, 1983, some 300 United States and French troops were killed by a suicide bomber who drove a truck laden with explosives into the U.S. Marine headquarters at the Beirut airport. Within a year all Western forces were pulled out, leaving behind a power vacuum and unsolved problems that would plague the world community for the rest of the century. Barry had enjoyed an archaeological adventure to ancient sites in Lebanon and neighboring countries in 1968 and had been scheduled to return to Beirut in 1975 to participate in a World Conference of his church. The event had to be canceled because of the outbreak of war there. Religiously fueled hatreds were blocking constructive religious efforts.

Beyond contamination of the earth and bloody hatred among many of its peoples, a third source of potential disaster now loomed on the world's horizon. Scientific advances, while impressive, held very negative potential. Splitting the atom had led both to power plants and lethal weapons, lighted cities and devastated cities. Space exploration held such exciting potential, but suffered from the public's lessening tolerance for its very high costs. Then came the tragic explosion of the space shuttle *Challenger* on January 28, 1986. NASA weathered the storm of criticism and renewed flights within three years. Nonetheless, with the horrific meltdown of the Chernobyl power plant also in mind, the safety and wisdom of big science projects was in question.

With this worry came developments in biology that brought new possibilities and moral dilemmas never before faced by humans. "Genetic engineering" was the popular designation for this whole new world of frightening fascination. What if errors or accidents were to occur as happened in the nuclear power and space programs? A genetically engineered virus, for example, might mutate into a toxic plague; modified plant life might destroy the world's food stocks. Worse yet, what about the new potential of modifying the genetic structure of human beings themselves, producing "superhumans" or eradicating a type of human judged undesirable by someone in power?

Surely the world had not already forgotten Nazi Germany and the "final solution" of Hitler's gas chambers. If evil is indeed a reality in human experience, then the positive potential in dramatic scientific advance is always paralleled by frightening negative potential.

These global-scale developments and dilemmas, however, were hardly everyday issues for most Americans. While it was true that relative affluence and leisure time allowed people from the U.S. to be frequent world travelers, they usually chose to be hotel-oriented tourists. Americans were not often given to learning "foreign" languages and studying seriously the international arena. Several members of the J-M class of 1959, for instance, had never traveled more than a few hundred miles from their old high school, and then often only for family vacations in U.S. tourist centers. Other than the clear exceptions of Francis, Betty, Ian, Larry, and Barry,[41] in nearly every case those who had traveled internationally had done so only in connection with their military service in the 1960s.

Concluded David Wallechinsky in 1986: "Americans, on the whole, are frighteningly ill-informed, and especially so about foreign countries, about which most Americans are not only painfully ignorant but also needlessly paranoid."[42] What most Americans were concentrating on was what they perceived to be impacting them directly. For instance, according to the 1990 census, Ohio had 10,847,000 inhabitants, only a very slight increase over the total in 1980. Whites comprised eighty-eight percent of this population. While a major agricultural state, about seventy-four percent of Ohio's people now lived in areas defined as urban. In 1990, whites constituted 49.5 percent of Cleveland's population and blacks 46.6, with the population of the city proper decreasing from 573,800 in 1980 to 505,600 in 1990. Here could be seen the struggle of America's inner cities, the continuing racial tension fueled in large part by economic inequity, and the shifting industrial base that was changing the face of the nation. This is where most Americans tended to really live.

---

[41]Betty had traveled to India several times to visit with her husband's family. Francis at various times had extended work experiences in Australia, Algeria, etc. Ian had lived and studied in New Zealand and Canada. Larry soon would be traveling in Asian countries for his electronics firm. I had visited Australia, China, England, Germany, Japan, Israel, Italy, South Korea, Switzerland, and elsewhere in relation to church work and the international education program of Anderson University (Indiana).

[42]David Wallechinsky, *The Class of '65: Chronicles of an American Generation—Midterm Report* (N.Y.: Viking Penguin, 1986), 415. By contrast, Ian reports that the average student he has encountered in recent years as a faculty member in a university in the Northeast has had a truly global mentality.

When All Foundations Crumble

Looking back now, what happened serves as a revealing symbol. In towering thunderstorms on May 31, 1985, were supercells that at first concealed tornadoes with winds too high to record. This weather system developed to its highest pitch of fury as it moved eastward across Indiana into the area of Northeastern Ohio. Ugly fingers suddenly reached down with a rain of devastation. Right in the path was the Newton Falls High School where many members of the Jackson-Milton class of 1959 had attended as freshmen. What was left would never be used as a high school again. The Jackson-Milton school, just a few miles away, was pressed into service to house people brutally dislocated from what minutes before had helped define their existence. Soon parts of Pennsylvania, New York, and Ontario would come under the same violent attack of nature. The storm was a symbol of what soon would be a shaking of the political world by the collapse of walls that had divided much of humanity for decades. An early warming of the Cold War between the U.S. and the U.S.S.R. came, of all places, from the world of great music.

A lanky, unpretentious, and incredibly gifted pianist from Texas named Van Cliburn took Moscow by musical storm in 1958. He won the first Soviet-sponsored Tchaikovsky International Piano Competition and, at the height of the Cold War, became a beloved and rare bridge between dangerously diverse cultures. He represented to Russians a hope that what they understood to be the evil capitalists of the West may have a humble gentleness and warmth that they had not even imagined possible. His person became a small crack in the awful ice of East-West relations. Then in 1987, more mature than that twenty-three-year-old that captured the Russian heart in 1958, something similar happened again. Van Cliburn was invited to perform at a state dinner where Mikhail and Raisa Gorbachev would be the honored Russian guests of Ronald and Nancy Reagan. Having played beautifully, Cliburn bounded off the platform in the East Room of the White House and kissed the first ladies of the world's two super-powers. Then Mrs. Gorbachev requested that he play something else. He quickly chose "Moscow Nights," one of the beloved Soviet songs he had performed during his first incredible journey to Moscow in 1958. With millions of Americans watching on television, the Gorbachevs quickly joined Van Cliburn in singing as he played, with the whole room of dignitaries dissolving into tears. When the playing and singing ended, Gorbachev, visibly tired from his first full day of summit meetings with Reagan, burst into applause, then came to his feet and embraced the pianist with a bear hug and kisses on both cheeks. Van Cliburn

November 11, 1989—Taking down the Berlin wall, as East German border guards watch from the top of the Branden-berg Gate.

was more than a musical genius. He communicated a simple and rich humanity that was hope itself. The Soviet Union and the United States, for at least a few magic moments, joined voices and hearts. It was a sign of much soon to come on the political scene of the Cold-War world.[43]

The horrors and political results of World War II brought about the shape of the world that had existed ever since. That world, defined largely by the Cold War, began to change radically as the final decade of the 20th century was about to dawn. The change was symbolized by a Tuesday evening in October 1989, when much of the American public turned on their televisions to watch a much-hyped baseball game about to be played in San Francisco. Something, however, was radically wrong. The 58,000 high-spirited specta-tors present in Candlestick Park had watched both teams finish their batting practices. Then some distant rumble had grown louder. The TV cameras were now on so that the whole country could watch the big game. Instead, the sta-dium shuddered and the foul-line poles in left and right fields whipped back and forth. The people were told by bullhorns that there would be no game. As they left in fear and bewilderment, the TV cameras, rather than the

---

[43]For a biography of Van Cliburn, see Howard Reich, *Van Cliburn* (Nashville: Thomas Nelson, 1993).

expected game, were showing the nation a bizarre development. Clouds of smoke could be seen from the stadium. It was the Great Quake of 1989. In some fifteen seconds, an estimated 100 people had been killed and 3,000 more injured in the San Francisco area. Most dramatic was the crumbled concrete of I-880 in Oakland. The upper deck of this busy city highway had collapsed on the lower, flattening some cars to a thickness of only six inches. This was surely no game, no typical TV soap opera. It was harsh reality. For many people the world had shifted very quickly!

Another kind of dramatic shaking was happening in the political world. A key event of this multinational "revolution" happened the following month in Berlin. Since World War II this great city had been divided, with the ugly Berlin Wall first built in 1961 to keep East Germans from escaping to the West. By 1989 the East Germans were no longer content with the broken promises and failed ideals of communism. They had been encouraged by the 1985 coming to power in the Soviet Union of Mikhail Gorbachev. He promised *perestroika* (economic reform, restructuring) and *glasnost* (openness) at home, a cutting of Soviet aid to Third World countries, and a withdrawing of Soviet troops from eastern Europe. Gorbachev gave limited autonomy to the fifteen republics that made up the Union of Soviet Socialist Republics. But events were running ahead of even him and soon the Soviet Union would no longer stay a united and tightly-controlled empire.

Demand for political reform and freedom of travel spread quickly across Eastern Europe. On November 9, 1989, the East German government gave in and opened the borders to West Berlin and West Germany. Crowds surged toward freedom. In West Berlin, East Germans headed for the banks where approximately fifty-four U.S. dollars were given to each as a "welcome to the West." Soon the huge wall was dismantled by gleeful Germans. What had started in the 1940s as a multinational squabble over the spoils of war and had at times escalated into disputes threatening World War III finally ended on October 3, 1990, with the reunification of Germany. Much of the world rejoiced. Apparently the Cold War that had dominated global politics since World War II finally was winding down. At least it no longer would serve as the organizing principle of American and Soviet foreign policies. In December 1991, Gorbachev agreed to dissolve the Soviet Union in favor of the new Commonwealth of Independent States. Much would change rapidly. One major worry in the West was who, if anyone, now had firm control over the numerous nuclear weapons stored in various locations within the Commonwealth. Hopefully, they would not become items on the world's black market! Some declared the Cold War won by an America now fully vindicated. For example: "I must say that the events of 1989—the 'Communist meltdown' in the Soviet Union and Eastern Europe, the brutal massacre in Tiananmen Square [China]—provide additional support...for the proposition that the fundamentals of our system—political democracy, economic freedoms tempered by government protections—really are at the basis of any good society."[44]

For at least Christians and Jews, the following quotation from the Bible tends to anticipate correctly the dilemma of our present time. Psalm 11:3 poses this profound question: "When the foundations are being destroyed, what can the righteous do?" Clearly the experience of recent decades has been one of the culture actively destroying old foundations of truth and morality and trying to build some new foundation on the rubble. Today we actually see the attempt to reject virtually *all foundations* and thus the frustrating and probably ill-fated attempt to live with a radical relativism, avoiding foundational judgments altogether. In the past people often argued about what is right and what is wrong, what is true and what is not. Now people commonly dismiss the very concepts of fixed moral standards and claims to absolute truth. Presumably all such things are just social creations, always changing as society changes. Is a time such as this the right opportunity to finally bury or to finally accept the truly radical claim of the Christian faith? The claim is that the church is "built upon the foundation of the apostles and prophets, with Christ Jesus himself as the cornerstone" (Ephesians 2:20). "Each builder," warned the Apostle Paul, "must choose with care how to build.... For no one can lay any foundation other than the one that has been laid; that foundation is Jesus Christ" (1 Corinthians 3:10-11).

This instinct for a sturdy and enduring foundation for life and society now extends well beyond the borders of the faithful in the Christian church. There is, for instance, a worldwide resurgence of Islam that is crying out in the face of secularized governments. Prophetic voices are daring to speak even in the wilderness of postmodern relativism. The issue was joined clearly in 1978 when Alexander Solzhenitsyn gave the commencement address at Harvard University. He began by invoking Harvard's motto, "Veritas" (Latin for "truth"). He proceeded to excoriate the West's immorality, materialism, and godlessness. The feathers of the intellectual establishment were now ruffled. Soon outrage appeared among the academics. Indignant editorials peppered the liberal media. The *New York Times* scoffed that this man "believes himself to be in possession of The Truth"[45] (an outrageous idea for

---

[44]Michael Barone, *Our Country*, xvi.
[45]"The Obsession of Solzhenitsyn," June 13, 1978.

our times). But Michael Novak called Solzhenitsyn's address "the most important religious document of our time."[46]

The 1980s was a decade in search of fundamentals. Secretary of Education William Bennett called for a return to "excellence" and the fundamentals of education. Allan Bloom argued for a return to the ancient truths still found in the great books of Plato and Saint Augustine.[47] Experiments with "alternative lifestyles" had largely fizzled out in the face of the renewed hope for a realization of "traditional" family structures. Old-time patriotism was in vogue again. Christian fundamentalists were pushing for "Creationism" to replace "Darwinism" in public classroom textbooks, while many families were shifting to private education or even home schooling for their children. Ronald Sider was dramatizing the unacceptable irony of mass starvation in the world and the presence of many rich Christians who seemed somehow to have missed or rationalized the biblical perspecive on the poor and possessions.[48] The Oscar-winning movies *Chariots of Fire* (1981) and *Gandhi* (1982) raised again the options of courageous morality and dramatic self-sacrifice in the face of human greed and social injustice. Apparently the only viable way forward involved a going back to some select basics.

The decade closed with the deaths of two people very much a part of the U.S. way of life since the 1940s, Lucille Ball (1911-1989) and Irving Berlin (1888-1989). For decades the one had made Americans laugh with abandon and the other had enabled Americans to sing with pride.[49] Who or what now would bring joy and harmony to the land? From what source would come credible vision (faith) that could yield adequate foundations for personal and social life in a nation flaunting a fragile economic success and floundering in widening moral confusion?

Living Is Serving

Most Americans in the 1980s reached a fresh level of pride in the nation and relative comfort with Ronald Reagan as their president. When Reagan's loyal vice-president was nominated to replace him in the election of 1988,

---

[46]"On God and Man," in *Solzhenitsyn at Harvard*, ed. Ronald Berman (Washington, D. C.: Ethics and Public Policy Center, 1980), 131.

[47]Allan Bloom, op. cit.

[48]Ronald J. Sider, *Rich Christians In An Age of Hunger* (Downers Grove, Ill.: InterVarsity Press, 1977).

[49]Lucille Ball was the star of the *I Love Lucy* television show (1951-1957) that is still seen regularly on television in the 1990s. Irving Berlin wrote some 1,500 songs, best loved of which are "There's No Business Like Show Business," "God Bless America," "White Christmas," and "Easter Parade."

On Nov. 5, 1994, President Ronald Reagan, then retired and suffering from Alzheimer's disease, wrote the following to "my fellow Americans": "When the Lord calls me home, whenever that may be, I will leave with the greatest love for this country of ours, and eternal optimism for its future. I now begin the journey that will lead me into the sunset of my life. I know that for America, there will always be a bright dawn ahead."

George Bush told the Republican National Convention in New Orleans on August 18, 1988:

> …the most important work of my life is to complete the mission we started in 1980…. Eight years ago, I stood here with Ronald Reagan and we promised, together, to break with the past and return America to her greatness. Eight years later, look at what the American people have produced: the highest level of economic growth in our entire history, and the lowest level of world tensions in more than 50 years…. My friends, eight years ago this economy was flat on its back—intensive care. We came in and gave it emergency treatment—got the temperature down by lowering regulation, got the blood pressure down when we lowered taxes…. This has been called the American century because in it we were the dominant force for good in the world. We saved Europe, cured polio, we went to the moon and lit the world with our culture. Now we are on the verge of a new century, and what country's name will it bear? I say it will be another American century.

Bush's first act as president (during his address at the nation's Bicentennial Inauguration on January 20, 1989) was to offer this prayer:

> Heavenly Father, we bow our heads and thank You for Your love. Accept our thanks for the peace that yields this day and the shared faith that makes its continuance likely. Make us strong to do Your work, willing to heed and hear Your will, and write on our hearts these words: "Use power to help people." For we are given power not to advance our own purposes, nor to make a great show in the world, nor a name. There is but one just use of power, and it is to serve people. Help us to remember it, Lord. Amen.

People dedicated to genuine service to others had hardly been a central characteristic of the 1980s. Early in the decade, a Michelob beer commercial declared that "you can have it all."[50] Many believed this and tried hard to test the limits of outright greed, yielding an ever-wider gulf between the very wealthy and those on the streets with no homes. According to Art Levine, "Even religion became, for many, just another lite commodity. Forget the time-consuming devotion to '70s gurus; salvation and healing could be yours instantly." Further, "as AIDS began to claim more lives than Vietnam, the joy of free sex transmuted into the fear of sex."[51]

Most members of the J-M class of 1959 had come to that time in their lives when they were settled in for the "long haul." While the class now had only fifty living members and about half of them were still living within a twenty-mile radius of the high school, there were members who by now had lived for many years in California, Florida, Indiana, Minnesota, New Mexico, New York, Texas, Vermont, and Virginia. In 1989 one member, Charles, moved from Florida with his wife to a rural setting in Hawaii—they were looking for and found less crowding and crime in this new setting that in many ways was like their original homes in Ohio and Pennsylvania, except that the Pacific Ocean slightly outclassed Lake Milton! Over the years, this class had tended to follow national migration patterns. This was also true of their even more mobile children.

Frank lived next door to the old home of his parents, a semi-rural setting between Craig Beach and Pricetown. Carol, his wife and classmate, enjoyed the fact that both her siblings and children still lived in the immediate area. John's three children were all close by, as were all four of Tom's. Another Tom in the class, now a single man again, had grown up in a house just down the road from Frank. Over the following decades (except for his four years around the world in the military) he had never lived more than a mile away. Nancy was living in the family home her father had built years before in a semi-rural setting near North Jackson and her two grown sons were still with her. More typical of the increasingly mobile society, two of Dorothy's four children were still close to her, but the other two lived in North Carolina and California. Stan's two children were in Ohio and South Carolina and his

---

[50]The tension may be seen in the titles of two top-selling records. The one for 1984 was Tina Turner's *What's Love Got To Do With It?* For 1985 it was the service-oriented *We Are the World* by USA for Africa. Maybe true service for others requires that love has everything to do with it.

[51]Art Levine, in *US News and World Report*, December 25, 1989/January 1, 1990, 112-113.

five stepchildren were scattered in Ohio and Michigan. Jane's three ranged from one living next door (between Lake Milton and North Jackson) to one each in South Carolina and Louisiana. Similarly, Judy's three sons were still close by her and the old high school, while her daughter lived in Colorado. Larry's son lived near him in the prosperous Silicon Valley of California, while his daughter and five grandchildren lived in Florida.

Like the larger society, this mixed picture of settledness and mobility was not without sudden jolts for some, like the dozen or more divorces suffered by members of the J-M class of 1959. Many in this class, then in their mid-forties, were finding ways to rise above the self-serving attitudes and sometimes destabilizing shifts of the general society. Jesse is a good example. A Roman Catholic from North Jackson, Ohio, he and his wife Judy (a classmate) years before had found their way to the State of New York in the service of a large corporation. Now a local Vietnamese priest encouraged Jesse to take formal training for the role of church deacon. He did so on a part-time basis from 1983-1985. It was a time of real testing with an epileptic daughter permanently at home, the company getting into the "downsizing" mood, and his father's death in 1982. Here was something of a new identity for Jesse

RECENT PRESIDENTS
of the
UNITED STATES OF AMERICA

Name	Number	State of Birth	Years of Service
Franklin D. Roosevelt	32nd	New York	1933-1945
Harry S. Truman	33rd	Missouri	1945-1953
Dwight D. Eisenhower	34th	Kansas	1953-1961
John F. Kennedy	35th	Massachusetts	1961-1963
Lyndon B. Johnson	36th	Texas	1963-1969
Richard M. Nixon	37th	California	1969-1974
Gerald R. Ford	38th	Nebraska	1974-1977
Jimmy Carter	39th	Georgia	1977-1981
Ronald Reagan	40th	Illinois	1981-1989
George Bush	41st	Massachusetts	1989-1993
William Clinton	42nd	Arkansas	1993-

TABLE 20

beyond the usual corporate rat race. It was a way of service instead of constant and aggressive ambition, a way that allowed him the unusual and difficult opportunity in 1988 of returning to Northeast Ohio to plan and conduct the funeral of his own mother.

Judy and her husband had settled into a lovely old farmhouse some miles from the North Jackson High School, intending to stay there for life. Because of her settledness and sensitivity to people, she soon was being called on often to be friend and private counselor to a series of neighbors who struggled with various issues of daily life and sometimes death. Charlotte and her husband were running a day-care center for children in Texas. Shirley, now located in Florida, had become "a very strong woman" because as a nurse "I have had to live in a man's world." She had come to own a nursing agency, but soon found it a real struggle. When her husband Charles, a high school classmate, decided to end the marriage and later start a new family in Hawaii, she sold out, went to school to learn to be a professional clown (one way to bring laughter to troubled people), and spent a year on the beach as a "bum" reconnecting with herself and life. Soon she was back in her profession, now helping to set up special units for Alzheimer's patients around Florida. Back in Ohio, classmate Jane recently had chosen to be a practical nurse in a prison setting—a new and freshly fulfilling challenge.

Maybe the society as a whole could somehow get beyond its recent decades of apathy, radicalism, deterioration of national institutions and traditions, failed idealisms, and faulty foundations on which to secure justice, maintain peace, and find personal happiness. Maybe vision and faith could be found again, found in the midst of giving oneself away, a rooted and reasoned faith in the nation itself, in other people, maybe even in God. Maybe. When David Wallechinsky published his "midterm report" in 1986 as part of his ongoing task of chronicling the baby boomer generation (class of 1965), he insisted that he did not find "a generation of hippies turned yuppies and. . .self-indulgent acquirers." What he did find was "far more complex and far more provocative." This class of 1965 "had done some wild and weird things as it had struggled through the first half of its life, but now it is on track and preparing for power."[52] The country certainly needed this power to be used well.

---

[52]Wallechinsky, op. cit., 3, 418.

Taking Time To Reflect

1. Is the government's encouraging of the public's pursuit of self-interest really the best path to a truly good society? Was Ronald Reagan's reversing of Franklin Roosevelt's "New Deal" really a good deal for the U.S.? Did the collapse of communism in 1989 and 1990 "prove" that the American system of government is right for all the world's peoples?

2. Is science the path to a people's justice and prosperity? Given the Chernobyl, K219, and Challenger disasters of 1986, the Pan Am 103 terrorism of 1988, and the new potential of "genetic engineering," what or who can really be trusted? Is "evil" a continuing reality in human experience? Should it be understood in theological as well as political terms?

3. Perception is functional reality for the perceiver. Are we humans socially controlled by the incidentals of where we live and which advertisements we see, editorial "spins" we read, and talk shows we hear? Is there such a thing as "the truth" apart from the maze of limited human perceptions?

4. Given "plastic" money, computers, and the mounting national debt of the 1980s, can people really spend their way to happiness? Can a nation long survive its constant consumption in the present by borrowing from the future?

5. What can be learned from the conviction and imprisonment of Christian evangelist Jim Bakker and the failed presidential candidacies of Pat Robertson and Jesse Jackson? Does too much money corrupt even the best of public leaders? Can an authentic witness to Jesus Christ survive for long in a culture committed to prosperity as the symbol of "success"? Should religion and politics attempt to mix? What about racial identity?

6. Is style a subtle and sinister form of modern social control? Are we humans what we wear or own? Have concrete possibility and short-lived style become hopelessly confused?

7. Does the constant pursuit of material possessions and entertainment finally satisfy the deepest human needs? How did the "New Age" movement try to offer a fresh "faith" option that addresses an obvious emptiness of busy and affluent Americans? Had more traditional faith communities failed to fill this emptiness?

8. Was George Bush right in 1988 when he claimed that the 20th century has been the American century because "in it we were the dominant force for good in the world"? If the U.S. has "lit the world with our culture," has it been a good and enduring light? Why do so many people in the world dislike Americans?

Chapter Seven

The Dim Horizon

1990s

———

As we approach the year 2000, the millennium is reemerging
as a metaphor for the future.... The modern millennium
ignites our vision for a better world—alongside
our nightmares of the world's end.[1]

———

Your ancient ruins shall be rebuilt; you shall raise up the foundations
of many generations; you shall be called the repairer of the breach,
the restorer of streets to live in. (Psalm 58:12)[2]

———

One hundred years ago numerous analysts anticipated the twentieth century with an almost unbridled optimism. This perspective was shared among
Christians, the dominant religious tradition in the United States. Common
slogans were "ever onward and upward," "the evangelization of the world in
our generation," and "the absoluteness of Christianity." A new journal
launched by some broad-minded believers in 1900 was called *The Christian
Century*. Doomsayers were pushed to the margins as industrialization mushroomed and faith in the future was robust. Now, at the end of the twentieth
century, things appear very different. The century once so anticipated has
turned out to be an era of massive brutality and moral meltdown, a most un-

———

[1]John Naisbitt and Patricia Aburdene, *Megatrends 2000: Ten New Directions for the
1990s* (N.Y.: William Morrow, 1990), 16. For Christian perspectives on "millennium," see
Barry Callen, *Faithful In the Meantime* (Nappanee, Ind.: Evangel Publishing House,
1997).

[2]This biblical quotation was highlighted by President Bill Clinton in his State of the
Union address to the United States Congress, February 4, 1997. He commented: "For no
matter what our differences—in our faiths, our backgrounds, our politics—we must all
be repairers of the breach."

Christian century if one judges by the standards of social justice and world peace. The awful word is genocide. Joseph Stalin's genocidal rampage during the 1930s is known as the "Great Purge." Aleksandr Solzhenitsyn[3] has estimated that sixty million Soviets were killed between 1930 and 1938. Soon after, Adolf Hitler began his mass extermination of Jews across Europe. His "final solution" destroyed millions of human beings of various nationalities.

Cambodia in the 1970s suffered some 1.5 million deaths at the brutal hands of the Khmer Rouge. In only ten weeks in 1994, Rwanda lost at least 500,000 of its citizens by ugly killings as one tribe, the Hutus, sought to exterminate another, the Tutsis. Now has come Bosnia, with human nature making it likely that even more is on its way somewhere. Summarized one recent interpreter in a mood of sadness about the way the century actually has gone:

> The Christian century suffocated in the gas chambers at Auschwitz. Compassion was crushed at Pearl Harbor and conscience vaporized in the sky over Hiroshima. Civility bled to death in the fields of Cambodia and was interred in the hills of Bosnia. Back home, the American character was shot from a passing car and lies bleeding in front of a burning church.[4]

The 1990s offered a chance for a much-less-than-ideal century to end on a better note. The chance was hardly a good one, however. From its very beginning, trouble was brewing internationally and culture wars were still raging in the United States. Even nature had its say, with Hurricane Andrew slamming into South Florida in August, 1992, driving a million people from their homes and using its sustained winds of 135 miles an hour to do $15-20 billion worth of property damage—the costliest storm in U.S. history. The J-M class of 1959 had passed their mid-fifties and the oldest of the baby boomers, that "pig in a python" generation, were reaching their fifties. For the society in general, it was not clear whether it was early morning or late evening. There was hope on many fronts, but the light was diffused and the horizon still uncomfortably dim.

Military and Economic Storms

George Bush, who had served for eight years as vice-president alongside an enormously popular President Ronald Reagan, was the country's choice for president in 1988. Americans were generally happy with the status quo,

---

[3]Solzhenitsyn was exiled to Siberia in 1953, won the Nobel Prize for literature in 1970, and completed his famous *Gulag Archipelago* in 1973.

[4]Address by Dr. Eugene F. Roop, President of Bethany Theological Seminary, to the chapel of Anderson University School of Theology, April 23, 1997.

including a leader like Bush who had a gentle public image (said by opponents to be a "wimp") and who said he wanted a "kinder, gentler nation." He was very respected worldwide.[5] The sour Vietnam memory still weighed heavily on America's readiness to get involved again militarily in the problems of others. But, as General Colin Powell said: "One of the fondest expressions around is that we can't be the world's policeman. But guess who gets called when suddenly someone needs a cop?" The call came in August 1990. Iraqi leader Saddam Hussein invaded neighboring and wealthy little Kuwait and shocked the world with the threat of his going on into Saudi Arabia (allowing him to take control of much of the world's oil supply). Ironically, between 1985 to 1990, Iraq had been supported with some $500 million worth of new American technology to strengthen it as a buffer against Iran. Now the tables turned. President Bush condemned this "naked aggression" and declared the integrity of Saudi Arabia a vital American interest. In conjunction with the Security Council of the United Nations, he worked quickly to constitute a 28-nation alliance, including several Islamic countries. "Operation Desert Storm" was unleashed on January 16, 1991, with on-site television coverage, flying cruise missiles, falling "smart bombs," and high-tech stealth bombers helping to bring a stunning military victory within weeks. Kuwait was liberated, although Hussein remained in power as a continuing irritant for American foreign policy.

The stigma of Vietnam now seemed erased. America had again led an international force, like in World War II, in a "righteous" and victorious war. The nagging problem for Bush was on the homefront. While his popularity with the public had skyrocketed as he led the alliance in the Middle East conflict, the American economy was suffering. The savings and loan crisis would have to be bailed out at the immense cost of some $500 billion. The biggest hangover from the binge years of the 1980s, however, was the national debt that had tripled during the Reagan years to some $2.6 trillion. Corporations were "downsizing." Recalling the Great Depression of the 1930s, some analysts called this phenomenon of the 1990s the "Great Compression." One in ten Americans was on food stamps and real estate prices were skidding. On the eve of the 1992 election, just months after the president's impressive popularity because of the Desert Storm victory, Bush's approval rating had sunk from a high of 91 to a mere 36 percent. The 1992 Republican Convention hardly helped. It was dominated by harsh right-wing rhetoric that pushed Bush's image away from the political center. Pat Robertson, for

---

[5]George Bush had previously been envoy to China, U.S. ambassador to the United Nations, and director of the Central Intelligence Agency.

instance, told the convention that the proposed Equal Rights Amendment was "a socialistic, anti-family political movement that encourages women to leave their husbands, kill their children [abortion], practice witchcraft, destroy capitalism, and become lesbians."[6] Activists on behalf of women's rights passed off such comments as ridiculous and irresponsible, and pointed rather to events like the one to come in 1997 when the Women's National Basketball Association was launched. Reflected to the public by the WNBA was the maturation of female professional-level sports skills now supported by corporate finances and network TV exposure.

The Democrats presented a more centrist image and nominated a relatively unknown baby boomer from Arkansas, Bill Clinton, who out-campaigned Bush and replaced him in the White House. He was younger (46) when elected than any other president in history except his idol, John F. Kennedy. Clinton represented a shift in generations, the first president born after World War II. He came "from a place called Hope," he announced idealistically about both his hometown in Arkansas and his intent of reviving the optimism and social horizons of the nation. Many Americans danced in the streets when the election results were in. Others read Clinton's election less optimistically:

> The cultural seepages of the Fifties strengthened and became a torrent that swept through the nation in the Sixties, only to seem to die away in the Seventies. The election of Ronald Reagan in 1980 and the defeat of several of the most liberal senators seemed a reaffirmation of traditional values and proof that the Sixties were dead. They were not. The spirit of the Sixties revived in the Eighties and brought us at last to Bill and Hillary Clinton, the very personifications of the Sixties generation arrived at early middle age with its ideological baggage intact.[7]

The mystique of the "great war" (World War II) that had launched a new world and a new historical cycle for the U.S. had faded from public consciousness. Increasingly, key leaders of the nation were people who had been shaped by the 1960s, including a one-time antiwar (Vietnam) activist now living in the White House. In fact, in many ways the 1960s is what the 1992 election was all about. For Clinton,

> ...the 1960s represented an apogee of hope, a surge of moral commitment to make the world better. To George Bush, they represented traitorous dissent from "the American way," unwarranted government

---

[6]As quoted in George Tindall and David Shi, *America: A Narrative History*, 1996, 1542.
[7]Robert Bork, *Slouching Towards Gomorrah: Modern Liberalism and American Decline* (N.Y.: ReganBooks, HarperCollins, 1996), 2.

intervention and special favors on behalf of the poor and the black, and the kind of carping criticism of traditional values and institutions that threatened to ruin a great country.[8]

Clinton won the 1992 election, but certainly not with a large mandate. Ross Perot's third-party candidacy managed to get an impressive nineteen percent of the vote, suggesting that many Americans were disaffected with traditional party politics. The early months of the new administration did not help this negative environment as Clinton ran into trouble with some of his major appointments, while the inexperience of his staff blundered into some controversy that gained much media attention. His own personal and professional history and that of his wife Hillary provided the grounds for a "Whitewater" investigation and suggestions of scandal that would trouble both terms of his presidency.

Americans remained distrustful and were increasingly insecure about their own economic well-being. A vastly changing world economy now was demanding significant adjustments nearly everywhere. Beginning especially in the early 1980s in the face of an awkward if short-lived economic downturn, leaders of America's businesses made a national bestseller of the book *In Search of Excellence*. What could be learned from the country's best-run companies that could provide the secret for the survival of many others? The authors featured an old quote of F. Scott Fitzgerald: "The test of a first-rate intelligence is the ability to hold two opposed ideas in mind at the same time and still retain the ability to function." Rational models of organizational life were said to have their limits. Executives must dare again—dare to be untidy, dare to innovate, be obsessed with service to the customer, have a bias for action, risk with a slogan like "Ready. Fire. Aim."[9]

The company for which Mac had worked for over two decades now was struggling with employees about issues of pay, benefits, and pensions. It seemed to him that the workplace had become the troubled location where there is much more greed than respect for people. This was so divisive that he concluded it "probably will take some catastrophe to pull us together again." It was announced in 1997, for example, that the RCA assembly plant in Bloomington, Indiana, was closing and moving to Mexico after fifty-seven years of local operation. This plant had produced the first black-and-white and then the first color TVs and in the 1990s was the world's largest TV

---

[8]William Chafe, *The Unfinished Journey: America Since World War II* (N.Y.: Oxford University Press, 3rd ed., 1995), 504.

[9]Thomas Peters and Robert Waterman, Jr., *In Search of Excellence* (Warner Books, 1984), 89, 119.

assembly site. Now part of a multinational corporation owned by the French government, the corporate justification for the move was that it no longer could afford the labor and production costs in the United States. Hoosier anger at such a decision was aimed at the French in this case, although more often the target had become the North American Free Trade Agreement (NAFTA).

Approval of NAFTA had been strongly supported by the Clinton administration. When it became effective on January 1, 1994, supported by con-

---

Preamble
North American Free Trade Agreement–1994

The Government of Canada, the Government of the United Mexican States, and the Government of the United States of America resolved to:

STRENGTHEN the special bonds of friendship and cooperation among their nations;

CONTRIBUTE to the harmonious development and expansion of world trade and provide a catalyst to broader international cooperation;

CREATE an expanded and secure market for the goods and services produced in their territories;

REDUCE distortions to trade;

ESTABLISH clear and mutually advantageous rules governing their trade;

ENSURE a predictable commercial framework for business planning and investment;

BUILD on their respective rights and obligations under the General Agreement on Tariffs and Trade and other multilateral and bilateral instruments of cooperation;

ENHANCE the competitiveness of their firms in global markets;

FOSTER creativity and innovation, and promote trade in goods and services that are the subject of intellectual property rights;

CREATE new employment opportunities and improve working conditions and living standards in their respective territories;

UNDERTAKE each of the preceding in a manner consistent with environmental protection and conservation;

PRESERVE their flexibility to safeguard the public welfare;

PROMOTE sustainable development;

STRENGTHEN the development and enforcement of environmental laws and regulations; and

PROTECT, enhance and enforce basic worker's rights.

TABLE 21

siderable idealism about its intent and significance (see Table 21), Ross Perot warned that with NAFTA the U.S. would hear "a giant sucking sound" as American jobs flowed away to the cheap labor available on foreign shores. Given such a fearsome view, its passage had been opposed vigorously by many American workers because to them it seemed just another open door for American companies to increase their "out-sourcing"—securing parts and services from cheaper suppliers, often outside the United States and often at the apparent expense of employment at home. Could and should the globalization of the economy be stopped? Reporting frankly, the executive of one major U.S. company put it this way: "We at NCR think of ourselves as a globally competitive company that happens to be headquartered in the United States."[10] In fact, NAFTA made North America the largest free trade area in the world and to date has not interrupted the ongoing economic boom in the U.S. (it might even be one of the reasons for it).

A dramatic example of internationalized business came from Northeast Ohio. In May 1997, about 8,500 members of the International Union of Electronic Workers went on strike at GM's Delphi Packard Electric Systems complex in Warren, Ohio.[11] The dispute was largely over job security and fear that GM was planning to shift more jobs to Mexico. Such a strike near the Jackson-Milton High School threatened to quickly cripple GM assembly plants across North America and those of some other auto makers worldwide. The shape and demands of the workplace of the 1990s certainly were shifting and some of the resulting dilemmas can be understood in this larger context:

> The peasantry, which had formed the majority of the human race throughout recorded history, had been made redundant by agricultural revolution, but the millions no longer needed on the land had in the past been readily absorbed by labor-hungry occupations elsewhere, which required only a willingness to work, the adaptation of country skills, like digging and building walls, or the capacity to learn on the job. What would happen to the workers in those occupations when they in turn become unnecessary? Even if some could be re-trained for the high-grade jobs of the information age which continued to expand (most of which increasingly demanded a higher education), there were not enough of these to compensate.[12]

---

[10]Jonathan Schell, *N.Y. Newsday*, 1993.

[11]GM's 18 plants in the Warren-Youngstown area produce printed circuit boards, battery and ignition cables, and other electronic parts used in nearly all GM vehicles.

[12]Eric Hobsbawm, *The Age of Extremes: A History of the World, 1914-1991* (N.Y.: Vintage Books, Random House, 1994), 415.

In 1995 Wall Street set a record for records. The list includes the greatest number of corporate mergers and a record number of highs (69) reached by the Dow Jones Industrial Average on Wall Street (overcoming the previous record of 65 in 1925). This combination of 1925 and 1995 is one ready symbol of the irony, exhilaration, and foreboding of our times. Four years after the 1925 economic surge the country plunged into a great depression. Four years after 1995, the J-M class of 1959 will be marking its fortieth-year reunion. The century will be bringing to a close its large and troubled books. Is something quite depressing just ahead again? Many commentators are speaking of the crumbling of Western civilization. Meanwhile, and paradoxically, headlines in 1998 told of the nation's jobless rate at a 25-year low, consumer confidence at a 29-year high, with Wall Street cheering as stock prices rose to record levels.

Was this the surge upward before the plunge downward? The world increasingly is one interrelated market. Plunges now can be triggered by problems abroad. This was dramatized in October 1997 when Asian stock markets (especially Hong Kong) suddenly plunged and the U.S. Dow Jones industrial average reacted with a quick 7.18 percent loss of its value. The economic circumstance in the United States stabilized quickly because most domestic financial indicators remained fundamentally strong. Even so, America's vulnerability was obvious.

In a conservative turn in American politics, the Republican Party gained majorities in both houses of Congress in 1995, the first time in forty years. The victorious Republicans claimed they had a "Contract With America." Here Newt Gingrich, Speaker of the House, and other Republicans celebrate at a rally on Capital Hill.

A Volatile Political Climate

With such significant changes economically, the political climate naturally would be volatile. When the parents of the class of 1959 were teenagers, the United States was giving thanks for a "New Deal" coming from the nation's capital. When the class itself was in second grade, their parents were looking for another new deal in the aftermath of war. Most of them found it in the growing U.S. economy that stretched from the late 1940s into the 1970s. Now that the class members had become grandparents, the New Deal of the 1930s and the sustained economic boom of the 1950s and 1960s were history. The societal circumstance soon turned from a rush of "liberal" government programs in 1992 to a Rush Limbaugh[13] and a resurgent Republican Party's "Contract With America" in 1995. According to Rush Limbaugh, said by *Time* magazine to be "the loudest voice in the crucial conversation America is now having with itself":

> Today liberalism, because of its utter philosophical bankruptcy, has had to resort to magic tricks, to illusions, to distortions…. With experiential truth and empirical evidence refuting their credo at every imaginable turn, they're reduced to faith: faith in a set of beliefs long since discredited; faith in a lifestyle long since proven to be harmful; faith in a valueless value system; faith in a secular nihilistic world devoid of answers but full of trendiness, chic-ness, Hollywood glitter, pseudo-elitism, and arts-and-croissants self-adulation.[14]

This conservative resurgence was confident, even arrogant, and was prepared to take back the country for the people.[15] The claimed "contract" assumed that the American people were ready to dismantle big government and discard failed "give-away" programs that were judged to take away liberties and create a degrading dependence on welfare. Such an agenda helped focus the 1994 campaign and then provided direction for victorious conservatives now comprising the first Congress controlled by the Republicans in forty years. The contract included applying all the laws of the nation to Congress itself, a balanced budget amendment to the U.S. Constitution, a line-item veto for the president, welfare reform, term limits in Congress, a tax credit for children, and an enforceable death penalty for convicted criminals

---

[13]Rush Limbaugh, an abrasive and infectious personality with a vigorous conservative agenda and skill in the use of radio and television, authored the bestselling nonfiction book of 1992, *The Way Things Ought To Be*, and the one of 1993, *See, I Told You*.

[14]Rush Limbaugh, *See, I Told You So* (N.Y.: Pocket Books, 1993), 287-288.

[15]The political style of the new breed of conservatives reminded one of the best motion picture of 1995, *Braveheart*. It was a full-throated, red-blooded battle epic about a legendary Scots warrior who led his nation into battle.

in certain categories. This political agenda leaned in the direction of limited government, private initiative, and a stable society of law. Some observers pointed to the apparent impact of baby boomers who were growing older and often more conservative, and were very ready to champion at least some old-fashioned values and finish the job of the 1960s of subduing big government.

As the society took a conservative turn, it also was becoming more fractious. Newt Gingrich of Georgia was launched into the national spotlight as the powerful new Speaker of the House of Representatives. His speech was direct, even confrontational. About the poor of the nation, Gingrich would write: "The poor today are trapped both in a bureaucratic maze and in a culture of poverty and violence. No simple steps will suffice. It will take an immense effort and a lot of volunteers to replace the current *welfare state* with an *opportunity society*."[16] On the opposite political pole was Mario Cuomo, an eloquent voice of the Democratic Party who was capsized himself by the Republican tide of 1994. In defeat he was left at least with the hope that soon a great chorus of voices would arise to state loudly what to him was obvious:

> Of course the middle class, and most of America for that matter, has been unhappy with the direction this country was taking, but the new conservative Republican agenda won't solve our problems. It is a New Harshness that will make them worse, while stirring our meanest instincts and trampling upon our best impulses.[17]

In his characteristic eloquence, Cuomo challenged the "Contract" of the 1994 Republicans:

> The signers of the Contract tempt me and other fortunate Americans with all the luxuries of individualism and indifference to the wider world.... How dare they prey on our fears and frustration! How dare they behave as if we won't notice the evasion and simplistics! How dare they think so little of us and what we're capable of!... I don't want to leave behind me an America that is not as good as the one I was given.... I'm humiliated to think that my children and theirs would inherit a shrunken, desiccated vision of what this place can be, withered in opportunity and quality of life, diminished in justice, hope, and aspiration.... I cannot face the idea that mine would be the first generation of Americans in our modern history who failed to see that our immediate convenience was not necessarily identical with the nation's greatest good.[18]

---

[16]Newt Gingrich, *To Renew America* (N.Y.: HarperCollins, 1995), 84. Emphasis added.
[17]Mario Cuomo, *Reason To Believe* (N.Y.: Simon & Schuster, 1995), 7.
[18]Ibid., 177-178.

Not only did a wave of conservative Republicans arrive as new members of Congress in 1995, but they soon were vocal and action-oriented. The Republicans brought to Congress with them a determination to act definitively and quickly on a range of conservative subjects that were to change the very way the federal government works. Their sometimes strident rhetoric was echoed by a Christian minister, Brother Joe, in his surprisingly direct prayer at the Kansas state house in 1996 (see Table 22 and the Appendix).

In 1996 the Democratic president, Bill Clinton, signed a bill to bring many of the desired major changes to the nation's welfare system. The new call was to limit the automatic and unending "right" of people to be supported by the public when work is an option for them. The paying public had had enough of being "cheated" by some who appeared to them to be just lazy. Another target of conservatives was "affirmative action," a network of laws supporting special advantages for citizens previously discriminated against because of their gender or race. Increasingly, these laws were being seen by the general public as unfair policy. Was it now time to stop making up for past injustices by being unjust to the majority in the present? Is not such focusing on the sins of the past not hurtful to all people in the present, male and female, white and black? Shelby Steele's 1990 bestseller *The Content of Our Character* argued that preferential government treatment of blacks raised doubts in the minds of blacks and whites about the inherent worth of any black achievement. Blacks needed to stop viewing themselves as "victims" and start achieving the American dream.[19] President Clinton hoped to hold the line here—black and female voters were among his key supporters. But attitudes shared by two Toms from the J-M class of 1959, each employees at GM's Lordstown Assembly Plant since 1968, were getting a wider hearing all the time. These "backlash" whites agreed that blacks and women should not have been held down in the past. That, however, does not now justify giving them special advantages they do not deserve. "I am tired of a blatant double standard," said one. "Blacks, for instance, are allowed to collect in the plant for Black colleges. That would never be allowed for other colleges."

---

[19]Shelby Steele, *The Content of Our Character: A New Vision of Race in America* (N.Y.: HarperPerennial, 1990). One black who certainly had achieved the American dream by mid-decade was Oprah Winfrey. Actress and television talk-show hostess, her influence and credibility among everyday Americans soon appeared greater than that of politicians, press, and clergy. The best-selling nonfiction books for 1994 and 1996 were either about or by her. The first, *In the Kitchen with Rosie*, was a collection of Winfrey's favorite recipes by her personal chef, Rosie Daley. The second, *Make the Connection*, described ten steps to a better body and life.

A PRAYER OF BROTHER JOE
State House in Topeka, Kansas
January 23, 1996

Heavenly Father, we come before you today to ask Your forgiveness and seek Your direction and guidance. We know Your Word says, "Woe to those who call evil good," but that's exactly what we have done. We have lost our spiritual equilibrium and inverted our values. We confess that:

We have ridiculed the absolute truth of Your Word and called it moral pluralism;

We have worshipped other gods and called it multi-culturalism;

We have endorsed perversion and called it an alternative lifestyle;

We have exploited the poor and called it the lottery;

We have neglected the needy and called it self-preservation;

We have rewarded laziness and called it welfare;

We have killed our unborn and called it choice;

We have shot abortionists and called it justifiable;

We have neglected to discipline our children and called it building esteem;

We have abused power and called it political savvy;

We have coveted our neighbors' possessions and called it ambition;

We have polluted the air with profanity and pornography and called it freedom of expression;

We have ridiculed the time-honored values of our forefathers and called it enlightenment.

Search us, O God, and know our hearts today; try us and see if there be some wicked way in us; cleanse us from every sin and set us free. Guide and bless these men and women who have been sent here by the people of Kansas, and who have been ordained by You to govern this great state. Grant them Your wisdom to rule and may their decisions direct us to the center of Your will.

I ask it in the name of Your Son, the Living Savior, Jesus Christ. Amen.

TABLE 22

The perceived unfairness extended to other population groups as well. Jesse is generally an open-minded and tolerant person. He insists that he is without racial prejudice, but quickly admits to real prejudice against those many illegal aliens who these days slip into this country, manage to stay, and unfairly "suck dry the nation's resources" that are much needed for numerous struggling Americans. Legal immigration increased from 297,000 in 1965 to over 720,000 in 1995, with 300,000 or more illegal aliens added annually to the total of newcomers, numbers rivaling the historically high levels just before World War I. In 1994, some two million illegal aliens were estimated to be living in California alone. "Somehow," laments Jesse, "we have lost control, have lost our sense of balance, reward the wrong people and the wrong things." He was speaking from the harsh experiences of his own life in the shifting society of America in the 1990s. In 1966 he had been laid off at a Youngstown-area steel mill, refused to accept unemployment, got an interview with IBM, and soon traveled with his young family in their little VW Beetle to New York state. There they lived in a trailer and he had his job as a maintenance technician. They would be there twenty-six years until the "Great Compression" of the reorganizing business world forced its way into their lives.

Jesse had his "mid-life crisis" at about age 30. Obviously he was not on the road to wealth. Rather than climbing the corporate ladder at IBM, he came to understand that his wealth was his wife and daughters. He found satisfaction in who he was and who they were together. Then came the downsizing of IBM in the 1990s. Jesse accepted early retirement in 1992 that included three years of no income before the regular retirement benefits would begin. Their plan was to sell the home, leave behind the cold winters, and join his wife's relatives now living in Florida. It took two years to sell the house. Meantime, now in their early fifties, Jesse worked on a golf driving range and Judy folded linen at a motel and then was a store cashier. Finally, in 1994 they moved to Sarasota, taking along their adult daughter with epilepsy and soon adding to their household their second daughter and granddaughter after an especially troubled divorce in 1995. More problems came. The family network in Florida proved dysfunctional in some ways. Then, because of decades of smoking and the stress of the last four years, Jesse had a heart attack and open heart surgery in 1996, followed the next year by Judy having to have a cancerous kidney removed. It was a bumpy road, but these people now knew who they were and what was really important.

Maureen, classmate of Jesse and Judy now beyond her middle fifties, is a divorced and hardworking fitness professional in Youngstown, Ohio. Her youngest of five children, when 29 in the middle 1990s, was again living at home with her. This daughter had married her high school sweetheart, was divorced within six months, and had a daughter then nine years old. Maureen was willing and devoted, ready to do whatever it took. That seemed a general attitude of the loyal but stressed generation that had left high school in 1959. Barry and his wife were grandparents twice by 1996. Their only child, a son, was a university graduate who had remained in the Indiana city where they lived, married a university classmate, and joined her as two active professionals building their young careers in a volatile corporate setting (another General Motors center). Their two infant children were cared for on weekdays by grandma, a willing and loving helper sometimes having to scramble to be helpful to the needs of the next generation. Like the nation as a whole, these people from the J-M class of 1959 were coping, sometimes suffering, and frequently reorganizing their lives as circumstances necessitated. It is the way the country was in the volatile political times of the 1990s. Maybe this helps explain the great popularity of the movie *Forrest Gump* in 1994. The hero, played by Tom Hanks, is a thoroughly decent man with an IQ of seventy-five who manages to become involved personally in every major event in American history between the 1950s and 1980s. The film is a highly entertaining meditation on these decades through the eyes of a simple and honest man who takes things for what they are. People were needing help in sorting out the times, minus all the media hype, self-deception, and pretense.

The Market Up, Absolutes Down

A basic reason for the volatility of politics was the paradoxical circumstance of the nation's economy and value systems. Slightly younger than the classes of 1959 were those many baby boomers now approaching their fifties. They had been born into the prosperity that followed World War II, and by the 1990s were living in a high-tech and high-flux global economy that their parents, who had flourished economically in the rosy Eisenhower era, could not have foreseen. By 1995 *The Wall Street Journal* would feature a story on the boomers with the title "Their Careers: Count on Nothing and Work Like a Demon."[20] The story included a sequence of cartoons showing the boomers as babies being pampered in the 1950s, being welcomed to their first professional positions in the 1970s, sitting contentedly in their lush corporate offices in the 1980s, and now cleaning their offices on the way out in the 1990s. Many of them already were casualties of corporate retrenchment.

---

[20]*The Wall Street Journal*, October 31, 1995, B1, B7.

They were part of a big demographic bulge that no longer could be afforded by companies, at least at the full-time and full-benefit level.

The pain hit the somewhat older generation also. During the recession of 1990-1992, job displacement among workers fifty-five and older surpassed that of younger workers for the first time. Often this apparent lack of company loyalty to experienced workers was justified on the basis of older people having only outdated technical skills. Many had done their college term papers with paper and pen and then on electric typewriters, and were reluctant to make a job-related, dramatic entrance into the computer age. Fortunately for some of them, their homes were paid for and they had good long-term pension plans—although often they were not yet old enough to draw on such plans or on Social Security—which itself was said to be threatened as the baby boomers approached retirement in numbers the system was never designed to service.

In spite of all this, there was some really good news on the economic front. The 1990s in general proved to be a boom time in the U.S.[21] All of the reorganization in the corporate world had been for a purpose, a goal justifying for executives the costs in dislocation to numerous employees. The purpose was to modernize industrial plants, introduce new technology, and streamline the workforce so that the companies could again be competitive in the world marketplace. Painful and chaotic as much of this was at times, overall it appeared successful. The Dow-Jones average on Wall Street soared from the 3,000 to the 8,000 range by 1997. Joblessness was reduced, although many of the new jobs were the minimum-wage kind. Inflation was kept under control and economic growth was modest but steady. The secret to all this? Key certainly was the end of the Cold War, related real reductions in military spending, and finally an actual shrinking of the annual federal budget deficits. In 1997 the red ink was less than 1.4 percent of gross national product, the lowest among all industrialized countries. The first seven years of the decade were expansionist, better even that the roaring 1920s and nostalgic 1950s. The idealisms found in the Preamble to NAFTA (see Table 21) seemed to be realizable on more than paper.

Deep cultural tensions continued, however, evidenced in part by the Republican take-over of Congress in 1995. But President Clinton was learning to compromise his "liberal" agenda (a nationalized health-care system, gays in the military, etc.) to fit the nation's mood. While many people were profiting from the strong economy, they nonetheless were nervous about it

---

[21]In 1997 Greg Maddux, pitcher for the Atlanta Braves baseball team, received a five-year contract extension that will pay him $57.5 million.

suddenly crashing around them. In the election of 1996, Clinton was returned to the White House[22] and the Republicans retained control of Congress. The nation apparently wanted no political extreme, valued the balance of power, and was tiring of the confrontational rhetoric in Washington. Politicians got the message and tried harder to work together. A prominent success story came in August 1997, when Clinton and Congress joined in finally passing "balanced budget" legislation. Possible only in a time when the economy was booming, the Republicans got taxes cut, the Democrats got more spending on select social programs, the president got to use his new line-item veto, and both got the politically valuable fact that soon the federal budget presumably would come into balance for the first time in nearly thirty years—all without much political bloodshed for anyone. With all its political maneuvering and compromising, the big budget deal of 1997 was viewed by most Americans as a welcome event, a hopeful sign that maybe government would start spending only what money it actually had, even though the accumulated national debt had risen to some $5 trillion, with massive interest payments required each year.

Events other than economic reports and political battles and compromises in Washington were capturing public attention. In 1994, O. J. Simpson, Hall of Fame professional football player, was charged in a bizarre set of televised circumstances with the brutal murders of his wife and her friend. No murder case in U.S. history has received such sensational and relentless publicity. Outside this California courtroom and beyond the earth itself, space exploration was active and freshly fascinating. People were watching television and making routine phone calls by means of satellite transmission. Numerous satellites and at least one space station[23] now circle high over our cities and farms. Through 1993, a total of 308 people had traveled into space, including 195 Americans. The U.S. had launched 1,004 spacecrafts, 89 of them manned flights. On July 4, 1997, the America's *Pathfinder* landed on Mars and began sending stunning pictures back to earth—seen instantly through the Internet by millions of fascinated people all over the world. Scientists have established sophisticated listening devices focused on outer

---

[22]Having been courted by both the Democrats and Republicans, in November 1995 General Colin Powell announced that he would not run for the presidency. He was a war hero (Desert Storm) and an articulate black man who had enormous public appeal across party and racial lines. Had he run, the 1996 election results might have been different. See his *An American Journey*.

[23]This was the Russian *Mir* that featured in the 1990s a joint Russian and American crew and suffered mechanical problems that made many headlines back on earth in 1997.

The surface of Mars in a picture transmitted July 4, 1997, from the Pathfinder spacecraft, which can be seen in the foreground.

space. Messages are being sent toward the 100 billion stars of the Milky Way. Hundreds of people have insisted that they have been in contact with, even abducted and examined by alien beings. Big questions were being posed publicly. Have we been visited?[24] Are we alone in this universe? Is there someone or something beyond our immediate living environment who (which) is coming to us, listening to us, studying us, possibly a threat to us? In fact, the earth, thought by the ancients to be the center of all things, is moving in human perception toward the margin of a reality more massive than mere earthlings can conceive. We who ride the earth through space now seem but a receding speck of sand on an endless stretch of beach that disappears from view into the distant blackness of outer space. While economic markets were soaring in the U.S., the arrogance of many was being humbled.

If there is or was life existing beyond planet Earth, this is news that has dramatic implications for the self-understanding, security, and future of human beings. In the summer of 1996, for instance, a potato-sized rock found near

---

[24]For example, something highly unusual happened in 1947 near Roswell, New Mexico. Was it actually the crash of an alien spacecraft, the death of several aliens, and a large government cover-up? Despite a 1997 report by the U.S. Air Force entitled *The Roswell Report: Case Closed*, the debate seems destined to continue.

the South Pole and presumably originating from Mars showed possible evidence that tiny bacteria may have lived in or near the rock billions of years ago. Some scientists announced this tentative finding as likely new evidence of a universe filled with life. In fact, excitement about apparent ancient life on Mars dates back to 1877, when an Italian astronomer first claimed to have seen a system of channels on Mars' surface, thought to be canals of water created by intelligent life to irrigate that planet's surface. *Pathfinder* revealed new evidence in 1997 that there indeed may once have been large quantities of water on Mars, an essential component for life. Might we humans be on the verge of a new view of life in the universe—and thus a new and more humble view of ourselves? Maybe. We at least know about the great changes in recent decades back on earth. The older segment of the population in the U.S. tended to view many of them with real concern.

One change is a highly mobile population, symbolized well by the shifts in geographic locations of two members of the J-M class of 1959. While in high school in the 1950s, Bill lived on a little farm in Northeast Ohio that had a few domestic animals and provided just enough grain to feed them. In sight were fields, trees, and the occasional passing of a car. The mid-1990s, however, found Bill retired to an orange grove in rural Florida. Now, when he looks eastward out his living room window, he sometimes sees more than the incidentals of nature. On select evenings he witnesses from his armchair the launching from Cape Kennedy of huge space rockets. We humans seem bent on being on our way to some other state or even world.

Charlotte still has two brothers living in the northeastern Ohio area. She, however, has been a long-time resident of Texas who retired in 1996 with her husband from the directorship of a day school for children. They are now "having a ball" traveling around the United States, maintaining a second home in Colorado and a third in Florida, and playing golf and skiing as much as possible. (Their e-mail address begins with "Ilovegolf"!) For them, health is still good and the resources and time are adequate to allow a busy and enjoyable life of leisure in a great and diverse country.

Studs Terkel is a Chicago journalist famous for telling history through the real-life medium of oral history. He has published an extended commentary based on his interviews with a diverse group of Americans over seventy. In 1995 he concluded this work by sharing a sober consensus of opinion among his elderly interviewees. For them and their (our) century, time is running out. All things considered, according to the "old," it has been a good, even if a hard life. But what about dreams for the future? What hope do they see for their children, grandchildren, and country? Summarizes Terkel: "There is a sense of loss. Their mourning is not so much for themselves as for those who follow."[25]

What do they say has been lost in these last decades of the twentieth century? Their grieving focuses on the downsides of the dramatic new high technology. Their constant complaints are about "the promiscuous use of the machine; the loss of the personal touch; the vanishing skills of the hand; the competitive edge rather than the cooperative center; the corporate credo as all-encompassing truth; the sound bite as instant wisdom; trivia as substance; and the denigration of language."[26] It is understandable that *Time* magazine would name Andrew Grove its "Man of the Year" for 1997—he was a leading representative of the "digital age." But there was fear of "cyber sabotage," a digital doomsday when one computer hacker could bring down banks, stock exchanges, even multi-state electric grids.

Even more, the young today lack a sense of history and a setting of real community. They doubt that the "primitive" past—everything before computers and space stations—really matters. They don't belong; they just begin. They don't remember and thrive; they just compete and survive. Further, they tend to relativize most things. Is anything absolute? Is there actually any *truth*, or only current perceptions and best guesses?

One play from the theater of the absurd aids in understanding what it feels like to live in the U.S. at the end of the twentieth century. Tom Stoppard took two minor characters from Shakespeare's *Hamlet* and put them on center stage in *Rosencrantz & Guildenstern Are Dead*. These two, fragile and fickle in the face of life's confusion, knew themselves to have been summoned—but for what? Life has so little direction. The characters have nothing but appearances to go on. Are there correct answers? Is life merely to be a frustrated living among unending questions? Even the rules of logic seem no longer to apply. We find ourselves in a new world with new rules—or maybe no rules at all. Rosencrantz and Guildenstern soon find themselves trapped on a boat carrying them to their sure, even predestined deaths. It was so senseless and unavoidable, like modern life is sometimes experienced. As a culture, do Americans any longer have a clear identity, a commonly intended destination, or is life now the playing of insignificant roles in some kind of global drama not in our control? Who is the author of this drama—or is it writing itself? Is this the last scene? Death comes as a mystery. Is it all as arbitrary and meaningless as the original call into life? Stoppard's play asks whether people are able to "live in the questions."

---

[25]Studs Terkel, *Coming of Age* (N.Y.: The New Press, 1995), xxv.
[26]Ibid., xiv.

Competing Absolutes in the America of the 1990s*

The *Old* Absolutes

1. Religion is the backbone of American culture.

2. Human life is sacred and worthy of protection, from conception to natural death.

3. Marriage is God-ordained, is between a man and a woman, and lasts until death.

4 The "normal" family is a married father and mother, with children.

5. Sexual intercourse belongs only within the marriage relationship.

6. Same-sex and bisexual intercourse is immoral and destructive.

7. Women should be loved and protected, but not granted social equality.

8. All white people should be treated with dignity and respect.

9. Western civilization and its heritage should be studied and valued above others.

10. Different perspectives should be heard and tolerated, but only the true and right ones should prevail in society.

The *New* Absolutes

1. Religion is the bane of public life.

2. Human life is valuable as long as wanted. It begins and ends when someone decides that it does.

3. Marriage is only a human contract, made between any two people, and can be terminated whenever desired for any reason.

4. Any grouping of two or more people, with or without children, is a family.

5. Sexual intercourse is a "right" regardless of marital status or level of commitment.

6. All forms of sexual activity are acceptable as long as between consenting parties.

7. Women are oppressed by men and should be liberated to control their own bodies and destinies.

8. People of color should receive preferential treatment.

9. Non-Western societies and their heritages should be studied and valued above Western civilization.

10. Only those viewpoints now deemed to be "politically correct" should be tolerated and encouraged to prevail.

*These pairings are adapted from those listed by William Watkins, *The New Absolutes* (1996), 45-46.

TABLE 23

A key question in the 1990s is whether there are any absolutes after all. John Leo joins many others in believing that multi-culturalism has played a role in spreading "the vapors of non-judgmentalism." Americans, he laments, have overdosed on the attitude that no one has the right to criticize the moral views of another group or culture.[27] Allan Bloom, a University of Chicago professor, claimed the following in his 1987 bestselling book: "There is one thing a professor can be absolutely certain of: almost every student entering the university believes, or says he believes, that truth is relative."[28] Many have come to call the new philosophic mood "post-modernism." Others see it as the subtle reign of a new set of floating guidelines of preference accepted as proper by those who decry the existence of any fixed absolutes. William Watkins, for instance, wants to help "push back the night"[29] by exposing a series of such new guidelines that he sees functioning as virtual absolutes by many Americans in the late 1990s. They are presented in Table 23.

Richard laments what he sees as the corrosive impact of "tolerance" in American society since the 1960s. By this he means the socially unraveling effects of such attitudes as "I'll do my own thing," "Rules are not for me," "No one tells me what to do," and "I have a right to do as I please." This trend toward radical individualism and disrespect for authority and tradition is the opposite of what Elton Trueblood insisted in the 1940s was essential for building a new world after the tragedy of world war and in the face of the atomic bomb (see chapter 2). Trueblood said that adherence to the Ten Commandments of the biblical tradition is a must. This adherence includes the "necessity of intolerance," the phrase used by Trueblood for the title of the chapter on commandment two, "Thou shalt not make unto thee any graven image. . .thou shalt not bow down thyself unto them nor serve them." In the 1990s, however, there has been at least one widely publicized court challenge to the legal right of a public official to even display the Ten Commandments in a public building—a supposed application of the need to keep church and state strictly separate.

In February 1997, U.S. Circuit Judge Charles Price, agreeing with a lawsuit brought by the American Civil Liberties Union, ordered Judge Roy Moore in Alabama to remove or modify a replica of the Ten Commandments that he

---

[27]"A No-Fault Holocaust," *U.S. News and World Report,* July 21, 1997, 14. Leo's years of college teaching had revealed that up to twenty percent of his students could not bring themselves to say that the Nazi killing of millions of Jews was wrong, even though they knew that it had happened and they deplored it personally.

[28]Allan Bloom, *The Closing of the American Mind* (N.Y.: Simon & Schuster, 1987), 25.

[29]William Watkins, *The New Absolutes* (Minneapolis: Bethany House Publishers, 1996), 249.

had hanging in his courtroom. Moore resisted and Alabama Governor Fob James vowed to defend the courtroom display with force if necessary. Price, arguing that the display was intended to promote religion (now unacceptable in the U.S.) said that they could stay if Judge Moore would add nonreligious items to make it a larger and religiously neutral display. The U.S. House of Representatives even got involved by passing a nonbinding resolution (295-125) introduced by a Republican from Alabama supporting Judge Moore and arguing that the Ten Commandments should be permitted in government offices and courthouses because they are "a declaration of fundamental principles that are the cornerstones of a fair and just society." (Early in 1998 the Alabama Supreme Court dismissed the lawsuit.) The role of religious belief in a diverse and relativistic society had become a major issue.

One Nation—Under God?

As the U.S. approaches the end of the 20th century, it is struggling with the current meaning of some of its most identifying traditions and slogans. Why does the nation's paper money and coins still carry the official phrase "In God We Trust"? Is this merely a holdover from a more religious past, one so ingrained in the cultural vocabulary that no one yet has had the political nerve to get it removed? What of *e pluribus unum*. In what sense is the nation now *one* nation from *many* peoples, cultures, and traditions? Should the English language be made the country's only official language, established as such by law? Are the U.S. shores still seen as points of welcome for the oppressed of the earth? How much diversity can be tolerated by the rich religious heritage of the nation, or does it matter anymore whether or not there is any common bond of values or religious belief?

For the last fifty years the Democrats and Republicans have debated the philosophic issues of the role of government in a free-market economy and the proper scope of entitlement programs and individual rights. But there are two even deeper concerns, really fears, that appear to lie at the root of the presently pervasive discontent. As worded by Michael Sandel:

> One is the fear that, individually and collectively, we are losing control of the forces that govern our lives. The other is the sense that, from family to neighborhood to nation, the moral fabric of community is unraveling around us. These two fears define the anxiety of the age.[30]

There was a clear covenant that held ancient Israel together. Later, the Apostle Paul, assuming a oneness in Christ, gloried in a diversity of gifts and

---

[30]Michael J. Sandel, "America's Search for a New Public Philosophy," *The Atlantic Monthly* (March 1996), 57-58.

functions in the church. But, in line with his Jewish heritage, he taught that without the oneness, the diversity quickly becomes chaos. What now holds the United States together? What holds together a nation of greedy individualists ready to sue anyone at any time for any perceived infringement on "my rights"? What has become of togetherness, mutual discipline, and a corporate covenant to be one people? Is the only common value now a toleration of virtually any value another wants to hold?

Traditionally the U.S. has had the image of the world's great "melting pot" society. People from all over the world have arrived on these shores and then were assimilated—sort of melted down to an amalgam, the standard all-purpose American. Was it really ever that way? Is it even a desirable ideal? Sometimes offered as a better option is the image of a "salad bowl" society in which varieties of peoples are in the same bowl without losing their separate identities. The resulting beauty is the coordinated range of tastes and colors that together create much more than any one cultural tradition could on its own.

What is the real identity, foundation, and destiny of the United States of America? There is a deep level of understanding at issue in the nation's public discourse, an understanding about the character and place in history of the nation itself. America's "legitimating myths" have evolved over many generations of citizens who usually have seen their nation beating enemies, aiding friends, attracting millions of immigrants, and rising as a great star on the stage of world economic, political, and military power. The end of World War II saw Americans feeling extremely good about their nation and their increased role in the big scheme of things. More recently, however, the position of the U.S. in the world has been changing. Particularly since the late 1960s, the social environment that grounded the nation's classic self-understanding has been shifting. International economic and political realities have become volatile and unpredictable, joining the changing value and religious commitments at home to pressure and reshape the self-perceptions of Americans as a people.

What have been these traditional self-perceptions of America? The two basic ones, according to Robert Bellah, are civil religion and a highly utilitarian secular ideology.[31] Civil religion consists of many Judeo-Christian symbols and values that link the nation to a plan of God. The secular ideology, rooting in the political philosophy of the Enlightenment (see Table 17), yields a sense of rightness to the way this nation rules itself and insists that

---

[31]See especially his book *The Broken Covenant* (N.Y.: Seabury Press, 1975).

life, liberty, and the pursuit of happiness are assured for all its citizens. These two "myths" of the nation are said to be "self-evident" in the country's Constitution. The nation is founded on the assumption that it is one people, under the gracious guidance of God, with freedom and justice that allow all citizens to seek happiness. In this overarching assumption are "sacred" and "secular" dimensions that often use the same language about themselves and sometimes are in conflict with each other. Typically, they function as one in identifying the United States as the best representative of what should be in all the world, a place of goodness, fairness, generosity, faith, and freedom.

A popular novel of the mid-nineteenth century described Americans as "the Israel of our time" and the United States as a "political Messiah" sent to "bear the ark of the liberties of the world."[32] America's leading role in World War II only enhanced this national self-image; but the reversals of the 1960s and 1970s brought new caution and national self-doubt. Even so, Dale Evans Rogers contended in 1975 that America "was in the mind of God before it became earthly reality" and that it was still "a part of His purpose for mankind."[33] While such assumptions have been basic and widespread, forcing Christian views on the general public has been a rare occurrence, although an isolated act of violence against abortion clinics have been justified by the name of Jesus. More typical has been Senator Mark Hatfield, an evangelical Christian who has stood for caution about any easy and idolatrous identification of America and the kingdom of God on earth or of associating God's will with given political decisions.[34] Very common nonetheless is the assumption that America's privileged position of wealth and power is a gift of God to be used to evangelize the world for Jesus Christ.

There are at least two reasons why strong Christian convictions, central to the lives of millions of Americans in all generations, have not led to a militant fundamentalism such as has Islam in modern Iran. One is the view of Jesus as a leader of love who chose gentle persuasion over violent action. The other is the influence of the second guiding principle of America. Beyond the Christian-shaped civil religion is the secular ideology of "with liberty and jus-

---

[32]Herman Melville, *White-Jacket, or, The World in a Man-of-War* (Boston: Page, 1982 [c.1850]), 144. Martin Marty cautions against any idealizing of America's religious history. "The America of the 'little white church and little red school house' was not, by any historical measure, more church-going, more religious, more literate, necessarily more moral, than is contemporary America" (*Religion and Republic: The American Circumstance*, Boston: Beacon Press, 1987, 346).

[33]Dale Evans Rogers, *Let Freedom Ring!* (Old Tappan, N.J.: Revell, 1975), 19-20.

[34]Mark Hatfield, *Between a Rock and a Hard Place* (Waco, Tex.: Word Books, 1976), 92.

The careers of both Billy Graham and Fidel Castro have spanned forty years. Graham (left) is shown during one of his early evangelistic crusades, inviting persons to commit themselves to Jesus Christ. Speaking in the Camaguey Central Park in 1959, Castro (right) promises change in Cuba.

tice for all." This "liberal" view of America usually avoids drawing directly from the Judeo-Christian tradition, speaking rather of a more secular salvation involving America's traditional commitment to individual freedom from a tyrannical government and its interdependence with the rest of the world, and its responsibility to represent and work everywhere for human rights, economic security, and international peace. Such things as freedom and peace often draw directly on biblical materials, but are more inclusive of a range of perspectives, some not consciously religious in nature.

Most Americans believe in God and freedom, while some believe in freedom apart from God. Americans take pride in the freedom to choose politically and religiously. When freedom reigns, "America is great because America is good." Put baldly in a materialistic way, America obviously is good because its way of life has yielded the most successful economy in the world's history. Warned Reinhold Niebuhr, however: "Our power will be used the more justly if we recognize that our possession of it is not a proof of our virtue."[35] Even with this caution, leading politicians of both major political parties hold the same general view in the final years of the 1990s: The Soviet Union has crumbled; America stands preeminent, rich, powerful and good, carrying the awesome responsibility of somehow leading the world into the next millennium.

---

[35]Reinhold Niebuhr, "America's Eminence," *Christianity and Society* 13 (1948), 3-4.

Two men have been prominent on the American and world scenes from the 1950s to the end of the 1990s. Each has outlasted eight U.S. presidents. One has been their friend and spiritual counselor,[36] while the other consistently has opposed all of them with bitter rhetoric. The first, Billy Graham, has been a Bible-centered American preacher of the Christian gospel, who in 1959 already was in his thirteenth year of public ministry and in that one year conducted thirteen major evangelistic crusades from Arkansas to Australia.[37] The other, Fidel Castro, has been a cigar-smoking Cuban revolutionary espousing the gospel of communism. Ian recalls Mr. Long talking about Castro in a 1959 civics class at Jackson-Milton High School and now reflects with interest on Castro's unusual longevity for a political strongman. In 1996 Castro celebrated his seventieth birthday while trying to maintain political power after the ending of years of massive Soviet subsidies to Cuba. His harsh rhetoric goes on still, but now with lessening credibility and with fewer serious listeners.

Graham is quite another story. He has never sought personal power and was the first Christian to preach in public behind the Iron Curtain after World War II, culminating in giant gatherings across the People's Republic of China and the Union of Soviet Socialist Republics (1988), in Budapest (1989), Moscow (1992), and North Korea (1994). Rather than an angry and isolated dictator, Graham has been on lists of the ten most-admired people in America and the world in virtually every year since the 1950s. He packed people into Madison Square Garden for sixteen weeks in 1957, where an amazing range of people were willing to hear the straight and simple word of biblical salvation. Then in 1995, at age seventy-six, the distinctive voice of this beloved evangelist soared upward from a pulpit in San Juan, Puerto Rico, to a network of 30 satellites that relayed his Christian messages to 185 countries in 116 languages.[38] Said Graham of this "Global Mission" campaign that had as many as one billion listeners, there is no conflict between "the old, old story" and the newest means of transmitting it. "It is time," he observed, "for the church to use the technology to make a statement that in the midst of chaos, emptiness, and despair, there is hope in the person of Jesus Christ."

---

[36]See *U.S. News & World Report* (May 5, 1997), 56-70, for a story and photos on Billy Graham and his relationships with every contemporary President from Harry Truman to Bill Clinton.

[37]See Billy Graham, *Just As I Am: The Autobiography of Billy Graham* (San Francisco: HarperCollins, 1997).

[38]A close Italian friend of Barry (J-M class of 1959) functioned on this and other occasions as the worldwide Italian interpreter for Billy Graham.

Communist ideology has about breathed its last; the Christian gospel still stands as a potential source of hope for the future.

Representing Roman Catholicism recently has been Pope John Paul II, elevated to the papacy in 1978. This Polish pope (the first non-Italian pope since 1523) survived an assassination attempt in Rome in 1981 and since has traveled the world widely and spoken to huge crowds on his opposition to abortion, birth control, genetic engineering, and euthanasia, as well as his concerns for the destructive effects of superpower rivalry, the need to reconcile capitalism with social justice, and the wrongness of moral relativism. He was named by *Time* magazine as 1994's "Man of the Year." Why would this secular publication choose the Pope? Because it recognized the timeliness of his relentless support for the sanctity of the human being and his unquestioned ability to be a moral force in a time when so many people lament the decline in moral values and the rise of humanly destructive behavior. Pope John Paul apparently sees it as his God-given duty to trouble "modernity," especially its assumption that individuals are equal with God in deciding who will be born (abortion) and its too easy accommodation to the great distance between the wealthy and the wretchedly poor of the world. He argues forcefully that "rationalism" by itself is not enough:

> This world, which appears to be a great workshop in which knowledge is developed by man, which appears as progress and civilization, as a modern system of communications, as a structure of democratic freedoms without any limitations, this world is not capable of making man happy.[39]

Charles Colson certainly agrees with this judgment of the Pope. He has expressed concern that the now secularized United States, particularly the apparently anti-religion recent decisions of the Supreme Court, is slowly ending a true democracy in which the views of people with clear religious perspectives are respected and at least heard. Christians who are serious about their faith and its life implications always risk being viewed as "an enemy" because they maintain a dual identity (Christians and Americans) and their loyalty to the faith will be seen as disloyalty to a tolerant and pluralistic society.[40]

---

[39]*Time* magazine, December 26, 1994-January 2, 1995, 57.

[40]Charles Colson, "Can We Still Pledge Allegiance?" *Christianity Today*, April 28, 1997, 96. See the Appendix "We Hold These Truths" (1997) at the end of this volume. Here Colson and other religious leaders in the United States express major concern about the well-being of American democracy in the late 1990s.

Judy speaks for most of the J-M class of 1959. She still has faith in the country, sure that available alternatives are worse. But she is upset deeply at how things now are. While in high school in the late 1950s, she and many others in her class disliked and even feared the Principal, Mary Lucy Lauban. Expectations from "the office" were high, limits clear, discipline sometimes swift and harsh. Now Judy has generated some real respect for her memory of "Lucy." After all, today "it is very sad that adults have so little control of their own children. Teachers are afraid to discipline at all. Ironically, children want and need love and limits. And taking prayer out of the schools was a tragic mistake." Something destructive is happening to the young. There was a twenty-seven percent increase in births to girls ages fifteen to seventeen from 1986 to 1991, "kids having kids." Some sixty-seven percent of the births to teens in 1990 were to unmarried mothers. In 1960 only fifteen percent were born to the unmarried. Of course, there should be no forcing of religion on anyone; but neither should the nation act like humility and faith in a higher power are not important to national identity and human life. Discipline should be measured and humane, of course; but lack of it is destructive to human well-being.

Pressing social questions persist. How can we live together well? How can we humans survive our own greed and lust for power? Can hope continue to exist, or will the nation and increasing numbers of its citizens become exhausted in places where there seem to be no exits?[41] Maybe what we dread most, as G. K. Chesterton's amateur sleuth once observed, is finding ourselves in a maze with no center. That is why "atheism is only a nightmare."[42] What if it should turn out to be the case that nothing ultimately does mean anything after all? Are we moderns done with the very idea of God, or will we inevitably be done ourselves apart from God? Certainly the journey to discover the sure center of things, that which allows all else to have meaning and direction, is yet unfinished. Note, for instance, that in a two-week period in 1997 there appeared cover stories in national news periodicals on "Does Heaven Exist?" "Life After Death," and "Lost Souls."[43]

---

[41]See, for instance, the celebrated although dark presentations of the modern condition titled *No Exit and Nausea* by Jean-Paul Sartre.

[42]G. K. Chesterton, *The Complete Father Brown* (London: Penguin Books, Ltd., 1981), 235.

[43]*Time*, "Does Heaven Exist?" (March 24, 1997); *U.S. News and World Report*, "Life After Death" (March 31, 1997); and *U.S. News and World Report*, "Lost Souls," (April 7, 1997).

At that time there also was a popular prime-time television series called *Touched By An Angel*. In each episode, angels appearing as caring humans were assigned by God to become involved in the troubled lives of selected Americans of the late twentieth century. These troubled people would be forced to face their gone-wrongness in the light of God's freshly communicated presence, love, and forgiveness. Most so touched were surprised and, while finding belief hard in their worlds, finally welcomed it. On the much more negative side, the great success in 1991 of the film *The Silence of the Lambs* made dramatically clear that evil still lurks in this world. People were "entertained" by watching a graphic portrayal of mass murderers, one who ate his human victims and one, "Buffalo Bill," who skinned his.

Worse than what was on the big screens, such things were really happening outside the theaters. Brutal and sometimes indiscriminate criminal activity became an urgent social problem in the 1990s. Youth gangs evolved in even smaller cities. Drive-by shootings, serial killers, and "road rage" potentially threatened anyone just going to work or the grocery store. It was happening in the big cities and small towns. Just west of Dixville, New Hampshire, for instance, where the nation's first presidential votes are cast every four years, sits the little town of Colebrook. The August 20, 1997, headline in Colebrook's weekly newspaper deviated sharply from its usual range of small-town happenings and curiosities. It read: "Four Gunned Down in Colebrook; Editor, Lawyer, Two Officers Dead." The killer, finally cornered and shot to death himself, was local resident Carl Drega who had a grudge against a part-time judge, an AR-15 assault rifle, and a secret bomb factory at his rural home. Shortly, as an act of a shocked community's grief, a sign out on Route 3 read: "The Moose Festival Has Been Canceled." What had not been changed was the fierce independence of Americans, their frequent love of guns, and too often their willingness to resort to violence for a wide range of reasons.

Ian lives in rural Vermont and it happened even there in 1997. His house doors were never locked and keys often stayed in family automobiles—traditionally no problem in the area. A flashing light was noticed down the road one night, however. It turned out that a pick-up truck was being consumed by fire. Then a car suddenly was missing from Ian's property. The police soon solved the night's crime spree, which included an irrationally angry man stealing and torching three area vehicles. On the corporate scene, the huge tobacco industry in the U.S. finally admitted in 1997 that their products are addictive, harmful to human health, and that they had misled the public for years in these regards. States began demanding massive repayments for tobacco-related medical costs that the states had carried.[44] White-collar crime was notoriously rampant and less often detected and stopped.

Gross inhumanity, seen in such ugly fashion in Nazi Germany in the 1940s, was very much present in the U.S. of the 1990s. But what had remained of America's self-authenticating idealism? What is the bonding factor that defines and holds together the United States in its problems and challenges? Is it in fact what one of its official slogans claims, one nation under God? Martin Marty observes that the U.S. is continuing its quest for coherence and consensus. He traces the record of a people "that has grown ever more pluralist and has still found reasons to develop enough common spirit to have creative arguments—and has survived."[45] Less dispassionately, James Kennedy doubts that the nation can last much longer by affirming together only enough to have creative arguments. To the contrary: "But when any society chucks God out of its public life and slaps up a patchwork structure of humanism and idealism in the place of God, the soul of its people can only grow weaker and its character atrophy and die."[46]

What Is Worth Remembering?

One way to avoid national atrophy is to focus unfailingly on select lessons from the past. In the 1990s, Jim developed Alzheimer's disease, that frightful problem that degrades memory and slowly removes one's functional identity. What about the remembering ability and identity of the United States? Is there a *will* to remember and the wisdom needed to know what is worth remembering in the bewildering maze of information clogging all media today? True communities are built on shared memories, stories, and values. Forgetting is easy when the future beckons constantly with tantalizing newness and tempts one to dismiss yesterday as too primitive to be of value anymore. Since the 1940s, technological changes and cultural shifts have come at a pace too fast for many people to even comprehend, let alone remember and relate to the ongoing meaning of their lives. Little stays in place long enough to merit serious commitment. Effective remembering often is just a matter of time and priorities. Members of the J-M class of 1959, for instance, became preoccupied with their own lives soon after graduation.

---

[44]A settlement was reached that further limits cigarette advertising and will cost the industry some $360 billion over the next 25 years (something it can afford!). In return, the industry appeared successful in its search for protection from further legal liability.

[45]Martin Marty, *Religion and Republic: The American Experience* (Boston: Beacon Press, 1987), Epilogue.

[46]James Kennedy, *Character and Destiny: A Nation In Search of Its Soul* (Grand Rapids: Zondervan, 1994), 11.

Even the many who remained over the years within the immediate area of their high school have seen each other only rarely. Barry had to take the initiative for the only three reunions the class has had in thirty-seven years, working from his home in Indiana, three hundred miles away. What is really worth putting effort into? What must not be forgotten? The 1990s saw several significant attempts to identity and dramatize a few such things.

Key people, of course, are worth the investment of memory time. For the J-M class of 1959, to date there has been the loss of five members by death (see the dedication page). In addition, the decade of the 1990s has endured the deaths of many prominent figures who have been central to the American culture for decades. Included have been President Richard Nixon (1994), First Lady Jacqueline Kennedy Onasis (1994), baseball legend Mickey Mantle (1995), folksinger Burl Ives (1995), naturalist Jacques Cousteau (1997), and beloved actor Jimmy Stewart (1997). Stewart's leading roles in *Mr. Smith Goes To Washington* (1939) and *It's A Wonderful Life* (1946) made him a true American in the eyes of millions, a national symbol of decency and moral courage. In 1996 alone, death came to Spiro Agnew, Cardinal Joseph Bernardin, Erma Bombeck, George Burns, Ella Fitzgerald, Greer Garson, Barbara Jordan, Gene Kelly, Timothy Leary, and Carl Sagan. This passing parade of the prominent left behind political idealism (Jordan), political shame (Agnew), stage and film masterpieces (Fitzgerald, Garson, Kelly), models of faith (Bernardin), humor (Bombeck, Burns), drug-induced radicalism (Leary), and a fascination with the universe in which we humans live (Sagan).

In September 1997, the two most prominent women in the world died at almost the same time, in very different sets of circumstances, with both events receiving intense worldwide attention. Princess Diana of England (1961-1997) was killed tragically in an auto accident in Paris and Mother Teresa of India (1910-1997) died of a heart attack. These women were mourned openly by much of the world. Both were loved as models of compassion for human misery. The princess was associated awkwardly with a royal family and was featured by constant media attention as the "peoples' princess" who was the epitome of grace and glamour. Diana was elegance coupled with the common touch. At her elaborate funeral in London's Westminster Abbey, her brother called her "a symbol of selfless humanity, a standard-bearer for the rights of the truly downtrodden, a very British girl who transcended nationality, someone with a natural nobility who was classless." The other, a nun with no glamour interest for the media, lived selflessly with the poor and dying in Calcutta, India. She was an unassuming angel

(Left) Prince William, Earl Spencer, Prince Harry and Prince Charles follow the coffin of Diana, Princess of Wales, into Westminster Abbey on Sept. 6, 1997. Princess Diana was killed in a car crash a week earlier in Paris.

(Right) Sister Nirmala, who succeeded Mother Teresa as the superior-general of the Missionaries of Charity, pays her respects to Mother Teresa at her state funeral service at India's Netaji Stadium, Sept. 13, 1997.

of mercy who had founded the Missionaries of Charity in 1950, received the Nobel Peace Prize in 1979, and by the 1990s was generally acclaimed a "living saint." Both of these women had cared deeply, communicated effectively with the common person, and became public icons of good in a world sorely in need of a loving touch. In death as in life, they helped millions across religious, national, and class lines to rethink what is truly worthy, noble, and valuable in life. They brought light into some traditionally dark places.

Beyond the people are key historical episodes that must remain living memory for the sake of a just and viable future. One tragic episode is the Holocaust in Europe during the 1940s. The classes of 1959 were mere babies as this tragedy began and not yet ready for school when the horror finally ceased. Now they are grandparents as voices are heard actually denying that it ever happened (!) and vigorous efforts are being made to be sure that such a thing is never forgotten. Memory is surely being helped by the new Holocaust Museum that opened in Washington, D. C., in April 1993, close to the Washington Monument.[47] Then there was Steven Spielberg's dramatic

---

[47]The $194 million needed to build and equip the museum was raised by a national campaign for private donations. Told in impressive exhibits is the story of the six million Jews targeted for annihilation in state-sponsored genocide and of other Nazi victims— Gypsies, Poles, the handicapped, Soviet POWs, etc. The museum's primary mission is to share knowledge, preserve memory, raise spiritual and moral questions, and highlight the responsibilities of being citizens of a democracy in a less-than-ideal world.

1993 movie, *Schindler's List*. Winning seven Academy Awards, here was a moving depiction of the Holocaust horrors and the courageous behavior of a war-profiteering Nazi industrialist who discovered, in the midst of making money, that he had a heart and conscience. As a Jew and a socially sensitive modern man, Spielberg was convinced that this film conveyed a story needing told "because the generations forget and every new generation needs to face their past all over again." He was right. Forgetting is made easy when, for instance, in 1997 the Cold War reversed political alignments and NATO invited into its membership three ex-Soviet satellites, Poland, Hungary, and the Czech Republic. Soon the horrors of how it was will fade, increasing the chance of their return.

What, for instance, is the future for the black baby born in 1996, a grandchild of a white grandmother, member of the J-M class of 1959? Will the price of traditional racial prejudice yet have to be paid by the newly born? *Life* magazine (July 1966) identified Steven Spielberg as the most influential of all the baby boomers born between 1946 and 1964. Why? Because he has become our "mythmaker," our Hans Christian Anderson, "an epic fairytale maker with a Midas touch." The films *E. T.* and *Schindler's List* made us aware that warmth and hope still live, even in unlikely places like in the presence of an ugly little creature from outer space or in a Nazi concentration camp. Light is where you find it—and it is still to be found! American movie goers were further helped to face their fears and live their fantasies by watching Spielberg's *Jurassic Park*, *Jaws*, and *Raiders of the Lost Ark*. These films have become vehicles (myths) by which millions have tried to come to terms with themselves and their times.

Another thing worth remembering is the American Civil War. A moving television special by Ken Burns has brought back to life hundreds of ordinary Americans who got caught up in the nation's worst internal tragedy. Somehow this war remains a paradigm of what the U.S. must never allow to happen again. Yet another vital memory, coming from even earlier in U.S. history, has to do with the brutal mistreatment of Native Americans. Kevin Costner was featured in 1990 in the award-winning film *Dances With Wolves*. He played an isolated Union Army lieutenant who encounters the Sioux Indians and comes to learn their civilization and suffering firsthand. Then in 1992, on the 500th anniversary of Christopher Columbus having "discovered" America, a debate broke out about the treatment of the earliest Americans. It was both a time of national celebration and soul-searching. Would America have been better off without Columbus and the rest of the Europeans? Had it become politically correct by the 1990s to think of Columbus as a greedy

Tall ships crowd the water in front of the Statue of Liberty in New York harbor. Over thirty tall ships took part in Operation Sail '92 to observe the 500th anniversary of Columbus' first voyage to the New World.

Italian explorer who "brought nothing to the peaceful New World 'paradise' but oppression, disease, brutality, and genocide?"[48] Avoiding historical revisionism as much as possible, can we remember in a way that sobers us, leading to a fresh resolve to be one people with justice for all?

What Do We Tell Our Grandchildren?

Social security in the U.S. used to mean being part of an extended, loving, supportive family. The aging could rely on the young to be close and helpful as needed. More recently, social security has come to mean the federal government's guarantee of a modest income and basic health care for older citizens who have been productive during their working lifetimes. In our competitive, mobile society, often the aging have no children, or they live far away, are strapped with debt, and are very busy indeed, not feeling that they have the time to care for needy parents. Numerous parents of class members are now dead, in care facilities of various kinds, or still are active and independent. Retirement centers, nursing homes, and isolated older adults have become standards in this society. The J-M class of 1959 is just now beginning to deal personally with such issues. Richard, living in the Minneapolis area, retired in April 1997. About the same time, Tom had a heart attack and open heart surgery and Frank suffered a stroke and had to retire early. Meanwhile, the children were close by and far away. Judy has four children, three living

---

[48]Rush Limbaugh, *See, I Told You So* (N.Y.: Pocket Books, 1993), 67.

within a few miles of her in Ohio and one in Colorado. Shirley has three children, two living close by her home in Florida and the third also in Colorado. Another Richard, now living in Georgia, has three, two still close to the home high school area and one in nearby Cleveland. Another Judy lives in Virginia and has all three of her sons and their three daughters very close by. There are even larger extended families which are scattered widely. To date the class has a total of about 125 grandchildren.

What will the classes of 1959 tell their numerous grandchildren? This book is dedicated to my own beloved granddaughter, Emily, highlighting my perception of the importance of the question for the nation's future. Members of the J-M class of 1959 offer their pieces of wisdom. Betty: "Take risks, don't sell yourself short, but give yourself a chance to be all you can be." Jane: "Trust in God, get a good education, be patient, don't marry too early, and explore what's in the world." Charles reports that "the value of money is limited—it can't buy joy." He now sees that he has chosen to work too much, failing out of his own economic insecurity to go and do enough things with his family. Stan: "Learn all you can while in school. Don't mess around like I did." Mac adds: "Kids need to learn to adjust, be happy, and do what they want as long as it doesn't hurt others." Much being said by this class is pragmatic, with little philosophic or religious perspective showing in some and much showing in others. The importance of education is a constant theme. Being less materialistic is another. Being yourself is yet another. The call is to be "happy," with faith in God being essential in the judgment of many, but not for all. Numerous class members have bolted earlier faith commitments, finding them too binding, artificial, and self-serving, choosing rather to go on individualized and non-institutionally related spiritual journeys. Some have moved toward classic faith communities for the first time in their lives. Nearly all would admit readily to believing in God.

In the mid-1960s, Judy and David bought an old farmhouse in Berlin township a few miles from the North Jackson High School where she graduated in 1959. In 1995 she made this comment: "It is an old house, a sturdy old house, and we'll stay here until we're dead." In this home they keep an outstanding collection of beautiful glassware, objects that Judy is consciously preserving for the enjoyment of another generation. "I really don't own this glass," she says. "I'm just holding it for the next people." She raises a crucial question. Beautiful glass, yes; but what else is so beautiful in life that another generation deserves to see it? Judy, class salutatorian, was present at her class reunion at the Wranglers Olde Country Restaurant marking the 35th year out of high school. She didn't tell most of us at the time that she had a significant health worry that evening. In previous weeks she had been suf-

Milestones of the Decade

Best Movie of the Year#	Bestselling Nonfiction Book of the Year	*Time* Magazine's Person of the Year*
1990 *Dances With Wolves*	*Wealth Without Risk*, Charles Givens	George Bush, President of the U.S.
1991 *The Silence of the Lambs*	*Iron John: A Book About Men*, Robert Bly	Ted Turner, Communications Leader
1992 *Unforgiven*	*The Way Things Ought To Be*, Rush Limbaugh	William "Bill" Clinton, President of the U.S.
1993 *Schindler's List*	*See, I Told You*, Rush Limbaugh	Yitzhak Rabin, Nelson Mandela, F. W. DeKlerk, Yasser Arafat, the Peacemakers
1994 *Forrest Gump*	*In the Kitchen with Rosie*, Rosie Daley	John Paul II, Pope of Rome
1995 *Braveheart*	*Men Are From Mars, Women Are From Venus*, John Gray	Newt Gingrich, Speaker, House of Representatives
1996 *English Patient*	*Make the Connection*, Oprah Winfrey	Dr. David Ho, AIDS Research
1997 *Titanic*†	*Don't Sweat the Small Stuff…And It's All Small Stuff*, Richard Carlson	Andrew Grove, The Digital Age

Recipient of the Oscar from the Academy of Motion Picture Arts and Sciences.

† Although the Oscars for 1997 had not been announced when this edition went to press, *Titanic* won four Golden Globe Awards (including "Best Drama") and was widely expected to receive an Oscar as Best Movie of the Year. The three-hour film has become the highest-grossing movie in history.

* A designation on the part of the editors of *Time* of the person, people, or thing that, for better or worse, most significantly influenced the course of world events in the preceding twelve months.

TABLE 24

fering from terrible nose bleeding, probably the result of a change in medication. But there also was a negative reading on a stress test. Her mother had died in 1990 from an ailment that might now be making its fearful appearance in Judy. The reunion evening went well for Judy, but nearly a year later she finally agreed to listen to her doctor's advice to have a heart catheterization. On March 9, 1995, on the very anniversary of her mother's death, she went to the famed Cleveland Clinic and had the invasive heart test. The finding was encouraging, but there certainly had been no advance guarantees. So in a little letter dated March 7, Judy had left a message for her children and grandchildren—just in case Cleveland turned out to be her final stop in this life. Ending with "Love Always, Mom," it read in part:

> Try always to treat others with kindness and compassion. Try to think before you act—is this an action I can at least be satisfied with, if not proud of? Satisfaction with your life should be your goal. This is the true measure of happiness—not the amount of money you have or what you own. *You control your own life!* Take hold of it and make it what you want it to be.
>
> The Ten Commandments are good rules to live by, whatever your religion. Life is too short to worry about the "what might have beens." Enjoy each day as it comes. See the beauty of nature always around you. This truly is the first day of the rest of your life. Have a dream and always work towards it.
>
> My proudest accomplishment was to raise four children to the best of my ability and to try to instill good values in them and to set them a good example. I hope they will do the same with their children. If all else fails, I tell myself: *This too will pass.*

Not everyone in the J-M class of 1959, of course, has yet faced a health crisis as life-threatening as Judy's well might have been, nor would some of them be as articulate as she in putting their reflections on paper for family members. Some would put less emphasis on traditional, family-oriented values. Some would be far more specific and affirmative about particular religious commitments. Nevertheless, it has become very clear to all that life is fragile and rather brief. Yes, the average life-span of Americans has increased considerably. Medical advances in recent decades have been marvelous and most welcome.[49] Life, nonetheless, still is a precious and passing gift.

As of this writing, most members of the class of 1959 are only fifty-seven years old, still staying about five years ahead of the oldest baby boomers. Even so, nine percent of the class has died—two in the 1970s, one in the 1980s, and two in the 1990s. Disability has sidelined four others. Increasingly these

---

[49]In late 1997, Bobbi McCaughey in Iowa, having put her faith in God and in a fertility drug, gave birth to seven babies, the world's only surviving septuplets.

classmates are aware of their own mortality. For instance, in 1997 Judy had a kidney removed because of a cancerous tumor. The cancer might come back, of course, but she is optimistic. Life is not forever—at least not here. The large majority of the class probably will see at least the first few years of a new century—if, of course, the world lasts that long.

One way or another, in one year or another, the end will come for each of these classmates from 1959. What—if anything—then? Judy is very articulate about her view of things. She and her husband, who came from a religiously active Protestant family, have never attended church in their married lives. They never took their children to church, although two of them currently are attending a church on their own. Judy's philosophy is simple: "If you live a good life, follow the Ten Commandments—good rules for anybody—and instill good values in your children, that's the important thing and all a person can do." She adds this: "My goal is not to be rich and famous, but to make a positive difference in someone else's life." She is sensitive about the religious hypocrisy she has seen. Her observation is that too many religiously active people are involved in a church for poor reasons and often have less real love and compassion for people than some who do the right things just because they are right.

She lost a good friend because that lady became a "born again" Christian and turned aggressively toward Judy and her needed "conversion." Tolerance for honest differences seemed to just disappear. By contrast, Judy is the good listener, the community "bartender" who hears and counsels gently with a range of local people who seek her out. "Who's to say that a Hindu won't go to heaven [if there is such a place] just because she or he doesn't believe what Christians do?" That's been Judy's view ever since college days at Ohio State when she counseled her high school friend and college roommate Betty about Betty's new friendship with an Indian young man. The important thing is who the man is and whether he really loved Betty, not his creed, color, or country of origin. Betty did marry him and embraced his Hinduism.[50]

What about life after death? What witness is to be left before this life ends? The American culture at large remains curious and fascinated with the hope of something beyond. A best-selling book released in 1992 told of a personal after-death experience and employed a rather common "light" theme—

---

[50]Actually, Betty has generally avoided active religious association ("any religion made up by man for self-serving reasons") in favor of reverencing the universal and living in gentle and loving ways. She resides with her family near a state university campus which has had a broadening effect on her, increasing toleration for the differences among people.

there was said to be a warm and welcoming light on the other side.[51] On a more bizarre note, Timothy Leary (LSD guru of the 1960s) died in the 1990s. Near the end of his life he saw a video showing a rocket's fiery re-entry into the earth's atmosphere. He is said to have cried, "Finally, I will be light! Everyone will know I am light!" He arranged for his cremated remains to be flown on a commercial rocket in 1997. It is to circle earth for about ten years, then re-enter, "blazing like a shooting star in final tribute" according to the company's promotional literature. Expectations for life after death are less grandiose for members of the J-M Class of 1959, and for most other Americans.

For Judy there may be nothing after, nothing at all. On the other hand, she's not sure. She at least entertains the idea of reincarnation. So does Betty, who believes that nothing created is destroyed, including human souls. For her, there is no fear since "death is just a part of living." She is concerned that she and others be allowed to die with dignity. Whatever the truth turns out to be, Judy concludes this: "If there is a heaven and hell, I've lived a moral and compassionate life and can't believe I'd go to hell." Others like James, Francis, Stan, and Barry remain real believers in classic Christianity and its teachings about the afterlife.[52] Francis judges with gratitude that he has had a good marriage and career and now is left with hope for much fishing in retirement and life with God after death. Stan has no fear of death because "I know where I'm going. Sometimes I think it would be good to get out of this world." John has no worry about dying since "when your time comes, you'll go, and that's all." Dallas is confident that there is another life after this, so he is not afraid and will just wait to see. Ian is most interested in waiting and seeing. Death to him "is like Christmas—I don't yet know what the wrapped present will turn out to be?" Jane has a living will on file, thinks that there cannot be the extraordinary now apart from real hope for the hereafter, and gladly affirms her strong love for God who cares for the present and is in charge of the future.

The Century (and World?) At Its End

The twentieth century has been full of idealism and sickness. No better example exists than the Summer Olympic Games that were staged in Atlanta, Georgia, in July and August of 1996. These were the centennial games of the modern Olympics with athletes gathered from 197 nations, the most com-

---

[51]Betty Eadie, *Embraced by the Light* (Carson City, Nev.: Gold Leaf Press, 1992).

[52]I have written a widely distributed book expressing my views on life now and hope for after this life (Barry Callen, *Faithful in the Meantime: A Biblical View of Final Things and Present Responsibilities*, Nappanee, Ind.: Evangel Publishing House, 1997).

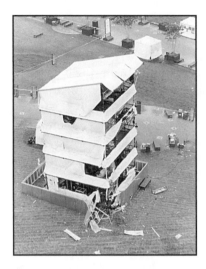

Debris scattered around a broadcast tower in Atlanta's Centennial Olympic Park after a bomb disrupted Olympic activities in 1996, killing two and injuring at least 100.

prehensive representation of the world at any event in history. The pageantry of the opening ceremony was stunning and the competition exhilarating. But there also was the terrorist pipe-bomb that exploded in the middle of a celebrating crowd in Centennial Park in Atlanta and, at the same time, the tragic crash of TWA Flight 800 off Long Island, New York.[53] Richard and Delores had just watched the U.S. "Dream Team" shine in basketball. They exited the arena and walked into crowded Centennial Park, moving right past the spot where the bomb would explode just minutes later. Life and death, victory and defeat, waving flags and bloodied bystanders, powerful takeoffs and shattered oblivion—that's the tortured world today. Judged an ominous editorial in *The Jerusalem Post*:

> The one world so beloved of speechmakers at the games [1996 Summer Olympics] is a world none of us lives in any more, if it ever existed. We live in a world being slowly closed in by security checks, iron gates and fear of flying…. The purveyors of false dawns will continue leading everyone into ever-darker nights of terror.[54]

There it is. The world at the end of the 20th century is still seeking the light of peace and justice. Too often, however, what is being found are false dawns

---

[53]The public fear was that this crash and large loss of life had been caused either by a bomb or even a missile. The long investigation of the wreckage recovered from the sea floor yielded the conclusion that apparently the actual cause was massive mechanical failure of the aircraft itself.

[54]Editorial, "Marching Into Darkness," Sunday, July 28, 1996, in *The Jerusalem Post*, International English Edition, for the week ending August 3, 1996, 10.

and even nights of terror. The Hubble telescope was first launched into space in 1990 and has since given humans the eyes to see distant reality like never before. It has helped revolutionize astronomy and maybe even increased humanity's understanding of the nature and origin of the universe and of themselves. The horizon of outer space now is less dim. Unfortunately, the source of human happiness and fulfillment, the source of justice and peace on earth, may be as dim as ever. In the 1960s it was the race to space. In the 1990s it is the race to cyberspace. The new potential boggles the mind—and brings with it many of the same old problems, only now on a bigger scale. For example, Ted Turner was named "Man of the Year" in 1991 by *Time* magazine because of his Cable News Network (CNN) that was the first global news company. It was influencing the dynamic of world events by turning viewers in 150 countries into instant witnesses of history as it happened. Observed the magazine: CNN "gives everyone the same information, the same basis for discussion, at the same moment. That change in communication has in turn affected journalism, intelligence gathering, economics, diplomacy and even, in the minds of some scholars, the very concept of what it is to be a nation."[55] Logging on to the Internet is like joining a worldwide town meeting of tens of millions from everywhere who are saying, showing, and selling virtually whatever they want to whomever is interested. The issues of access, free speech, accuracy of information, censorship, and personal identity in this electronic maze are urgently real.

People of the 1990s have been dazzled by amazing computer simulations and mountains of information flow. Humans have never been so "advanced," and never so threatened. There is serious overpopulation, deforestation, new and deadlier strains of disease, ethnic bloodbaths on a devastating scale, and still the reality of unimaginable weapons of mass destruction. One likely reflection of how this overwhelms is the extraordinary popularity among today's Americans of the TV quiz show *Jeopardy!* and the board game *Trivial Pursuit*. Trivia are bits of "objective" and usually marginal information from the past. Seeking them usually is an act of nostalgia and sometimes a subtle acknowledgment of unpreparedness to deal effectively with larger issues. Americans now are building narrower and narrower pools of knowledge and are being forced to engage in compensatory surface-fact learning in the

---

[55] *Time*, January 6, 1992, 24. Geographic boundaries now are less limiting and thus less defining of what it means to be a nation. In 1997 Ted Turner made the dramatic announcement that over a ten-year period he would be donating $1 billion to humanitarian programs of the United Nations.

many fields in which they necessarily are severely deficient. The demand for trivia, beyond an easy desire for escapism in the midst of frustration, is an attempt to cope at least in a rote and shallow way with worlds of learning far beyond one's own specialization.[56]

As we finish this century and face the next, there are two central questions to be faced squarely. Has living through all the turmoil of the 1940s, '50s, '60s, '70s, '80s, and '90s surfaced any wisdom for life that might help the world face constructively whatever future it yet has? Can the America of today sort out its deep social and spiritual dilemmas and find viable paths to lasting peace, genuine community, and sustainable life in this kind of world? Persistent impasses in political and social life certainly continue to confuse and torment. In 1940, the parents of the J-M class of 1959 looked fearfully at the headlines as the German Luftwaffe sought to bring England to her knees with brutal bombing. In 1996, the class members saw a very different headline: "Luftwaffe Puts Base In U.S. To Train Its Fighter Pilots."[57] What a change to see a row of Tornado ground-attack jets, each stenciled with the Iron Cross of Germany's modern air force, sitting quietly at Holloman Air Force Base at Alamogordo, New Mexico. This was the first foreign military base in the U.S. since the British finally were ejected in 1814.

One past event in America serves well as a sad paradigm of what could be the coming future. It happened in Pennsylvania in 1889. Johnstown was a booming coal-and-steel community filled with families striving for at least a modest piece of the nation's burgeoning industrial prosperity. In the mountains above town was an old earth dam that had been rebuilt hastily to create an exclusive resort lake patronized by the Pittsburgh-based tycoons—among them Andrew Carnegie, Henry Clay Frick, and Andrew Mellon. Despite repeated warnings of possible danger, nothing was done about the dam. After all, it was serving well the pleasure needs of the rich. Then came May 31, 1889. The dam burst, sending a wall of water thundering down the mountain and smashing through Johnstown. More than 2,000 helpless residents below were dead in minutes. It was a tragedy that immediately became a national scandal.[58] Something like it may be preparing to happen again, although on a much bigger scale.

Leonard Sweet has announced that "the world has come to an end—at least the world we knew. The lay of the land has fundamentally changed,

---

[56]See Mark Wexler and Ron Sept, "The Psyco-Social Significance of Trivia," *Journal of Popular Culture* (Fall, 1994).

[57]In Cleveland's *The Plain Dealer* (August 15, 1996).

[58]See David McCullough, *The Johnstown Flood* (N.Y.: Simon & Schuster, 1968, 1987).

never to return to its original form. This earthquake has made us strangers in our own land."[59] What comes next? One assessment judges this way:

> As we approach the year 2000, the millennium is reemerging as a metaphor for the future.... The modern millennium ignites our vision for a better world—alongside our nightmares of the world's end.... Beneath the specter of nuclear weapons is a growing sense of hope that if we can just "make it to the year 2000," we will have proved ourselves capable of solving our problems and living harmoniously on this fragile planet.... [Already] the magnet year 2000 is pulling forth bold experiments in market socialism, a spiritual revival, and a burst of economic growth around the Pacific Rim.[60]

Howard Snyder's *EarthCurrents* is more cautious and probably a little more realistic since it takes note of the persistent depravity of human beings.[61] We all know that there are numerous ballistic missile submarines, the ultimate killers, prowling in secrecy through the world's oceans and carrying enough destructive force to make the atomic bombs dropped on Japan in 1945 appear by comparison to be mere firecrackers. The question is whether and when one of them will be launched by direct order or freak accident.

Another urgent question is whether a doomsday asteroid will take aim at earth and alter the earth's surface and weather in a life-changing way. Apparently it has happened before and remains a real possibility. It was reported in 1997 that, with only ten percent of the sky systematically searched to that date, 99 asteroids had been found, each capable of causing massive destruction if it should collide with the earth. The earth's fossil record seems to show that this actually happens every ten to thirty million years, usually with devastating results. We now are about ten million years overdue for another major collision.

Speculations about the future are notoriously suspect. For instance, highbrow critics commonly deplored the mass culture of the 1950s—Hollywood spectaculars, "horror" comics, hammering rock-and-roll music, and increased television watching. Columnist Harriet Van Horne was crying cultural doom: "Our people are becoming less literate by the minute.... As old habits decline, such as reading books and thinking thoughts, TV will absorb their time. By the 21st Century our people doubtless will be squint-eyed, hunchbacked

---

[59]Leonard Sweet, *FaithQuakes* (Nashville: Abingdon Press, 1994), 8.
[60]Naisbitt and Aburdene, ibid.
[61]Howard Snyder, *EarthCurrents: The Struggle for the World's Soul* (Nashville: Abingdon Press, 1995).

and fond of the dark."[62] Jim now insists that "the biblical prophecies have been fulfilled before our very eyes, meaning that we are living in the last days." Those who are not aware of this apparently lack faith, fail to study their Bibles, are spiritually "squint-eyed," and may even be fond of the dark. Van Horne was right and wrong. Is Jim?

The U.S. finally had to say good-bye to George Burns (1896-1996), the last of a generation who grew up in vaudeville, helped inaugurate sound films and radio, and adapted successfully to the age of television. In his late 90s in the early 1990s, his longevity was often the subject of his comedy. "It's nice to be here," he would announce to an adoring audience. "At my age, it's nice to be anywhere!" Also, "I get a standing ovation for just standing!" Turning his gags just a little, what of the nation? Where is it in its life-cycle? How long will it keep standing—at least in a way recognizable to those who have known and loved it for decades? Francis expressed his feelings this way: "Some days I'm encouraged; some days I'm appalled. Politics are just ridiculous." Alexander Solzhenitsyn was probably right in this prophetic pronouncement in 1993:

> Although the earthly ideal of Socialism-Communism has collapsed, the problems it purported to solve remain: the brazen use of social advantage and the inordinate power of money, which often direct the very course of events. And if the global lesson of the twentieth century does not serve as a healing inoculation, then the vast red whirlwind may repeat itself in entirety.[63]

Speaking generally, the twentieth century has been one of world wars, hot and cold, conducted by great powers threatening each other regularly. Despite—or maybe because of—the sheer terror of mutual assured destruction if nuclear war ever began, so far there has been no worldwide conflagration. The world actually has survived fifty years of the nuclear age. But, as one historian concludes: "The century ended in a global disorder whose nature was unclear, and without an obvious mechanism for either ending it or keeping it under control." He adds soberly:

> If humanity is to have a recognizable future, it cannot be by prolonging the past or the present. If we try to build the third millennium on that basis, we shall fail. And the price of failure, that is to say, the alternative to a changed society, is darkness.[64]

---

[62]As quoted in *This Fabulous Century*, vol. 6, The Fifties (N.Y.: Time-Life Books, 1970), 176.

[63]As quoted by Eric Hobsbawm, *The Age of Extremes* (N.Y.: Vintage Books, Random House, 1994), 558.

[64]Hobsbawm, op. cit., 585.

Yes, darkness! Humanity is still seeking the light. At least a hint of the yet-needed light was suggested by the *Star Wars* trilogy, three of the most action-packed and popular films of all time (*Star Wars*, 1977; *The Empire Strikes Back*, 1981; and *The Return of the Jedi*, 1983). The hero, young Luke Skywalker, knew that no military advantage or technical superiority can finally insure victory. Luke's compassion proves to be the strength that topples the evil Empire. To change the historical time frame but not the subject, after all was said and done, Jesus hanging on a Roman cross was not the final defeat of goodness, as all surface observations suggested, but only the beginning of true and finally triumphant goodness. I venture the personal witness that this "light-of-the-world" Jesus remains a viable option for our frequently lightless and often empty world.

This dark side of our world is symbolized well by one fictional figure who has been present in the American imagination since 1940 when he first was given his own magazine. Batman is a great crime-fighting detective shaped as a creature of the night to instill fear in criminals. Residing in Gotham City, Batman was equipped with a series of special gadgets to confound criminals (Batmobile, Batcave, Utility Belt, Batplane, etc.). This character now has maintained a significant popularity with the American public for six decades, with three of the highest grossing movies of all time being *Batman* (1989), *Batman Returns* (1992), and *Batman Forever* (1995). Another in this series was released in 1997, *Batman and Robin*. Like its predecessors, it was a special effects extravaganza that critic Roger Ebert said "is wonderful to look at, and has nothing authentic at its core."[65] Is that dark possibility (an essentially empty world of wild and pointless action) characteristic of the U.S. as the twenty-first century dawns?

The famous French physician and astrologer Nostradamus (1503-1566) predicted that the world would end when Easter fell on April 25. So far this has happened in 1666, 1734, 1886, and 1943—and we are still here. It happens again in 2038. A series of doomsday prophets have punctuated the twentieth century with their dire predictions. In 1954, just as the J-M class of 1959 was preparing to begin its high school experience, many in Italy thought that all experience was about to end. An old Italian adage reports that Rome and the world are safe as long as the Coliseum stands. This hulk of a building, with such a dramatic 1,800-year-old past, suddenly developed huge cracks on May 18. Someone said it was a "sign" that Monday, May 24, 1954, would be the day of world destruction. Thousands flooded the Vatican, pleading for the

---

[65]Roger Ebert, as quoted in *The Herald Bulletin*, Anderson, Ind., June 20, 1997.

Pope to absolve them of their sins. What happened? Engineers repaired the ailing Coliseum so that it could continue being a tourist attraction.

What about "signs of the times"? Hope, fear, and doomsday predictions have stayed very much with us. On October 28, 1992, the sprawling capital city of South Korea virtually closed down. The streets of Seoul were filled with riot police and ambulances as followers of Lee Jang-rim waited on the "rapture" to signal the end of the world. Nothing happened—except that this "prophet" was later convicted of fraud (he had collected $4.4 million from his followers and bought bonds that would mature long after October 28!). Widely read books written by fundamentalistic Christian writers on the supposed contemporary meanings of biblical prophecy have included those by Jack Van Impe and Hal Lindsey.[66] In January 1995, members of a Japanese religious sect released a toxic nerve gas in Tokyo subway cars, killing 12, injuring 5,000, and sending fear into millions. Earlier in the decade there had been death and major destruction caused by a bombing at the World Trade Center in New York City.

David Koresh gathered his community of about 130 Branch Davidians outside Waco, Texas, to live communally and absorb a steady diet of his privately constructed and self-serving biblical interpretations. An earlier leader of this "church" had predicted that the last days of creation would begin on April 22, 1959, just as members of the J-M class of that year were hoping to begin their own creative lives. That Davidian was wrong, obviously. Then successor Koresh[67] took full control in 1988 and gained public attention in April 1993, when he and 81 of his members (some of them children) met a fiery death, apparently self-inflicted after a highly-publicized and controversial 51-day standoff with frustrated and finally aggressive FBI agents. In many ways this tragedy was a repeat of the mass suicide inspired by religious fanatic Jim Jones in 1978. In other ways it was an instance of growing sentiment in the U.S. that government had grown too invasive of private life, too big, strong, even violent. The April 1993 tragedy in Texas may have been the inspiration for an even more terrible event on Waco's second anniversary. A devastating explosion tore at the heart of Oklahoma City and shocked the heart of the nation. Timothy McVeigh had deliberately bombed the Murrah

---

[66]Examples are Jack Van Impe, *2001: On the Edge of Eternity* (Dallas: Word Publishing, 1996) and Hal Lindsey, *Planet Earth—2000 A.D.* (Palos Verdes, CA: Western Front, Ltd., 1994).

[67]His original name was Vernon Howell, but in 1990 he changed it to Koresh, Hebrew for "Cyrus," the Persian king who allowed the Jews to return to Israel after their captivity in Babylon.

A bomb destroyed the Murrah Federal Building in Oklahoma City in 1995, killing 168 people.

Federal Building, killing 168 people. In another violent anti-government event in April of 1997, a heavily armed separatist group holed up in a compound in Texas. They were prepared, they said, to die in the cause of Texas becoming a sovereign nation apart from the United States. Frequently in the news were heavily armed militia groups using the language of anti-government rage.[68]

Is this only the beginning? Are we seeing early evidence of what in the next few years will be a major cultural turning in the United States? Such a possible turning has been described as the end of the troubled era of the 1960s through the 1990s when rampant individualism has been dominant in the midst of crumbling institutions. In place of such a personal-rights revolution likely will be a perilous gate through which the nation will walk into some new social arrangement, some new starting over. By about 2005, the following scenario is suggested as one of several plausible catalysts for such major change:

> Beset by a fiscal crisis, a state lays claim to its residents' federal tax monies. Declaring this an act of secession, the president obtains a federal injunction. The governor refuses to back down. Federal marshals enforce the court order. Similar tax rebellions spring up in other states.

---

[68]See, for instance, "Mainstreaming the Militia," *U.S. News and World Report,* April 21, 1997, 24-37. This report concludes: "The roots of this broad antigovernment movement, in both the violent and nonviolent forms, lie in the sense of alienation some Americans feel toward their national institutions. The sense of vulnerability and anger is now being fed by a small industry. That means the mainstreaming of the militia movement has just begun" (37).

Treasury bill auctions are suspended. Militia violence breaks out. Cyberterrorists destroy IRS databases. U.S. special forces are put on alert. Demands issue for a new Constitutional Convention.[69]

Such a scenario, while unlikely to happen in just this way, represents a significant turning that in some form is likely in a few years. The elements of debt, civic decay, global disorder, and values confusion are major and threatening. The hope is that a time of real crisis can yield a new rendezvous with destiny, a new social contract in which national identity and trust are reborn.

Unfinished Journey

Quite unfinished is America's quest for peace, justice, prosperity, and faith. People generally want one or two without the price of the others—something that experience appears to say is an impossibility. When only some people are prosperous at the expense of others, there is no justice and will be no peace for long. When a people lacks a common vision of togetherness and faith in something greater than its momentary time and place in the sun, there is no firm basis on which to build toward all that humanity holds most precious. A provocative symbol of the unfinished journey of the U.S. flashed across the nation's television screens on January 28, 1996. It was Super Bowl Sunday. Featured in the pre-game ceremonies was a dramatic fly-over of screaming jets that swooped toward the cheering stadium in perfect formation, then suddenly, right on cue, lunged upward, still in formation. It was a heart-stopping display of the most sophisticated of human machinery excitedly streaking into the limitless sky as mere mortals below were thrilled and about to watch well-paid men kicking, throwing, and running somewhere with a football. This special moment of dramatic pageantry marked the tenth anniversary of the frightful explosion soon after launch of the *Challenger* space shuttle, an event that had shocked and humbled the U.S. Now, on this Sunday of the big game, the son of one of the dead astronauts was piloting the plane leading the gleaming formation skyward. He was carrying on the journey that his father never finished! So it must be with the nation itself.

The Jackson-Milton class of 1959, and especially the "baby boomers" who soon joined this class as a dominant force in the culture, are now left to carry on the quest unfinished by those who went before. The tens of millions of Americans born between 1946 and 1964 have become a perennial fasci-

---

[69]William Strauss and Neil Howe, *The Fourth Turning* (N.Y.: Broadway Books, 1997), 272.

nation of the mass media. As children of the post-war boom of the 1940s and 1950s, these baby boomers are said to have invented free sex in the 1960s, frequent divorce in the 1970s, and unlimited consumption in the 1980s. The youngest of them turned 50 in the mid-1990s. Some critics claim that already they have bankrupted the moral fiber of the nation. Now the question is whether their retirements after the turn of the century will bankrupt federal programs like Social Security and Medicare. In 1950 there were seventeen workers paying into the Social Security system for every one drawing out benefits. The alarming projection is that by 2006, there will be only three putting in for every one taking out.

Just a little younger than the high school classes of 1959, the boomers have a somewhat less firm rootage in the traditions, institutions, and the values traditional in America before the 1960s. During recent decades they have ridden and sometimes whipped to a full run the wild horse of social change. And what change it has been! Between 1930 and 1990, fewer than one-half as many cows have been helped to produce nearly one and one-half times as much milk. The number of Americans living on farms dropped from 30.5 million in 1940 to 4.6 million in 1990, with the nation's citizens age 65 and over doubling from 1960 to 1992. Registered passenger cars per 1,000 population jumped from 265 in 1950 to 612 in 1993, while overseas telephone calls made by Americans mushroomed from 23.4 million in 1970 to over one billion in 1990.

Much more than numbers has changed. Basic outlooks on the world have shifted greatly. In the key arena of faith, the phrase "post-Christian" has become disorientingly relevant for a large segment of the American population still deeply rooted in the Judeo-Christian tradition. The thirty-eight million young men and women born between 1964 and 1977, the wave following the flood of baby boomers, has been called "Generation X," taken from Douglas Coupland's 1991 novel by that title.[70] The "X" signifies an unknown variable, a generation still in search of its identity, the first to grow up in a "postmodern"[71] and "post-Christian" America. In a more recent novel, the same author offers additional snapshots of an aimlessly wandering genera-

---

[70]Douglas Coupland, *Generation X: Tales of An Accelerated Culture* (N.Y.: St. Martin's Press, 1991).

[71]"Postmodern" refers to a radical reaction against the "Enlightenment" understanding of truth. Rather than truth being rational, dependable, quantifiable, systematically available, the new mood of our time is much more relativistic. Meaning depends on the perceiver and is defined by each individual and the community of which he or she is a part. Intuition now invades the earlier dominance of the rational as a key way of coming to know truth. See Table 17.

tion raised by parents who no longer even took the trouble not to believe in God.

I have never really felt like I was "from" anywhere; home to me. . .is a shared electronic dream of cartoon memories, half-hour sitcoms and national tragedies. I have always prided myself on my lack of accent—my lack of any discernible regional flavor. I used to think mine was a Pacific Northwest accent, from where I grew up, but then I realized my accent was simply the accent of nowhere—the accent of a person who has no fixed home in their mind.[72]

Here is a new generation of Americans, many of whom have never had enough sense of place, roots, or identity to be able to even consider themselves "lost." Lost means that you had some locating perspective to begin with. These young people, however, are lacking even the memory of anything like a hope-giving Christian gospel; they are shaped by default with the givens of social phenomena like AIDS, MTV, a multi-trillion-dollar federal deficit, and impending environmental if not military catastrophe. They frequently are the children of divorced or working and often absentee parents. "I am homesick for the home I never had," screams out the lead singer for the rock group Soul Asylum as part of the lyrics of its hit song "Homesick." Today's young are said to be the most ignored, misunderstood, and disheartened generation in history. When the boomers were twenty-something, they were ready to save the world. Members of the "X" generation feel barely able to save themselves. Given the very large crowds still gathering at Billy Graham crusades, maybe his view may be both right and timely. Having ministered to hundreds of millions of people since the 1940s, he reports in his recent autobiography:

> About one thing I have absolutely no regrets, however, and that is my commitment many years ago to accept God's calling to serve him as an evangelist of the gospel of Christ. We live in a world of confusion. Competing and often contradictory intellectual and religious voices clamor for our attention and allegiance. In the midst of so many crosscurrents, how can we assert that *anything* is true?. . . Since I first committed my life to Jesus Christ some sixty years ago, I have crossed paths with people who hold virtually every kind of religious and philosophical view imaginable. Often I am moved by the intensity of their spiritual searching and by the depth of their commitment. At the same time, as the years have gone by, I myself have become even more convinced of the uniqueness and truth of the gospel of Christ.[73]

---

[72]Douglas Coupland, *Life After God* (N.Y.: Pocket Books, 1994), 174.
[73]Billy Graham, *Just As I Am* (HarperSanFrancisco, Zondervan, 1997), 724-725.

At least some of the surface things are being turned in a better direction. One can see it in the area where the J-M class of 1959 grew up and went to school. Yes, Northeast Ohio had become part of the "Rust Bowl." Yes, near-by Lake Erie had become a virtual "dead sea" and Cleveland was joked about as the "Mistake on the Lake." But in the late 1990s there was new life. Lake Erie has been helped to make a remarkable comeback and Cleveland's Cuyahoga River no longer is the fire hazard it was in 1960 when its industrial runoff was consumed in an historic conflagration.[74] Some manufacturing operations that in the 1970s and 1980s had been moving to the South, the West, and to Mexico in search of cheaper labor and open-shop environments were coming back because of the strong industrial infrastructure in Ohio. The area being abandoned by some was proving resilient. Cleveland gained national attention with its remarkable progress in urban renewal. Jacobs Field and the Gund Arena opened in 1994 as the new city-center homes of baseball's Cleveland Indians and basketball's Cleveland Cavaliers. That year the Indians averaged over 39,000 fans per home game in a modern facility with many luxury boxes that greatly increased revenue to a professional sport paying gigantic salaries. The new stadium was praised as state-of-the-art.[75] In 1997, Cleveland's mayor, Michael White, was praised nationally as one of the new breed or urban leaders making City Hall a hothouse for innovation.[76]

The new Rock and Roll Hall of Fame and Museum opened in Cleveland in 1995. Although Art Modell took his NFL franchise, the legendary Cleveland Browns, to Baltimore, the city fought back and brokered a deal that kept the Browns name in Cleveland, got assurance of a new team in 1999, and are now building a wonderful 72,000-seat stadium to house it. After constructing more neighborhood homes in recent years than in the previous forty-five, Cleveland was cited by Harvard Business School as a "leader in urban renaissance." The area's renewal was represented well one evening in July 1997. Baseball's annual All-Star game was being played at Cleveland's Jacobs Field. Pride was everywhere. The capstone was a classic game, won dramatically in the final inning when the catcher of the Cleveland Indians, all-star at that position for the American League, came to the plate in front of the

---

[74]In the same ceremony in which I was inducted into the Jackson-Milton High School Hall of Fame (April 1987), another of the school's graduates was honored for his key role in the dramatic clean-up of Lake Erie.

[75]Ironically, one casualty of the big money driving professional sports in recent years was Cleveland's loss of its beloved Browns football team (moved to Baltimore, a city that earlier had lost its Colts to Indianapolis). The team will be replaced in Cleveland in 1999 and retain the name "Browns."

[76]*Time* magazine, August 18, 1997, 21-24.

home crowd. The place went wild when Sandy Alomar's home run ended it all in a blaze of glory.

Just days later in nearby Pittsburgh, Francisco Cordova and Ricardo Rincon[77] combined to pitch a 10-inning no-hitter for the Pirates in front of 44,000 cheering fans. It was second best only to the greatest game ever pitched in the majors, Harvey Haddix's twelve perfect innings for Pittsburgh against Milwaukee in 1959. Not far away and close to North Jackson High School, Lake Milton, after sad decades of neglect and decay following the early 1960s, became a beautiful state park in the 1990s with new facilities and attractive new homes along its shorelines. Craig Beach may have lost its historic amusement park in the mid-1960s, with the ground sitting scarred and abandoned for nearly thirty years, but now it is being covered with new condominiums that have a lovely lake view. The rust was being rubbed off an area that had suffered decline.

What has all this American history meant since World War II? Where is the unfinished journey now going? Here is the observation of one current historian:

> In some ways, America seems to face the greatest moment of possibility in all of its post-World War II history as the twentieth century nears its end. So much positive change had already occurred since 1945—the material progress of prosperity, victories against discrimination, the new horizons that had opened for education and creativity. On the other hand, so much remained to be done in a society where homelessness, poverty, drug addiction, and crime reflect the abiding power of race, class, and gender to block people's quest for a better life.[78]

The quest goes on for the fuller realization of peace, prosperity, justice, and faith. The first three may be out of reach apart from a serious addressing of the fourth, faith. The irony is that the frustrated quest for the better life continues despite the stunning wealth of the United States. In 1995, the real gross national product (in billions of U.S. dollars) of the four largest economies in the world were the U.S. ($7,248), China ($3,500), Japan ($2,679), and Germany ($1,452). The United States' GNP was nearly as large as the next

---

[77]This surely was a sign of the times. Here in "middle America" were former Mexican League pitchers who could barely speak English making history in the United States. But there was even more. The Cleveland Indians made it to the seventh game of the 1997 against the Florida Marlins, having lost twice in the series to the young Cuban-exile pitcher Livan Hernandez and finally being eliminated by the dramatic hit of Edgar Renteria from Colombia.

[78]William Chafe, *The Unfinished Journey: America Since World War II*, 3rd ed. (N.Y.: Oxford University Press, 1986, 1991, 1995), 517.

three combined, yet the U.S. remained unable or unwilling to care adequately for the basic needs of all its citizens. Obviously, dollars alone are not the answer. Urgently required is the necessary vision, will, faith, and the commitment to justice in the midst of prosperity. There will be no real peace without them all.

What we as modern humans seek are the intangibles of hope and wholeness, an existence with meaning that yields happiness, a society that is encouraging and enabling the search of all its people for the highest in human life.[79] Finally, what we seek is "a city that hath foundations." The author of the Epistle to the Hebrews in the New Testament reports that the only builder of such a city is God (Heb. 11:8-10). Nathan Scott is right: "Indeed, we do perceive, intermittently and anxiously, that our severances from one another may be a reflection of some profounder dislocation and that perhaps the former will not be healed until the latter has been repaired."[80] Increasingly it is perceived that it is time for some basic repair of profound human dislocations. As Bernice King says: "Now it's morning time. The alarm clock has already gone off, and we've worn out the snooze button. It's time to get up, turn off the alarm clock, and start a new day."[81]

People still are seeking the better life. Most Americans, however, are far less euphoric about the prospects than were the joyous American soldiers flooding back to their homes in 1945. Then there was victory, hope, relief from economic depression and war, a real chance to get on with life in a world now being reborn. In the seasons of history, the late 1940s was springtime. The late 1990s struggles with the chill of winter. Culturally speaking, the days now are shorter, the light more limited. There is widespread anxiety and significant amounts of confusion over values and understandings of reality, meaning, identity, and national direction. A deep disconnectedness and quiet despair haunt the land. A generation has arisen for whom all gods are dead, all faiths shaken, all inner hell let loose.

The beloved comic Red Skelton died in September 1997. In the 1950s and 1960s few Americans with access to a television set were unfamiliar with his

---

[79]The search was dramatized well by Viktor Frankl, the inspirational Austrian psychiatrist who survived Nazism's concentration camps of the 1940s, although his parents, brother, and first wife did not. Dying in 1997 at age 92, he left behind his classic book of the modern age, *Man's Search for Meaning* (1963). Faith had helped him survive the camps. Is there a sturdy meaning in which people yet can believe, a meaning that can enable a truly human future?

[80]Nathan Scott, Jr., *Craters of the Spirit: Studies in the Modern Novel* (Washington, D.C.: Corpus Books, 1968), 27.

[81]Bernice A. King, *Hard Questions, Heart Answers* (N.Y.: Broadway Books, 1996), 16.

trademark line at the end of each show: "Good night, and God bless." Was the American culture moving into night along with Skelton. Would God bless? Madonna gives popular voice to the perceived incoherence of life and the common desire for personal gratification—because it is assumed that *me* and *now* are all that there is. The nation is looking for the foundations of some new springtime. There appeared in 1997 the book *Nearer My God: An Autobiography of Faith* by William F. Buckley, Jr., one of the more prominent American conservative figures in recent decades (b. 1925).[82] In these pages Buckley shares a deeply personal defense of his Roman Catholic faith, continuing a conversation he began in 1951 with his earlier book, *God and Man at Yale.* The subject is the place of faith in people's lives. Maybe there still should be a place, all contrary public policy notwithstanding.

What of the near future and the successful achievement of the nation's perennial goals of peace, prosperity, justice, and faith? America at the end of the 1990s suffers from a deep dis-ease, an uncomfortable feeling that the light for which the society longs is still little more than a dim flicker on a distant horizon. In fact, it is widely perceived that the desired future may not come as a natural next step from where the culture now is. Something radical may need to happen, some dramatic new face-off, maybe a "fourth turning."[83] As the members of the J-M class of 1959 now reflect more soberly in the grand-parenting stage of their lives, so the culture as a whole is sobered, cautious, streetwise about the shallowness of easy answers, groping for cohesion in the midst of its pluralism, open again to a role for religious foundations to provide some real solutions.

The U.S. has been blessed with an era of unprecedented material abundance and world leadership since the 1940s. It now is clear, however, that prosperity is not all that is needed for human happiness; mere dollars will not earn respect around the world. Fortunately, peace, at least the avoidance of a third world war, has been managed since the 1940s. But lasting peace is always elusive apart from justice being provided to all citizens, something not yet achieved. Justice is always elusive unless the universal tendency to human

---

[82]N.Y.: Doubleday, 1997. Buckley founded the conservative journal *The National Review* in 1955 and, beginning in 1966, has served as host of *Firing Line,* a weekly television program on politics and public affairs.

[83]See William Strauss and Neil Howe, *The Fourth Turning: An American Prophecy* (N.Y.: Broadway Books, 1997). Stressing that generational dynamics is a key to understanding the cycles of American history, these authors project that, early into the twenty-first century, the society will pass through a great and perilous gate in its history. The hope is that on the other side is a new beginning full of fresh vitality and potential.

greed and arrogance has been addressed effectively. Faith in something (Someone) beyond the individual and the moment appears essential if there again is to be real community and shared values that nurture the best in humanity. Reaching this goal is always an unfinished journey.

Taking Time To Reflect

1. One member of the J-M class of 1959 judges that the following is a central problem in the U.S. today: "We have perfected the art of blaming everybody else for our own faults. My *greed* takes precedence over your *need*." Do you agree with this judgment?

2. What about "affirmative action" policies? Is it proper and necessary to give special advantages in the present to some people who have been treated unfairly in the past? Does doing so degrade everyone involved, as Shelby Steele argues? Is there a better way to achieve justice.

3. Are there such things as "absolutes," fixed rights and wrongs? Is all valuing and believing only a matter of personal choice and best guess given the individual's current knowledge?

4. Billy Graham and Pope John Paul II have been major spokespersons for the relevance of Christian faith to modern life. What issues have concerned them most? Why have they gotten such a wide hearing despite the "secular" setting of recent decades in the Western world?

5. Why was the 1992 celebration of the 500th anniversary of the first arrival of Christopher Columbus in the New World so controversial? Were Native Americans better off before the Europeans came? Was justice done in relation to these earliest Americans?

6. What do you consider important enough wisdom about life to pass on to the next generation? Do the thoughts of the J-M class of 1959 seem right to you?

7. What really is worth a new generation remembering from America's experience of recent decades? Name one person, event, and film that capture something worth never forgetting. What is at the heart of these crucial memories?

8. Is it justified to assume that the U.S. is facing some major changes, a difficult transitional time that can yield a hopeful new beginning for the country in the new century?

Appendix

We Hold These Truths[1]
A Statement of Christian Conscience and Citizenship
July 4, 1997

The most fundamental constitutional question is: Who ultimately decides what is constitutional?. . . Not only is religious liberty in peril, so is democratic self-government.[2]

On this two hundred and twenty-first anniversary of the Declaration of Independence, we join in giving thanks to Almighty God for what the Founders called this American experiment in ordered liberty. In the Year of Our Lord 1997, the experiment is deeply troubled, but it has not failed and, please God, will not fail. As America has been a blessing to our forebears and to us, so will it be a blessing to future generations, if we keep faith with the founding vision.

Invoking "the law of nature and of nature's God," the Founders declared, "We hold these truths to be self-evident." This Fourth of July Americans must ask themselves whether they hold them still. We, for our part, answer emphatically in the affirmative. We affirm that before God and the law all are equal, "endowed by their Creator with certain unalienable Rights, that among these are Life, Liberty and the pursuit of Happiness." In recent years it has become increasingly manifest that these truths cannot be taken for granted. Indeed, there is ominous evidence of their rejection in our public life and law.

As leaders of diverse churches and Christian communities, we address our fellow citizens with no partisan political purpose. Our purpose is to help repair a contract too often broken and a covenant too often betrayed....

---

[1]An abridged edition of the July, 1997, booklet *We Hold These Truths* that was signed by forty-three prominent Catholic, Orthodox, and Protestant Christian leaders representing a range of political, ethnic, and racial identities. Also adding their names were representatives of the Notre Dame and Harvard Law Schools. Distributed by Prison Fellowship Ministries, these excerpts are used by permission.

[2]Excerpts from an August 15, 1997, letter from Charles Colson that accompanied mailed copies of the *We Hold These Truths* booklet.

Religion and morality are not an alien intrusion upon our public life, but the source and foundation of our pursuit of the common good....

Nations are ultimately judged not by their military might or economic wealth but by their fidelity to "the laws of nature and nature's God." In the view of the founders, just government is self government. Liberty is not license but is "ordered liberty"—liberty in response to moral truth. The great threat to the American experiment today is not from enemies abroad but from disordered liberty. That disorder is increasingly expressed in a denial of the very concept of moral truth. The cynical question of Pontius Pilate, "What is truth?" is today frequently taken to be a mark of sophistication in our political discourse and even in the jurisprudence of our courts.

The bitter consequences of disordered liberty resulting from the denial of moral truth are by now painfully familiar. Abortion, crime, consumerism, drug abuse, family disintegration, teenage suicide, neglect of the poor, pornography, racial prejudice, ethnic separatism and suspicion—all are rampant in our society. In politics, the public interest is too often sacrificed to private advantage; in economic and foreign policy, the lust for profits overrides concern for the well-being of families at home and the protection of human rights abroad. The powerful forget their obligation to the powerless, and the politics of the common good is abandoned in the interminable contention of special interests. We cannot boast of what we have made of the experiment entrusted to our hands.

While we are all responsible for the state of the nation, and while our ills no doubt have many causes, on this Fourth of July our attention must be directed to the role of the courts in the disordering of our liberty. Our nation was constituted by agreement that "we the people," through the representative institutions of republican government, would deliberate and decide how we ought to order our life together. In recent years, that agreement has been broken. The Declaration declares that "governments are instituted among men, deriving their just powers from the consent of the governed." In recent years, power has again and again been wielded, notably by the courts, without the consent of the governed.

The most egregious instance of such usurpation of power is the 1973 decision of the Supreme Court [*Roe v. Wade*] in which it claimed to have discovered a "privacy" right to abortion and by which it abolished, in what many constitutional scholars have called an act of raw judicial power, the abortion law of all fifty states. Traditionally in our jurisprudence, the law reflected the moral traditions by which people govern their lives. This decision was a radical departure, arbitrarily uprooting those moral traditions as they had been enacted in law through our representative political process. Our concern is for both the integrity of our constitutional order and for the unborn whom the Court has unjustly excluded from the protection of law....

In its stated effort to end the national debate over abortion, the Supreme Court in *Planned Parenthood v. Casey* (1992) transferred the legal ground for the abortion license from the implied right of privacy to an explicit liberty right under the Fourteenth Amendment. The Court there proposed a sweeping redefinition of liberty: "At the heart of liberty is the right to define one's own concept of existence, of meaning, of the universe, and of the mystery of human life." The doctrine declared by the Court would seem to mean that liberty is nothing more or less than what is chosen by the autonomous, unencumbered self.

This is the very antithesis of the ordered liberty affirmed by the Founders. Liberty in this debased sense is utterly disengaged from the concepts of responsibility and community, and is pitted against the "laws of nature and of nature's God." Such liberty degenerates into license for the oppression of the vulnerable while the government looks the other way, and throws into question the very possibility of the rule of law itself. *Casey* raises the serious question as to whether any law can be enacted in pursuit of the common good, for virtually any law can offend some individuals' definition of selfhood, existence, and the meaning of life. Under the doctrine declared by the Court, it would seem that individual choice can always take precedence over the common good.

Moreover, in *Casey* the Court admonished pro-life dissenters, chastising them for continuing the debate and suggesting that the very legitimacy of the law depends upon the American people obeying the Court's decisions, even though no evidence is offered that those decisions are supported by the Constitution or accepted by a moral consensus of the citizenry.... It is exceedingly hard to avoid the conclusion that the Court is declaring that laws or policies informed by religion or religiously-based morality are unconstitutional for that reason alone. In this view, religion is simply a bias, and therefore inadmissible in law. Obviously, this was not the belief of those who wrote and ratified our Constitution. Just as obviously, the Court's view is not accepted by the people today. For the Founders and for the overwhelming majority of Americans today, ethics and morality transcend human invention and are typically grounded in religion.... Already it seems that people who are motivated by religion or religiously-inspired morality are relegated to a category of second-class citizenship....

[President George] Washington spoke of "the experiment entrusted to the hands of the American people." We cannot simply blame the courts for what has gone wrong. We are all responsible. The communications media, the entertainment industry, and educators bear a particular burden of responsibility, as do we Christian leaders and our churches when we fail to instill the hard discipline of ordered liberty in the service of the common good.

A most particular responsibility belongs also to our elected officials in state and national government. Too often, legislators prefer to leave difficult and controverted questions to the courts. This must be called what it is: an abdication of their duty in our representative form of democratic government. Too often, too, Christian legislators separate their convictions from their public actions, thus depriving our politics of their informed moral judgment....

Let no one mistake this statement as an instance of special pleading for Christians or even for religious people more generally. Our purpose is to revitalize a polity in which all the people of "we the people" are full participants. Let no one fear this call for our fellow Christians to more vibrantly exercise their citizenship responsibilities. We reject the idea that ours should be declared a "Christian" nation. We do not seek a sacred public square but a civil separation of church and state, which must never be interpreted as the separation of religion from public life. Knowing that the protection of minorities is only secure when such protections are supported by the majority, we urge Christians to renewed opposition to every form of invidious prejudice or discrimination. In the civil public square we must all respectfully engage one another in civil friendship as we deliberate and decide how we ought to order our life together.

The [43] signers of this statement are by no means agreed on all aspects of law and public policy. We are Catholics, Orthodox, and Protestants of differing convictions on many issues. We are conservatives and progressives of various ethnic and racial identities and with differing political views. We are agreed that we must seek together an America that respects the sanctity of human life, enables the poor to be full participants in our society, strives to overcome racism, and is committed to rebuilding the family. We are agreed that government by the consent of the governed has been thrown into question, and as a result, our constitutional order is in crisis. We are agreed that—whether the question be protection of the unborn, providing for the poor, restoring the family, or racial justice—we can and must bring law and public policy into greater harmony with the "laws of nature and of nature's God."

Not all Americans are agreed on the implications of those laws, and some doubt that there are such laws. But all can exercise the gift of reason to discern the moral truth that serves the common good. All can attempt to persuade their fellow citizens of the truth that they discern. We Americans are a political community bound to one another in civil argument. Such is the experiment in ordered liberty that has been entrusted to our hands. That experiment is today imperiled, but we are resolved that it continue and flourish, for as it was said two hundred and twenty-one years ago, so also it is the case today that "We hold these truths."

SELECT BIBLIOGRAPHY

Books only. All of these sources and many others are cited in the text.

Recent American History:
Select General Studies

Alexander, Charles. *Holding the Line: The Eisenhower Era, 1952-1961.* Bloomington, Ind.: Indiana University Press, 1975.

Baldwin, James. *Notes of a Native Son.* Boston, 1955.

Barlett, Donald, and James Steele. *America: Who Stole the Dream?* Kansas City: Andrews and McMeel, 1996.

Barone, Michael. *Our Country: The Shaping of America from Roosevelt to Reagan.* New York: The Free Press, Macmillan, 1990.

Bell, Daniel. *The Cultural Contradictions of Capitalism.* N.Y.: 1976.

Bellah, Robert, et al. *Habits of the Heart: Individualism and Commitment in American Life.* Berkeley: University of California Press, 1985.

Bellah, Robert, Phillip Hammond. *Varieties of Civil Religion.* N.Y.: Harper & Row, 1980.

Biskind, Peter. *Seeing Is Believing: How Hollywood Taught Us to Stop Worrying and Love the Fifties.* New York, 1983.

Bloom, Allan. *The Closing of the American Mind.* N.Y.: Simon and Schuster, 1987.

Blum, John. *Years of Discord: American Politics and Society, 1961-1974.* New York, 1991.

Bondi, Victor, ed., *American Decades: 1970-1979.* Detroit: Gale Research, a Manly Book, 1995.

Bondi, Victor, ed., *American Decades: 1980-1989.* Detroit: Gale Research, a Manly Book, 1996.

Bork, Robert H., *Slouching Towards Gomorrah: Modern Liberalism and American Decline.* N.Y.: Regan Books, HarperCollins, 1996.

Burner, David. *John F. Kennedy and a New Generation.* Boston, 1988.

Carroll, Peter. *It Seemed Like Nothing Happened: The Tragedy and Promise of American Life in the 1970s.* New York, 1982, rev. ed., 1990.

Carter, Dan. *The Politics of Rage: George Wallace, The Origins of the New Conservatism, and the Transformation of American Politics.* New York: Simon & Schuster, 1995.

Chafe, William. *The Unfinished Journey: America Since World War II* . N.Y.: Oxford University Press, 3rd ed., 1995.

Colson, Charles, and Jack Eckerd. *Why America Doesn't Work*. Dallas: Word Publishing, 1991.

Commager, Henry Steele. *The American Mind: An Interpretation of American Thought and Character Since the 1880s*. New Haven: Yale University Press, 1950.

Coupland, Douglas. *Generation X: Tales of An Accelerated Culture*. N.Y.: St. Martin's Press, 1991.

Coupland, Douglas. *Life After God*. N.Y.: Pocket Books, 1994.

Cuomo, Mario. *Reason To Believe*. N.Y.: Simon & Schuster, 1995.

Ely, Melvin. *The Adventures of Amos 'n' Andy: A Social History of an American Phenomenon*. N.Y.: The Free Press, 1992.

Ewen, Stuart. *All Consuming Images: The Politics of Style in Contemporary Culture*. NY: BasicBooks, 1988.

Fried, Richard. *Nightmare in Red: The McCarthy Era in Perspective*. New York, 1990.

Friedman, Benjamin. *Day of Reckoning: The Consequences of Economic Policy Under Reagan and After*. N.Y.: Random House, 1988.

Gingrich, Newt. *To Renew America*. N.Y.: HarperCollins, 1995.

Glassman, ed. *The Macmillan Visual Almanac*. N.Y.: Macmillan, Blackbirch Press, 1996.

Goulden, Joseph. *The Best Years, 1945-1950*. N.Y.: Atheneum, 1976.

Halberstam, David. *The Fifties*. N.Y.: Fawcett Columbine, 1993.

Harrington, Michael. *The Other America: Poverty in the U.S.* Baltimore: Penguin Books, 1971, first ed. 1962.

Harrison, Cynthia. *On Account of Sex*. Berkeley, 1988.

Harvey, Edmund, Jr., ed. *Our Glorious Century*. Pleasantville, N.Y.: The Readers Digest Association, 1994.

Hersh, Seymour M. *The Dark Side of Camelot*. Boston: Little, Brown & Co., 1997.

Hobsbawm, Eric. *The Age of Extremes: A History of the World, 1914-1991*. N.Y.: Vintage Books, Random House, 1994, 1996.

Hoover, Dwight. *Middletown Revisited*. Muncie, Ind.: Ball State University, monograph 34, 1990.

Hunter, James Davison. *Culture Wars: The Struggle to Define America*. N.Y.: BasicBooks, HarperCollins, 1991.

Lasch, Christopher. *The Culture of Narcissism: American Life in an Age of Diminishing Expectations*. N.Y.: Norton, 1979.

Layman, Richard, ed., *American Decades: 1960-1969*. Detroit: Gale Research, a Manly Book, 1995.

Limbaugh, Rush. *See, I Told You So*. N.Y.: Pocket Books, 1993.

Manchester, William. *The Glory and the Dream: A Narrative History of America 1932-1972*. Boston: Little, Brown & Co. 1974.

Marling, Karal Ann. *As Seen on TV: The Visual Culture of Everyday Life in the 1950s*. Cambridge, Mass., 1994.

Matthews, Christopher, *Kennedy & Nixon: The Rivalry That Shaped Postwar America*. N.Y.: Simon & Schuster, 1996.

Matusow, Allen. *The Unraveling of America: A History of Liberalism in the 1960s*. N.Y.: Harper & Row, 1964.

Miller, Timothy. *The Hippies and American Values: The Utopian Ethics of the Counterculture, 1965-1970*. 1991.

Morris, Charles. *A Time of Passion: America, 1960-1980*. N.Y.: Harper & Row, 1984.

Naisbitt, John, and Patricia Aburdene, *Megatrends 2000: Ten New Directions for the 1990s*. N.Y.: William Morrow, 1990.

Norberg, John. *A Force for Change: The Class of 1950*. West Lafayette, Ind.: Purdue University, 1995.

Oakley, J. Ronald. *God's Country: America in the Fifties*. N.Y.: December Books, 1986.

Orwell, George. *Nineteen Eighty-Four*. N.Y.: New American Library ed., 1961; original ed., 1949.

Patterson, James T. *Grand Expectations: The United States, 1945-1974*. N.Y.: Oxford University Press, 1996.

Reich, Charles. *The Greening of America*. N.Y.: Bantam Books, 1970.

Risen, James, and Judy Thomas. *Wrath of Angels: The American Abortion War*. N.Y.: BasicBooks, 1998.

Rosenberg, Rosalind. *Divided Lives: American Women in the Twentieth Century*. N.Y.: 1992.

Salinger, Pierre. *John F. Kennedy: Commander in Chief*. N.Y.: Penguin Studio, 1997.

Scammon, Richard, Ben Wattenberg. *The Real Majority*. N.Y.: Coward-McCann, 1970.

Schlesinger, Arthur, Jr. *The Cycles of American History*. Boston: Houghton Mifflin Co., 1986.

Siegel, Frederick. *Troubled Journey: From Pearl Harbor to Ronald Reagan*. New York, 1984.

Skolnick, Arlene. *Embattled Paradise: The American Family in an Age of Uncertainty*. N.Y.: BasicBooks, HarperCollins, 1991.

Steele, Shelby. *The Content of Our Character: A New Vision of Race in America*. N.Y.: HarperPerennial, 1990.

Strauss, William, and Neil Howe. *The Fourth Turning: An American Prophecy*. N.Y.: Broadway Books, 1997.

Terkel, Studs. *The Great Divide: Second Thoughts on the American Dream*. N.Y.: Avon Books, 1988.

Terkel, Studs. *The Good War: An Oral History of World War II*. N.Y.: Pantheon Books, 1984.

Terkel, Studs. *Coming of Age: The Story of Our Century by Those Who've Lived It*. N.Y.: The New Press, 1995.

This Fabulous Century, vol. 6, The Fifties. N.Y.: Time-Life Books, 1970.

Tindall, George Brown, and David Shi. *America: A Narrative History*. N.Y.: W.W. Norton & Co., fourth ed., 1996.

Tofler, Alvin. *The Third Wave*. N.Y.: Morrow, 1980.

Van der Vat, Dan. *Stealth At Sea: The History of the Submarine*. Boston: Houghton Mifflin, 1995.

White, Theodore. *The Making of the President, 1960*. N.Y.: Pocket Books, 1961.

Witcover, Jules. *The Year the Dream Died: Revisiting 1968 in America*. N.Y.: Warner Books, 1997.

Wright, Gordon. *The Ordeal of Total War, 1939-1945*. N.Y.: Harper & Row, 1968.

Wrynn, V. Dennis. *Coke Goes To War*. Missoula, Mont: Pictorial Histories Pub. Co., 1996.

Yankelovich, Daniel. *New Rules: Searching for Self-Fulfillment in a World Turned Upside Down*. N.Y.: Random House, 1981.

Recent American History:
Select Religious Perspective Studies

Allen, Diogenes. *Christian Belief in a Postmodern World*. Louisville, Ky.: Westminster/John Knox Press, 1989.

Altizer, Thomas. *The Gospel of Christian Atheism*. Philadelphia: Westminster Press, 1966.

Bellah, Robert. *The Broken Covenant*. N.Y.: Seabury Press, 1975.

Bellah, Robert, and Phillip Hammond. *Varieties of Civil Religion*. San Francisco: Harper & Row, 1980.

Berman, Ronald, ed. "On God and Man," in *Solzhenitsyn at Harvard*. Washington, D.C.: Ethics and Public Policy Center, 1980.

Boyer, Paul. *When Time Shall Be No More: Prophecy Belief in Modern American Culture*. Cambridge, Mass.: Belknap Press of Harvard University, 1992.

Brueggemann, Walter. *Finally Comes the Poet*. Fortress Press, 1989.

Callen, Barry. *Guide of Soul and Mind: The Story of Anderson University*. Anderson, Ind.: Anderson University and Warner Press, 1992.

Callen, Barry. *God As Loving Grace: The Biblically Revealed Nature and Work of God*. Nappanee, Ind.: Evangel Publishing House, 1996.

Callen, Barry. *Faithful in the Meantime*. Nappanee, Ind.: Evangel Publishing House, 1997.

Cherry, Conrad. *God's New Israel: Religious Interpretations of American Destiny*. Englewood Cliffs, N.J.: Prentice-Hall, 1971.

Colson, Charles. *Burden of Truth: Defending Truth in an Age of Unbelief*. Wheaton, Ill.: Tyndale House Publishers, 1997.

Colson, Charles. *Kingdoms In Conflict*. William Morrow and Zondervan Publishing, 1987.

Das, Lama Surya. *Awakening the Buddha Within: Tibetan Wisdom for the Western World*. N.Y.: Broadway Books, 1997.

Ellwood, Robert. *The Fifties: Spiritual Marketplace*. New Brunswick, N.J.: Rutgers University Press, 1997.

Ellwood, Robert. *The Sixties: Spiritual Awakening*. New Brunswick, N.J.: Rutgers University Press, 1994.

Fletcher, Joseph. *Situation Ethics: The New Morality*. Philadelphia: Westminster Press, 1966.

Flowers, Ronald. *Religion In Strange Times: The 1960s and 1970s.* Macon, Georgia: Mercer University Press, 1984.

Forest, Jim. *Living With Wisdom: A Life of Thomas Merton.* Maryknoll, N.Y.: Orbis Books, 1991.

Frankl, Viktor. *Man's Search For Meaning.* Boston: Beacon Press, 1963.

Grenz, Stanley and Roger Olson. *20th-Century Theology: God & the World in a Transitional Age.* Downers Grove, Ill.: InterVarsity Press, 1992.

Hatfield, Mark. *Between a Rock and a Hard Place.* Waco, Tex.: Word Books, 1976.

Hauerwas, Stanley, and William Willimon. *Resident Aliens: Life in the Christian Colony.* Abingdon Press, 1989.

Heelas, Paul. *The New Age Movement.* Cambridge, Mass.: Blackwell, 1996.

Herberg, Will. *Protestant, Catholic, Jew: An Essay in American Religious Sociology.* Garden City, N.Y., 1955.

Hughes, Richard, and C. Leonard Allen. *Illusions of Innocence: Protestant Primitivism in America, 1630-1875.* Chicago: University of Chicago Press, 1988.

Kelley, Dean. *Why Conservative Churches Are Growing.* N.Y.: Harper & Row, 1972, rev. 1977.

Kennedy, James. *Character and Destiny: A Nation in Search of Its Soul.* Grand Rapids: Zondervan, 1994.

Kuhlman, Kathryn. *I Believe in Miracles.* Englewood Cliffs, N.J.: Prentice-Hall, 1962.

Küng, Hans. *Reforming the Church Today: Keeping Hope Alive.* N.Y.: Crossroad, 1990.

LaHaye, Tim. *The Battle for the Mind.* Old Tappan, N.J.: Fleming Revell Co, 1980.

Lindsey, Hal. *The Late Great Planet Earth.* Grand Rapids: Zondervan, 1970.

Lippy, Charles. *Being Religious, American Style: A History of Popular Religiosity in the United States.* Westport, Conn.: Greenwood Press, 1994.

Marty, Martin. *Religion & Republic: The American Experience.* Boston: Beacon Press, 1987.

Melton, J. Gordon, Phillip Charles Lucas, Jon R. Stone. *Prime-Time Religion: An Encyclopedia of Religious Broadcasting.* Phoenix, Ariz.: Oryx Press, 1997.

Neuhaus, Richard John, *The Naked Public Square: Religion and Democracy in America.* Grand Rapids: William Eerdmans, 1984.

Niebuhr, Reinhold. *Moral Man and Immoral Society.* N.Y.: Charles Scribner's Sons, 1932.

Noll, Mark. *A History of Christianity in the United States and Canada.* Grand Rapids: William B. Eerdmans, 1992.

Oden, Thomas. *Two Worlds: Notes on the Death of Modernity in America and Russia.* InterVarsity Press, 1992.

Robertson, Pat. *America's Dates With Destiny.* Nashville: Thomas Nelson, 1986.

Rogers, Dale Evans. *Let Freedom Ring!* Old Tappan, N.J.: Fleming Revell, 1975.

Schaeffer, Francis A. *How Should We Then Live?: The Rise and Decline of Western Thought and Culture.* Old Tappan, N.J.: Fleming Revell, 1976.

Schuller, Robert. *Move Ahead with Possibility Thinking.* Old Tappan, N.J.: Spire Books, 1967.

Scott, Nathan, Jr. *Craters of the Spirit: Studies in the Modern Novel.* Washington, D.C.: Corpus Books, 1968.

Sider, Ronald J. *Rich Christians in an Age of Hunger.* Dallas: Word Publishing, 4th ed., 1997.

Snyder, Howard A. *EarthCurrents: The Struggle for the World's Soul.* Nashville: Abingdon Press, 1995.

Sweet, Leonard I. *FaithQuakes.* Nashville: Abingdon Press, 1994.

Trueblood, D. Elton. *Foundations for Reconstruction.* N.Y.: Harper & Brothers, 1946.

Trueblood, D. Elton. *Alternative to Futility.* N.Y.: Harper & Brothers, 1948.

Van Impe, Jack. *2001: On the Edge of Eternity.* Dallas: Word Publishing, 1996.

Veith, Gene Edward, Jr. *Postmodern Times: A Christian Guide to Contemporary Thought and Culture.* Wheaton, Ill.: Crossway Books, 1994.

Wagner, C. Peter. *The Third Wave of the Holy Spirit: Encountering the Power of Signs and Wonders Today.* Ann Arbor, Mich.: Servant Publications, Vine Books.

Watkins, William. *The New Absolutes.* Minneapolis: Bethany House Publishers, 1996.

Wells, Ronald. *History: Through the Eyes of Faith.* Christian College Coalition, Harper SanFrancisco, 1989.

Wolterstorff, Nicholas. *Until Justice & Peace Embrace.* Grand Rapids: Wm. B. Eerdmans, 1983.

Wuthnow, Robert. *The Restructuring of American Religion.* Princeton, 1988.

Recent American History:
Select Regional Studies, Northeastern Ohio
and Western Pennsylvania

Alberts, Robert C. Pitt: *The Story of the University of Pittsburgh, 1787-1987.* Pittsburgh: University of Pittsburgh Press, 1986.

Aley, Howard. *A Heritage To Share: The Bicentennial History of Youngstown and Mahoning County, Ohio.* Youngstown: The Bicentennial Commission, 1975.

Aley, Howard. *The Time of Your Life: The One Hundred Twenty-Fifth Anniversary History of the Mahoning County Agricultural Society.* (Canfield Fair, 1846-1971.)

Balog, John R., with editor Mary Ann Abey. *The History of Jackson Township.* Boardman, Ohio: Pub. privately, 1992.

Billett, Dominic. *20 Years at the Crossroads.* N.Y.: Carlton Press, 1973. Refers to North Jackson, Ohio.

Blue, Frederick, et. al. Mahoning Memories: *A History of Youngstown and Mahoning County.* Virginia Beach, Va.: The Donning Company Publishers, with the Mahoning Valley Historical Society, 1995.

Buss, Terry, and F. Stevens Redburn, *Shutdown at Youngstown.* Albany: State University of New York Press, 1983.

Gordon, William. *Four Dead In Ohio.* Laguna Hills, Calif.: North Ridge Books, 1995.

Havighurst, Walter. *River to the West: Three Centuries of the Ohio.* N.Y.: G. P. Putnam's Sons, 1970.

Hildebrand, William, and others, eds., *A Book of Memories: Kent State University, 1910-1992.* Kent, Ohio: Kent State University Press, 1993.

History of Trumbull and Mahoning Counties, vol. 2. Cleveland: H. Z. Williams & Brothers, 1882.

Hoerr, John P. *And the Wolf Finally Came: The Decline of the American Steel Industry.* Pittsburgh: University of Pittsburgh Press, 1988.

Lorant, Stefan. *Pittsburgh: The Story of an American City.* Lenox, Mass.: Authors Edition, 1964, rev. 1975.

Lubove, Roy. *Twentieth-Century Pittsburgh: The Post-Steel Era,* Vol. II Pittsburgh: University of Pittsburgh Press, 1996.

Lynd, Staughton. *The Fight Against Shutdowns: Youngstown's Steel Mill Closings.* San Pedro: Singlejack Books, 1982.

Michener, James. *Kent State: What Happened and Why.* N.Y.: Random House, 1971.

Reid, Robert, ed. *Always a River: The Ohio River and the American Experience.* Bloomington: Indiana University Press, 1991.

Serrin, William. *The Company and the Union.* N.Y.: Alfred Knopf, 1973.

Skardon, Alvin. *Steel Valley University: The Origin of Youngstown State.* Youngstown: Youngstown State University, 1983.

Recent American History: Life Journeys, Beliefs, and Values of Select Groups (1940s to 1990s)

Jackson-Milton High School, Class of 1959 (Ohio)

Select biographical information drawn from numerous taped interviews, letters, and telephone calls with most living members of the Jackson-Milton High School class of 1959 (North Jackson, Ohio).

Palisades High School, Class of 1965 (California)

Medved, Michael and David Wallechinsky, *What Really Happened to the Class of '65?* N.Y.: Random House, 1976.

Wallechinsky, David. *The Class of '65: Chronicles of an American Generation— Midterm Report.* N.Y.: Viking Penguin, 1986.

Baby Boomer Generation (Born Between 1946 and 1964)

Miller, Craig. *Baby Boomer Spirituality: Ten Essential Values of a Generation.* Nashville: Discipleship Resources, 1992.

Roof, Wade. *A Generation of Seekers.* San Francisco: Harper, 1993.

Autobiographies

Bakker, Jim. *I Was Wrong.* Nashville: Thomas Nelson, 1996.

Berle, Milton. *Milton Berle: An Autobiography.* N.Y.: Delacorte Press, 1974.

Buckley, William, Jr. *Nearer, My God: An Autobiography of Faith.* N.Y.: Doubleday, 1997.

Colson, Charles. *Born Again.* Old Tappan, N.J.: Revell, 1976.

Eisenhower, Dwight. Ferrell, Robert, ed. *The Eisenhower Diaries.* N.Y.: W.W. Norton & Co., 1981.

Graham, Billy. *Just As I Am: The Autobiography of Billy Graham*. Harper-SanFrancisco, 1997.

Humbard, Rex, with Joyce Parks. *Put God on Main Street: An Autobiography*. Akron, Ohio: The Cathedral of Tomorrow, 1970.

Iacocca, Lee. *Iacocca: An Autobiography*. New York: Bantam Books, 1984.

Powell, Colin. *My American Journey*. N.Y.: Random House, 1995.

Mays, Benjamin. *Born To Rebel: An Autobiography*. N.Y.: Charles Scribner's Sons, 1971.

Merton, Thomas. *The Seven Storey Mountain*. N.Y.: Harcourt, Brace, 1948.

Ten Boom, Corrie. *Corrie ten Boom: Her Story*. N.Y.: Inspirational Press, 1995.

Trueblood, Elton. *While It Is Day: An Autobiography*. N.Y.: Harper & Row, 1974.

Warren, Earl. *The Memoirs of Earl Warren*. Garden City, N.Y.: Doubleday & Co., 1977.

Biographies

Armstrong, Louis. Laurence Bergreen, *Louis Armstrong: An Extravagant Life*. N.Y.: Broadway Books, 1997.

Bonhoeffer, Dietrich. Mary Bosanquet, *The Life and Death of Dietrich Bonhoeffer*. N.Y.: Harper & Row, 1968.

Cliburn, Van. Howard Reich, *Van Cliburn*. Nashville: Thomas Nelson, 1993.

Einstein, Albert. Abraham Pais, *Subtle Is the Lord*. N.Y.: Oxford University Press, 1982.

Jefferson, Thomas. Gilbert Chinard, *Thomas Jefferson: The Apostle of Americanism*. Ann Arbor, 1929, 1957.

John, Pope, XXIII. Lawrence Elliott, *I Will Be Called John: A Biography of Pope John XXIII*. N.Y.: Reader's Digest Press, 1973.

Kennedy, John. F. Richard Reeves, *President Kennedy: Profile of Power*. N.Y.: Simon & Schuster, 1993.

King, Martin Luther, Jr. James Haskins, *I Have a Dream: The Life and Words of Martin Luther King, Jr.* Brookfield, Conn.: Millbrook Press, 1992.

Kuhlman, Kathryn. Helen Hosier, *Kathryn Kuhlman: The Life She Led, the Legacy She Left*. Old Tappan, N.J.: Fleming Revell, 1976.

McCutcheon, Lillie. Barry Callen, *She Came Preaching*. Anderson, Ind.: Warner Press, 1992.

Martin, Dean. Nick Tosches, *Dino: Living High in the Dirty Business of Dreams*. N.Y.: Dell Publishing, 1992.

Merton, Thomas. Jim Forest, *Living With Wisdom: A Life of Thomas Merton*. Maryknoll, N.Y.: Orbis Books, 1991.

INDEX

Italicized page numbers refer to photographs.

A Brief History of Time, 252, 258
A Prairie Home Companion, 186, 243
Abington Township School District v. Schempp, 171
abortion, 94, 216, 222-225, *223*, 227, 246, 284, 304, 307, 338-339
Abstract Expressionism, 74
AC/DC, 255
Adams, President John, 20
affirmative action policies, 225, 291, 317, 335, 337
Afghanistan, 237
African-Americans, 27-28, 66-68, 70, 74, 101-105, 134, 136, 146, 153, 156, 159-161, 169, 178-179, 206, 209, 241, 263
Age of Aquarius, 168
Agnew, Spiro, 197, 311
AIDS, 106, 152, 245, 261-262, 276, 316, 330
Akron (Ohio), 11-12, 27, 99, 108, 123
Alda, Alan, 208, 247
Aldrin, Buzz, 203
Ali, Muhammad, 148, 190
All Creatures Great and Small, 211
All in the Family, 207-208, *208*
"All Shook Up!", 115, 125
All Things Wise and Wonderful, 211
Allen, Diogenes, 19
Alliance (Ohio), 148
Altizer, Thomas, 150
American Assoc. of Retired Persons (AARP), 204
American Express cards, 206
Ames brothers, 93

amnesia (social memory), 9
Amos 'n' Andy, 68
Anatevka (Russia), 145
Anderson, Hans Christian, 313
Anderson University, 34, 140, 169, 178, 187, 217, 240, 269, 282
Anderson, Sherwood, 10
Andrews sisters, 93
Anka, Paul, 93
Annie Get Your Gun, 60
apartheid, 139
Arcaro, Eddie, 70
arms race, 58, 81
Armstrong, Neil, 180, 203
Arnold, Matthew, 239
Atlantic Charter, 52
atomic bomb, 39, 46, 48-49, *49*, 52, 71, 73, 81, 84, 116, 301
Auerbach, Red, 153
Auschwitz, 282
Austintown (Ohio), 24, 125
Autobiography of Malcolm X, 157
automobiles, 81, 86, 92, *94*, 94-95, 99, 108, 115-116, 119-120, 125, 132, 135, 150-151, 192, 212-214, 244, 246, 248, 253, 255, 272, 309, 312, 326, 329

baby boomers, 19, 31, 51, 62-63, 80, 136-137, 167, 206, 246, 251, 256, 264, 278, 282, 284, 290, 294-295, 313, 317, 328-329
Baldwin's Market, 124
Baldwin, James, 106, 147
Baez, Joan, 172
Bakker, Jim, 253, 257, 279
Ball, Lucille, *90*, 90-91, 274

Barbie dolls, 126
Barcelona (Spain), 252
Barnard, Christiaan, 218
Barone, Michael, 58, 243, 248, 256, 273
Bastille, 19
Batman, 325
Bay of Pigs, invasion of, 143, 148
Beatles, 151-152, *152*
Beaver Falls (Pa.), 40, 138-139, 150, 178
Bell, Daniel, 151
Bellah, Robert, 20, 129, 184, 260-261, 303
Ben-Hur, 114, 116
Bennett, Tony, 93, 264
Bennett, William, 274
Benny, Jack, 68
Berle, Milton, 90-91
Berlin airlift, 55
Berlin Diary, 42, 72
Berlin (Germany), 7, 19, 55, 141, 247, 272
Berlin, Irving, 46, 60, 274
Berlin Wall, 7, 19, 247, *271*, 271-272
Berrigan, Daniel, 175
Berrigan, Philip, 175
Berry, Chuck, 102
Betty Crocker's Picture Cook Book, 89, 114-115
Bible, 32, 106-107, 114-115, 144, 178, 205, 208, 210, 217, 227, 257, 259, 273
Bicentennial (1976), 232, 275
Bierstadt, Albert, 17
Bill of Rights (U.S.), 20
Bill Haley and the Comets, 115
Birmingham (Ala.), 154, 156, 158
Black Monday, 213, 249
Black Muslims, 147-148
Black Panthers, 181
Black power, 157, 168
Blair House, 54

Blood, Sweat and Tears (book), 42
Blood, Sweat and Tears (music group), 172
Bloom, Alan, 262-263, 274, 301
Blue Denim, 94
Blue laws, 107
boats, 57, 99, 112, 124, 299
Bob Jones University v. United States, 216
Boesky, Ivan, 248
Bonhoeffer, Dietrich, 176, 182
Boone, Pat, 93, 114
Bork, Robert, 75, 194, 236
Boston Celtics, 153
Bosnia, 282
Branch Davidians, 326
Brando, Marlon, 115
Brandt, Willy, 210
Braveheart, 289, 316
Brave Men, 44, 72
Bridge (card game), 61
Brigadoon, 75
Brooklyn Bridge, 90
Brooklyn Dodgers, 69
Brown v. Board of Education, 100, 102, 128
Brown, Helen Gurley, 154
Brown, Rap, 164
Bryan, William Jennings, 20, 207
Buchanan, Patrick, 262
Buckley, William, Jr., 334
Buddhism, 174, 188, 256
Bunker, Archie, 207-208, *208*
Burns, George, 311, 324
Burns, Ken, 313
Bush, President George, 14, 241, 251, 275, 277, 279, 282-284, 316

Cable News Network (CNN), 321
Callen, Emily Elizabeth, 34, 315
Callen, Ian Patrick, 34
Calypso, 219-220

Cambodia, bombing of, 141, 184,
  193, 199, 267, 282
Cambridge University, 101
Camelot, 133-134, 136
Canasta (card game), 74
Candlestick Park, 271
Canfield Fair, 88, 95
Canton (Ohio) 11
Captain and Tennille, 211
Carmichael, Stokely, 156
Carnegie, Andrew, 322
Carnegie, Dale, 65
cars (see automobile)
Carousel, 73
Carroll, Peter, 183, 232, 235
Carson, Rachel, 147, 219
Carter, President Jimmy, 185, 203,
  210, 215, 218, 221-222, 227-228,
  232, 236-237, 241, 267, 277
Castro, Fidel, 97, 130, 148, *305*, 305-
  306
Catch-22, 147
Catcher in the Rye, 172-173
Cathedral of Tomorrow, 108
Chiang Kai-shek, 96
Challenger (shuttle), 268, 279, 328
Chariots of Fire, 258, 274
Charles, Ezzard, 90
Charles, Ray, 102
Chavez, Cesar, 159
Checkpoint Charlie, 142
Chernobyl, 265, 268, 279
China, 40-41, 81-83, 96-97, 166,
  197-198, 258, 269, 273, 283, 306,
  332
Christian Broadcasting Network,
  217, 227, 248
Christian Century, 96, 281-282
Christianity Today, 218, 227, 307
Christians, Evangelical, 20, 215, 218,
  227 (See also Protestant Church)
Christmas, 46, 87, 93, 112, 178-179,
  253, 274, 319

Christmas Is Together-Time, 178
Chrysler Corporation, 245
Churchill, Winston, 42, 52, 54, 72,
  147, 186
cigarettes, advertising ban, 115, 224
Civil Air Patrol, 121, 125, 142
civil religion, 20, 129, 184, 303-304
Civil Rights movement, 68, 104,
  106, 158, 161, 196
Civil War, 6, 25-26, 38, 76, 101, 129,
  134, 138, 153, 155, 200, 313
class photos, Class of 1959, Jackson-
  Milton High School, 2, *30*, *126*
Clay, Cassius (see Ali)
Cleaver, Eldridge, 181
Cleveland (Ohio), 24, 44, 119, 240
Cleveland Browns, 119, 331
Cleveland Indians, 70, 119, 331-332
Cliburn, Van, 270
Clinton, President William Jefferson
  (Bill), 33, 141, 277, 281, 284-286,
  291, 295-296, 306, 316
Clooney, Rosemary, 93
Coca-Cola, 44-45
Cold War, 7, 41, 54-55, 71, 73, 79,
  82-83, 85, 87, 97, 101, 103, 130-
  132, 134, 141, 148, 163, 165-166,
  178, 198, 236-237, 247, 266, 270-
  272, 295, 313
Cole, Nat King, 93
colonialism, European, 39-40, 55,
  166
Colson, Charles, 227, 307, 337
Columbus, Christopher, 313, 335
Columbus, (Ohio), 137, 139
Commager, Henry Steele, 20
Commission on the State of
  Women, 154
communism, 54-55, 61, 70-71, 73,
  87-88, 96, 98, 109, 128, 163, 199,
  245, 272, 279, 306, 324
Como, Perry, 93, 125
Compulsion, 94

computers, 70, 98, 101, 279, 299
Constitution of the U.S., 5-7, 20,
    102, 151, 216, 222, 226, 289, 304,
    339
Contract With America, *288*, 288-
    289
Cooper, D. B., 186, 239
Corvair (Chevrolet car), 86
Cosby, Bill, 258, 261
Cosmos, 179, 252, 258
Costner, Kevin, 313
Cousteau, Jacques, 219, 311
Craig Beach (Ohio), 28, 57, 90, 95,
    105, 123-125, 149, 160, 169, 191,
    231, 276, 332
creationism, 274
credit cards, 254
Crockett, Davy, 91, 93, *93*, 126
Crosby, Bing, 46, 93
Crystal Cathedral, 108
Cuba, 97, 130, 143, 148-149, 250,
    305-306
Cuban missile crisis, 148-149
cults, 206, 212, 226
cultural cycles, 5, 12, 129
Cuomo, Mario, 290

DeBartolo, Edward, 191
DeGaulle, Charles, 39, 114
Daley, Richard, 169
Dallas (television show), 162-163,
    264
Daniels, Jonathan, 161
Davis, Al, 252
Davis, Ossie, 39
Day, Doris, 125
Dayton (Ohio), 170, 196, 230
Dead Sea Scrolls, 69
Dean, James, 115, 150
Death of a Salesman, 64, 77
debt, national, 204, 279, 283, 296
Deep Throat, 204

Delphi Packard Electric, 287
Denver, John, 219
Depression babies, 19
Depression, Great (1930s), 22, 40-
    41, 58, 63, 126, 155, 212, 228,
    283, 288
deprogrammers, 206
Desert Storm, Operation, 283, 296
Dewey, Thomas, 54
Diana, Princess of Wales, 33, 311-
    312, *312*
Dickens, Charles, 98
Dietrich, Marlene, 46
DiMaggio, Joe, 42
Disney, Walt, 91
Disneyland, 91-92, *92*
DNA, 101
Doby, Larry, 70
Domino, Fats, 102
Don Quixote, 145
Douglas, Lloyd, 43
draft resisters, evaders, *141*, 202
drugs, illegal, 101, 168, 171, 176,
    185, 226-227, 264
DuBois, W. E. B., 68
Dukakis, Michael, 251
Dulles, John Foster, 114, 117, 164
Dylan, Bob, 152

Eagle (lunar lander), 180
Earth (photo from the Moon), *177*
EarthCurrents, 323
Earth Day, 219
earthquake, San Francisco Bay Area
    (1989), 271-272
Easy Rider, 180
Einstein, Albert, 41, 116
Eisenhower, David, 201, *201*
Eisenhower, President Dwight D.,
    71-72, 79, 85-86, *86*, 90, 114, 277
Elizabeth, Queen, 164
Elmer Gantry, 110, 128

Emancipation Proclamation, 155
Emerson, Ralph Waldo, 8
Emigrants Crossing the Plains (painting), 17
Engel v. Vitale, 171, 216, 218
England, 39, 42, 44, 72, 101, 114, 151, 186, 269, 311, 322
Enlightenment, 13-14, 19, 168, 237-238, 292, 303, 329
"entitlement", psychology of, 126, 128, 302
Environmental Protection Agency (EPA), 219
Equal Pay Act, 154
Equal Rights Amendment (ERA), 226, 284
E.T., 313
euthanasia, 307
Evers, Medgar, 154
Everything's Coming Up Roses, 93
Exxon Valdez, 267

Falcon (Ford car), 86
Falwell, Jerry, 206, 217, 227, 241, 257
Family Channel, 217
Fatal Attraction, 249
Father Knows Best, 91, 263
Fatherhood, 258, 261
Faubus, Orval, 104
feminism, 10, 185, 225-226
Ferraro, Geraldine, 242, *242*
Fiddler on the Roof, 145
Final Solution (Nazi), 269, 282
First Amendment, U.S. Constitution, 151, 216, 226
First Federated Church (North Jackson, Ohio), 111-112
Fisher, Eddie, 93
Fletcher, Joseph, 171
Flight 103 (Pan Am), 251
Flight 800 (TWA), 320

flower children, 168, 172
Forbes Field, 68, 136
Ford, President Gerald, 197, 202-203, 227-228, 277
Forrest Gump, 294, 316
Foundations For Reconstruction, 48, 52-53
Fourth Turning (cultural shift), 5, 75, 110, 127, 236, 241, 328, 334
Freedom 7, 143
Friedan, Betty, 154
Fromm, Eric, 113, 128
Fuchida, Mitsuo, 46
Fun and Frolics, 121

Galbraith, John Kenneth, 131
Gandhi, Indira, 267
Gandhi, Mahatma, 55, 159
Garroway, Dave, 96
gay rights, 106, 224
General Motors, 65-66, 95, 114, 132, 204, 214, 230, 294
genetic engineering, 268, 279, 307
Geneva College, 137, 139, 150, 178
Germany, 13, 27, 35, 39-41, 43, 54-55, 68, 114, 116, 141, 150, 176, 190, 220, 241, 269, 272, 310, 322, 332
Gethsemani, Abbey of, 53, 85, 161
Gettysburg Address, 6
GI Bill, 59, 62, 128, 136
Gingrich, Newt, 198, 288, 290, 316
Gleason, Jackie, 91, 94
God, 3-4, 6, 10, 17, 19-22, 26, 32, 37-38, 53, 63, 65, 69, 71, 73, 77, 81, 88, 97, 103, 107-110, 128, 149-150, 152, 156, 158-159, 161, 175-176, 179, 182, 187-188, 190, 202, 216, 218, 231, 233, 236, 246-248, 253, 257, 259, 261, 267, 274, 278, 292, 300, 302-305, 307-310, 315, 317, 319, 330, 333-334, 337-340

"gods," false, 183-184, 187, 259, 292, 333

"God Bless the U.S.A.", 247

Golden Gate Bridge, 66, 90

Goldwater, Barry, 132, 155, 181

Goldwyn, Samuel, 61

Goodman, Benny, 57

Gorbachev, Mikhail, 251, 258, 270, 272

Gore, Tipper, 255

Gorgeous George, 90

Graham, Billy, 53, 65, 106-107, 110, 128, 150, 164, 210, 218, 227, 239, 257, *305*, 305-306, 330, 335

Grant Park (Chicago), 169

Grateful Dead, 168, 264

Gray Panthers, 204

"Great Society", 146, 155, 166, 172, 245

Greenwood, Lee, 247

Gregory, Dick, 136

Grenada, 250

Guideposts, 108

Gund Arena, 331

Gunsmoke, 94

Guthrie, Arlo, 172

Habitat for Humanity, 221

Habits of the Heart, 260-261

Hagman, Larry, 264

Haight-Ashbury (San Francisco), 168, 236

Hair, 168

Haley, Alex, 157, 209

Hamilton, William, 150

Hamlet, 72, 299

Hanks, Tom, 294

Happy Days, 186

Hare Krishna, 174, *174*, 206

Harrison, George, 264

Harvard University, 95, 132, 273-274, 331, 337

Hatfield, Mark, 201, 227, 304

Hauser, Gayelord, 89, 114

Have Gun—Will Travel, 94

Hawking, Stephen, 252, 258

Hay, Harry, 106

Hayes, Gabby, 95

Heartbreak Ridge, 82

Heavy Metal music, 255

Heller, Joseph, 147

Hello Dolly!, 172

Hendrix, Jimi, 172-173

Henry, Patrick, 20

Herberg, Will, 110, 128

Herriot, James, 210-211

higher education, 62, 64, 117, 136-141, 167, 190, 287

Hindu faith, 55, 139, 175, 256-257, 318

Hinckley, John, Jr., 250

hippies, 174, 206, 226, 236, 278

Hiroshima (Japan), 39, 46, 63, 282

Hispanic Americans, 29, 146, 159

Hitler, Adolf, 25, 41, 46, 72, 85, 247, 269, 282

Hobsbawm, Eric, 40, 80, 235, 287, 324

Ho Chi Minh, 83

Hoff, Marcian, 218

Hoffman, Dustin, 150

Hollywood, 61, 84, 97, 107, 180, 264, 289, 323

Holocaust, 32, 35, 55, 71, 116, 220, 224, 301, 312-313

Holocaust Museum, 312

homeless people, 54, 157, 211, 236, 245

homosexuality, 94, 224, 262

Honduras, 142

Hoover, Barbara, 34

Hoover, J. Edgar, 107, 110

Hoover, President Herbert, 241

Hope, Bob, 44, 72, 197

How to Stop Worrying and Start Living, 65
Howe, Neil, 5, 75, 110, 127, 236, 241, 328, 334
Hubble telescope, 321
Hudson, Rock, 262
hula hoops, 126
human potential movement, 212
Humanae Vitae, 171
Humbard, Maude Aimee, 108
Humbard, Rex, 108, 257
Humphrey, Hubert, 169-170, 173, 231
Hungarian Freedom Fighters, 122
Hunt v. McNair, 216
Hunter, James, 20
Hussein, Saddam, 283

"I Have a Dream" speech, 156-157
I Love Lucy, 90, 90-91, 94, 274
I Need All the Friends I Can Get, 178
I Never Left Home, 44, 72
Iacocca, Lee, 245, 258
In Search of Excellence, 258, 285
immigration, 15, 17, 55, 159, 293
India, 40, 52, 55, 69, 139, 159, 175, 206, 211, 267, 269, 311-312
inflation, 59, 65-66, 83, 98, 128, 183, 189, 211, 241, 244, 254, 295
integrated circuit, 137
Intel, 218
Internet, 296, 321
Interstate Highway Act, 98
Iran, 10, 22, 114, 221-222, 228, 237, 243, 250, 267, 283, 304
Iran-Contra affair, 250
Iran hostage crisis, 222, 228, 237, 243, 250
Iraq, 267, 283
Islam, 22, 157, 273, 304
Island in the Sun, 94
isolationism, 41-43, 163

Israel, 3, 9-10, 55-56, 168, 170, 221, 250, 267-269, 302, 304, 326
It Seemed Like Nothing Happened, 183, 232, 235
It's A Wonderful Life, 311
Ives, Burl, 311

Jackson, Jesse, 169, 241, *241*, 279
Jackson, President Andrew, 23
Jackson-Milton High School, 1-2, 12, 22-23, *23*, 28, 34, 40, 62, 98-99, 101, 112, 118, 120, 123, 126, 132, 134, 139, 146, 153, 160, 162, 191, 193, 214, 270, 278, 287, 306, 315, 331-332
Jackson State College, 195
Jacobs Field, 331
Jagger, Mick, 177
Japan, 40-41, 43, 46-47, 49, 63, 66, 68, 81-83, 86, 167, 190, 204, 244, 269, 323, 332
Japanese Americans, 66-67, *67*
Jaws, 313
Jefferson, President Thomas, 3, 18, 35, 111, 238
Jeopardy! (quiz show), 321
Jesus Christ, 4, 13, 21, 53, 69, 77, 157-159, 175-177, 179, 186-187, 211, 227, 248, 252-253, 273, 279, 292, 302, 304-306, 325, 330
Jesus Freaks, 206
Jesus Movement, 176
Jews, 13, 55-56, 176, 227, 273, 282, 301, 312, 326
Jitterbug, 46
Joan of Arc, 186
John XXIII, see Pope John XXIII
John Paul II, see Pope John Paul II
Johnson, President Andrew, 201
Johnson, President Lyndon, 134, 144, 146, 154-155, 164-166, *165*, 173, 208, 222, 245, 277

Johnstown (Pa.), 322
Jones, Jim, 207, 214, 234, 326
Joplin, Janis, 173
Judeo-Christian tradition, 3-4, 52,
    56, 106, 111, 303, 305, 329
Judaism, 3, 21, 71, 111, 144-145,
    220, 257, 303
Jurassic Park, 313
justice, 1, 3-4, 6-8, 13, 15, 17-19, 25,
    46, 48-53, 71, 74-75, 102, 104,
    147, 154-155, 157-159, 161, 165,
    169, 173, 176, 181-182, 196, 221,
    224, 238, 278-279, 282, 290, 304,
    307, 314, 320-321, 328, 332-335,
    340

K-219 (submarine), 265
Kandinsky, Wassily, 74
Keillor, Garrison, 186, 243
Kelley, Dean, 217
Kelly, Gene, 93, 311
Kennedy, Edward, 197, 232
Kennedy, Jacqueline, *133*, 164-165,
    165, 311
Kennedy, James, 310
Kennedy, President John F., 130-
    134, *133*, 136, 144-145, 148-150,
    153-154, 156, 161-166, 172-173,
    179, 181-182, 184-186, 188, 192,
    197-198, 232, 250, 277, 284
Kennedy, Robert, 153, 165, 170, 181,
    189
Kent (Ohio), 137, 193-194
Kent State University, 123, 137
    shooting of student protesters,
        173, 184, 188, 193-195, *194*
Khmer Rouge, 199, 282
Khomeini, Ayatollah, 210, 221, 267
Khrushchev, Nikita, 87, 114, 130
Kids Say the Darndest Things!, 114-
    115
Kinchlow, Ben, 248

King Arthur, 133
King, Martin Luther, Jr., 55, 104,
    128, 144, 156-158, *157*, 165, 168-
    169, 182, 186
Kissinger, Henry, 210
Kmart, 236
Knievel, Evel, 191
Korean Conflict, 80, 82, *82*, 97, 127,
    208
Koresh, David, 326
Kovachik, Florence, 121
Kramer vs. Kramer, 210
Kuhlman, Kathryn, 108-109
Kunta Kinte, 209
Kuwait, 283

Lady Chatterley's Lover, 151
LaHaye, Tim, 20, 225
Lake Erie, 26, 331
Lake Milton (Ohio), 23, 27-29, 57,
    74, 90, 92, 95, 99-100, 105, 112,
    117-119, 123-124, 137, 186, 199,
    230-231, 276-277, 332
Lake Wobegon, 186, 243
Larson, Don, 119
Lasch, Christopher, 215, 260
Lauban, Mary Lucy, 117, 120, *120*,
    122, 138, 145-146, 308
League of Nations, 148
Leary, Timothy, 168, 311, 319
Leave It To Beaver, 89
Lebanon, 66, 169, 250, 267-268
Lend-Lease Act, 42
Lennon, John, 151
Lennon sisters, 95
Lewis, C. S., 9, 227
Lewis, Jerry, 93-94
Liberace, 262
Libya, 251
Liebman, Rabbi Joshua, 65
Life Is Worth Living, 108

Light, theme of, 3, 7, 13-14, 16, 19, 30, 75, 174, 177, 179-180, 183-184, 187, 190, 200, 235, 238, 255, 266, 270, 272, 279, 282, 309, 312-313, 318-320, 325, 333-334
Limbaugh, Rush, 289, 316
Lincoln, President Abraham, 6, 20, 38, 76, 111, 134, 155-156, 158, 164, 201
Lindsey, Hal, 187, 326
Linkletter, Art, 114-115
Liston, Sonny, 148, 157
Little Rock, Ark., Central High School, 104
Lockerbie (Scotland), 251
Lodge, Henry Cabot, 166
Lord of the Flies, 172-173
Lordstown Army Depot, 42
Lordstown assembly plant, 66, 132, 291
Loop (Chicago), 164
Los Angeles, 12, 106, 109, 157, 165, 255
Los Angeles Times, 213
Louis, Joe, 68, 102
Love Canal (New York State), 202, 219, 234
"Love Me Tender", 93
"Love Will Keep Us Together", 211
LSD, 196, 226, 319
Lucas, George, 201, 264
Luftwaffe, 322
lunar landing, *179*, 180
Lykes Corporation, 213

MacArthur, Gen. Douglas, 82-83
McCague, George, 98
McCarthy, Eugene, 189
McCarthy, Joseph, 96, *96*
McCutcheon, Lillie, 108, 140
McDonalds (restaurant), 95
McGovern, George, 170, 197

McGuffey Readers, 25
McKinley, President William, 25
McVeigh, Timothy, 326
Macbeth, 138
MacLaine, Shirley, 256
MacLeish, Archibald, 180
Maddux, Greg, 295
Madonna, 251, 334
Mahoning County (Ohio), 28, 33, 67, 88, 95, 121, 213
Mahoning River, 25-27, 213
Maine, 198
Malcolm X, 157
Man in the Gray Flannel Suit, 89
Man of LaMancha, 145
Manifest Destiny, 9-10, 17
Manson, Charles, 171
Mantle, Mickey, 311
Mao Tse-tung, 96
Marty, Martin, 304, 310
"Material Girl", 251
March on Washington, 156-157
Marciano, Rocky, 90
Marines, U.S., 164, 250
Mars, 161, 232, 296-298
M*A*S*H (television series), 208-209, 247
Marshall, Gen. George, 44
Marshall, Thurgood, 102-103, *103*
Marshall Plan, 54-55, 72
Martin, Dean, 93-94, 264
Martin, Mary, 73
Maryland, 197-198, 216
Maverick, 94
Mays, Willie, 102
Mazeroski, Bill, 136
Mellon, Andrew, 322
Melville, Herman, 20
Memphis (Tenn.), 159, 165, 229
Merton, Thomas, 53, 55, 85, 175
Metalious, Grace, 94
Methodist Episcopal Church, 111, 138

Mexico City, 266
microprocessor, 218
Middletown (Muncie, Ind.), 71, 205
Miller, Arthur, 64, 77
Miller's Marina, 99
Missionaries of Charity, 211, 312
Missouri River, 17
Modernism, 301
Modungo, Domenico, 121
"Moments To Remember", 116
Mondale, Walter, 242
Monroe, Marilyn, 94, 115
Montreal (Canada), 252
Moral Majority, 206, 227, 257
Morgan, Marabel, 210, 214
motels, 95, 99, 293
Montgomery (Ala.), 103-105, 153, 156
bus boycott, 104
Moonies (Unification Church), 206-207
Moore, Archie, 90
Moore, Roy (Judge), 301
Mostel, Zero, 145
Mother Teresa, 211, 311-312, *312*
Motley Crue, 255
Mount St. Helens, 239, 266, *266*
Mount Union College, 137-138, 148, 160, 162
Moynihan, Daniel Patrick, 165
MTV (music television), 252, 330
Mulroney, Brian, 16
Muncie (Ind.) (see Middletown)
Murrah Federal Building (Oklahoma City) bombing, 326-327, *327*
Murrow, Edward R., 90
Musial, Stan, 70
Muskie, Edmund, 198
Mussolini, Benito, 41

Nader, Ralph, 191, 232
Nagasaki (Japan), 39, 46, 49, *49*
Namath, Joe, 178
National Association for the Advancement of Colored People (NAACP), 103, 153-154
National Council of Churches, 110
national debt, 204, 279, 283, 296
National Football League, 11, 178, 252, 331
National Honor Society, 121-122
National Security Council, 250
Native Americans, 146, 313, 335
NCR, 287
Nelson, Ricky, 93
Neuhaus, Richard, 21
New Age religion, 256-257, 279
New Frontier, 131, 133, 166
New Right, 225, 227, 241, 254
New York Times, 150, 192, 273
New York World's Fair (1939), 41
New York Yankees, 119, 136
Newton, Isaac, 9
Newton Falls (Ohio), 40, 42, 57, 98, 105, 108, 140, 270
Nicaragua, 250
Niebuhr, Reinhold, 110, 128, 305
Nineteen Eighty-Four, 113
Nixon, President Richard, 85, 161, 170, 173, 180-181, 183, 185, 188-190, 192-193, 196-204, *201*, 210, 212, 218-219, 227-229, 236, 243, 277, 311
presidential resignation, 200
Nobel Peace Prize, 130, 139, 157, 211, 312
non-violent resistance, 55, 104
Normandy (France), 130, 247
normative reflection, 4
North American Free Trade Agreement (NAFTA), 286-287, 295
North Atlantic Treaty Organization (NATO), 55, 313

North Jackson (Ohio), 11-12, 22-24, 26-29, 31, 40, 57, 62, 74, 90, 95, 99, 101, 105, 108-109, 111-112, 118-119, 123, 138-139, 149, 153, 163, 193, 276-278, 315, 332
North Korea, 82-83, 306
North, Oliver, 250
North Vietnam, 193
Northwood (Ohio), 138
Nostradamus, 325

Oakland Raiders, 252
Ohio National Guard (at Kent State Univ.), *194*, 194-195
Ohio River, 26
Ohio State University, 119, 137, 139, 229
Ohio Turnpike, 98
oil embargo, 211, 234
Oklahoma, 73
Oklahoma City bombing (see Murrah Federal Building bombing)
Olympic Games,
    Olympics of 1960, 148
    Olympics of 1973, 220, 234
    Olympics of 1980, 237
    Olympics of 1984, 267
    Olympics of 1996, 190, 319-320
    Olympic Park bombing (Atlanta, Ga.), 320, *320*
Operation Breadbasket, 169
Operation PUSH, 169
organized crime, 100, 213
Orwell, George, 113
Oswald, Lee Harvey, 164

pacifism, 85
Packard Electric, 229-230, 287
Page, Patti, 93
Paine, Thomas, 18, 35

Palisades High School (Calif.), 2, 12, 228
Pan Am Flight 103, 251
Panama Canal, 164
Parker, Fess, 91, 93
Parks, Rosa, 103, 105, 153
Pathfinder, 296-298, *297*
Patinkin, Mandy, 81
patriotism, 18, 46, 61, 97, 141, 147, 170, 182, 189, 192, 225, 243, 246, 274
Patti, Sandi, 203
Patton, 210
peace, 1, 3-4, 7-8, 14-15, 17, 19, 25, 39, 41, 46, 49-53, 55, 58, 63, 65, 70-72, 74-75, 77, 79-80, 85, 87, 95-96, 108, 118, 124, 127-131, 134, 139, 147-148, 157-158, 163, 166, 168, 172, 175, 180, 182, 188, 197-200, 211, 221, 237-238, 244, 246, 256, 267, 275, 278, 282, 305, 312, 320-322, 328, 332-334
Peace Corps, 163, 172, 192, 197
Peace of Mind, 65, 72
Peace of Soul, 65
Peace With God, 65
Peale, Norman Vincent, 65, 108
Pearl Harbor, 31, 38, 42-43, *43*, 46-47, 51, 66, 84, 282
People's Temple Church, 207, 226
Perot, Ross, 285, 287
Peter, Paul, and Mary, 152
pill, the, 106, 152
Pittsburgh (Pa.), 56
Pittsburgh Pirates, 135
Pittsburgh, University of, 101, 240
Pizza Hut, 236
Platoon, 248, 258
Playboy magazine, 94, 168
pluralism (diversity), 4, 7, 18, 20, 28, 66, 121, 176, 182, 232, 247, 256, 292, 302-303, 334
Pledge of Allegiance (U.S.), 6, 107

Plessy v. Ferguson, 100, 102, 153
polio, 14, 98, 101, 275
politics, 17, 22, 25, 54, 79, 90, 115,
    171, 174, 182, 185, 189, 197-198,
    200, 225-226, 232, 237, 240, 248-
    249, 272, 279, 281, 285, 288, 294,
    324, 334, 338, 340
Pope John XXIII, 112, 144, 149
Pope John Paul II, 246, 307, 316,
    335
Porgy and Bess, 79
Pork Chop Hill, 82
pornography, 185, 204, 225, 248,
    250, 292, 338
Postmodernism, 256
Powell, Colin, 283, 296
Powers, Francis Gary, 130
prayer in public schools, 107, 122,
    216, 225, 308
Presley, Elvis, 93, 113, *113,* 115-116,
    229
Pricetown, (Ohio) 105, 107, 276
Prince Edward Sound (Alaska), 267
Princeton University, 117
Profiles In Courage, 131, 164
prosperity, 1, 3-4, 7-8, 17-19, 25, 49,
    51, 53, 58-59, 71, 74, 98-99, 102,
    108, 115, 117, 125-128, 134, 142,
    147, 173, 175, 181, 244, 253, 279,
    294, 322, 328, 332-334
Protestant-Catholic-Jew, 110
Protestant Church, 15, 56, 110-111,
    130, 149-150, 176, 206, 257, 259-
    260, 318, 337, 340
psychology of "entitlement", 126,
    128, 302
PTL, 253
Pulitzer Prize, 73, 131
Puritans, 21, 74
Pyle, Ernest, 44

Quo Vadis, 107

Raiders of the Lost Ark, 313
Ravenna Ordnance Plant, 42
Rayburn, John, 117-118
Reagan, President Ronald, 58, 184,
    186, 198, 218, 222, 228, 235-237,
    240-245, 247-251, 254, 258, 264,
    270, 274-275, *275,* 277, 279, 282-
    284
Rebel Without a Cause, 115, 150
Reformed Presbyterian Church, 137
Regent University, 217
Reich, Charles, 184, 215
reincarnation, 256, 319
released time, religious instruction,
    122
religion and American life, 18
Republic Steel (Warren, Ohio), 120,
    230
Resident Aliens, 259
Reynolds, Burt, 127
Reynolds, Debbie, 121
Rhodes, James, 193
Rickey, Branch, 69
Riesman, David, 64, 260
Robertson, Pat, 217, 222, 227, 242,
    253, 257, 279, 283
Robinson, Jackie, 69, *69,* 102
Robinson, Sugar Ray, 90
Rocky, 210
rock 'n' roll music, 102, 115, 229,
    323, 331
Rock Around the Clock, 115
Rockwell, Norman, 60-61, 94
Roddenberry, Gene, 178
Roe v. Wade, 216, 222, 338
*Roemer v. Board of Public Works of
    Maryland,* 216
Rogers, Dale Evans, 304
Rolling Stone magazine, 172, 255
Roman Catholic Church, 71, 110-
    112, 122, 130, 148-150, 152, 171,
    223, 227, 246, 260, 277, 334, 337
Roosevelt, Eleanor, 60

Roosevelt, President Franklin D., 38, 41, 52, 58, 66, 72, 75-76, 116, 155, 231, 243, 277, 279
Roots (television series), 209, *209*
Roseanne, 264
Rosemary's Baby, 218
Rosencrantz & Guildenstern Are Dead, 299
Rosie the Riveter, 60, *60*
Rubin, Jerry, 251
Ruby, Jack, 164
Russell, Bill, 153
Russia, see Soviet Union
Rust Belt, 212

Sadat, Anwar, 210, 267
Sagan, Carl, 252, 258, 311
Salk, Jonas, 101
Sandburg, Carl, 212
Sands of Iwo Jima, 73
San Francisco, 50, 52, 66, 106, 168, 271-272
Satanism, 255
Saturday Evening Post, 60, 94
Saudi Arabia, 283
Schaeffer, Francis, 225, 227, 260
Schindler's List, 313, 316
Schulz, Charles, 178
Schuller, Robert, 108, 253, 257
science, 41, 48, 98, 101, 131, 137, 152, 179, 182, 202, 222, 234, 252, 268, 279
Scranton Commission, 195
Seale, Bobby, 181
Security Is a Thumb and a Blanket, 178
See It Now, 90
segregation, racial, 51, 68-69, 100-104, 153, 158
Selective Training and Service Bill, 42
Seltzer, Louis, 107

seminaries, seminarians, 110, 161, 169, 217, 282
Sex and the Single Girl, 154
sexual liberation, 154
Sheen, Bishop Fulton, 65, 108
Shephard, Alan, 143
Shining Light (Peru), 267
Shirer, William, 42, 72
Shriver, Sargent, 197
shopping mall, 191, *191*
shopping, mail-order, 253
Shultz's Store, 124
Sider, Ronald J., 274
Silent Majority, 174, 181, 184, 188, 198, 229
Silent Spring, 147, 219
Simpson, O. J., 296
sin, 4, 32, 150, 176, 182, 201, 224, 238, 292
Sinatra, Frank, 46, 264
Singing in the Rain, 93
Situation Ethics (book), 171,
situation ethics, 182
Six-Day Arab-Israel War, 168
Smith, Bailey, 257
Solzhenitsyn, Alexander, 273, 324
Southern Park Mall, (Boardman, Ohio), 191
South Dakota, 197
South Korea, 82-83, 207, 269, 326
South Pacific, 73
Southern Baptist Convention, 257
Southern Manifesto, 153
Soviet Union, 7, 19, 39-40, 49, 54-55, 58, 71, 87, 97, 114, 122, 131, 141, 143, 163, 178-179, 197, 228, 236, 243, 247, 250-251, 258, 265, 271-273, 305-306
Spielberg, Steven, 264, 312-313
Spitz, Mark, 220
Spock, Benjamin, 65, 80
Springsteen, Bruce, 25, 264
Sputnik, 83-84, *84*

St. Catherine's Catholic Church
(Lake Milton, Ohio), 112
St. Lawrence Seaway, 26, 87
Stalin, Joseph, 49, 52, 54, 72, 282
Star Trek, 178, 245
Star Wars (air defense system), 249
Star Wars (film), 201, 249, 257, 325
Starr, Kay, 93
Stategic Arms Limitation Treaty
(SALT), 197
Statue of Liberty, 16-17, 203, 314,
314
steel industry, 25-28, 40, 44, 66, 86,
88, 105, 120, 132, 138, 143, 212-
213, 230, 240, 265, 293, 322
Stewart, Jimmy, 62, 311
Strauss, William, 5, 75, 334
Stokes, Carl, 161
Stoppard, Tom, 299
Stuart, M. Lyle, 210, 214
Steubenville (Ohio)., 93
Student Non-Violent Coordinating
Committee (SNCC), 157
Students for a Democratic Society
(SDS), 167
submarines, 42, 45, 66, 143, 165,
265, 323
suburbs, 59, 59, 73, 95, 98, 105, 107,
196
"Summertime", 79
Sun Belt, population shift, 185
Sun Myung Moon, 207
Sunday, Billy, 107
Super Bowl III, 178
Supreme Court, U.S., 5, 100, 102-
105, 128, 151, 153, 158, 171, 200,
204, 216, 218, 222, 233, 307, 338-
339
Swaggart, Jimmy, 253, 257
Swit, Loretta, 208
"Sympathy for the Devil", 177

Tales of Wells Fargo, 94
"Tammy", 121, 253
technology, 33, 41, 63, 84, 98, 127,
131, 171, 202, 234, 240, 246, 255,
264, 283, 295, 299, 306
telephones, cellular, 248, 253
televangelists, 185, 257
television, 41, 70, 86, 88-91, 93-97,
102, 104, 108-109, 113, 119, 126,
150, 154, 156, 161, 164, 166, 173-
174, 178, 186, 192-193, 200, 207-
209, 211, 217, 219, 224-225, 227,
237, 245-248, 252-253, 255-257,
263-264, 270-272, 274, 283-285,
289, 291, 296, 309, 313, 321, 323-
324, 328, 333-334
Ten Boom, Corrie, 53
Ten Commandments, 48, 52, 301-
302, 317-318
Terkel, Studs, 15, 34, 38, 101, 207,
298
terrorism, 220, 234, 251, 279
Terry, Ralph, 136
Tet Offensive, 192
Texaco Star Theater, 90
Texas School Book Depository
building, 163
The 700 Club, 217, 253
The Affluent Society, 131
The Battle for the Mind, 20, 225
The Best Years of Our Lives, 61
The Big Chill, 261
The Bonfire of the Vanities, 251
The Closing of the American Mind,
262-263, 301
The Common Sense Book of Baby and
Child Care, 65
The Conscience of a Conservative, 132
The Cosby Show, 263
The Culture of Narcissism, 215
The Deer Hunter, 210
The Echo, 120-121
The Exorcist, 218

The Feminine Mystique, 154
The Fire Next Time, 147
The French Connection, 210
The Godfather, 210
The Graduate, 150
The Greening of America, 184, 215
The Honeymooners, 91
The Invasion of the Body Snatchers, 101
The Jackie Gleason Show, 94
The Late Great Planet Earth, 187
The Lone Ranger, 91
The Lonely Crowd, 64, 260
The Music Man, 125
"The Old Rugged Cross", 25
The Power of Positive Thinking, 65, 108
The Red Skelton Show, 94
The Rifleman, 94
The Robe, 43, 107
The Sensuous Man, 210, 214
The Seven Storey Mountain, 53, 175
The Silence of the Lambs, 309
The Song of Bernadette, 43
The Sound of Music, 125
The Sting, 210
The Ten Commandments, 107
The Total Woman, 210, 214
The Wild Ones, 115
Three Mile Island (nuclear facility), 202, 219, 232, 234
Tianamen Square, 273
Tilton v. Richardson, 216
Times Square (N.Y.), 57, 198
Today Show, 96
tolerance, 21, 50, 66, 71, 73, 94, 205, 224, 263, 268, 301, 318
Tomorrowland, 91, 127
Tower Commission, 250
trains, 99, 256
Transcendental Meditation, 174, 190, 212, 256
transistors, 101

Trinity Project, 63
Trivial Pursuit (game), 321
Trueblood, David Elton, 48, 52-53, 64, 77, 301
Truman, President Harry, 54, 68, 72, 81-83, 102, 111, 166-167, 277, 306
Truman Doctrine, 54
Trump, Donald, 248
Truth Or Consequences, 126
Tupperware, 107
Turner, Frederick Jackson, 9
Turner, Ted, 33, 316, 321
Tussaud's Wax Museum, 186
Tutu, Desmond, 139
TV dinners, 89
TWA Flight 800, 320

Ueberroth, Peter, 255, 258
Underground Railroad, 138
unemployment, 40, 86, 128, 205, 212, 241, 244, 246, 293
Unification Church (see Moonies)
Union of Soviet Socialist Republics (see Soviet Union)
United Auto Workers, 65, 246
United Nations, 52, 68, 82, 97, 130, 148, 182, 250-251, 254, 259, 281, 283, 321
Charter of, 50
Security Council of, 82, 250-251, 283
University of Alabama, 178
University of California (Berkeley), 248
University of Chicago, 15, 169, 254, 301
University of Vermont, 220, 230
U.S. Steel (Youngstown, Ohio), 143
U.S.S. *Champlain*, 143
U.S.S. *Constellation*, 143
U.S.S. *Enterprise (Star Trek)*, 179

Valiant (Chrysler car), 86
Van Dyke, Henry, 8
Vatican Council II, 112, 149
V-E Day, 46
V-J Day, 47, 97, 198
Van Buren, Paul, 150
Vega (General Motors car), 132
veterans, 57-59, 61-62, 82, 136-138,
    198-199, 202, 247
Vietnam Veterans Memorial, 199,
    247, *247*
Vietnam War, 82, 137, 141, 148,
    155, 167, 169, 175, 190, 193, 196-
    197, 199, 201, 203, 215, 233, 247,
    251, 264
violence, 13, 22, 73, 100, 118, 141,
    154, 157, 159, 163-166, 170, 183,
    188, 193-194, 196, 217, 221, 234,
    290, 304, 309, 328
Volare, 121
Volkswagen, 150-151, *151*

Wagon Train, 94, 178
Wallace, George, 169-170, 173, 197-
    198, 225
Wall Street, 236, 249, 251, 288, 295
Waltons, 209
War on Poverty, 134, 155, 172
Warren, Earl, 102-103
Warren (Ohio), 47, 135, 287
Washington, President George, 18,
    20, 35, 340
Washington Post, 192
Watergate Hotel, 189, 200-201, 204,
    236, 242, 250
Watts (Los Angeles), 157
Wayne, John, 73
Welk, Lawrence, 95
West Berlin, 55, 141-142, 272
West Side Story, 125, 144
Western Reserve, 23
"Whatever Will Be, Will Be", 125

Wheeling (W.V.), 96
Whirlaway, 42
white backlash, 198
"White Christmas", 46, 274
White, Theodore, 133
Whitewater, 285
Whitman, Walt, 20
*Why Conservative Churches Are
    Growing*, 217
Wiesel, Elie, 13
William Tell Overture, 91
Williams, G. Mennen, 84
Williams, Ted, 42
Wilson, Charles E., 58
Wilson, Sloan, 89
Wilson, President Woodrow, 20
Windsong, 219
Winesburg, Ohio, 10
Winfrey, Oprah, 291, 316
Wisconsin v. Yoder, 216
Witcover, Jules, 165, 170
WNBA, 284
Wolfe, Tom, 251
Wolterstorff, Nicholas, 4
Woodstock Rock Festival, 172-173,
    188
Working Girl, 249
World Trade Center (bombing), 326
World War I, 7, 22, 27, 38-39, 70,
    72-73, 120, 159, 293
World War II, 1, 7, 13, 22-23, 25, 31,
    34, 37-53, *47*, 55-56, 64-67, 71,
    73-75, 77, 79-83, 87, 89, 99, 101-
    102, 112, 115, 130, 136-137, 139,
    141-142, 146-147, 150, 154, 170,
    172, 184, 187, 189, 198, 203, 211-
    212, 228, 253, 260, 267, 271-272,
    283-285, 294, 303-304, 306, 332
World Aflame, 164
Wyoming, 220, 230

Yalu River, 83
Yankelovich, Daniel, 203, 206, 214
Year of the Evangelicals, 215
Young, John, 25-26, 132
Youngstown (Ohio), 12, 23, 25-29,
    33, 44-46, 56-57, 62, 66-68, 88,
    93, 96, 98-100, 105, 109, 112,
    121, 123, 125, 136-138, 140, 143,
    159, 165, 191, 212-214, 230, 240,
    257, 259, 287, 293
Youngstown College (Univ.), 62,
    136-138, 143, 162
Youngstown Sheet and Tube Co.,
    27, 213-214
Yugoslavia, 267
Yuppie, 251

Zen Buddhism, 174, 190
Zionism, 55